AZMAT
MOHAMMED

LEARN THE LANGUAGE OF THE HOLY QUR'ĀN

SENIOR LEVEL / AND ADULTS

IQRA' PROGRAM OF ARABIC AND QUR'ĀNIC STUDIES

Revised Edition

Dr. ABDULLAH ABBAS NADWI

INTERNATIONAL DISTRIBUTOR

IQRA' Book Center, 6408 North Campbell, Chicago, IL 60645
Tel: (312) 274-2665, 1-800-521-4272 Fax: (312) 274-8733

IQRA's NOTE

We are greatly honored to publish the revised edition of our prestigious publication Learn the Language of the Qur'an by Dr. Abdullah Abbas Nadvi.

Ever since its initial publication in 1989 this book has grown in popularity and is currently being used by many schools and colleges across the world to teach the classical Arabic of the Qur'an. Its author is not only an Alim of great eminence, a graduate of Nadwah al-Ulama', Lucknow, India but also holds a Ph.D in Arabic Studies. He was Professor of Arabic Literature at Umm al-Qura' University, Makkah Mukarramah and an Special Educational Consultant to Sheik Abul Hasan Ali Nadvi and to Nadwat al Ulama'.

This work represents a life-long efforts in teaching Arabic and developing educational material based upon the Qur'an. This textbook along with its companion volume The Vocabulary of The Qur'an (A dictionary of the Qur'anic Arabic words and terms) constitutes a major contribution of the author to the teaching of Arabic language and understanding of the Qur'an.

This revised and enlarged edition is a major improvement on its previous publication. Since its first publication the textbook had not been revised and a need was felt for a thorough revision to make some necessary corrections, incorporate new ideas by the author and discerning readers, make further additions, improve type-setting quality and graphic presentation and to make the transliteration system consistent with the present standard of the Library of Congress System.

On our request Professor Assad Busool, Head of the Arabic Department of American Islamic College and Mr. Fadel Abdullah, Head of the Arabic Studies, Iqra' International Educational Foundation, two well known educators and linguists, field tested the book, offered valuable suggestions and proposed some useful addition to the textbook. Dr. Nadvi spent considerable time and effort in reviewing each suggestion and incorporating all useful information.

I am also grateful to Mr. Zubair Surati, who in spite of his various preoccupations and genuine excuses, conceded to our fervent request and did this beautiful type-setting and designing.

We are confident that in its present form this textbook offers a unique and comprehensible Program of Arabic Studies to benefit both a layperson and a scholar. May Allah (SWT) reward Dr. Nadvi for his painstaking efforts and Dr. Busool, Mr. Abdullah and other students and scholars for participating in the revision and improvement efforts.

The Chief Editors:

Friday, 3 February 1995
    3 Ramadan 1415

Part of a Comprehensive and Systematic Program of Islamic Studies

A Textbook for Arabic and Qur'anic Studies Level: Senior/ Géneral

Revised Edition 1995

First Print: Cairo 1979
Second Print: India 1981
Third Print: Lebanon 1989
Fourth Print: Lebanon 1995
Fifth Print: Malaysia 1997

Learn the Language of the Holy Qur'an
Fourth Edition
First Revised Edition 1995

Chief Program Editors

Dr. Abidullah al-Ansari Ghazi
(Ph.D., History of Religion
Harvard University)

Tasneema Ghazi
(Ph.D., Curriculum-Reading
University of Minnesota)

Reviewed & Field-tested by

Assad N. Busool
(Ph.D., Islamic and Arabic Studies,
University of California, Berkeley)

Fadel Abdallah
(M.A., Arabic Islamic Studies,
University of Minnesota)

ISBN # 1-56316-009-9

Design, Typesetting and Page make-up by

Zubair G.K. Surati
P.O. Box 20197
Jeddah 21455
Saudi Arabia

Printed in Malaysia by
Percetakan Zafar Sdn Bhd

PREFACE

Arabic, as the famous linguist A.L. Schlozer (d. 1781) has pointed out, belongs to the Semitic group of languages. More specifically, it is an offshoot of the languages of south-west Arabia. While its origins lie buried in remote antiquity, by the third century (C.E.), Arabic has developed into a full-fledged language.

In our time most of the Semitic languages have disappeared. In addition to Arabic, the only living Semitic languages are modern Hebrew, Amheric and a dialect of Aramaic. As for Arabic, it remains not only a fully living language but also enjoys a unique importance. It alone can serve as the source of knowledge of all Semitic languages. Whenever the grammarians of these languages are faced with intricate grammatical problems, they are forced to have recourse to consulting parallel grammatical rules in Arabic, particularly as they are exemplified in the Qur'ān.* Moreover, enormous change has taken place in the vocabulary of all Semitic languages. Change in word-meaning alone is considered. The present versions of these languages have little resemblance with their original versions. The only exception is Arabic, the language of the Qur'ān, which retains its old grammar, syntax and vocabulary that makes it the archetype of the entire family of Semitic languages.

Since the language of the Qur'ān is Arabic, it is the main source of knowledge about Islam. About one billion Muslims of the world recite the Qur'ān in its original language regardless of whether they understand it or not, and a good number of them do cherish the desire to comprehend the Qur'ān without the medium of translation. Moreover, there are a large number of people around the globe who wish to learn this language because of its political importance, for it is the official language of no less than the twenty-one member states of the Arab League. Gradually the importance of Arabic has also been enhanced because of the overwhelming importance of the Arab countries in international commerce and finance. Thanks to these, a number of text books and grammars for learning Arabic have been appearing in the Western countries and the volume of these publications is on the increase. The authors of these works have taken pains to make the learning of the language easy for beginners. The process of learning that one encounters in these works appears somewhat mechanical as many of these authors had little appreciation for the literary beauty of Arabic. Some, one might even suspect that their intrinsic prejudice against

---

* **Sabatino Moscati,** *An Introduction to the Comparative Grammar of Semitic Studies,* amply illustrates this.

Arabic had convinced them that it could not be presented in an interesting, systematic and simple manner. This being the state of affairs, it is the duty of Muslim scholars to make concerted efforts to produce good text books that would facilitate and speed up the process of learning Arabic among those that are conversant with English and other international languages. Unfortunately, this challenging task has not been taken up by many scholars. Mine is thus an effort which has been taken up to fill the gap.

Professor Abdus Salam Kidwai* of India pioneered a method for teaching Arabic in 1942. His main idea was to make the Qur'ān the prime source of teaching Arabic language. He compiled a book consisting of ten primary lessons for this purpose and it proved very useful. The present work is an adoption of the idea originated by Professor Kidwai.** His work was designed for Urdu-speaking adults of the Subcontinent who were acquainted with the Arabic alphabet and with some Arabic vocabulary. While attempting to present this language to English-speaking people, the present author was in a far less advantageous position since the greater number of readers will presumably have little or no knowledge of Arabic alphabet and vocabulary. This made my task an exceedingly difficult one.

The lessons of this book have been arranged in simple grammatic classifications supported by verses of the Holy Qur'ān as illustrations of the postulated rules in Philology, Morphology and Syntax. It is an attempt to assist those who wish to acquire proficiency in this language for the sake of understanding the Qur'ān. It is hoped that they will get used to the Qur'ānic style and language and in the process of learning be able to develop a degree of familiarity with Arabic idioms as well.

This is an experimental attempt which, the author hopes, will be conducive to a speedier and easier learning of Arabic. The author has made efforts to cover all the essential elements for learning the language. It goes without saying that there will always be scope for improvement. Suggestions or advice that would enable me to improve this work will be more than welcome and will be greatly appreciated.

The author is greatly indebted to Mr. Sayyid Muhsin Ba-Roum for publishing the first edition of this book through the famous publishing house of *Dār Al-Shurouq*. I am also greatful to IQRĀ' International Educational Foundation for adopting this work in their series, *The Arabic and Qur'ānic Studies* as part of their *Comprehensive and Systematic Program of Islamic Studies*.

Makkah al-Mukarramah   1986   **Abdullah Abbas Nadwi**

---

* Incharge of Education, Nadwat al-Ulama, Lucknow, India and Academic Secretary of Dar al-Musannifin, (Shibli Academy), India died in 1979.

** His way of explanation is also adopted in the first three chapters.

بسم الله الرحمن الرحيم

ABOUT THE WORK :

… It is a very interesting and useful work which meets the requirement of both students and general readers to learn the basic mode and structure system of the language of the Last Revealed Book… I congratulate the author on his impressive attempt and presentation and recommend that all non-Arabic speaking people study it thoroughly.

Saiyyid Abdul Hasan Nadwi

☆ ☆ ☆

… A precise and easy-to-grasp methodology to familiarize oneself with the approach, diction and nuances of the Arabic language, particularly relating to the Islamic epitomes and principles so beautifully conveyed by the Glorious Qur'ān. With a pleasant and rather informal treatment of the subject, the book will go a long way to help and instruct the English-knowing beginners everywhere.

Dr. Abdullah Omar Nasseef
Secretary-General
Muslim World League
Makkah al-Mukarramah

☆ ☆ ☆

The work of Dr. Nadwi accomplishes remarkably well the numerous spiritual, intellectual and educational purposes which he had set out to accomplish. He has also taken care to avoid verbal extravagance and dilettantism and has attempted to make the book as easy and simple as possible. He indeed deserves the gratitude of the world of learning for the great contribution he has made to the Arabic language.

Muhsin Ba-Roum

☆ ☆ ☆

The revised and enlarged edition of this pioneering work is a major improvement on its previous publication. Since its first publication the textbook had not been revised and a need was felt for a thorough revision to make some necessary corrections, incorporate new ideas by the author and discerning readers, make further additions, improve type-setting quality and graphic presentation and to make the transliteration system consistent with the present standard of the Library of Congress System.

Dr. Abidullah Ghazi

٨

تعلّم
لغة القرآن الكريم

دكتور عبد الله عبّاس الندوي

IQRA'
TRANSLITERATION CHART

أ ء	'	*	ز	z		ق	q	*
ب	b		س	s		ك	k	
ت	t		ش	sh		ل	l	
ث	th	*	ص	ṣ	*	م	m	
ج	j		ض	ḍ	*	ن	n	
ح	ḥ	*	ط	ṭ	*	هـ	h	
خ	kh	*	ظ	ẓ	*	و	w	
د	d		ع	'	*	ي	y	
ذ	dh	*	غ	gh	*			
ر	r		ف	f				

SHORT VOWELS	LONG VOWELS	DIPHTHONGS
ـَ / a	ـَا / ā	ـَوْ / aw
ـُ / u	ـُو / ū	ـَيْ / ai
ـِ / i	ـِي / ī	

* Special attention should be given to the symbols marked with stars for they have no equivalent in the English sounds.

THE ALPHABET

The Arabic Alphabet (حُرُوفُ الهِجَاء / *Ḥuruf-ul-Hijā'*) consists of 28 letters (29 if hamza is counted as a separate letter). Three of them : وَاو *wāw,* أَلِفْ *'alif* and يَاء *yā'* are used as long vowels or dipthongs and also as weak consonants.

The following table shows the various forms of these letters according to whether the letter is isolated, initial, medial or final.

Care has to be taken to distinguish letters which are similar to each other in form and differ in discritical pionts or dots.

Name of the Letter and Transcription			Isolated Form	Final Letter	Medial Letter	Initial Letter
⇩			⇩	⇩	⇩	⇩
*	ألف	'alif **a**	أ	أ	ـأ	أ
	باء	bā' **b**	ب	ـب	ـبـ	بـ
	تاء	tā' **t**	ت	ـت	ـتـ	تـ
	ثاء	thā' **th**	ث	ـث	ـثـ	ثـ
	جيم	jīm **j**	ج	ـج	ـجـ	جـ
	حاء	ḥā' **ḥ**	ح	ـح	ـحـ	حـ
	خاء	khā' **kh**	خ	ـخ	ـخـ	خـ
	دال	dāl **d**	د	ـد	ـد	د
	ذال	dhāl **dh**	ذ	ـذ	ـذ	ذ
	راء	rā' **r**	ر	ـر	ـر	ر

* In fact, this is a hamzah (ء) and the 'alif (أ) is just a seat for it.
For more details, see under the Hamzah, pp. 19-20.

Name of the Letter and Transcription			Isolated Form	Final Letter	Medial Letter	Initial Letter
زاي	zā' zāy	z	ز	ـز	ـزـ	ز
سين	sīn	s	س	ـس	ـسـ	سـ
شين	shīn	sh	ش	ـش	ـشـ	شـ
صاد	ṣād	ṣ	ص	ـص	ـصـ	صـ
ضاد	ḍād	ḍ	ض	ـض	ـضـ	ضـ
طاء	ṭā'	ṭ	ط	ـط	ـطـ	طـ
ظاء	ẓā'	ẓ	ظ	ـظ	ـظـ	ظـ
عين	'ayn	'	ع	ـع	ـعـ	عـ
غين	ghayn	gh	غ	ـغ	ـغـ	غـ
فاء	fā'	f	ف	ـف	ـفـ	فـ

Name of the Letter and Transcription			Isolated Form	Final Letter	Medial Letter	Initial Letter
قاف	qāf	q	ق	ـق	ـقـ	قـ
كاف	kāf	k	ك	ـك	ـكـ	كـ
لام	lām	l	ل	ـل	ـلـ	لـ
ميم	mīm	m	م	ـم	ـمـ	مـ
نون	nūn	n	ن	ـن	ـنـ	نـ
هاء	hā'	h	ه	ـه	ـهـ	هـ
واو	wāw	w	و	ـو	ـو	و
ياء	yā'	y	ي	ـي	ـيـ	يـ

Most of the Arabic letters are connectors; that is, that they connect both to a preceding and a following letter. However, there are six letters that do not connect to a following letter, though they connect to preceding letters. Let us call them 'non-connectors', and they are :

Letter	Example	Letter	Example	Letter	Example
ا	قَالَ	ذ	مَذْمُومٌ	ز	تَزْكِيةٌ
د	مَعْدُودَاتُ	ر	ألرَّحْمٰنُ	و	مَوْعُودٌ

VOWELS

فَتْحَة *fatḥah*	signed as ◌َ on top of a letter and pronounced as **a** in "**above**"
كَسْرَة *kasrah*	signed as ◌ِ under a letter and pronounced as **i** in "**if**"
ضَمَّة *ḍammah*	signed as ◌ُ on top of a letter and pronounced as **u** in "**put**"

سُكُون *sukūn*	signed as ◌ْ or ◌ْ on top of a letter is a stop or stress; it indicates that the consonant is vowelless.

For the transcription (a) stands for *fatḥah* (i) for *kasrah* and (u) for *ḍammah*.

Long vowels or dipthongs are three :

Name of the letter		Transliteration Symbols
أَلِف	'*alif*	**ā**
وَاو	*wāw*	**ū**
يَاء	*yā'*	**ī**

Examples : **Note :** For 'nunation' at the end of some of these examples, see chapter 1.

عَالِـمٌ	'ālimun; a learned man.
كَاتِبٌ	kātibun; a writer.
نَائِمٌ	nā'imun; sleeping one.
بَعِيدٌ	ba'idun; far
سَعِيدٌ	sa'idun; a male proper name; also an adjective meaning "happy"
يَعُودُ	ya'ūdu (3rd Pers. Imperfect); he returns or will return.
مَمْنُونٌ	mamnūn (Part Passive); an obliged one; thankful; indebted.
يَكُونُ	yakūnu (Imperfect, 3rd Pers.); he is or will be.

Students should carefully note all the signs on the following letters.

ثْ	ثُ	ثِ	ثَ
جْ	جُ	جِ	جَ
دْ	دُ	دِ	دَ
رْ	رُ	رِ	رَ
شْ	شُ	شِ	شَ

EXERCISE

أرض	أب	أخ	أ

إله	إلى	إذا	إِ

أسرة	أخت	أم	اُ

اِهدأ	امـلأ	إبـدأ	أْ

كتبَ	بَاب	بَدأ	بَ

بِسم	كتابِي	أبِي	بِ

كَتَبُوا	بُشرىٰ	أبُوك	بُ

اذهبْ	اكتبْ	اركـبْ	بْ

نَبَتَ	تَعِبَ	تَرَكَ	تَ

تِمْسَاح	بِنْتِي	بَيْتِي	تِ

تُفَّاح	فَهِمْتُ	أَكَلْتُ	تُ

رَجَعَتْ	قَالَتْ	ذَهَبَتْ	تْ

The Hamzah ألـهَـمْـزَة

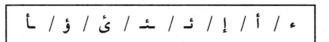

أَ / إ / أ / ئَ / ـئـ / ئ / ؤ / أَ / ء

The *hamzah,* represented by the symbol (ء) , is a separate consonant that should not be mixed up with the *'alif* (ا).

As a sound, the *hamzah* is a glottal stop that has no single letter equivalent in most other languages. It is produced by blocking off the air stream at the top of the windpipe, and then releasing it.

At the beginning of a word, *'alif* (ا) is always used as a chair for the *hamzah.* It the following vowel is ‗ *(kasra),* the *hamzah* is written then under *'alif*; thus إ . Otherwise, the *hamzah* is written over *'alif*; thus أ or أ .

Examples :

أَرْضٌ	(**'arḍun**) = earth.
أُخْتٌ	(**'ukhtun**) = a sister.
إِبْنٌ	(**'ibnun**) = a son.

In addition, however, one of the other weak letters, *yā'* (ى , without dots, known also as *nabrah* / نَـبْرَة) and *wāw* (و), may be the chair. Further, *hamzah* sometimes occurs without a chair and is then written over the line·connecting the letters, on either side of it or by itself.

The rules governing the chair of the *hamzah* may be summarized as follows :

1. At the beginning of a word the chair is always *alif* (ا) .

2. In the middle of a word :

    (a) If only one of the vowels ﹷ or ﹹ or ﹻ (or two identical vowels) is contiguous to the *hamzah* (i.e. precedes or is borne by it) the chair will be, respectively, ى (actually ـ or ﹻ) or و or ا .

    Example :

رَئِيسٌ	بِئْرٌ
رَؤُوفٌ	يُؤْمِنُ
فَأْرٌ	يَسْأَلُ

    (b) If two different vowels are contiguous to the *hamzah,* the vowel which determines the chair (in accordance with the correspondence in 1, 2a) is governed by the following order of preference :

    ﹻ ﹹ ﹷ (e.g. سَئِمَ سُؤَالٌ سُئِلَ); in the first example the contiguous vowels are ﹹ and ﹻ , then the ﹻ takes preference, and therefore the chair is ى (actually ـ) .

    (c) If the *hamzah* is preceded by a long vowel and bears ﹷ , it has no chair (e.g. مُرُوءَة سَاءَلَ). If, however, the *hamzah* is preceded by a long vowel and bears ﹻ or ﹹ , the chair usually corresponds to the vowel the *hamzah* bears (e.g. تَسَاؤُلٌ سَائِلٌ).

(3) At the end of a word :

(a) The preceding vowel determines the chair (in accordance
with the correspondence given in 1, 2a).

Example :

بَـدَأ	قَـرَأ
بَطُؤ	دَفُؤ
قُـرِئ	فَتِئ

(b) If there is no preceding short vowel (i.e. if there is "sukūn"
or a long vowel), there is no chair (e.g. شَيْءٌ بَطِيءٌ).

(c) A *hamzah*, occuring at the end of a word after a long 'alif,
is written on the line after the 'alif, e.g.

هَـوَاء ، سَمَـاء ، حَـوَّاء ، بَـطْحَـاء

Exercise

Copy the following, putting in the correct chair for the *hamzah;*
join letters as required :

	وَءَدَ		ءْكْرَمَ		ءَكَلَ
	رَءَسٌ		إِسْمٌ		ءَخَذَ
	رَءِيسٌ		سَـءَلَ		ءَمِنَ
	شَاطِىء		يَـءِس		نَشَءَ
	سَيَمَاء		فُـءَاد		هَدَءَ
	لُـءْلُـء		قَرَءَ		مَلَءَ
	بُـءْسٌ		بِـءْر		مُـءْمِنٌ

Exercise

Recite and compare the following sets of words. Notice that in the list to your right the *'alif* is a long vowel; in the list to your left, it is just a seat for the *hamzah* ·

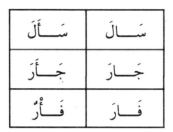

سَـــأَلَ	سَـــالَ
جَـــأَرَ	جَـــارَ
فَـــأْرُ	فَـــارَ

هَمْـزَةُ ٱلْقَطْعِ وَ هَمْـزَةُ ٱلْـوَصْلِ

Hamẓat-ul-qaṭ'i wa hamẓat-ul-waṣli

I. *Hamẓat-ul-qaṭ'i* is the ordinary *hamzah* which is always pronounced and written at the beginning of a word initiating a sequence of sounds. The symbol for this *hamzah* is the (ء) on top or under an *alif*, e.g.

أَسْمِعْ بِـهِ وَ أَبْصِرْ .

أَبْشِرُوا بِـٱلْـجَـنَّـةِ .

إِذَا جَـاءَ نَصْرُ الله وَٱلْـفَـتْـحِ .

II. The definite article in Arabic is respresented by the sound *'al;* (أَلْ) which is a combination of a *hamzah* on top of the *'alif* and a *lām*, (ل) i.e. ل + أ . If the *hamzah* of the definite article is at the beginning of a word to initiate a sequence of sounds, then this is a *hamzat-ul-qaṭ'i* which is fully pronounced as well as written.

However, if a word having the definite article أَلـ is preceded by other sounds, then the *hamzah* of the أَلـ is elided (i.e. not fully pronounced), and is written then without the (ء) or with a special symbol, called *hamzat-ul-waṣl*, which is (ٓ) on top of the *'alif;* thus آ .

Examine the following example :

| أَلْـقُرْآنُ يَـهْـدِي إلى آلـخَـيْـرِ | The Qur'ān guides to the goods. |

The above example contains a *hamzat-ul-qaṭ'* in the word أَلْـقُرْآنُ and a *hamzat-ul-waṣl* in the word آلـخَـيْـرِ .

The following example (from the Holy Qur'ān) contains several illustrations of *hamzat-ul-waṣl :*

| هُوَ آللهُ آلـخَالِقُ آلبَـارِئُ آلـمُصَوّرُ لَهُ آلأَسْمَـاءُ آلحُسْنَى | He is Allah, the Creator, the Shaper out of naught, the Fashioner, His are the most beautiful names. |
| يُسَبِّحُ لَـهُ مَا فِي آلسَّمٰواتِ وَآلأَرْضِ وَهُوَ آلـعَزِيـزُ آلـحَكِيمُ . | All that is in the heavens and the earth glorifieth Him and He is the Mighty, the Wise. (59 : 24) |

EXERCISE

The Nunation *(Tanween)*

See Chapter 1

أُ	اٍ إ	أً
مَبْدَأً	مَبْدَإٍ	مَبْدَأً

أ

بُ	بٍ بِ	بًا
بَابٌ	بَابٍ	بَابًا

ب

جُ	جٍ جِ	جًا
زُجَاجٌ	زُجَاجٍ	زُجَاجًا

ج

24

٢٤

SHADDAH

Shaddah is a sound of double consonant, e.g in English words. such as i**rr**egular or i**nn**ocent etc. but in Arabic one letter is not written twice, it is written single with a mark of *Shaddah*, above the letter, that means this letter should be pronounced twice, e.g. مَرَّ *marra*, instead of writing مَرْرَ or قَلَّ *qalla*, instead of writing قَلْلَ This type of verbs have the appearance of being biliteral, e.g. حَجَّ *hajja*, جَرَّ *jarra*, مَرَّ *marra*, etc.

The following table should be carefully exercised by the students :

بُّ	بِّ	بَّ	بَ
رَبُّهُ	رَبِّي	رَبَّكَ	

لُّ	لِّ	لَّ	لَ
يَقِلُّ	مُعَلِّمٌ	عَلَّمَ	

نُّ	نِّ	نَّ	نَ
يَرِنُّ	إِنِّي	إِنَّهُ	

MADDAH

آ

If a *hamzah*, vowelled with *fathah*, and followed by the long vowel; *'alif* (the hamzated *fathah*) is dropped in writing and the long vowel *'alif* is written over the *'alif* horizontally as آ *aa*, this sign is called *Maddah*.

Examples : قُرآن instead of writing قُرأان , or رآه instead of رأاه .

EXERCISE

Practice the pronunciation of the following words which contain *maddah* in different positions :

آثَارٌ	آلافٌ	تَآمَنَ	قَرَآ	أْلآنَ	آلآمُ	آمَالٌ	آدَمُ
آمَنَ	آبٌ	آتِي	ألآتِي	آبَاءُ	آبَارٌ	آبَادٌ	آبَدِ

The Dagger 'Alif

In a few very common words the long vowel *aa* (ــ) is represented not with the letter *'alif* after the consonant, but with the sign ــ written over the **consonant**. This sign is a short vertical stroke with the appearance of a small *'alif*.

Examples :

هٰذا	هٰذِهِ	ألله	ذٰلِكَ	هٰؤُلاءِ
أَلرَّحْمٰن	ألسَّمٰوات	إِبْرٰاهِيمُ	لٰكِنَّ	إِسْمٰعِيلُ

This dagger *'alif* is usually omitted in unvowelled texts.

SOME IMPORTANT RULES OF ARABIC CHARACTERS

I. أَلتَّاءُ آلـمَرْبُوطَـةُ *at-Tā'-ul-Marbūṭah* (ـة ، ة) :

When we introduced the Arabic characters, we learned that
the third letter was تَاء *(Tā')*, written in its terminal form
as ـت . We must add now that the original form of *tā'* is called
at-Tā'-ul-Maftūḥah to distinguish it from the other form of *tā'*
which we are introducing now.

The character ة or ـة (called in Arabic *at-Tā'-ul-Marbūṭah*
'tied t') serves a double function. Phonologically, it represents the sound *t*, exactly the same sound as the one represented
by ت .

Examples :

أَلـجَنَّـةُ	*'al-Jannatu*	The Paradise
مَـلِكَـةٌ	*malikatun*	Queen
فَـتَاةٌ	*fatātun*	Girl
طَـالِبَـةٌ	*ṭālibatun*	Female student

Grammatically, it mostly (but not always) indicates a
feminine gender in the noun or adjective in which it appears
as illustrated by the examples above.

There are some additional points to be noted about
'at-Tā'-ul-Marbūṭah:

1. It occurs only as the last consonant of a word. If a suffix in-
   volving additional letters is added to such a word, the ة
   is changed to ت .

Examples :

مَلِكَةٌ	*malikatun*	'queen'
مَلِكَتُهُمْ	*malikatuhum*	'their queen'

فَتَاةٌ	*fatātun*	'girl'
فَتَاتُهُ	*fatātuhu*	'his girl'

2. It is always preceded by either the short vowel ﹷ *a* or, in much smaller number of words by the long vowel ا *ā* as illustrated earlier.

3. The *'alif* which is normally written with the accusative nunation is not written after ة ; thus : مَلِكَةً *malikatan* and جَنَّةً *jannatan*.

4. The pausal form of ة at the end of a sentence will result in pronouncing it as the sound ه hā' (26th letter). Thus the pause form of الْجَنَّةُ *al-jannatu* is *al-jannah*.

Study the expanded following examples :

Full Form		Pause Form
مَلِكَةٌ	*malikatun*	
مَلِكَةً	*malikatan*	*malikah*
مَلِكَةٍ	*malikatin*	

28   ٢٨

II. الحُرُوفُ ٱلْقَمَرِيَّة ’al-ḥurūfush shamsiyyah and الحُرُوفُ ٱلشَّمْسِيَّة ’al-ḥurūful qamariyyah

The Definite Article :
The Sun Letters and The Moon Letters :

In relation to the pronunciation of the consonants when preceded by the Definite Article (ال) *al*, Arabic letters are divided into two groups: 1) Sun Letters, and 2) Moon Letters.

When we introduce the Definite Article (ال) *al* to a noun starting with a Sun Letter we do not pronounce the letter (ل) *lām* of the Definite Article; this *lām* is assimilated into the first letter of the noun and thus this first letter is doubled and consequently written with a *shaddah* (ـّ) sign.

On the other hand, if a noun starts with a Moon Letter, the *lām* (ل) of the Definite Article is fully pronounced and there is no further modification in relation to the pronunciation of the first letter of the defined noun.

Sun Letters الحُرُوفُ ٱلشَّمْسِيَّة ’al-ḥurūfush shamsiyyah

ألشَّمْسُ	شَمْسٌ	ش	ألتُّوتُ	تُوتٌ	ت
ألصَّيْفُ	صَيْفٌ	ص	ألثَّانِي	ثَانِي	ث
ألضَّرْبُ	ضَرْبٌ	ض	ألدَّارُ	دَارٌ	د
ألطَّيْرُ	طَيْرٌ	ط	ألذَّنْبُ	ذَنْبٌ	ذ
ألظُّهْرُ	ظُهْرٌ	ظ	ألرَّسُولُ	رَسُولٌ	ر
أللَّيْلُ	لَيْلٌ	ل	ألزَّيْتُ	زَيْتٌ	ز
ألنَّهَارُ	نَهَارٌ	ن	ألسَّلَامُ	سَلَامٌ	س

Moon Letters اَلْحُرُوفُ ٱلْقَمَرِيَّةُ *al-ḥurūful qamariyyah*

أَلْفِيلُ	فِيلٌ	ف	ٱلْأَمِيرُ	أَمِيرٌ	ء
أَلْقَمَرُ	قَمَرٌ	ق	ٱلْبِنْتُ	بِنْتٌ	ب
أَلْكَلْبُ	كَلْبٌ	ك	ٱلْجَمَلُ	جَمَلٌ	ج
أَلْمَسَاءُ	مَسَاءٌ	م	ٱلْحِمَارُ	حِمَارٌ	ح
أَلْهَوَاءُ	هَوَاءٌ	هـ	ٱلْخَيْرُ	خَيْرٌ	خ
أَلْوَلَدُ	وَلَدٌ	و	ٱلْعَيْنُ	عَيْنٌ	ع
أَلْيَمِينُ	يَمِينٌ	ي	ٱلْغَرْبُ	غَرْبٌ	غ

III. *'Al-Alif-ul-Maqṣūratu* أَلْأَلِفُ ٱلْمَقْصُورَةُ

In a considerable number of Arabic words, a final long vowel (ـا) *ā* is represented not by the usual *'alif*, but by a special symbol ى called أَلْأَلِفُ ٱلْمَقْصُورَةُ *'al-'alif-ul-maqṣūrah* (shortened *'alif*). It has the shape of the letter ي *yā'* but without the two dots.

Examples :

قَضَىٰ	مُوسَىٰ	يَحْيَىٰ	هُدَىٰ

Three points may be particularly noted about ى :

1. The long *ā* sound represented by ى is exactly the same sound as that represented by the regular *'alif*, thus no new pronunciation feature is involved.

2. In the classical Arabic writing system, especially that of the Qur'ān, the ى appears with a short vertical stroke on top of it as shown in the four examples above. In the

modern printing system, however, this short vertical stroke is dropped.

3. The ى occurs only as the last letter of a word; if a suffix is added to such a word the ى is changed to ١.

Contrast :

هُـدَى	hudā	right guidance.
هُـدَانَا	hudānā	our right guidance.

بَـنَى	banā	he built.
بَـنَاهُ	banāhu	he built it.

Exercise

قَـضَى	سَعَى	رَأَى	إِلَى	عَـلَى	مَـتى
أَلْقُـرَى	هُـدَى	لَـيْلَى	يَـحْيَى	مُـوسَى	رَوَى
أَلأُوَلَى	إِسْتَوْلَى	إِسْتَوَى	إِنْـبَرَى	رَمَى	نَـدَى

CHAPTER 1

THE NOUN AND THE ARTICLE

1. The Noun :

مُحَمَّد Mohammad, حَامِد Ḥāmid, مَحْمُود Maḥmūd, بَشِير Bashīr, نَاصِر Nāṣir, and خَالِد Khālid are the names of persons. They are called Proper Nouns.

In a formal language this type of name is pronounced with a suffix of a **nūn** sound. Thus: The word 'Mohammad' will be pronounced as مُحَمَّدٌ Muḥammad**un** and :

حَامِد	Ḥāmid	as	حَامِدٌ	Ḥāmid**un**
مَحْمُود	Maḥmūd	as	مَحْمُودٌ	Maḥmūd**un**
بَشِير	Bashīr	as	بَشِيرٌ	Bashīr**un**
نَاصِر	Nāṣir	as	نَاصِرٌ	Nāṣir**un**
خَالِد	Khālid	as	خَالِدٌ	Khālid**un**

The **nūn** sound, say "Nunization" is marked here as "un"; it may be changed to "in" or "an" according to the noun in the construction of a sentence as will be explained later.

Common nouns such as شَجَر Shajar (tree), حَجَر Hajar (stone), تُفَّاح Tuffāḥ (apple), بَيْت Bait (house), رَبّ Rabb (Lord), رَسُول Rasūl (messenger), are also subject to the nunization, unless the definite أل ('al) is prefixed. In case a word is made a proper noun through prefixing أل ('al), The nunization will be removed. Compare :

شَجَرٌ	shajarun	as	الشَّجَرُ	'ashshajaru
حَجَرٌ	hajarun	as	الْحَجَرُ	'alhajaru
تُفَّاحٌ	tuffāhun	as	التُّفَّاحُ	'attuffāhu
بَيْتٌ	baitun	as	البَيْتُ	'albaitu
كِتَابٌ	kitābun	as	الكِتَابُ	'alkitābu

2. The Article :

Arabic has only one definite article to turn a common noun into a proper one, i.e. الـ ('al) as it is illustrated above. The indefiniteness of a common noun is indicated by **nunization.** Thus تُفَّاحٌ tuffā**h**un means any apple, while التُّفَّاحُ'attuffāhu means a particular apple. The informal usage of noun is free from nunization. Also it occurs only on a word of Arabic origin. Thus a non-Arabic word or dual or plural will not be suffixed with **nūn** sound.

3. Gender :

Arabic has two genders, i.e. masculine and feminine. There is no common gender in this language as in English.

A common sign of a feminine noun is ة (tā') that is to be suffixed to the final letter of a noun, e.g.

عَاقِلٌ	'āqilun	a wise man	Masc.
عَاقِلَةٌ	'āqilatun	a wise woman	Fem.
نَافِعٌ	nāfi'un	useful person or thing	Masc.
نَافِعَةٌ	nāfi'atun	a useful woman or thing	Fem.
عَالِمٌ	'ālimun	a man of knowledge	Masc.
عَالِمَةٌ	'ālimatun	a woman of knowledge	Fem.
مَحْمُودٌ	maḥmūdun	a praised person	Masc.
مَحْمُودَةٌ	maḥmūdatun	a praised person	Fem.

This ة (tā') of feminine gender is changed into a ه (hā') sound in speech; also in formal language when it occurs at the end of a sentence e.g. :

كَانَتْ ضَرْبَةً قَاضِيَه	kānat ḍarbatan qāḍiyah	it was a decisive stroke.

Example from the Holy Qur'ān :

أُدْخُلُوا فِي السِّلْمِ كَافَه	'udkhulū fis silmi kāffah	(People !) Enter in peace all of you. (2-208)

The feminine gender nouns كَافَه (kāffah) and قَاضِيَه (qāḍiyah) were كَافَّةً (kāffatan) and قَاضِيَةً (qāḍiyatan) respectively, but their ة (tā') has been changed to ه (hā') because they occurred at the end of sentence.

4. Numbers :

Apart from singular and plural numbers which is common to all languages, Arabic has an additional number, between singular and plural that is 'the dual' for two, e.g.

Singular	Dual	Plural
مُسْلِمٌ *Muslimun*	مُسْلِمَان *Muslimāni*	مُسْلِمُونَ *Muslimūna*
كَاتِبٌ *Kātibun*	كَاتِبَان *Kātibāni*	كَاتِبُونَ *Kātibūna*
قَادِمٌ *Qādimun*	قَادِمَان *Qādimāni*	قَادِمُونَ *Qādimūna*

In case of a feminine gender the additional infixed vowel shows the number i.e. **'āni'** or **'ūna'**. This takes place after ة *(tā')* of feminine gender, thus :

Masculine	Feminine
مُسْلِمٌ *Muslimun*	مُسْلِمَةٌ *Muslimatun*
مُسْلِمَانِ *Muslimāni*	مُسْلِمَتَانِ *Muslimatāni*

But the plural مُسْلِمُونَ *(Muslimūna)* will be turned to مُسْلِمَاتٌ *(Muslimātun)* e.g. :

	Singular	Dual	Plural
Masc.	قَادِمٌ *Qādimun*	قَادِمَانِ *Qādimāni*	قَادِمُونَ *Qādimūna*
Fem.	قَادِمَةٌ *Qādimatun*	قَادِمَتَانِ *Qādimatāni*	قَادِمَاتٌ *Qādimātun*
Masc.	كَاتِبٌ *Kātibun*	كَاتِبَان *Kātibāni*	كَاتِبُونَ *Kātibūna*
Fem.	كَاتِبَةٌ *Kātibatun*	كَاتِبَتَانِ *Kātibatāni*	كَاتِبَاتٌ *Kātibātun*

EXERCISE

1. Write in Arabic and put 'nunization' accordingly :

   Khālid, Sharīf, Nāṣir, Ḥabīb, Rashīd, 'Alī, 'Ubaid, Karīm, 'Āliah, Ḥussain.

2. Write the following names with and without article الـ (al) :

دَارٌ Dārun	House	حُجْرَةٌ Hujratun	Room
أَرْضٌ 'Arḍun	Earth	بَيْتٌ Baitun	House
سَقْفٌ Saqfun	Roof	جِدَارٌ Jidārun	Wall
فِرْدَوْسٌ Firdawsun	Paradise	نَارٌ Nārun	Fire
نَافِعٌ Nāfi'un	useful one	سَمَاءٌ Samā'un	Heaven
رَسُولٌ Rasūlun	Messenger	قُرْآنٌ Qur'anun	Qur'ān
رَحِيمٌ Raḥīmun	Merciful	فَضْلٌ Faḍlun	Grace
رَافِعٌ Rāfi'un	The one who raise in esteem		

3. Give the dual number of the following nouns for both masculine and feminine :

   كَاتِبٌ ، شَاعِرٌ ، طَبِيبٌ ، طَبَّاخٌ ، نَجَّارٌ ، حَكِيمٌ

4. Mention the plural form of these :

   مُسْلِمٌ ، مُؤْمِنٌ ، عَاقِلٌ ، حَكِيمٌ ، شَهِيدٌ ، سَائِقٌ ، شَاعِرٌ ، خَطِيبٌ ، كَاتِبٌ

CHAPTER 2

THE SIMPLE NOMINATIVE SENTENCES

رَسُولٌ	*Rasūlun*	Messenger
وَاسِعٌ	*Wāsi'un*	Wide
رَبٌّ	*Rabbun*	Lord
خَلِيفَةٌ	*Khalīfatun*	Caliph
نَاضِجٌ	*Nāḍijun*	Ripe
حَكِيمٌ	*Ḥakīmun*	A wise man
كَرِيمٌ	*Karīmun*	A kind man, generous; also a male proper name
صَادِقٌ	*Ṣādiqun*	A true man
دِينٌ	*Dīnun*	Religion
لَذِيذٌ	*Ladhīdhun*	Delicious
شَاعِرٌ	*Shā'irun*	A poet

خَالِدٌ حَكِيمٌ	Khālid is a wise man.
بَشِيرٌ شَاعِرٌ	Bashīr is a poet.

مَحْمُودٌ عَالِمٌ	Maḥmūd is a learned man.
حَامِدٌ كَرِيمٌ	Ḥāmid is a kind man.
مُحَمَّدٌ رَسُولٌ	Muḥammad is a messenger.

1. These types of sentences are formed by two nouns. The first word of each sentence is a proper name (marked with 'un' Nunization) that needs no article الـ ('al). The second word which is called the predicate, is a common noun. To form such sentences you have only to 'nunize' the last letters of both words and remove « is, a, an » of English construction. Thus if you want to translate :

Ḥāfiẓ is a poet. & 'Alī is a writer.

a) Put the Arabic word شَاعِرٌ for poet, (the common noun) and كَاتِبٌ for writer (the common noun).

b) Nunize the endings of each word so that will be :

حَافِظٌ شَاعِرٌ	Ḥāfiẓun Shāʿirun.
عَلِيٌّ كَاتِبٌ	ʿAliyyun Kātibun.

2. In case the first word (the subject of the sentence) is not a proper noun, the article الـ ('al) will be prefixed while the second word will remain 'nunized', thus :

ألقُرآنُ كِتَابٌ	'al-Qur'ānu kitābun	Qur'ān is a book.
ألإسْلامُ دِيْنٌ	'al-Islāmu dīnun	Islam is a religion.
ألرَّسُولُ صَادِقٌ	'ar-Rasūlu ṣādiqun	The Messenger is a true man.

There should be an agreement in number and gender between subject and predicate, i.e. If a subject is a feminine, dual or plural, the predicate should be the same accordingly.

EXAMPLES :

Singular Masculine

سَعِيدٌ عَالِمٌ	Sa'īdun 'ālimun	Sa'īd (A proper name) is a learned man.
الطَّالِبُ مُجْتَهِدٌ	'at-Ṭālibu mujtahidun	The student is a hard worker.

Singular Feminine

سَعِيدَةُ عَالِمَةٌ	Sa'īdatu 'ālimatun	Sa'īdah (A proper name) is a learned woman.
الطَّالِبَةُ مُجْتَهِدَةٌ	Attālibatu mujtahidatun	The student (Female) is a hard worker.

A female proper name does not accept nunation as shown above.

Dual Masculine

ألرَّجُلَانِ مُؤْمِنَانِ	'ar-Rajulāni mu'mināni	The (two) men are believers.

Dual Feminine

ألطَّالِبَتَانِ مُجْتَهِدَتَانِ	'at-Ṭālibatāni mujtahidatāni	The (two female) students are hard workers.

Plural Masculine

ألرِّجَالُ مُؤْمِنُونَ	'ar-Rijālu mu'minūna	The men are believers.

Plural Feminine

ألطَّالِبَاتُ مُجْتَهِدَاتٌ	'at-Ṭalibātu mujtahidātu	The (female) students are hard workers.

RULES :

1. A complete sentece formed by nouns i.e. a simple Nominal sentence is called in Arabic جُمْلَةٌ إِسْمِيَّةٌ *Jumlatun 'Ismiyyatun* or ألْجُمْلَةُ الإِسْمِيَّةُ *'al-Jumlatul 'Ismiyyatu.*

   It has مُبْتَدَأ *Mubtada'un* (Subject) and خَبَرٌ *Khabarun* (Predicate).

2. Predicate should agree with the subject in number and gender.

EXERCISE

1. **Translate into English,** using as reference the vocabulary introduced in this chapter as well as the vocabulary list at the end of this chapter.

اللهُ رَبٌّ ، مُحَمَّدٌ رَسُولٌ ، الْقُرْآنُ كِتَابٌ ، ألْجَنَّةُ حَقٌّ ، ألنَّارُ حَقٌّ ،

ألدِّيْنُ حَقٌّ ، ألدُّنْيَا فَانِيَةٌ ، الآخِرَةُ بَاقِيَةٌ ، ألْخُلَفَاءُ صَادِقُونَ ،

ألنِّسَاءُ مُؤْمِنَاتٌ ، ألْمَرْأَةُ تَقِيَّةٌ ، ألْبِنْتُ مُؤَدَّبَةٌ ، ألرِّسَالَةُ سَمَاوِيَّةٌ ،

ألْكَعْبَةُ قِبْلَةٌ ، ألْعِلْمُ نُورٌ ، ألْجَهْلُ ظَلاَمٌ ، ألْحَدِيثُ صَحِيحٌ ،

أَلْجَـوَابُ كَامِـلٌ ، أَلْخَـطِيبُ وَاعِظٌ ، أَلْعَبْدُ مُطِيعٌ ، أَلْحُكُومَةُ إِسْلَامِيَّةٌ ،

أَلشَّرِيعَةُ نَافِعَةٌ ، أَلرِّجَالُ قَـوَّامُونَ ، أَلْجَنَّتَانِ عَالِيَتَانِ ، أَلْبَابَانِ وَاسِعَانِ ،

أَلْكَلِمَتَانِ خَفِيفَتَانِ ، أَلْمُؤْمِنَاتُ قَانِـتَاتٌ ، أَلْبَنَاتُ حَافِظَاتٌ .

2. **Translate into Arabic :**

Ḥāmid is a wise man.

The physician is clever.

The translation is excellent.

Fāṭimah is a learned (woman).

The boy is tall.

Both of the two boys are successful.

Both of the two travellers are coming.

The wealth is gone   (ذَاهِبَـةٌ) .

Houses are large.

The women believers are fortunate.

Ḥāfiẓ is a poet.

Both of the two friends are close to each other.   use: (قَرِيـبَانِ)

Rashīd is a traveller.

The surgeon is an expert.

The work is useful.

The house is wide.

The girl is small.

Ḥabīb is a surgeon.

The faith is firm.   (ثَابِت)

Both of the two (female) students are hard workers.

The streets are narrow.

The way is clean.

Both of the two sisters are God-fearing.   (تَقِيَّتَانِ)

3. (a) Form dual forms of the following words :

مُؤَدَّبَةٌ	أَلْمَرْأَةُ	أَلْخَلِيفَةُ	أَلْجَنَّةُ
أَلْخَطِيبُ	أَلْجَوَابُ	أَلْحَدِيثُ	سَمَاوِيَّةٌ

(b) Write the singular of the following words :

أَلْخُلَفَاءُ	أَلنِّسَاءُ	أَلْبَابَانِ	أَلْمُؤْمِنَاتُ	أَلرِّجَالُ
أَلْقَانِتَاتُ	أَلرَّاشِدُونَ	أَلْجَنَّاتُ	أَلْخُطَبَاءُ	أَلْعِبَادُ

(c) Write the plurals of the following words :

أَلْجِدَارُ	ثَابِتٌ	صَادِقٌ	أَلْكِتَابُ
أَلْعَبْدُ	أَلْقَلَمُ	أَلْبَيْتُ	أَلـدَّارُ

4. Make ten sentences from the following words :

أَلْلَيْلُ . . .	أَلصَّبَاحُ . . .	صَادِقَةُ . . .	أَحْمَد . . .
أَلنَّهَارُ . . .	أَلْمَسَاءُ . . .	أَلْأُخْتُ . . .	شَاعِرٌ . . .

VOCABULARY

أَلْجَنَّةُ	heaven
حَــقُّ	fact, true
أَلْآخِـرَةُ	the Hereafter
فَانِيَـةٌ / فَانٍ	going, gone
أَلْخُلَـفَاءُ	Caliphs
أَلنِّسَاءُ	women
سَمَاوِيَّةٌ / سَمَاوِيٌّ	heavenly
أَلْعِلْمُ	wisdom, knowledge
ظَـلَامٌ	darkness
أَلْـوَلَـدُ	the boy
صَحِيحٌ	right, correct
كَامِـلٌ	complete
وَاعِـظٌ	advisor, preacher
مُطِـيعٌ	obedient
أَلشَّرِيعَـةُ	The Islamic law

أَلنَّارُ	The Hell, the fire
أَلدُّنْيَا	the world
بَاقِيَةٌ / بَاقٍ	remaining
أَلرِّسَالَةُ	the message
خَلِيفَةٌ	Caliph
أَلْمَرْأَةُ	the woman
أَلْقِبْلَةُ	the direction of prayers
نُورٌ	light
أَلْبِنْتُ	the girl
أَلْحَدِيثُ	the talk
أَلْجَوَابُ	the answer
أَلْخَطِيبُ	the speaker
أَلْعَبْدُ	the slave or servant of Allah; the worshiper
أَلْحُكُومَةُ	the government

CHAPTER 3

THE POSSESSIVE CASE OR GENETIVE

'Al-'Iḍāfatu   ألإضَافَـــة

God's messenger. Prophet's order. Girl's school. Ḥāmid's house. Khālid's book. Men's souls. In English, this kind of sentence is formed with nouns by adding a simple apostrophe (s) (---'s) to the singular and the irregular plurals (e.g. men's souls). To form this kind of sentence in Arabic we have to follow the rules below :

1. (a) Replace the English words by the Arabic words; e.g. :

   God = أَلله 'Allāhu'   Messenger = رَسُولٌ Rasūlun

   Girl = بِنْتٌ Bintun   Prophet = نَبِيٌّ Nabiyyun

   Men = بَشَرٌ Basharun   or   نَاسٌ nāsun

   (b) Interchange the place of words i.e. the word which occurs first in English, put it later and vice versa, thus God's messenger in Arabic will be : رَسُولُ / أَلله

   (c) Omit the apostrophe (s). Thus God's messenger will become in Arabic "messenger God" e.g. : رَسُــولُ اللهِ (Rasūlullāhi) and Prophet's order will be read : "order prophet" أَمْـرُ النَّبِيِّ ('amrunnabiyyi).

   (d) Put a short 'u' vowel sign (ـُ) on the final letter of the first vowel e.g. in above sentences :

   Rasūlullāhi رَسُولُ اللهِ . The Lām of رَسُول is the point of

*. _dammah_ (ضَمَّة)

(e) Put a short ' i ' vowel sign (—) under the final letter of the second name, that is _hā'_ in the word "Allāh" of this sentence. Thus _Rasūlullahi_ رَسُـولُ الله would be exact translation of "God's messenger".

The second sentence is "Prophet's order", after applying the above process, it would be in Arabic : أَمْـرُ النَّبِــيِّ (_'amrunnabiyyi_).

Note :

The first noun is called مُضَاف (_mudāfun_). It will remain always as a common noun and in no case will take an article, but the second noun that is مُضَـافٌ إِلَـيْهِ (_mudāfun 'ilaihi_) should be proper noun or be particularized by الـ (_'al_) as shown above in نَبِيٌّ (_nabiyyun_) which is read أَلنَّبِـيُّ (_'annabiyyu_).

2. The other form of genitive in English is formed by using a particle 'of' between two nouns, e.g. House of Lords, Land of Peace, Field of activity, etc. In Arabic there is no particle of this kind. The rule mentioned above will be applied here too, but you need not interchange the places of nouns. Thus House of Lords will be rendered in Arabic.

دَارٌ = house,   الْأَمَـرَاءُ = lords :

---

* The final letter of each word is the point where vowel is changed according to the formation of a sentence. It is called إِعْـرَابْ _i'rāb_ (declension) that will be dealt with in chapter 22.

46   ٤٦

House of Lords	دَارُ الأُمَرَاءِ	*dārul'umarā'i*
Land of Peace	أَرْضُ السَّلَامِ	*arḍussalāmi*
Field of Activity	مَيْدَانُ النَّشَاطِ	*maidānunnishāṭi*

Examples from The Holy Qur'ān :

رَسُولُ الله	Allāh's messenger.
نَاقَةُ الله	Allāh's she-camel.
حَدِيثُ ٱلْجُنُودِ	The story of the hosts.
عَذَابُ ٱلْحَرِيقِ	The chastisement of burning.
حِزْبُ ٱلشَّيْطَانِ	The group of satan.
عَذَابُ ٱلنَّارِ	The chastisement of the Fire.
صَاحِبُ ٱلْحُوتِ	The companion of the fish.
يَوْمُ ٱلْفَصْلِ	The day of decision.
نَصْرُ الله	Allāh's help.
لَيْلَةُ ٱلْقَدْرِ	The Night of Power.
حَبُّ ٱلْحَصِيدِ	The grain of crops.
أَصْحَابُ ٱلسَّعِيرِ	The people of the Hell.

EXERCISE

1. **Translate into Arabic :**
   (Note : words in brackets are not to be followed in Arabic).

   (a) The teacher's son.   The merchant's shop.

   The girl's dress.   The boy's school.

   The house of Allāh.   The book of Islām.

   The door of the house.   The pen of the writer.

   Aḥmad's pen.   Ḥāmid's watch.

   The eyes of the bird.   The bird's eye.

   The wood of the chair.   The President's chair.

   (b) with the combination of chapter 11.

   The teacher's son is a student.

   (The) merchant's shop is (a) big (one).

   The girl's dress is fine.

   The boy's school is (a) famous (one).

   The pen of the writer is known.

   Allāh's book is the Qur'ān.

   The Messenger's tradition is the Sunnah.

   The King's order is to be obeyed.

   Ramaḍān's fasting is prescribed.

   The morning prayer is a must.

   Muḥammad is Allāh's Messenger.

   Qur'ān is Allāh's book.

2. Translate into English :

(a)
  أَصْحَابُ ٱلْيَمِينِ ،   يَوْمُ ٱلدِّينِ ،   حَدِيثُ ٱلرَّسُولِ ،

  سَوْطُ عَذَابٍ ،   أَصْحَابُ ٱلْكَهْفِ ،   أَصْحَابُ ٱلْأُخْدُودِ ،

  مِثْقَالُ ذَرَّةٍ ،   أَصْحَابُ ٱلْفِيلِ ،   شَرُّ ٱلْبَرِيَّةِ ،

  نَضْرَةُ ٱلنَّعِيمِ ،   عِمَارَةُ ٱلْمَسْجِدِ ،   حَدِيثُ ٱلْغَاشِيَةِ ،

  فَكُّ رَقَبَةٍ ،   نَكَالُ ٱلْآخِرَةِ ،   كِتَابُ ٱلْفُجَّارِ ،

    وَادِ ٱلنَّمْلِ ،   سِقَايَةُ ٱلْحَاجِّ ،

(b)
  يَوْمُ ٱلدِّينِ شَدِيدٌ ،   حَدِيثُ ٱلرَّسُولِ مَعْلُومٌ ،

  أَصْحَابُ ٱلْأُخْدُودِ مَيِّتُونَ ،   أَصْحَابُ ٱلْيَمِينِ مُسْلِمُونَ ،

  أَصْحَابُ ٱلْفِيلِ خَاسِرُونَ .   أَصْحَابُ ٱلْكَهْفِ شَبَابٌ ،

3. Compare the two sentences and mention the difference between them:

  عِمَارَةُ مَسْجِدٍ / عِمَارَةُ ٱلْمَسْجِدِ .   فَكُّ رَقَبَةٍ / فَكُّ ٱلرَّقَبَةِ .

  سَوْطُ عَذَابٍ / سَوْطُ ٱلْعَذَابِ .   كِتَابُ ٱلْفُجَّارِ / كِتَابُ فُجَّارٍ .

4. Correct the following sentences if there is any mistake :

  حَدِيثُ ٱلْآخِرَةِ مَعْلُومَةٌ ،   حَدِيثُ ٱلرَّسُولِ مَعْلُومٌ ،

  أَصْحَابُ ٱلْفِيلِ رِجَالٌ ،   سَوْطُ ٱلْعَذَابِ شَدِيدٌ ،

  ضَوْءُ ٱلْقَمَرِ مَطْلُوبٌ ،   شَمْسُ ٱلنَّهَارِ طَالِعٌ ،

  عَمُّ مَحْمُودٍ ذَاهِبَةٌ .   خَالَةُ حَمِيدٍ قَادِمٌ ،

VOCABULARY

	Singular	**Plural**
teacher	مُعَلِّمٌ *Muʿallimun*	*Muʿallimūna* مُعَلِّمُونَ
merchant	تَاجِرٌ *Tājirun*	*Tujjārun* تُجَّارٌ
girl	بِنْتٌ *Bintun*	*Banātun* بَنَاتٌ
boy	وَلَدٌ *Waladun*	*'Awlādun* أَوْلَادٌ
house	دَارٌ *Dārun*	*Diyārun, Dūrun* دُورٌ، دِيَارٌ
house	بَيْتٌ *Baytun*	*Buyūtun* بُيُوتٌ
book	كِتَابٌ *Kitābun*	*Kutubun* كُتُبٌ
door	بَابٌ *Bābun*	*'Abwābun* أَبْوَابٌ
pen	قَلَمٌ *Qalamun*	*'Aqlāmun* أَقْلَامٌ
writer	كَاتِبٌ *Kātibun*	*Kuttābun* كُتَّابٌ
watch	سَاعَةٌ *Sāʿatun*	*Sāʿātun* سَاعَاتٌ
eye	عَيْنٌ *ʿAynun*	*ʿUyūnun* عُيُونٌ
wood	خَشَبٌ *Khashabun*	*'Akhshābun* أَخْشَابٌ
chair	كُرْسِيٌّ *Kursiyyun*	*Karāsin* كَرَاسٍ
president	رَئِيسٌ *Ra'īsun*	*Ru'asā'u* رُؤَسَاءُ
student	طَالِبٌ *Ṭālibun*	*Ṭullābun* طُلَّابٌ
shop	دُكَّانٌ *Dukkānun*	*Dakākīnu* دَكَاكِيْنُ

	Singular		**Plural**	
king	Malikun	مَلِكٌ	Mulūkun	مُلُوكٌ
order	'Amrun	أَمْرٌ	'Awāmirun	أَوَامِرٌ
prescribed	Farḍun	فَرْضٌ	Furūḍun	فُرُوضٌ
obligatory	Wājibun	وَاجِبٌ	Wājibātun	وَاجِبَاتٌ
son	'Ibnun	إِبْنٌ	'Abnā'un Banūna	أَبْنَاءٌ ، بَنُونَ
companion	Sāhibun	صَاحِبٌ	'Ashābun	أَصْحَابٌ
wicked	Fājirun	فَاجِرٌ	Fujjārun	فُجَّارٌ

أَلـدِّيْنُ	the judgement, the religion	يَوْمٌ	a day
أَلْأُخْدُودُ	the trench	سَوْطٌ	a portion
عَذَابٌ	chastisement	شَـرٌّ	worst, evil
خَيْرٌ	best, good	أَلـبَرِيَّةُ	The creature
أَلْفِيلُ	the elephant	مِثْقَالٌ	atom's weight
أَلْغَاشِيَّةُ	overwhelming	عَمَارَةٌ	building
أَلْمَسْجِدُ	the mosque	نَضْرَةٌ	brightness
أَلنَّعِيمُ	the bliss	كِتَابٌ	the devine writ, a record, a book
نَكَالٌ	punishment (an example of punished one)		

فَــكُ	to make free	رَقَبَةٌ	neck
سِقَايَةُ	to give drink	أَلْحَاجُّ	the pilgrim
وَادٍ	valley	نَمْلٌ	ant
أَلتَّلاقِيُّ	the meeting	حَدِيثٌ	talk, story

CHAPTER 4
THE VERB

1. The Root System

Arabic verbs are mostly tri-literal, that is, they are bsed on roots of three consonants. Thus the basic meaning of the verb فَتَحَ which means "opening", is given by three consonants ف ت ح *f t ḥ*. The basic meaning of "writing" is given by three consonants ك ت ب *k t b*. The basic meaning of "helping" is expressed by three consonants ن ص ر *n ṣ r*. Thus, *kataba* means "he wrote or has written". كَتَبَ زَيْدٌ (*kataba Zaidun*) "Zaid has written" or "Zaid wrote". كَاتِبٌ (*kātibun*) "writer", مَكْتُوبٌ (*maktūbun*) "a letter", مَكْتَبٌ (*maktabun*) "an office or writing table". Similarly, نَصَرَ (*naṣra*) "he helped". نَصَرَ رَاشِدٌ (*naṣara Rāshidun*) "Rāshid helped", نَصَرَتْ فَاطِمَةُ (*naṣarat Fāṭimatu*) "Fāṭimah helped". نَاصِرٌ (*nāṣirun*) "helper", مَنْصُورٌ (*manṣūrun*) "one who has been helped" and so on. In an Arabic dictionary all words are derived from a root form (in English; infinitive verb, and in Persian and Urdu as well as Arabic مَصْدَر *maṣdar*). Thus you will find مِفْتَاحٌ (*miftāhun*) "a key or an opener", under the part of verb ف ت ح *f t ḥ* the basic meaning of which is "opening".

2. The Morpheme

(a) To indicate patterns of verbs, the grammarians use the three consonants of the verb فَعَلَ (*fa'ala*) "to do". The ف

of which represents the first radical, the ع of which represents the second radical and the ل the third. Thus in the verb كَتَبَ *k t b*, ك is ف radical, ت is ع radical and ب is the ل radical; in نَصَرَ (*n ṣ r*), ن is ف radical, ص is ع radical and ر is ل radical. You can also refer to these radicals by numbers as initial, middle and final radicals.

(b) In a simple tri-literal verb the first and third radicals are vowelled with *fatḥah* (a short "a" vowel sign : ﹷ) but the second radical may be vowelled with *fatḥah* or *kasrah* (a short "i" vowel sign : ﹻ) or with *ḍammah* (a short "u" vowel sign : ﹹ). Thus a verb كَتَبَ (*kataba*), نَصَرَ (*naṣara*), or فَتَحَ (*fataḥa*) may be symbolized as :

I. فَعَلَ *fa'ala* (i.e. CaCaCa)* as كَتَبَ (*kataba*) "he wrote", نَصَرَ (*naṣara*) 'he helped', فَتَحَ (*fataḥa*) "he opened".

II. فَعِلَ *fa'ila*, type (CaCiCa) as فَرِحَ (*fariḥa*) "he became glad", سَمِعَ (*sami'a*) "he heard", عَلِمَ (*'alima*) "he knew".

III. فَعُلَ *fa'ula*, type (CaCuCa) as شَرُفَ (*sharufa*) "he was or has been honoured", نَبُلَ (*nabula*) "he was or became noble", عَظُمَ (*'aẓuma*) "he was or became great".

---

* C = consonant,　a = a short vowel "a",　i = a short vowel "i",　u = a short vowel "u". In Arabic *fatḥah, kasrah* and *ḍammah* respectively.

3. Tenses

The main tenses of the Arabic verb are the perfect and the imperfect. The perfect denotes a completed action, often referring to the past, while the imperfect denotes an incomplete action, most often referring to the present or the future.

The conjugation of verb begins in Arabic with the third person, and the order for the persons in the conjugation is third, second, first.

The Arabic verb also has a dual-form for the second and third persons, (see chapter 1). As to the first person, it has no dual form.

4. Added-Form

There are also derived forms in which additions to the tri-literal root give different shades of meaning. These will be dealt with in chapter 16-18. Each root form makes certain stock patterns and produces its own particular modifications of the basic meaning of the root.

5. Modifications of the verb

The modified morphemes of the verb are produced by prefixing, suffixing, or infixing of the vowels or fixed pronouns. In perfect tense suffixes denote the number and the gender.

Masculine   3rd person

Singular	I	فَعَلَ	*fa'ala*	He did
Dual	II	فَعَلَا	*fa'alā*	They (two) did
Plural	III	فَعَلُوا	*fa'alū*	They (all) did

Feminine

Singular	IV	فَعَلَتْ	*fa'alat*	She did
Dual	V	فَعَلَتَا	*fa'alatā*	They (two Fem.) did
Plural	VI	فَعَلْنَ	*fa'alna*	They (all Fem.) did

Masculine   2rd person

Singular	VII	فَعَلْتَ	*fa'alta*	You (one) did
Dual	VIII & XI	فَعَلْتُمَا	*fa'altumā*	You (two) did (both Masc. & Fem.)
Plural	IX	فَعَلْتُمْ	*fa'altum*	You (all) did

Feminine

Singular	X	فَعَلْتِ	*fa'alti*	You (one Fem.) did
Plural	XII	فَعَلْتُنَّ	*fa'altunna*	You (all Fem.) did

Dual case is shown above.

Masculine & Feminine   1st person

Singular	XIII	فَعَلْتُ	*fa'altu*	I did
Plural	XIV	فَعَلْنَا	*fa'alnā*	We did

There is no dual in First Person.

On the same pattern any root of the tri-literal consonants can be formed. e.g. from نَصَرَ *(n ṣ r)* :

		3rd Person		2nd Person		1st Person
		Masculine	**Feminine**	**Masculine**	**Feminine**	**Masc. & Fem.**
Singular		*naṣara* نَصَرَ	*naṣarat* نَصَرَتْ	*naṣarta* نَصَرْتَ	*naṣarti* نَصَرْتِ	*naṣartu* نَصَرْتُ
Dual		*naṣarā* نَصَرَا	*naṣaratā* نَصَرَتَا	*naṣartumā* نَصَرْتُمَا	*naṣartumā* نَصَرْتُمَا	*naṣarnā* نَصَرْنَا
Plural		*naṣarū* نَصَرُوا	*naṣarna* نَصَرْنَ	*naṣartum* نَصَرْتُمْ	*naṣartunna* نَصَرْتُنَّ	

from لَمَسَ *(l m s)* :

		3rd Person		2nd Person		1st Person
		Masculine	**Feminine**	**Masculine**	**Feminine**	**Masc. & Fem.**
Singular		*lamasa* لَمَسَ	*lamasat* لَمَسَتْ	*lamasta* لَمَسْتَ	*lamasti* لَمَسْتِ	*lamastu* لَمَسْتُ
Dual		*lamasā* لَمَسَا	*lamasatā* لَمَسَتَا	*lamastumā* لَمَسْتُمَا	*lamastumā* لَمَسْتُمَا	*lamasnā* لَمَسْنَا
Plural		*lamasū* لَمَسُوا	*lamasna* لَمَسْنَ	*lamastum* لَمَسْتُمْ	*lamastunna* لَمَسْتُنَّ	

and so on. These verbal morphems of the Past perfect tense are formed by suffixing the vowels and fixed pronouns. They are : *"t"* in IV, *"tā"* in V, *"na"* in VI, *"ta"* in VII, *"tuma"* in VIII & XI, *"tum"* in IX, *"ti"* in X, *"tunna"* in XII, *"tu"* in XIII, and *"nā"* in XIV.

Note : For reference, see the "perfect verb conjugation chart" on page 66.

Examples from the Holy Qur'ān :

	Form I فَعَلَ

مَنْ فَعَلَ هٰـذَا بِآلِـهَتِـنَآ	21-59 : who **has done** this to our gods ?
كَيْفَ فَعَلَ رَبُّكَ	105-1 : How thy Lord **did**.
وَإِذْ أَخَـذَ اللهُ مِيثَاقَ ٱلنَّبِـيِّـيْنَ	3-81 : Recall the time when Allah **took** the Covenant of the Prophets.
وَقَتَـلَ دَاوُوْدُ جَالُوْتَ	2-251 : And Dāwūd **killed** Jālūt.

	Form II فَعَلَا

فَأَكَـلَا مِنْهَا فَبَدَتْ لَهُمَا سَوْءَاتُهُمَا	20-121 : And **they both ate** from the tree, so that their nakedness dawned upon them.
فَلَمَّا بَلَـغَا مَجْمَعَ بَيْنِهِمَا	18-61 : When **both of them reached** the confluence.

	Form III فَعَلُوا

خَرَجُوا مِنْ دِيَارِهِمْ	2-243 : **They** (people) **came out** of their land.
رِجَالٌ صَدَقُوا مَا عَاهَدُوا اللهَ عَلَيْـهِ	33-23 : They are men among the believers **who have been true** to the covenant they made with Allah.
الَّذِيْنَ قَتَلُوا اَوْلَادَهُمْ	6-140 : Those who **killed** their children.

Form IV فَعَلَتْ	
كُلَّمَا دَخَلَتْ أُمَّةٌ لَعَنَتْ أُخْتَهَا	7-38 : As often as a nation **enters** hell it **curses** its sister nation.
Note : The word أُمَّة ('ummah) "nation" is feminine in Arabic.	
فَلَمَّا تَغَشَّاهَا حَمَلَتْ	7-189 : When he covered her, **she conceived**.
فَلَمَّا سَمِعَتْ بِمَكْرِهِنَّ	12-31 : When **she heard** of their back biting...

Form V فَعَلَتَا	
كَانَتَا رَتْقًا فَفَتَقْنَاهُمَا	21-30 : The heavens and earth **where** one mass and We rent them apart.

Note : The word كَانَتَا *(kānatā)* does not belong to the tri-literal consonantal verb; it represents a weak verb but in Holy Qur'ān this form has not occured with consonants.

Form VI فَعَلْنَ	
وَأَخَذْنَ مِنْكُمْ مِيْثَاقًا غَلِيْظًا	4-21 : And **they (women) have taken** from you a strong covenant.
فَإِنْ خَرَجْنَ فَلَا جُنَاحَ عَلَيْكُمْ فِيْمَافَعَلْنَ فِي أَنْفُسِهِنَّ مِنْ مَعْرُوفٍ	2-240 : Then if (these ladies) **go away** there is no blame on you for what **they did** of lawful deeds.

Form VII فَعَلْتَ	
وَمِنْ حَيْثُ خَرَجْتَ فَوَلِّ وَجْهَكَ شَطْرَ ٱلْمَسْجِدِ ٱلْحَرَامِ	2-149 : And from whatsover place, **thou came** from, turn thy face towards the sacred Mosque.
وَإِنْ حَكَمْتَ فَٱحْكُمْ بَيْنَهُمْ بِٱلْقِسْطِ	5-42 : And if **thou judge,** judge between them with equity.
قَالُوا : أَ أَنْتَ فَعَلْتَ هَذَا بِآلِهَتِنَا يَا إِبْرَاهِيمُ	21-62 : They said: Hast **thou done** this to our gods, O 'Ibrāhīm.

Form VIII & XI فَعَلْتُمَا

Not in accordance with that in the Holy Qur'ān.

Form IX فَعَلْتُمْ	
وَإِذَا حَكَمْتُمْ بَيْنَ ٱلنَّاسِ أَنْ تَحْكُمُوا بِٱلْعَدْلِ	4-58 : And when **you judge** between people, you judge with justice.
قَالَ هَلْ عَلِمْتُمْ مَا فَعَلْتُمْ بِيُوسُفَ وَأَخِيهِ	12-89 : He said: Do **you know,** how you **treated** (but, did) Yūsuf and his brother ?

Form X فَعَلْتِ	
إِنَّكِ كُنْتِ مِنَ ٱلْخَاطِئِينَ	2-72 : Surely **thou wast** (a lady is addressed) one of the sinful.

Note : Not in accordance with the Holy Qur'ān from the consonantal verb. Therefore, an example is given from a weak verb as in case of form V.

```
┌─────────────────────────────────────┐
│   Form  XI        فَـعَلْتُـمَا        │
└─────────────────────────────────────┘
```

(2nd person Feminine) see form VIII (2nd person Masculine).

```
┌─────────────────────────────────────┐
│   Form  XII       فَـعَلْتُـنَّ         │
└─────────────────────────────────────┘
```

Not in accordance with the tri-literal consonants, but with the weak and added patterns. There are some examples in the Holy Qur'ān.

يَا نِسَاءَ ٱلنَّبِيِّ ! لَسْتُنَّ كَأَحَدٍ مِنَ ٱلنِّسَاءِ إِنِ ٱتَّقَيْتُنَّ	33-32 : O! Wives of the Prophet, **you are not** like any other woman if you keep your duty (to Allāh).
وَإِنْ كُنْتُنَّ تُرِدْنَ الله وَرَسُولَهُ وَٱلدَّارَ ٱلْآخِرَةَ فَإِنَّ الله أَعَدَّ لِلْمُحْسِنَاتِ مِنْكُنَّ أَجْرًا عَظِيمًا	33-29 : And if **you are** desiring Allah and His Messenger and the abode of the Hereafter, then surely Allah has prepared for the doers of good among you a mighty reward.

Note : The verbs لَيْسَ (laisa) and كَانَ (kāna) are not full-fledged verbs in Arabic. They are auxilary verbs with their own conjugation rules and characteristics. Accordingly they should be treated separately.

```
┌─────────────────────────────────────┐
│   Form  XIII      فَـعَلْتُ            │
└─────────────────────────────────────┘
```

قَالَتْ : رَبِّ إِنِّي ظَلَمْتُ نَفْسِي	27-44 : She said: My Lord! Surely **I have wronged** myself.
قَالَ : بَصُرْتُ بِمَالَمْ يَبْصُرُوا بِهِ فَقَبَضْتُ قَبْضَةً مِّنْ أَثَرِ ٱلرَّسُولِ فَنَبَذْتُهَا	20-96 : He said: **I perceived** what they perceived not, so **I took** a handful from the foot prints of the Messenger, then **I cast** it away.
قَالَ رَبِّ إِنِّي قَتَلْتُ مِنْهُمْ نَفْسًا	28-33 : He said: My Lord! **I killed** one of them.

Form XIV فَـعَلْنَا	
قَالَا : رَبَّـنَا ظَـلَمْنَا أَنْـفُسَنَا	7-23 : They said: Our Lord, **we have wronged** ourselves;
مَا عَلِمْنَا عَلَيْـهِ مِنْ سُوءٍ	12-51 : Those (ladies) said: **We knew** of no evil on his part.

Note 1 : The particle قَدْ (*qad*) which often occurs before a Perfect verb, expresses the completion or certainty of the action and can sometimes be translated as "indeed" or "verily", but is generally omitted in translation.

Examples from the Holy Qur'ān	
قَدْ جَاءَكُمْ بَصَائِرُ مِنْ رَبِّكُمْ	6-104 : Indeed came to you clear proofs from your Lord.
قَدْ خَسِرَ الَّذِيْنَ كَذَّبُوا بِـلِقَاءِ الله	6-31 : They are losers indeed, who rejected the meeting with Allah.
قَـدْ سَمِـعَ اللهُ	58-1 : Indeed Allah has heard.
قَدْ عَلِمْنَا مَا تَنْقُصُ الْأَرْضُ مِنْهُمْ	50-4 : Indeed We knew what earth diminishes of them.

Note 2 : Often an additional ل is prefixed to قَـدْ (*qad*) which becomes لَقَدْ (*laqad*) to add further emphasis to the meaning of the verb.

Examples from the Holy Qur'ān	
لَقَدْ أَخَذْنَا مِيْثَاقَ بَنِي إِسْرَائِيْلَ	5-70 : Certainly We made a covenant with the children of Israel.
لَقَدْ خَلَقْـنَا الْإِنْسَانَ فِي أَحْسَنِ تَـقْوِيْمٍ	95-4 : Certainly We made man in the best form.

Note 3 : One way to negate the Perfect is formed by placing the negative particle مَا *(mā)* before the verb e.g. مَاكَتَبَ *(mā kataba)* "he did not write".

<table>
<tr><td colspan="2" align="center">**Example from the Holy Qur'ān**</td></tr>
<tr><td>مَا أَنْـزَلْـنَا عَلَيْكَ ٱلْقُرْآنَ لِتَشْقَىٰ</td><td>20-2 : We have not revealed upon thee the Qur'ān that thou mayst be in hardship.</td></tr>
<tr><td>مَا جَعَلَ اللهُ لِرَجُلٍ مِنْ قَلْـبَـيْنَ فِي جَـوْفِهِ</td><td>33-4 : Allah has not made for anyone two hearts within him.</td></tr>
<tr><td>مَا قَدَرُوا اللهُ حَقَّ قَـدْرِهِ</td><td>22-74 : They estimate not Allah with His due estimation.</td></tr>
</table>

EXERCISE

(a) Conjugate the following verbs :

ذَهَبَ	جَمَعَ	فَتَحَ	قَتَـلَ

Name the patterns, giving their numbers and the standard form *(fa'ala)* e.g. بَلَغَتْ *(balaghat)* 3rd person Sing. Fem. IV.

دَخَلْتُنَّ	دَخَلْتُمْ	دَخَلُوا	نَصَرْنَ	نَصَرَتَا	نَصَرْنَا	نَصَرَ
جَمَعْتُمَا	جَمَعَا	بَرَزْتَا	بَرَزْتِ	بَرَزْتَ	بَرَزْتُ	دَخَلْتُ

(b) Translate into English :

ذَهَبَ مُوسَى إِلَى ٱلْجَبَلِ	قَتَـلَ دَاوُودُ جَالُوْتَ
قَالَتَا لَا نَسْقِي حَتَّى يُصْدِرَ ٱلرِّعَاءُ	ذَهَبَ رَاشِدٌ إِلَى ٱلْحَدِيقَةِ
سَمِعَا نِدَاءَ ٱلْحَقِّ	قَالَا إِنَّا رَسُولَا رَبِّكَ

قُلْتُمْ مَا أَرَدْنَا إِلَّا ٱلْخَيْرَ	رَحِمَ اللهُ عَبْدًا قَالَ آمِيْنَا
تَلَوْتُ جُزْءًا مِنْ ٱلْقُرْآنِ ٱلْكَرِيْمِ	قُلْتُنَّ ذَهَبْنَا إِلَى أَقْرِبَائِنَا
دَخَلْنَا ٱلْمَسْجِدَ مَعَ وَالِدِي وَأَخِي	سَمِعْتُ الْأَذَانَ فَقُمْتُ لِلصَّلَاةِ
يَا هَارُونُ وَيَا رَاشِدُ لِمَ ذَهَبْتُمَا إِلَى ٱلسُّوقِ؟	خَرَجْتُ مِنَ ٱلْمَدْرَسَةِ ظُهْرًا
أَلْبَنَاتُ ذَهَبْنَ إِلَى ٱلْمَدْرَسَةِ	ٱلنِّسَاءُ سَمِعْنَ ٱلنَّصِيحَةَ

(c) Translate into Arabic :

1. Have you written (هَلْ كَتَبْتَ) your article on Arabic language ? Yes (نَعَمْ). I did and put it on that big table.
2. The maid opened the door of the house.
3. The beggar sought food from me.
4. Have you been (هَلْ كُنْتَ) out today ?
5. I went to the mosque to pray.
6. My uncle performed Ḥajj this year.
7. My sister visited me at home.
8. I received the guests at my house.
9. I used to stay with Ḥasan. (كُنْتُ أَسْكُنُ)
10. She used to write on long papers. (كَانَت تَكْتُبُ)
11. She was a good girl in her manners.

(d) Distinguish the following patterns putting their number from the stable verb (fa'l) :

قَالَتْ	كَانَتْ	قُلْتُ	قُلْتَ	كَانَتَا	قُلْنَ	كُنَّ

VOCABULARY

قَـتَـلَ	(3rd person Masc.) to kill.
دَاوُود	David *(Dāwūd)* (Proper name).
جَالُوتَ	Goliath *(Jālūt)* (Proper name).
الحَدِيْـقَـةُ	the garden.
لَا نَسْقِي	we do not give water (to our flocks).
يَصْدِرُ	(Imperfect, from صَدَرْ) to come out.
الرِّعَـاءُ	shepherds.
رَسُولا + رَسُولَانِ	two Messengers.
سَمِعْـنَا	(1st person Plural) we heard.
نِـدَاءً	call.
أَلْحَـقُّ	the truth.
رَحِمَ	(3rd person Sing. Masc.) to have mercy.
آمِـيْـنَ	May God accept the prayer, Amen.
مَا أَرَدْنَـا	we did not intend.
أَقْـرِبَـاءُ	(plural of قَرِيب) relatives.
تَـلَوْتُ	(1st person Sing.) I recited.
جُـزْءًا	one part.
أَلسُّوقُ	the market.
نَصِيحَةٌ	good advice.
مَـقَالٌ	article.

Perfect Verb Chart

(Past Tense) (أَلْفِعْلُ ٱلْمَاضِي)

English Equivalent	Corresponding Pronoun	Subject Marker Suffix	Verb Form
Singular Forms			
He studied	هُوَ	‒ (above the last letter)	دَرَسَ
She studied	هِيَ	‒ــتْ	دَرَسَتْ
You (M) studied	أَنْتَ	‒ــتَ	دَرَسْتَ
You (F) studied	أَنْتِ	‒ــتِ	دَرَسْتِ
I (M+F) studied	أَنَا	‒ــتُ	دَرَسْتُ
Plural Forms			
They (M) studied	هُمْ	‒ــوا	دَرَسُوا
They (F) studied	هُنَّ	‒ــنَ	دَرَسْنَ
You (M) studied	أَنْتُمْ	‒ــتُمْ	دَرَسْتُمْ
You (F) studied	أَنْتُنَّ	‒ــتُنَّ	دَرَسْتُنَّ
We (M+F) studied	نَحْنُ	‒ــنَا	دَرَسْنَا
Dual Forms			
They (two M) studied	هُمَا	‒ــا	دَرَسَا
They (two F) studied	هُمَا	‒ــتَا	دَرَسَتَا
You (two M+F) studied	أَنْتُمَا	‒ــتُمَا	دَرَسْتُمَا

CHAPTER 5

DOUBLED AND WEAK VERBS

Arabic verbs are mostly tri-literal but some of them have the appearance of being bi-literal. It happens in the following cases :

1. Some verbs have the same letters as its second and third radicals.

   In this case the second radical has *Shaddah* (that is a sound of a doubled consonant), e.g. in English the words such as irregular, innocent etc. But in Arabic one letter is not written twice, it is written single with a mark ـّ on the head that means this letter should be pronounced twice, e.g. مَرَّ *(marra)*, instead of writing مَرْرَ .

   This type of verb has the appearance of being bi-literal, e.g. حَجَّ *(hajja)* "to perfom Ḥajj".

Example from the Holy Qur'ān

فَمَنْ حَجَّ ٱلْبَيْتَ	2-158 : who is on pilgrimage to the House (of God).
وَهِيَ تَمُرُّ مَرَّ ٱلسَّحَابِ	27-88 : (and it) flying with the flight of clouds.

جَـــرَّ	*jarra*	to drag, to draw.
مَـــرَّ	*marra*	to pass.

Note : When the third radical is not followed by any vowel sign, it is marked with *sukūn* (ـْ) .

Shaddah will be removed and both radical will be written and pronounced separately as in case of pattern VI through XIV.

I	*Marra*	مَـرَّ	He passed.
II	*Marrā*	مَـرَّا	They (2 M) passed.
III	*Marrū*	مَـرُّوا	They (plu. M) passed.
IV	*Marrat*	مَـرَّتْ	She (sing. F) passed.
V	*Marratā*	مَـرَّتَا	They (2 F) passed.
VI	*Mararna*	مَـرَرْنَ	They (plu. F) passed.
VII	*Mararta*	مَـرَرْتَ	You (sing. M) passed.
VIII + XI	*Mararatumā*	مَـرَرْتُمَا	You (2 M or F) passed.
IX	*Marartum*	مَـرَرْتُمْ	You (plu. M) passed.
X	*Mararti*	مَـرَرْتِ	You (sing. F) passed.
XII	*Marartunna*	مَـرَرْتُنَّ	You (plu. F) passed.
XIII	*Marartu*	مَـرَرْتُ	I (sing.) passed.
XIV	*Mararnā*	مَـرَرْنَا	We (plu.) passed.

Note : See the following conjugation chart for a full conjugation of the verb with all the persons, numbers and tenses.

CONJUGATION CHART

Verb : حَجَّ   Verb Form : Doubled اَلْمُضَعَّفْ

Verb Meaning : To perform Ḥajj

Imperative	Imperfect Subjunctive	Imperfect Jussive	Imperfect Indicative	Perfect	Pronoun
اَلْفِعْلُ الْأَمْرُ	اَلْفِعْلُ الْمُضَارِعُ الْمَنْصُوبُ	اَلْفِعْلُ الْمُضَارِعُ الْمَجْزُومُ	اَلْفِعْلُ الْمُضَارِعُ الْمَرْفُوعُ	اَلْفِعْلُ الْمَاضِي	
	(لَنْ) يَحُجَّ	(لَمْ) يَحُجَّ	يَحُجُّ	حَجَّ	هُوَ
	تَحُجَّ	تَحُجَّ	تَحُجُّ	حَجَّتْ	هِيَ
	يَحُجُّوا	يَحُجُّوا	يَحُجُّونَ	حَجُّوا	هُمْ
	يَحْجُجْنَ	يَحْجُجْنَ	يَحْجُجْنَ	حَجَجْنَ	هُنَّ
	يَحُجَّا	يَحُجَّا	يَحُجَّانِ	حَجَّا	هُمَا (M)
	تَحُجَّا	تَحُجَّا	تَحُجَّانِ	حَجَّتَا	هُمَا (F)
حُجَّ	تَحُجَّ	تَحُجَّ	تَحُجُّ	حَجَجْتَ	أَنْتَ
حُجِّي	تَحُجِّي	تَحُجِّي	تَحُجِّينَ	حَجَجْتِ	أَنْتِ
حُجُّوا	تَحُجُّوا	تَحُجُّوا	تَحُجُّونَ	حَجَجْتُمْ	أَنْتُمْ
أُحْجُجْنَ	تَحْجُجْنَ	تَحْجُجْنَ	تَحْجُجْنَ	حَجَجْتُنَّ	أَنْتُنَّ
حُجَّا	تَحُجَّا	تَحُجَّا	تَحُجَّانِ	حَجَجْتُمَا	أَنْتُمَا (M+F)
	أَحُجَّ	أَحُجَّ	أَحُجُّ	حَجَجْتُ	أَنَا
	نَحُجَّ	نَحُجَّ	نَحُجُّ	حَجَجْنَا	نَحْنُ

Verbal Noun : حَجٌّ

Active Participle : حَاجٌّ

Passive Participle : مَحْجُوجٌ

Verb Characteristics :
It has identical second and third radicals; in writing the letter is written once with a *shadda* on top of it.

2. **Hollow Verb :** أَلْفِعْلُ ٱلْأَجْوَفُ *('al fi'lul-'ajwafu)*

Verbs whose middle radical is of و *(w)* or ي *(y)* origin, have stems with a long or short vowel between the first and last radicals instead of a second consonant. For example, the verb كَانَ *(kān)* 'to be' (root ك و ن *K W N*) has the perfect stem *kān-* in كَانَ *(kāna)* 'he was', and *kun-* in كُنْتُ *(kuntu)* 'I was'. These are called **hollow verbs.** And all hollow verbs have two forms of the perfect stem and also two forms of the imperfect stem. One form has a long vowel, and this is used with suffixes beginning with a vowel, for example كَانَتْ *(kān-at)* 'she was'; the other has a short vowel, used with suffixes beginning with a consonant, for example كُنْتَ *(kun-ta)* 'you (sing. M) were'. The full conjugation of the perfect tense of the verb is given below :

I	كَانَ	Kāna	VIII	كُنْتُمَا	Kuntumā
II	كَانَا	Kānā	IX	كُنْتُمْ	Kuntum
III	كَانُوا	Kānū	X	كُنْتِ	Kunti
IV	كَانَتْ	Kānat	XI	كُنْتُمَا	Kuntumā
V	كَانَتَا	Kānatā	XII	كُنْتُنَّ	Kuntunna
VI	كُنَّ	Kunna	XIII	كُنْتُ	Kuntu
VII	كُنْتَ	Kunta	XIV	كُنَّا	Kunnā

(see chapters 9 and 30)

For a full conjugation of all the tenses, see the following conjugation chart.

CONJUGATION CHART

Verb : كَانَ   Verb Form : Hollow الأَجْوَف

Verb Meaning : To be

Imperative	Imperfect Subjunctive	Imperfect Jussive	Imperfect Indicative	Perfect	Pronoun
ألْفِعْلُ الأمْرُ	ألْفِعْلُ الْمُضَارِعُ الْمَنْصُوبُ	ألْفِعْلُ الْمُضَارِعُ الْمَجْزُومُ	ألْفِعْلُ الْمُضَارِعُ الْمَرْفُوعُ	ألْفِعْلُ الْمَاضِي	
	(لَنْ) يَكُونَ	(لَمْ) يَكُنْ	يَكُونُ	كَانَ	هُوَ
	تَكُونَ	تَكُنْ	تَكُونُ	كَانَتْ	هِيَ
	يَكُونُوا	يَكُونُوا	يَكُونُونَ	كَانُوا	هُمْ
	يَكُنَّ	يَكُنَّ	يَكُنَّ	كُنَّ	هُنَّ
	يَكُونَا	يَكُونَا	يَكُونَانِ	كَانَا	هُمَا (M)
	تَكُونَا	تَكُونَا	تَكُونَانِ	كَانَتَا	هُمَا (F)
كُنْ	تَكُونَ	تَكُنْ	تَكُونُ	كُنْتَ	أنْتَ
كُونِي	تَكُونِي	تَكُونِي	تَكُونِينَ	كُنْتِ	أنْتِ
كُونُوا	تَكُونُوا	تَكُونُوا	تَكُونُونَ	كُنْتُمْ	أنْتُمْ
كُنَّ	تَكُنَّ	تَكُنَّ	تَكُنَّ	كُنْتُنَّ	أنْتُنَّ
كُونَا	تَكُونَا	تَكُونَا	تَكُونَانِ	كُنْتُمَا	أنْتُمَا (M+F)
	أكُونَ	أكُنْ	أكُونُ	كُنْتُ	أنَا
	نَكُونَ	نَكُنْ	نَكُونُ	كُنَّا	نَحْنُ

Verbal Noun : كَوْنٌ   Active Participle : كَائِنٌ

Verb Characteristics : It is a verb whose middle radical is of *w* or *y* origin; it has a stem with a long or short vowel between the first and last radicals instead of a second consonant.

This is the most frequently used stem in the Holy Qur'ān as well as in all Arabic literature. The modified forms are to be adjusted with the verbs such as قَالَ (qāla) 'to say' (literal 'he said') خَاضَ (khāḍa) 'to think, to discuss' (literal 'he thought, he discussed').

The modification of these types of verbs are based on the second radical of the verbal noun or more exactly on the roots (not on the pattern of 3rd person singular masculine as observed in case of consonant verbs). Thus كَانَ (kāna) – قَالَ (qāla) is 3rd pers. sing. masc. of the root كَوْن (kawn) – قَوْل (qawl). When the second radical is ي (yā') e.g. بَيْعٌ (bay'un) 'to sell', the patterns from I to V will be the same as in كَانَ (kāna) and قَالَ (qāla) but from VI onward will be vocalized with *kasrah* as بِعْنَ (bi'na), بِعْتَ (bi'ta), بِعْتُ (bi'tu) and so on.

Examples from the Holy Qur'ān :

I قَـالَ (qāla) he said.	
قَالَ نُوحٌ رَبِّ إِنَّهُمْ عَصَوْنِي	71-21 Noah said : My Lord surely they disobeyed me.

كَانَ (kāna) he was, he is.	
وَكَانَ اللهُ غَفُورًا رَحِيمًا	4-152 And Allah is (was) Forgiving, Merciful.

طَـالَ (ṭāla) he prolonged.	
حَتَّى طَالَ عَلَيْهِمُ ٱلْعُمْرُ	21-44 Until life was prolonged (for them).

II قَالَا *(qālā)* they (two Masc.) said.	
قَالَا : رَبَّنَا إِنَّنَا نَخَافُ أَنْ يَفْرُطَ عَلَيْنَا	20-45 They (two) said : Our Lord, we fear lest he hasten to do evil to us.

كَانَا *(kānā)* they (two Masc.) were.	
كَانَا يَأْكُلَانِ ٱلطَّعَامَ	5-75 They (two) used to have food.

III قَالُوا *(qālū)* they (pl. Masc.) said.	
قَالُوا رَبُّنَا اللهُ ثُمَّ ٱسْتَقَامُوا	41-30 They said : Our Lord is Allah then continued in the right way.

كَانُوا *(kānū)* they (pl. Masc.) were.	
كَانُوا لَا يَتَنَاهَوْنَ عَنْ مُنْكَرٍ فَعَلُوهُ	5-79 They forbade not one another the hateful thing they did.

IV قَالَتْ *(qālat)* she (sing. Fem.) said.	
قَالَتْ : رَبِّ أَنَّى يَكُونُ لِى وَلَدٌ وَلَمْ يَمْسَسْنِي بَشَرٌ	3-47 She said : My Lord how I can have a son and man has not yet touched me.

كَانَتْ *(kānat)* she (sing. Fem.) was.	
كَانَتْ مِنَ ٱلْغَابِرِينَ	7-83 She was of those who remained behind.

V قَالَتَا (qālatā) they (dual Fem.) told.

قَالَتَا لَا نَسْقِى حَتَّىٰ يُصْدِرَ الرِّعَاءُ	28-23 They (two girls) said we can not water until the shepherds takes away (their sheep).

كَانَتَا (kānatā) they (dual Fem.) were.

كَانَتَا تَحْتَ عَبْدَيْنِ مِنْ عِبَادِنَا صَالِحَيْنِ	66-10 They were both under two of our righteous servants.

VI قُلْنَ (qulna) they (pl. Fem.) said.

قُلْنَ حَاشَ لله مَا عَلِمْنَا عَلَيْهِ مِنْ سُوءٍ	12-51 They (pl. Fem.) said : Holy Allah, we knew of no evil on his part.

كُنَّ (kunna) there be (pl. Fem.).

فَإِنْ كُنَّ نِسَاءً فَوْقَ اثْنَتَيْنِ	4-11 If there be more than two females.

VII قُلْتَ (qulta) you (sing. Masc.) told (said).

أَ أَنْتَ قُلْتَ لِلنَّاسِ	5-116 Didst thou say to people.

كُنْتَ (kunta) you (sing. Masc.) were.

وَمَا كُنْتَ بِجَانِبِ الْغَرْبِيِّ إِذْ قَضَيْنَا إِلَىٰ مُوسَى الْأَمْرَ وَمَا كُنْتَ مِنَ الشَّاهِدِينَ	28-44 And thou wast not on the western side when We revealed to Moses the commandment nor wast thou among those present.

| VIII & XI قُلْتُمَا *(qultumā)* | you (dual Masc. & Fem.) told or said. |

| كُنْتُمَا *(kuntumā)* | you (dual Masc. & Fem.) were. |

(Not occuring in the Holy Qur'ān but very often used in Arabic).

| IX قُلْتُمْ *(qultum)* | you (plural Masc.) told. |

| وَإِذْ قُلْتُمْ يَا مُوسَىٰ لَنْ نَصْبِرَ عَلَىٰ طَعَامٍ وَاحِدٍ | 2-61 And when you said O' Moses, we cannot endure one food. |

| كُنْتُمْ *(kuntum)* | you (plural Masc.) were. |

| وَكُنْتُمْ عَلَىٰ شَفَا حُفْرَةٍ مِنَ ٱلنَّارِ فَأَنْقَذَكُمْ مِنْهَا | 3-103 And you were on the brink of the pit then He saved you from it. |

| X قُلْتِ *(qulti)* you (sing. Fem.) told (said). |

(Not occuring in the Holy Qur'ān, but from the verb جَاءَ *(jā')* coming; to commit).

| لَقَدْ جِئْتِ شَيْئًا فَرِيًّا | 19-27 May! thou hast indeed committed a strange thing. |

| كُنْتِ *(kunti)* you (sing. Fem.) were. |

| إِنَّكِ كُنْتِ مِنَ ٱلْخَاطِئِينَ | 12-29 Surely, thou art one of the sinfuls. |

XII	قُلْتُنَّ	*(qultunna)*	you (plural Fem.) told.
	لَسْتُنَّ كَأَحَدٍ مِنَ ٱلنِّسَاءِ		33-32 You are not like other women.

كُنْتُنَّ	*(kuntunna)*	you (plural Fem.) were.
وَإِنْ كُنْتُنَّ تُرِدْنَ ٱللهَ وَرَسُولَهُ		33-29 And if you desire Allah and His Messenger.

XIII	قُلْتُ	*(qultu)*	I told (common to Masc. & Fem.)
	كُنْتُ	*(quntu)*	I was (common to Masc. & Fem.)
	إِنْ كُنْتُ قُلْتُهُ فَقَدْ عَلِمْتَهُ		5-116 If I had said it Thou wouldst indeed have known it.

XIV	قُلْنَا	*(qulnā)*	we (pl. Masc. & Fem.) told (said).
	وَقُلْنَا يَا آدَمُ ٱسْكُنْ أَنْتَ وَزَوْجُكَ ٱلْجَنَّةَ		2-35 And We said : O' Adam dwell thou and thy wife in the garden.

كُنَّا	*(kunnā)*	we (pl. Masc. & Fem.) were.
وَأَنَّا كُنَّا نَقْعُدُ مِنْهَا مَقَاعِدَ لِلسَّمْعِ		72-9 And that : we used to sit in some of the sitting places thereof to steal hearing.

Note : Patterns VI *(fa‘alna = kunna)* and XIV *(fa‘alnā = qulnā)*, have very slight difference, as the former has a short ending vowel while the later has a long one. Compare : *qulna, qulnā, kunna, kunnā*

EXERCISE

A. Translate into Arabic :

1. Ali said : There were many fine fruits in my garden.
2. Your father was a true Muslim.
3. My sister was a teacher.
4. All of you (Masc.) were present over there.
5. Both of them were good players.
6. There were two girls going to the school early in the morning.
7. You were successful in the examination.
8. She was learning the Qur'ān.
9. They (Fem.) were good in their manners.
10. I was very happy to see you here.
11. Did you write (هَلْ كَتَبْتَ) your article on Arabic language ? yes (نَعَمْ) I did, and put it on that big table.
12. The beggar sought food from me.
13. The maid opened the door of the house.
14. Have you been (هَلْ كُنْتَ) out today ?
15. I went to the mosque to pray.
16. My uncle performed Ḥajj this year.
17. My sister visited me at home.
18. I received the guests at my house.
19. I used to stay with Ḥasan.
20. She used to write on long papers.
21. She was a good girl in her manners.

B. Translate into English :

١ - جَحَدُوا بِآيَاتِ رَبِّهِمْ .

٢ - مَا سَمِعُوا نِدَاءَ ضَمِيرِهِمْ وَأَعْرَضُوا عَنْ أَدَاءِ ٱلْوَاجِبِ .

٣ - لَقَدْ تَابَ اللهُ عَلَى ٱلنَّبِيِّ وَٱلْمُهَاجِرِينَ وَالأَنْصَارِ .

٤ - يَا أَيُّهَا ٱلَّذِينَ آمَنُوا تُوبُوا إِلَى اللهِ .

٥ - وَقَالَ ٱلَّذِينَ كَفَرُوا لِلَّذِينَ آمَنُوا لَوْ كَانَ خَيْرًا مَا سَبَقُونَا إِلَيْهِ .

٦ - كُنْتُمْ خَيْرَ أُمَّةٍ أُخْرِجَتْ لِلنَّاسِ .

٧ - كَانَ اللهُ غَفُورًا رَحِيمًا .

٨ - قُولُوا حُسْنًا .

٩ - قُولُوا قَوْلًا مَعْرُوفًا .

١٠ - قَالَتِ النَّصَارَىٰ لَيْسَتِ الْيَهُودُ عَلَى شَيْءٍ ، وَقَالَتِ الْيَهُودُ لَيْسَتِ النَّصَارَىٰ عَلَى شَيْءٍ .

١١ - الْإِسْلَامُ دِينٌ كَامِلٌ لِكُلِّ زَمَانٍ وَمَكَانٍ .

١٢ - الْقُرْآنُ ثَرْوَةٌ لِلْبَشَرِ جَمِيعًا ، وَهِدَايَةٌ لِلْعَالَمِينَ .

١٣ - كَانَ النَّاسُ أُمَّةً وَاحِدَةً .

C. Distinguish the following patterns putting their number and the stable verb (i.e. فَعَلَ) :

كُنَّ ، قُلْنَ ، كَانَتَا ، كُنْتَ ، قُلْتَ ، قُلْتِ ، كُنْتِ ، قُلْتِ ، كُنْتَ ، كَانَتْ ، قَالَتْ .

D. Conjugate the following verbs :

جَرَّ *(J R R)*   بَصَرَ *(B Ṣ R)*   ثَوَبَ *(Th W B)*

VOCABULARY

مَرُّوا	(P. Masc. pl.) to pass (by).
آمَنُوا	(P. Masc. pl.) to believe.
إتَّقُوا	(P. Masc. pl.) to fear God.
قَالُوا	(P. Masc. pl.) to say, to speak, to tell.
سَدِيدٌ	accurate, right, correct.
اسْكُن	(command) live, dwell.
زَوْجُكَ	thy wife, thy spouse.
الْجَنَّة	The paradise.
جَحَدُوا	(P. Masc. pl.) They denied.
آيَاتٍ	signs. (singular آيَة (āyat))
تَابَ	as قَالَ (qāla) to turn from sin, to repent.
النَّبِيُّ	the Prophet.
الْمُهَاجِرِينَ	(Masc. pl.) immigrants, (sing. مُهَاجِر muhājir)
نَصُوحًا	sincere, true, faithful, loyal.
كَفَرُوا	(P. Masc. pl.) rejected, disbelieved.
لَا تَسْمَعُوا	do not listen.
الْغَوا فِيه	take it as false.

لَوْ كَانَ	if it was.
خَـيْر	good.
سَبَقُو + نَا	(P. Masc. + pl. pronoun) they preceded us, they did it before of us.
قَوم + ي = قَوْمِي	*qawm* + (I = mine) = *qawmi* my people.
إتَّخَذُوا	they put, adopted.
مَهْجُورٌ	forsaken thing.
نَسَوا	(P. Masc. pl.) they forgot.
ألذِّكْر	The Holy Qur'ān, lit. remembrance.
بُـورٌ	doomed to perish.
أَللُّغَةُ ٱلْعَرَبِيَّة	Arabic language.
ألْعَمّ	uncle عَمِّي = my uncle.
زَارَتْ	she visited (as قَالَتْ (*qālat*) she said).
كُنْتُ	I used to, I was.
كَانَتْ	she used to, she was, it was.
أَلْمُسْتَقْبَل	the received, the future.

مَقَالٌ	article.	أَلْخَادِمَةُ	the maid.
كَبِير	big.	أَلْخَارِج	the outside.
أَلطَّاوِلَةُ	the table.	أَلأُخْت	the sister.

CHAPTER 6

THE VERBAL SENTENCES

In Arabic language the sentences are of two kinds :

1. **The Nominal sentences** الجُمَلُ الإِسْمِيَّةُ: in which the subject appears first, e.g. :

اللهُ رَبٌّ	"Allah is a Lord",
مُحَمَّدٌ رَسُولٌ	"Muḥammad is a Messenger",
اَللهُ بَسَطَ الرِّزْقَ	"Allah has amplified the provision".

This type of sentences was already dealt with in chapter 2.

2. **The Verbal sentences** الجُمَلُ ٱلْفِعْلِـيَّـةُ : in which the verb appears before the subject, e.g. :

أَتَىٰ أَمْـرُ الله	"Allah's commandment has come",
خَلَقَ اللهُ ٱلسَّمَوَاتِ وَالأَرْضِ	"Allah has created the heavens and the earth",
أَرْسَلْنَـا مُوسَىٰ	"We have sent Moses",
بَعَثَ اللهُ رَسُولا	"Allah has sent a Messenger",
بَسَطَ اللهُ ٱلرِّزْقَ	"Allah has amplified the provision".

In verbal sentences the verb always appears in the singular even in cases where the subject following the verb is dual or plural, e.g.

فَعَصَىٰ فِرْعَوْنُ ٱلـرَّسُولَ	"(But) Pharaoh disobeyed the Messenger",
سَأَلَ سَائِلٌ	"a questioner asked",

دَخَلَ (مَعَهُ ٱلسِّجْنَ) فَتَيَانِ	"and two youths entered the prison with him",
سَجَدَ الْمَلَائِكَةُ كُلُّهُمْ أَجْمَعُونَ	"So the Angels bowed down one and all",
جَاءَ إِخْوَةُ يُوسُف	"Joseph's brothers came",
قَـالَتْ أَمْـرَأَةُ ٱلْعَزِيز	"The Chief's wife said",
سَجَدَتِ ٱلْبِنْتَانِ	"The two girls bowed down",
سَجَدَتِ ٱلنِّسَاءُ	"The women bowed down".

The verb appears in singular masculine even when the subject is plural feminine, e.g. قَالَ نِسْوَةٌ "the ladies said". It appears sometimes in singular feminine though the subject is plural masculine, e.g. قَالَتِ الأَعْرَابُ آمَنَّا "the bedouins said : We have believed". It should be noted however, that this rule applies when the plural form is broken. In case the plural is solid (sound), e.g. أَلمُسْلِمُونَ, only singular, masculine, will work.

Declension of the verbal sentence

A perfect verb has an established mark as observed in chapters 1 & 3.

The following nouns, if they are the subject of a sentence, take *ḍammah* mark, the object of the sentences vocalized with *fatḥah*, e.g. :

$$\text{دَخَـلَ خَـادِمٌ بَـابًا}$$
$$\text{جَمَـعَ اللهُ ٱلـرَّسُـولَ}$$
$$\text{دَخَـلَ ٱلْخَـادِمُ ٱلْبَـابَ}$$

Compare the nominal and verbal sentences :

أَلْجُمْلَةُ الإِسْمِيَّةُ Nominal Sentences	أَلْجُمْلَةُ ٱلْفِعْلِيَّةُ Verbal Sentences	
الْمُسْلِمُ فَتَحَ الْبَابَ	فَتَحَ الْمُسْلِمُ الْبَابَ	The Muslim opened the door.
الْمُسْلِمَانِ فَتَحَا الْبَابَ	فَتَحَ الْمُسْلِمَانِ الْبَابَ	The two Muslims opened the door.
الْمُسْلِمُونَ فَتَحُوا الْبَابَ	فَتَحَ الْمُسْلِمُونَ الْبَابَ	The Muslims opened the door.
الْمُسْلِمَةُ فَتَحَتِ الْبَابَ	فَتَحَتِ الْمُسْلِمَةُ الْبَابَ	The Muslim woman opened the door.
الْمُسْلِمَتَانِ فَتَحَتَا الْبَابَ	فَتَحَتِ الْمُسْلِمَتَانِ الْبَابَ	The two Muslim women opened the door.
الْمُسْلِمَاتُ فَتَحْنَ الْبَابَ	فَتَحَتِ الْمُسْلِمَاتُ الْبَابَ	The Muslim women opened the door.

When the plural form is broken, such as أَلْعُلَمَاءُ (sing. عَالِمٌ), you can say قَالَ ٱلْعُلَمَاءُ " 'ulamā' said" and vice versa, قَالَتِ نِسْوَةٌ "women told".

When a subject is broken into plural, the verb will be singular feminine unless they refer to male human beings, e.g. ظَهَرَتِ ٱلنُّجُومُ "the stars appeared" but ظَهَرَ ٱلرِّجَالُ "the men appeared" though ظَهَرَتِ ٱلرِّجَالُ is also endorsed by the grammarians.

The word order in a verbal sentence :

The normal order in an English verbal sentence is : subject, verb, object; e.g. "A girl has broken the glass". But in Arabic the order is : verb, subject, direct object. Thus the above sentence (A girl has broken the glass) will be placed as : "Broke a girl the glass".

The place of the adverbs and others is often a direct object, e.g. حَضَرَ ٱلْمُسْلِمُونَ ٱلصَّلاةَ "Muslims joined the prayer (Lit: arrived)".

Examples from the Holy Qur'ān :

قَدْ فَرَضَ اللهُ لَكُمْ تَحِلَّـةَ أَيْمَانِكُمْ	66-2 Allah indeed has sanctioned* for you the expiation of your oath.

(يَامَرْيَمُ) لَقَدْ جِئْتِ شَيْئًا فَرِيًّا	19-27 O' Mary thou has indeed committed a strange thing.

وَنَهَى ٱلنَّفْسَ عَنِ ٱلْهَوَىٰ	79-40 And (one who) restrained himself from low desires.

كَذَّبَتْ قَوْمُ نُوحٍ ٱلْمُرْسَلِينَ	26-105 The people of Noah have rejected the Messengers.

---

* The verb فَرَضَ signifies to prescribe; to impose; to sanction.

حَتَّىٰ زُرْتُمُ ٱلْمَقَابِرَ	102-2 Until you came to the grave.
إِنَّا أَعْطَيْنَاكَ ٱلْكَوْثَرَ	108-1 Surely, we have given thee the "Kawthar" * * The fount (of abundance).
أَخَذَ عَلَيْكُم مُّوثِقًا مِنَ اللهِ	12-80 (Your father) took from you a covenant in Allah's name.
أَمَّا مَنْ خَافَ مَقَامَ رَبِّهِ	79-40 And as for him who feared his Lord.
وَلَقَدْ أَضَلَّ مِنْكُمْ جِبِلًّا كَثِيرًا	36-62 And certainly he led astray numerous from among you.
وَلَقَدْ رَآهُ نَزْلَةً أُخْرَىٰ	53-13 And certainly he saw Him in another descent.
أَكْثَرُوا فِيهَا ٱلْفَسَادَ	89-12 And (they) made great mischief herein.
فَسَجَدَ الْمَلَائِكَةُ كُلُّهُمْ أَجْمَعُونَ	15-30 So the angels made obeisance all of them together.

قَالَتِ ٱلْأَعْرَابُ آمَنَّا	49-14	The dwellers of the desert said, "We believe".

قَالَ نِسْوَةٌ فِي ٱلْمَدِينَةِ	12-30	The women of the town said.

مَاكَانَ مُحَمَّدٌ أَبَا أَحَدٍ مِنْ رِجَالِكُمْ	33-40	Muḥammad is not father of any of your men.

EXERCISE

A. Translate into English :

أَسَّسَ بُنْيَانَهُ عَلَى ٱلتَّقْوَى	لَيْلَةُ ٱلْقَدْرِ خَيْرٌ مِنْ أَلْفِ شَهْرٍ
نَاجَيْتُمُ ٱلرَّسُولَ	فَعَصَى آدَمُ رَبَّهُ فَغَوَى
أَهْلَكْتُ مَالًا لُبَدًا	عَمِلُوا ٱلصَّالِحَاتِ
حَتَّى إِذَا بَلَغَتِ ٱلْحُلْقُومَ	نَهَى ٱلنَّفْسَ عَنِ ٱلْهَوَى
أَرْسَلَ عَلَيْهِمْ طَيْرًا أَبَابِيلَ	أَكْثَرُوا فِيهَا ٱلْفَسَادَ
ظَلَمْتُمْ أَنْفُسَكُمْ	أَذْهَبَ عَنَّا ٱلْحَزَنَ

B. Translate into Arabic :

Man has passed from a space of time.
We have created man of mixed semen.
We put him to the proof.
We show him the right path.
Allah saved them from the evil of that day.
I have come to give you plain warning.
We burdened no soul beyond its capacity.
He created men from nothing.
He is The Merciful, The Forgiver.

VOCABULARY

لَيْلَةُ ٱلْقَدْرِ	The Night of Majesty (or Power).		
خَيْرٌ	best.	أَلْفٌ	one thousand.
شَهْرٌ	month.	عَصَىٰ	disobeyed.
غَوَىٰ	he misguided.	عَمَلُوا	they did (Masc.).
نَهَىٰ	he restrained.	النَّفْسَ	soul, person (himself).
هَوَىٰ	he desired.	الفَسَادَ	mischief.
أَكْثَرُوا	they made great (overdoing).		
أَرْسَلَ	he sent.	طَيْرٌ	biru.
أَبَابِيل	name of a certain bird (Put as such).		

أَذْهَبَ	removed.	الْحَزَنَ	the sorrow.
ظَلَمْتُمْ	you (plural Masc.) did wrong.		
نَاجَيْتُمْ	you (plural Masc.) whispered.		
أَهْلَكْتُ	I distroyed.	أَسَّسَ	he established.
مَـالٌ	wealth.	لُبَـدَا	(adj.) a big sum.
بَلَغَتْ	she or it reached.	الْحُلْقُوم	the throat.

The prepositions and pronouns will be dealt with later, here are some of them to help you in the translation.

Preposition

مِنْ	from, than
عَنْ	about
فِي	in

Pronouns

ه	His	رَبَّـهُ	His Lord.
هَا	Her	فِيهَا	In her (it).
نَا	Us, our	عَنَّا	about us.

دَهْـــر	The space of time.
خَلَــقَ	to create (use XIV form).
هَـدَىٰ	(hadā) show the path.
إنْـقَاذ	Delivery, rescue.
أَنْـذَرَ	Warned (he).
وُسْـعٌ	Capacity.
الرَّحِيم	The Merciful.
دَلِـيلٌ	(noun) proof.
الصِّرَاطُ	Right path.
شَـــرٌّ	Evil.
فَـوْق	Beyond; up.
لَا شَىء	Nothing.
الغَـفَّارُ	The Forgiver.

CHAPTER 7

THE IMPERFECT TENSE

أَلْمُضَارِعْ *'Al-Muḍāri‘* :

1. This tense is formed by prefixing one of the four letter : أ *(a)* ن *(n)* ت *(t)* ي *(y)* to the root-form as أ *(a)* and ن *(n)* for 1st. person, ت *(t)* for 2nd and third persons, and ي *(y)* for third person as will be illustrated in the conjugation. These pronominal prefixes are termed "signs of the imperfect". It also has suffixes to denote number of the person; they are آنِ *(āni)*, ـونَ *(ūna)*, ـنَ *(na)*, ينَ *(īna)*.

2. The imperfect tense expresses an action still imcomplete at the time to which reference is being made. It refers to the present or future as generally is assumed.

   The conjugation of the imperfect indicative of فَعَلَ , the standard root-form, is as below :

	3rd person	
Imperfect I sing. Masc.	يَـفْعَلُ *yaf‘alu*	he does or will do.

Imperfect II dual Masc.	يَـفْعَلَانِ	yaf'alāni	they (two) do, or will do.
Imperfect III plural Masc.	يَـفْعَلُونَ	yaf'alūna	they (all) do, or will do.
Imperfect IV sing. Fem.	تَـفْعَلُ	taf'alu	she does, or will do.
Imperfect V dual Fem.	تَـفْعَلَانِ	taf'alāni	they (two) do, or will do.
Imperfect VI plural Fem.	يَـفْعَلْنَ	yaf'alna	they (all) do, or will do.

2nd person

Imperfect VII sing. Masc. (as 3rd person sing. Fem.)	تَـفْعَلُ	taf'alu	you do, or will do.
Imperfect VIII dual Masc. (as 3rd person dual Fem.)	تَـفْعَلَانِ	taf'alāni	you (two) do, or will do.
Imperfect IX plural Masc.	تَـفْعَلُونَ	taf'alūna	you (all) do, or will do.

Imperfect X sing. Fem.	تَفْعَلِينَ	taf'alīna	you do, or will do.

Imperfect XI dual Fem. (as 3rd person dual Fem. & 2nd person dual Masc.)	تَفْعَلَانِ	taf'alāni	you (two) do, or will do.

Imperfect XII plural Fem.	تَفْعَلْنَ	taf'alna	you (all) do, or will do.

First person

Imperfect XIII singular	أَفْعَلُ	'af'alu	I do, or will do.

Imperfect XIV dual and plural	نَفْعَلُ	naf'alu	We do, or will do.

3. Groups of the tri-literal verbs :

There are five groups or families of the triliteral verbs.

A. The vowel of the second radical of the Perfect is 'a' i.e.
ـَ (fathah) and the same radical in the Imperfect has 'u'
i.e. ـُ (dammah) e.g.

نَصَرَ ، يَنْصُرُ	Naṣara, Yanṣuru	to help.
بَلَغَ ، يَبْلُغُ	Balagha, Yablughu	to reach.
كَتَبَ ، يَكْتُبُ	Kataba, Yaktubu	to write.

B. The 2nd radical in Perfect has 'a' ﹷ (fathah) vowel and 'i' ﹻ (kasarah) in the Imperfect e.g.:

ضَرَبَ ، يَضْرِبُ	ḍaraba, yaḍribu	to beat.

C. The 2nd radical in the Perfect has 'i' ﹻ (kasarah) vowel and the Imperfect has 'a' ﹷ (fathah) vowel e.g.:

سَمِعَ ، يَسْمَعُ	sami'a, yasma'u	to listen.

D. The 2nd radical in both Perfect and Imperfect has vowel 'a' ﹷ (fathah) e.g.:

فَتَحَ ، يَفْتَحُ	fataḥa, yaftaḥu	to open.

E. The 2nd radical in both Perfect and Imperfect has vowel 'u' ﹹ (ḍammah) e.g.:

كَرُمَ ، يَكْرُمُ	karuma, yakrumu	to be generous

F. The 2nd radical in both Perfect and Imperfect has vowel 'i' ﹻ (kasrah) e.g.:

حَسِبَ ، يَحْسِبُ	ḥasiba, yaḥsibu	to think

The knowledge of these groups is useful for consulting an Arabic dictionary and it assists in forming an idea about the nature of a word and the shade of its meaning.

4. The Imperfect itself denotes only unfinished action but it may
   be made to indicate the future by putting a particle سَـوْفَ
   before it, or prefixing a letter سَ (sa).

   Examples from the Holy Qur'ān :

سَيَقُولُ ٱلسُّفَهَاءُ مِنَ ٱلنَّاسِ...	2-142 the fools among the people will say...

سَوْفَ يُحَاسَبُ حِسَابًا يَسِيرًا	84-8 His account will be taken by an easy reckoning.

5. When signifying present time, the imperfect most often gives
   the meaning of the habitual present, especially in the Holy
   Qur'ān, e.g.

يَفْعَلُ اللهُ مَا يَشَاءُ	14-27 Allah does what He pleases.

يُخْرِجُ ٱلْحَيَّ مِنَ ٱلْمَيِّتِ ، وَيُخْرِجُ ٱلْمَيَّتَ مِنَ ٱلْحَيِّ . وَيُحْيِ ٱلْأَرْضَ بَعْدَ مَوْتِهَا	30-19 He brings forth the living from the dead and brings forth the dead from the living and gives life to the earth after its death.

يَا أَهْلَ ٱلْكِتَابِ لِمَ تَلْبِسُونَ ٱلْحَقَّ بِالْبَاطِلِ وَتَكْتُمُونَ ٱلْحَقَّ وَأَنْتُمْ تَعْلَمُونَ	3-71 O' people of the book! Why do you confound the truth with falsehood, and hide the truth while you know.

The imperfect may give the meaning of the present continuous, e.g. (from the Holy Qur'ān) :

| أَتَـقْـتُلُونَ رَجُلًا أَنْ يَـقُولَ : رَبِّ اللهُ . | 40-28 Are you killing a man becasue he says : My Lord is Allah. |

Or may indicate the future, e.g. (from the Holy Qur'ān) :

| يَلْبَسُونَ مِنَ سُنْدُسٍ وَإِسْتَبْرَقٍ مُتَـقَابِـلِينَ | 44-53 They will wear fine and thick silk facing one another. |

Examples from the Holy Qur'ān :

| **Imperfect Form I** | يَفْعَلُ (yaf'alu) |

| وَيَـفْعَلُ اللهُ مَا يَشَاءُ | 14-27 And Allah does what He pleases. |
| يَخْلُقُ اللهُ مَا يَشَاءُ | 24-45 And Allah creates what He pleases. |

| **Imperfect Form II** | يَفْعَلَانِ (yaf'alāni) |

| كَانَا يَأْكُلَانِ ٱلطَّعَامَ | 5-75 They both used to eat food. |
| وَدَاوُودَ وَسُلَيْمَانَ إِذْ يَحْكُمَانِ فِي ٱلْحَرْثِ | 21-78 And David & Solomon, when they were giving judgement concerning the field. |

Imperfect Form III	يَفْعَلُونَ (yaf'alūna)

يَقُولُونَ مَا لَا يَفْعَلُونَ	26-226	They say what they do not.
فَالْيَوْمَ ٱلَّذِينَ آمَنُوا مِنَ ٱلْكُفَّارِ يَضْحَكُونَ	83-34	So this day those who believe laugh at the disbelievers.
فَوَيْلٌ لِّلَّذِينَ يَكْتُبُونَ ٱلْكِتَابَ بِأَيْدِيهِمْ ثُمَّ يَقُولُونَ هٰذَا مِنْ عِنْدِ اللهِ	2-79	Woe! then to those who write the Book with their own hands then say, "This is from Allah".

Imperfect Form IV	تَفْعَلُ (taf'alu)

يَوْمَ تَشْهَدُ عَلَيْهِمْ أَلْسِنَتُهُمْ وَأَيْدِيهِمْ وَأَرْجُلُهُمْ بِمَا كَانُوا يَعْمَلُونَ	24-24	On the day when their tongues and their hands and their feet bear witness against them as to what they used to do.

Note : Almost all plurals, especially of broken type, (see chapter 13) are treated as feminine and the verbs for such subjects will be a feminine singular conjugation.

Imperfect Form V	تَفْعَلانِ (taf'alāni)

وَوَجَدَ مِنْ دُونِهِمُ ٱمْرَأَتَيْنِ تَذُودَانِ	28-23	And he found besides them two women keeping back their (flocks).

Imperfect Form VI يَفْعَلْنَ *(yaf'alna)*	

وَلَا يَحِلُّ لَهُنَّ أَنْ يَكْتُمْنَ مَا خَلَقَ اللهُ فِي أَرْحَامِهِنَّ	2-228 And it is not lawful for them (women) to conceal what Allah has created in their wombs.

Imperfect Form VII تَفْعَلُ *(taf'alu)*	

وَإِذْ تَخْلُقُ مِنَ ٱلطِّينِ كَهَيْئَةِ ٱلطَّيْرِ بِإِذْنِي فَتَنْفُخُ فِيهَا فَتَكُونُ طَيْرًا بِإِذْنِي وَتُبْرِئُ ٱلْأَكْمَهَ وَٱلْأَبْرَصَ بِإِذْنِي	5-110 When thou created, out of clay, a thing like the form of a bird by My permission then thou didst breath into it and it became a bird by My permission and thou didst heal the blind and the leprous by My permission.

Imperfect Form VIII تَفْعَلَانِ *(taf'alāni)*	

فَبِأَيِّ آلَاءِ رَبِّكُمَا تُكَذِّبَانِ	55-13 (O' jinn and human beings!) Which of the bounties of your Lord will you deny ?

Note : The verb تُكَذِّبَانِ, though represents Form VIII but not from triliteral type. It is from one of the derived (added) verbs (فَعَّلَ / Form II) which will be dealt with later.

Imperfect Form XI تَـفْعَلُونَ *(tafʿalūna)*	

وَإِذْ أَخَذْنَا مِيثَاقَكُمْ لَا تَسْفِكُونَ دِمَاءَكُمْ وَلَا تُخْرِجُونَ أَنْفُسَكُمْ مِنْ دِيَارِكُمْ ثُمَّ أَقْرَرْتُمْ وَأَنْتُمْ تَشْهَدُونَ ثُمَّ أَنْتُمْ هَؤُلَاءِ تَقْتُلُونَ أَنْفُسَكُمْ	2-84 And when We made a covenant with you: you shall not shed your blood nor turn your people out of your cities; then you promised and you bear witness; yet, you it is who would slay your people.
أَفَتُؤْمِنُونَ بِبَعْضِ آلْكِتَابِ وَتَكْفُرُونَ بِبَعْضٍ	2-85 Do you then believe in a part of the Book and deny the other.

Imperfect Form X تَـفْعَلِينَ *(tafʿalīna)*	

قَالُوا أَتَعْجَبِينَ مِنْ أَمْرِ اللهِ	11-73 They said: Wonderest thou at Allah's commandment ?

Imperfect Form XI تَـفْعَلَانِ *(tafʿalāni)*	

Not occuring in triliteral indicative imperfect. An example may be given from subjunctive imperfect (which will be dealt within next chapter) of a weak verb.

إِنْ تَـتُوبَا إِلَى اللهِ . . .	66-4 If you both turn to Allah.

Imperfect Form XII	تَـفْعَلْنَ (taf'alna)

إِنْ كُنْـتُـنَّ تُرِدْنَ ٱلْحَيَاةَ ٱلدُّنْـيَا	33-28 If you (ladies) wish the worldly life.

Imperfect Form XIII	أَفْـعَلُ ('af'alu)

إِنَّـنِي مَعَكُمَا أَسْمَعُ وَأَرَىٰ	20-46 Surely, I am with you both, I hear and I see.

Imperfect Form XIV	نَـفْعَلُ (naf'alu)

يَـوْمَ نَحْشُرُهُمْ جَمِيعًا	6-22 When We shall gather them all together.
وَنَطْمَعُ أَنْ يُـدْخِلَنَا رَبُّـنَا مَـعَ ٱلْقَـوْمِ ٱلصَّالِحِينَ	5-84 And we desire that our Lord may cause us to enter with righteous people.

Note : See the imperfect indicative conjugation chart for easy reference on page 104.

EXERCISE

A. Conjugate the Imperfect tense from the following verbs :

كَـرُمَ	حَفِظَ	جَمَعَ	ضَـرَبَ	قَـتَلَ

B. Distinguish the following forms by their numbers and stable forms from :

تَـقْـتُلُونَ	تَسْجُدِينَ	تَسْجُدُونَ	تَعْبُثُونَ	نَـبْعَثُ	تَأْكُلُونَ
تَحْمَدَانِ	يَنْصُرُونَ	أَنْصُرُ	نَـأْكُلُ	تَحْفَظْنَ	يَـقْتُلْنَ

C. **Translate into English :**

١ - وَإِذْ قُلْنَا لِلْمَلَائِكَة اسْجُدُوا لآدَمَ فَسَجَدُوا إِلَّا إِبْلِيسَ أَبَى وَاسْتَكْبَرَ وَكَانَ مِنَ الْكَافِرِينَ .

٢ - وَإِذْ قَالَ مُوسَى لِقَوْمِهِ إِنَّ الله يَأْمُرُكُمْ أَنْ تَـذْبَحُوا بَقَرَةً قَالُوا أَتَتَّخِذُنَا هُزُوًا قَالَ أَعُوذُ بِالله أَنْ أَكُونَ مِنَ الْجَاهِلِينَ .

٣ - وَإِذْ أَخَذْنَا مِيثَاقَ بَنِي إِسْرَائِيل لَا تَعْبُدُونَ إِلَّا الله .

٤ - وَإِذْ أَخَـذْنَـا مِيثَاقَكُمْ لَا تَسْفِكُونَ دِمَاءَكُمْ وَلَا تُخْرِجُونَ أَنْـفُسَكُمْ مِنْ دِيَارِكُمْ ثُمَّ أَقْـرَرْتُمْ وَأَنْتُمْ تَشْهَدُونَ .

D. **Translate into Arabic :**

For the first three years, or rather less, of his mission, the Prophet preached only to his family and his intimate friends, while (use بَيْنَمَا) the people of Makkah as a whole regarded him as one who had become (أَصْبَحَ) a little mad. First of his converts was his wife Khadija, the second his cousin Ali whom he had adopted, the third his servant Zayd. His old friend Abu Bakr also was among those early converts with some of his dependents.

If you are in doubt concerning that which we revealed to Muhammad, produce a *Surah* like it and call your witnesses beside Allah if you are truthful.

VOCABULARY

إِذْ	when, remember that time when.
أَلْمَلاَئِكَةُ	Angels.
سَجَدُوا	they bowed their head in respect (Perf. 3 P. Masc.)
أَبَى	he refused (Perf. 3rd person sing. Masc.)
إِسْتَكْبَرَ	he was proud (Perf. 3rd person sing. Masc.)
ذَبَحَ	he sacrificed, slaughtered (Perf. 3 P. sing. Masc.)
أَعُوذُ	I seek refuge (Imperfect first person)
مِيثَاقَ	convenant.
سَفَكَ	to shed blood (he).
يَخْرُج	to turn out, cause to get out.
أَقْرَرْتُمْ	You (Masc. plural) promised.
تَشْهَدُونَ	You (Masc. plural) bear witness.

The people.	أَلْقَـوْمُ
Convert, he who converted to Islam.	الَّذِي أَسْلَمَ
Dependent	تَحْتَ آلْكِفَالَة
Concerning with (preposition)	عَمَّا / عَنْهُ
To produce	يَنْتِجُ / إِنْتَاجُ
Truthful	الصَّـادِقُ
The first of them	أَوَّلُهُمْ
The servant	أَلْخَادِمُ
Doubt	أَلشَّــكُ
You (sing. Masc.) bear witness	تَشْهَـدُ

Verb Chart : Imperfect Indicative*

(أَلْفِعْلُ ٱلْمُضَارِعُ ٱلْمَرْفُوعُ)

Corresponding Pronoun	Mood Marker	Subject Marker Suffix	Subject Marker Prefix	Verb Form
Singular Forms				
هُوَ	above the ُ last letter		يَـ	يَدْرُسُ
هِيَ	above the ُ last letter		تَـ	تَدْرُسُ
أَنْتَ	above the ُ last letter		تَـ	تَدْرُسُ
أَنْتِ	نَ	ـيـ	تَـ	تَدْرُسِينَ
أَنَا	above the ُ last letter		أ	أَدْرُسُ
Plural Forms				
هُمْ	نَ	ـو	يَـ	يَدْرُسُونَ
هُنَّ	No mood marker	ـنَ	يَـ	يَدْرُسْنَ
أَنْتُمْ	نَ	ـو	تَـ	تَدْرُسُونَ
أَنْتُنَّ	No mood marker	ـنَ	تَـ	تَدْرُسْنَ
نَحْنُ	above the ُ last letter		نَـ	نَدْرُسُ
Dual Forms				
هُمَا (m)	نِ	ـا	يَـ	يَدْرُسَانِ
هُمَا (f)	نِ	ـا	تَـ	تَدْرُسَانِ
أَنْتُمَا (m+f)	نِ	ـا	تَـ	تَدْرُسَانِ

* **Note :** Imperfect indicative verbs correspond to English simple present tense or to a progressive construction with "is/are/am" and a verb in the "-ing" form.

CHAPTER 8

MOODS OF IMPERFECT

Arabic has three kinds of moods :

1	Indicative	اَلْمُضَارِعُ ٱلْمَـرْفُـوعُ
2	Subjunctive	اَلْمُضَارِعُ ٱلْمَنْصُوبُ
3	Jussive	اَلْمُضَارِعُ ٱلْمَجْــزُومُ

- The Imperfect indicative has already been dealt with in chapter 7, which makes a plain statement, whether applicable to the present or the future. But the Imperfect, by slight changes may be in subjunctive or jussive moods. Arab grammarians take the indicative case as an absolute unit that is influenced and shaped according to the prefixed nouns or particles that are called in Arabic أَلْعَوَامِل *'al-'awāmil* (elements). The simple Imperfect tense, such as يَفْعَلُ *(yaf'alu)* "he does or will do", is vowelled with *dammah* in its final letter and gives the meaning of a plain statement, but when it is preceded by a particle such as لَنْ *(lan)* or لَمْ *(lam)*, its case ending will be changed and the meaning will differ from what it has in absolute case. However, the Indicative mood of the Imperfect could be introduced as أَلْفِعْلُ ٱلْمُضَارِعُ . The Imperfect tense, i.e., its simple case without an element. These عَـوَامِل (elements) that turn the indicative mood to the subjunctive one, are :

I	أَنْ	'an
e.g.	أَمَرْتُهُ أَنْ يَذْهَبَ	I ordered him to go.

II	أَلَّا (أَنْ + لَا = أَلَّا)	may not
e.g.	أَلَّا يَقُولَ إِنِّي لَا أَعْلَمُ	so he may not say I do not know.

III	لَنْ	will not
e.g.	لَنْ يَذْهَبَ مَحْمُودٌ	Maḥmūd will not go.

IV	لِأَنْ	in order to
e.g.	لِأَنْ يَفْعَلَ مَا يَشَاءُ	so he may do what he pleases.

V	حَتَّىٰ	until
e.g.	حَتَّىٰ يَعُودَ إِلَى ٱلْحَقِّ	until (or so that) he may return to the truth.

VI	كَيْ	so that, in order that
e.g.	كَيْ نُسَبِّحَكَ كَثِيرًا	that we may glorify thee much.

These particles which we may call العَوَامِلُ (elements) bring two-fold changes in the simple indicative forms of the Imperfect.

1. They change the vowel of the final letter from *dammah* to *fathah,* so that يَفْعُلُ becomes يَفْعَلَ and omit *"nūns"* of duals and plurals except those of feminine plurals :

   يَفْعَلْنَ (3rd Pers. pl. Fem.)   تَفْعَلْنَ (2nd Pers. pl. Fem.)

2. They give the meaning of subjunctive mode. The conjugation with لَنْ "will not" is as following :

	Singular	Corresponding Pronoun
3rd Person, Masc.	لَنْ يَـذْهَبَ	هُــوَ
3rd Person, Fem.	لَنْ تَـذْهَبَ	هِــيَ
2nd Person, Masc.	لَنْ تَـذْهَبَ	أَنْتَ
2nd Person, Fem.	لَنْ تَـذْهَبِي	أَنْتِ
1st Person, Masc. & Fem.	لَنْ أَذْهَبَ	أَنَــا

	Dual	Corresponding Pronoun
3rd Person, Masc.	لَنْ يَـذْهَبَا	هُمَــا
3rd Person, Fem.	لَنْ تَـذْهَبَا	هُمَــا
2nd Person, Masc.	لَنْ تَـذْهَبَا	أَنْـتُـمَا
2nd Person, Fem.	لَنْ تَـذْهَبَا	أَنْـتُـمَا

	Plural	**Corresponding Pronoun**
3rd Person, Masc.	لَنْ يَـذْهَبُوا	هُـمْ
3rd Person, Fem.	لَنْ يَـذْهَبْنَ	هُـنَّ
2nd Person, Masc.	لَنْ تَـذْهَبُوا	أَنْـتُمْ
2nd Person, Fem.	لَنْ تَـذْهَبْنَ	أَنْـتُنَّ
1st Person, Masc. & Fem.	لَنْ نَـذْهَبَ	نَحْنُ

The "nūn" of Fem. Plural is not omitted. The subjunctive is also made by placing one of the following elements before the indicative (مُضَارِع *muḍāri'*)

كَيْ (*kai*) ، لِ (*li*) ، أَنْ (*'an*)

Here are some examples from the Holy Qur'ān :

أَنْ	*'an*	lest, to...

أَنْ تَـقُولَ نَفْسٌ يَا حَسْرَتَىٰ	39-56 Lest a soul should say, "O, woe is me".
أَوَلَمْ يَـرَوْا أَنَّ اﷲ ٱلَّذِي خَلَـقَ ٱلسَّمَـٰوَاتِ وَٱلْأَرْضَ قَادِرٌ عَلَىٰ أَنْ يَخْلُـقَ مِثْلَهُمْ	17-99 See they not that Allah, Who created the heavens and the earth, is able to create the like of them.

أَلَّا (أَنْ + لَا = أَلَّا)	'alla	so may not

حَقِيقٌ عَلَىٰ أَنْ لَّا أَقُولَ عَلَىٰ اللهِ إِلَّا ٱلْحَقَّ	7-105	worthy of not saying about Allah except the truth.

لَنْ	lan	will never (will not)

فَلَنْ يَغْفِرَ اللهُ لَهُمْ	9-80	Allah will never forgive them.

لِ	li	for, that

لِيَعْلَمَ أَنِّي لَمْ أَخُنْهُ بِالْغَيْبِ	12-52	This is that he might know that I have not been unfaithful to him in secret.

لأَنْ	li'an	for, that

وَأُمِرْتُ لأَنْ أَكُونَ أَوَّلَ ٱلْمُسْلِمِينَ	39-12	And I am commanded to be the first of those who submit.

حَتَّىٰ	ḥatta	until

حَتَّىٰ يَمِيزَ ٱلْخَبِيثَ مِنَ ٱلطَّيِّبِ	3-179	until He separates the evil from the good.

كَيْلَا	*kaila*	so that, so that not

كَيْلَا يَكُونَ دُولَةً بَيْنَ ٱلْأَغْنِيَاءِ	59-7	so that it be not taken by turns by the rich among you.

لَنْ تَنَالُوا ٱلْبِرَّ حَتَّى تُنْفِقُوا مِمَّا تُحِبُّونَ	3-92	You cannot attain to righteousness unless you spend out of what you love.

قُلْتُمْ لَنْ يَبْعَثَ اللهُ مِنْ بَعْدِهِ رَسُولًا	40-34	You said Allah will never raise after him a messenger.

وَأَنَّا ظَنَنَّا أَنْ لَنْ تَقُولَ ٱلْإِنْسُ وَٱلْجِنُّ عَلَى اللهِ كَذِبًا	72-5	And we thought that men and jinn will not utter a lie against Allah.

لِيَغْفِرَ لَكَ اللهُ مَا تَقَدَّمَ مِنْ ذَنْبِكَ وَمَا تَأَخَّرَ	48-2	that Allah may cover for thee thy shortcomings in the past and those to come.

وَكَفَّ أَيْدِي ٱلنَّاسِ عَنْكُمْ وَلِتَكُونَ آيَةً لِلْمُؤْمِنِينَ	48-20	and He held back the hands of men from you and that it may be a sign for the believers.

لِيَقْطَعَ طَرَفًا مِنَ ٱلَّذِينَ كَفَرُوا	3-127	that He may cut off a part of those who disbelieve.

لِيَجْزِيَ اللهُ ٱلصَّادِقِينَ بِصِدْقِهِمْ وَيُعَذِّبَ ٱلْمُنَافِقِينَ إِنْ شَاءَ أَوْ يَتُوبَ عَلَيْهِمْ	33-24 that Allah may reward the truthful for their truth, chastise the hypocrites if He pleases, or turn to them (mercifully).
لَمَسْجِدٌ أُسِّسَ عَلَى ٱلتَّقْوَىٰ مِنْ أَوَّلِ يَوْمٍ أَحَقُّ أَنْ تَقُومَ فِيهِ	9-108 A Mosque founded on observance of duty from the first day, is more deserving that you shouldst stand in it.
يُرِيدُونَ أَنْ يُبَدِّلُوا كَلَامَ اللهِ	48-15 They desire to change the words of Allah.
أَلَّا تَخَافُوا وَلَا تَحْزَنُوا	41-30 Fear not, nor be grieved.
حَتَّىٰ يَلِجَ ٱلْجَمَلُ فِي سَمِّ ٱلْخِيَاطِ	7-40 Until the camel passes through the eye of the needle.
لَا تَدْخُلُوا بُيُوتًا غَيْرَ بُيُوتِكُمْ حَتَّىٰ تَسْتَأْنِسُوا	24-27 Enter not houses other than your own houses, until you have asked permission.
لِكَيْ لَا تَحْزَنُوا عَلَىٰ مَا فَاتَكُمْ	3-153 that you not grieve over what escaped you.

Note : For easy reference, see the Imperfect Subjunctive conjugation chart at the end of this chapter.

EXERCISE

A. Translate into Arabic :

I will never go over there.   (use لَنْ)

He came to me in order that we might go to school today to-gether.

My uncle came here this afternoon to recite the Holy Qur'ān.

I can not enter my brother's room because he locked the door of his room and took the key with him.

Why did they (Fem.) take this book ?

She took this to read it.

The boys who played football in front of my house came again today to play there.

Do they (Fem.) know that his teacher wants to go to Makkah this year to perform Ḥajj ?

My brother made mistakes in his calculation but he was afraid to say so lest his neighbour laughs at him (in order that his neighbour might not laugh at him).

He came here to be present at this session.

We went up the mountain this morning to play there with the boys and our neighbours.

Who took the key of my car ?

Your brother's knife is very sharp.

Your father will never agree to go somewhere at the time of prayers.

B. Translate into English :

أَمَرَ الله ٱلْمُسْلِمِينَ أَنْ يَتَّبِعُوا أَوَامِرَهُ وَأَنْ يَجْتَنِبُوا ٱلْمُنْكَرَاتِ وَأَنْ يَفْعَلُوا ٱلْخَيْرَ

وَيَأْمُرُوا بِهِ وَأَلَّا يَقُولُوا عَلَى الله إِلَّا ٱلْحَقَّ ، وَأَنْ يَعْدِلُوا بَيْنَ ٱلنَّاسِ ، وَأَلَّا

يَجْعَلُوا ٱلدِّينَ لَهْوًا . إِنَّ الله يَغْفِرُ ٱلذُّنُوبَ جَمِيعًا وَلَنْ يَغْفِرَ لِلْمُشْرِكِينَ لِأَنَّ

ٱلشِّرْكَ ظُلْمٌ عَظِيمٌ . لَا تَتْرُكِ ٱلطَّعَامَ مَكْشُوفًا حَتَّى يَقَعَ ٱلذُّبَابُ فِيهِ ، حَافِظْ

عَلَى صِحَّتَكَ كَي لَا تَمْرَضَ . لِأَنْ يَهْدِيَ الله إِنْسَانًا عَلَى يَدِكَ خَيْرٌ لَكَ مِنَ

ٱلْأَمْوَالِ ٱلطَّائِلَةِ . إِعْمَلْ لِدِينِكَ وَوَطَنِكَ قَبْلَ فَوَاتِ ٱلْأَوَانِ . . أَنْ تَقُولَ لَوْ

كُنْت قَوِيًّا شَابًا فَعَلْتُ كَذَا وَكَذَا .

VOCABULARY

In order to, that	لِأَنْ	li'an
To recite	تَلَا – يَتْلُوا	talā – yatlū
He locked	قَفَلَ – يَقْفِلُ	qafala – yaqfilu
To perform	أَدَّى – يُؤَدِّي	'addā – yu'addī
To make answerable, To hold responsible	حَاسَبَ – يُحَاسِبُ	hāsaba – yuhāsibu
The Neighbour	أَلْجَارُ (pl. جِيرَان)	'al-jāru (pl. jīrān)
The Session	أَلـدَّوْرَةُ	'ad-dawratu

The Knife	السِّكِّين	'as-sikkīn
To follow	إتَّبَعَ – يَتَّبِّعُ	'ittaba'a – yattabi'u
To avoid	أَعْرَضَ – يُعْرِضُ	'a'raḍa – yu'riḍu
Forbidden things	أَلْمُحَرَّمَاتُ	'al-muḥarramātu
The Truth	أَلصِّدْقُ	'aṣ-ṣidqu
To do justice, To be just	عَدَلَ – يَعْدِلُ	'adala – ya'dilu
Leisure	أَللَّهْوُ	'al-lahwu
Forgiveness	أَلْعَفْوُ	'al-'afwu
Sins	أَلذُّنُوبُ	'adh-dhunūbu
Wrong, injustice	الظُّلْمُ	'aẓ-ẓulmu
To open, opened	فَتَحَ – يَفْتَحُ – المَفْتُوحُ	fataha – yaftaḥu – 'al-maftūḥu
Uncounted	لاَ يُحْصَىٰ	lā yuḥṣā
To pass away	مَضَىٰ – يَمْضِي	maḍā – yamḍī
Youthful	الفَتُوَّةُ	'al-fatuwwatu
Flys	الذُّبَابُ	'adh-dhubābu
Polytheism, Idolatry	الشِّرْكُ	'ash-shirku

Verb Chart : Imperfect Subjunctive* (أَلْفِعْلُ ٱلْمُضَارِعُ ٱلْمَنْصُوبُ)

Corresponding Pronoun	Mood Marker	Subject Marker Suffix	Subject Marker Prefix	Verb Form
Singular Forms				
هُوَ	above the last letter ـَ		يَـ	لَنْ / يَدْرُسَ
هِيَ	above the last letter ـَ		تَـ	تَدْرُسَ
أَنْتَ	above the last letter ـَ		تَـ	تَدْرُسَ
أَنْتِ	absence of the final ن which is present in the indicative.	ـِي	تَـ	تَدْرُسِي
أَنَا	above the last letter ـَ		أَ	أَدْرُسَ
Plural Forms				
هُمْ	absence of the final ن which is present in the indicative.	ـُوا	يَـ	لَنْ / يَدْرُسُوا
هُنَّ	No mood marker	ـْـنَ	يَـ	يَدْرُسْنَ
أَنْتُمْ	absence of the final ن which is present in the indicative.	ـُوا	تَـ	تَدْرُسُوا
أَنْتُنَّ	No mood marker	ـْـنَ	تَـ	تَدْرُسْنَ
نَحْنُ	above the last letter ـَ		نَـ	نَـدْرُسَ
Dual Forms				
هُمَا (m)	absence of the final ن which is present in the indicative.	ـَـا	يَـ	لَنْ / يَدْرُسَا
هُمَا (f)	absence of the final ن which is present in the indicative.	ـَـا	تَـ	تَدْرُسَا
أَنْتُمَا (m+f)	absence of the final ن which is present in the indicative.	ـَـا	تَـ	تَدْرُسَا

* To justify the subjunctive mood, verbs should be preceded by a subjunctive particle, the most common of which are : لَنْ – أَنْ – لِـ – كَيْ – لِكَيْ – حَتَّى – لِئَلَّا – كَيْلَا – لِكَيْلَا .

CHAPTER 9

MOODS OF IMPERFECT – II

The Jussive الْمُضَارِعُ ٱلْمَجْزُومُ

1. The mood of negative (or jussive) does not vary from the subjunctive (Mood of statement) except that the final radical takes *sukūn* ـْ i.e. the final letter is closed and has no vowel. To justify the jussive mood, a verb must be preceded by a jussive particle, the most common of which are : لَمْ and لَا of the negative command.

Examples :

Conjugation	لَمْ	Conjugation	لَمْ
3rd P; sing. Masc.	يَكْتُبْ	2nd P; sing. Masc.	تَكْتُبْ
3rd P; dual Masc.	يَكْتُبَا	2nd P; dual Masc.	تَكْتُبَا
3rd P; pl. Masc.	يَكْتُبُوا	2nd P; pl. Masc.	تَكْتُبُوا
3rd P; sing. Fem.	تَكْتُبْ	2nd P; sing. Fem.	تَكْتُبِي
3rd P; dual Fem.	تَكْتُبَا	2nd P; dual Fem.	تَكْتُبَا
3rd P; pl. Fem.	يَكْتُبْنَ	2nd P; pl. Fem.	تَكْتُبْنَ
1st P; sing.	أَكْتُبْ	1st P; dual & pl.	نَكْتُبْ

2. The verb كَانَ "to be" in this mood loses its " و " when the last radical is vowelless, e.g.

2nd P; sing. Masc.	تَكُنْ		3rd P; sing. Masc.	يَكُنْ
2nd P; dual Masc.	تَكُونَا		3rd P; dual Masc.	يَكُونَا
2nd P; pl. Masc.	تَكُونُوا		3rd P; pl. Masc.	يَكُونُوا
2nd P; sing. Fem.	تَكُونِي		3rd P; sing. Fem.	تَكُنْ
2nd P; dual Fem.	تَكُونَا		3rd P; dual Fem.	تَكُونَا
2nd P; pl. Fem.	تَكُنَّ		3rd P; pl. Fem.	يَكُنَّ
1st P; dual & pl.	نَكُنْ		1st P; sing.	أَكُنْ

3. This mood is used after the following particles :

I.   لَا "do not" i.e. with prohibition, e.g.

لَا تَكُنْ كَذَّابًا don't be liar		لَا تَكْتُبْ do not write	

Holy Qur'ān :

لَا تَدْخُلُوا مِنْ بَابٍ وَاحِدٍ	12-67 Do not enter by one gate.
لَا تَكُنْ لِّلْخَائِنِينَ خَصِيمًا	3-104 And be not one pleading the cause of dishonest people.

II. لَمْ ; to deny a statement, when so used, it gives the meaning of the past perfect, e.g. :

Perfect مَا كَتَبَ "he did not write"

Imperfect (Jussive) لَمْ يَكْتُبْ "he did not write".

Holy Qur'ān :

مَا جَعَلَ اللهُ لِرَجُلٍ مِنْ قَلْبَيْنِ فِي جَوْفِهِ	33-4 Allah has not made for any man two hearts within him.
لَمْ نَجْعَلْ لَهُ مِنْ قَبْلُ سَمِيًّا	19-7 We have not made before any one his equal.

III. لَمَّا "not yet" e.g. لَمَّا يَكْتُبْ "he has not yet written".

Holy Qur'ān :

وَلَمَّا يَدْخُلِ ٱلْإِيمَانُ فِي قُلُوبِكُمْ	49-14 And faith has not yet entered into your hearts.

Note : A vowelless letter is changed to *kasrah* ⎯ when followed by a definite article as in لَمْ يَدْخُلِ ٱلْإِيمَانُ .

IV. After the "*lām* of command" لَام الأَمْر which expresses a command, e.g. : لِيَكْتُبْ رِسَالَةً إِلَى أَخِيهِ "let him write a letter to his brother".

Holy Qur'ān :

لِيُنْفِقْ ذُو سَعَةٍ مِنْ سَعَتِهِ	65-7 Let him who has abundance spend out of his abundance.

V. In the Protesis and Apodosis correlative conditional sentences* which are introduced by the particles إِنْ " if ",
مَنْ ''he who, if anyone'' e.g. :

إِنْ تَجْلِسْ أَجْلِسْ   "if you shall sit I shall sit"

مَنْ يَعْمَلْ سُوءًا يَـنْدَمْ   "he who does evil will regret".

Holy Qur'ān :

إِنْ يَشَأْ يُذْهِبْكُمْ أَيُّهَا ٱلنَّاسُ	4-133 If He please, He will cause you to vanish O! people.
مَنْ يَعْمَلْ سُوءًا يُجْزَ بِهِ	4-123 Whoever does evil will be requited for it.

VI. After particles أَيْنَ "where", أَيّ "which", attached to
مَا "to" e.g. :

Holy Qur'ān :

أَيْنَمَا تَكُونُوا يُدْرِككُّمُ ٱلْمَوْتُ	4-78 Wherever you are, death will overtake you.
أَيًّا مَّا تَدْعُوا فَلَهُ الأَسْمَاءُ ٱلْحُسْنَىٰ	17-110 By whatever (name) you call on Him, He has the best names.

4. The Jussive may be rendered more emphatic by adding a
"vowelless *nūn*" نُونٌ خَفِيفَة or a "doubled *nūn*" نُونٌ مُشَدَّدَة
this forms Energetic form (Modus Energicus).

---

* Conditional sentences will be dealt with in chapter 26.

Modus energicus I	Modus energicus II
يَكْتُبَنْ	يَكْتُبَنَّ

This is often strengthened by prefixing the particle لَ e.g. لِيَكْتُبَنَّ

Holy Qur'ān :

وَلَتَعْلَمُنَّ أَيُّنَا أَشَدُّ عَذَابًا وَأَبْقَى	20-71 Surely thou shalt know who among us will have severer chastisement and more lasting.

with negative particle لاَ may give the meaning of "thou shalt not" e.g. لَا تَقْتُلَنَّ "thou shalt not kill".

Holy Qur'ān :

وَلَا تَقُولُوا لِمَنْ يُقْتَلُ فِي سَبِيلِ اللهِ أَمْوَاتٌ	2-154 Thou shalt not say "dead" for these who are killed in the path of Allah.

Examples from the Holy Qur'ān :

فَلَا تَقُلْ لَهُمَا أُفٍّ وَلَا تَنْهَرْهُمَا	17-23 Do not say "Fie" to them (parents) nor chide them.
وَأَمَّا السَّائِلَ فَلَا تَنْهَرْ	93-10 And him who asks, do not chide.
وَلَا تَقْرَبُوا الْفَوَاحِشَ	6-15 Do not get nigh to indecencies.
لَا تَجْعَلْ مَعَ اللهِ إِلَهًا آخَرَ	17-22 Associate not any other god with Allah.

(خُـذْهَا وَ) لَا تَخَفْ	20-21 Seize it and fear not.
أَوَلَمْ يَـنْظُـرُوا فِي مَلَكُوتِ السَّمٰوَاتِ وَٱلْأَرْضِ	7-185 Do they not consider the kingdom of the heavens and and earth.
لَمْ نَـجْعَلْ لَـهُ مِنْ قَبْلُ سَمِيًّا	19-7 We have not made before any on his equal.
أَلَمْ أَقُـلْ لَّكَ إِنَّـكَ لَنْ تَسْتَطِـيعَ مَعِـيَ صَبْـرًا	18-75 Did I not say to thee that thou couldst not have patience with me ?
لِـيَعْلَمَ أَنِّي لَمْ أَخُـنْـهُ بِالْغَيْبِ	12-52 This is that he might learn that I have not been unfaithful to him.
لَا يَـنْفَعُ نَـفْسًا إِيمَانُهَا لَمْ تَكُنْ آمَنَتْ مِنْ قَبْلُ	6-158 Its faith will not profit a soul which believed not before.
لَمْ يَكُنِ ٱلَّذِينَ كَفَرُوا مِنْ أَهْلِ ٱلْكِتَابِ وَٱلْمُشْرِكِينَ مُنْفَكِّينَ حَتَّىٰ تَأْتِيَهُمُ ٱلْبَـيِّنَـةُ	98-1 Those who disbelieve from among the people of the book and the idolaters could not have been freed, till clear evidence came to them.
وَلَمَّا يَدْخُلِ ٱلْأِيمَانُ فِي قُلُوبِكُمْ	49-14 ...and faith has not yet entered in your hearts.
وَلَمَّا يَعْلَمِ اللهُ ٱلَّذِينَ جَاهَدُوا مِنْكُمْ	3-142 And Allah has not yet known those from among you who strive hard.

بَـلْ لَمَّا يَـذُوقُـوا عَـذَابِ	38-8　Nay, they have not yet tasted My chastisement.
لِـيَـقْضِ عَلَيْـنَا رَبُّـكَ	43-77　Let thy Lord make an end of us.
مَا نَـنْسَخْ مِنْ آيَةٍ أَوْ نُـنْسِهَا نَـأْتِ بِخَيْرٍ مِنْهَا	2-106　Whatever verses We abrogate or cause to be forgotten, We bring one better than it.
وَ إِنْ يَمْسَسْكَ بِخَيْرٍ فَهُوَ عَلَىٰ كُلِّ شَيْءٍ قَـدِيرٍ	6-17　And if He touch thee with good, He is the Possessor of Power over all things.
وَ إِنْ تُصِبْهُمْ سَيِّئَةٍ بِمَا قَـدَّمَتْ أَيْـدِيهِمْ إِذَا هُمْ يَقْنَطُونَ	30-36　And if an evil befalls them for what their hands have already wrongeth, Lo! They despair.

Note : For easy reference, see the Imperfect Jussive Conjugation Chart at the end of this chapter.

EXERCISE

A.　Translate into Arabic :

Let Makkah be the most beautiful city under the sun, students! He did not know (use لَمْ) any news from his home. O girl, do not go to market this time now. O boy don't open the window. I did not understand (use لَمْ) this argument. The lazy boys did not memorize conjugations. Do not leave your friends in anxiety. Do not prevent me from praying. Let us drink the Zamzam. The sister and mother were not able to go out. Let me be at your side among these groups. O 'Alī, I asked Bakr to come in, but some one else entered. Next month a visiting professor will come to the university. If Ḥasan goes home I will go with him. Whatever my father decides, I will obey him. My brother could not carry this heavy chair yesterday evening because he was very tired. Your friend Ḥabīb drank a cup of tea this morning. Do not open these two windows.

B. Translate into English :

١ - فَمَنْ يَعْمَلْ مِنَ ٱلصَّالِحَاتِ وَهُوَ مُؤْمِنٌ فَلَا كُفْرَانَ لِسَعْيِهِ وَإِنَّا لَهُ كَاتِبُونَ

٢ - قُلْ لَنْ يُصِيبَنَا إِلَّا مَا كَتَبَ الله لَنَا هُوَ مَوْلَانَا وَ عَلَىٰ اللهِ فَلْيَتَوَكَّلِ ٱلْمُؤْمِنُونَ

٣ - وَتَاللهِ لَأَكِيدَنَّ أَصْنَامَكُمْ

٤ - بِسْمِ اللهِ ٱلرَّحْمٰنِ ٱلرَّحِيمِ آلر كِتَابٌ أَنْزَلْنَاهُ إِلَيْكَ لِتُخْرِجَ ٱلنَّاسَ مِنَ ٱلظُّلُمَاتِ إِلَى ٱلنُّورِ بِإِذْنِ رَبِّهِمْ إِلَىٰ صِرَاطِ ٱلْعَزِيزِ ٱلْحَمِيدِ

٥ - قَالَ قَائِلٌ مِنْهُمْ لَا تَقْتُلُوا يُوسُفَ وَٱلْقُوهُ فِي غَيَابَتِ ٱلْجُبِّ يَلْتَقِطْهُ بَعْضُ ٱلسَّيَّارَةِ إِنْ كُنْتُمْ فَاعِلِينَ . قَالُوا يَا أَبَانَا مَا لَكَ لَا تَأْمَنَّا عَلَىٰ يُوسُفَ وَإِنَّا لَهُ لَنَاصِحُونَ أَرْسِلْهُ مَعَنَا غَدًا يَرْتَعْ وَيَلْعَبْ وَ إِنَّا لَهُ لَحَافِظُونَ

VOCABULARY

أَجْمَلُ ٱلْمُدُنِ	most beautiful cities	دَلِيلٌ	proof
كَسْلَان ، كَسَالى	lazy	حَفِظَ	to memorize
التَّصْرِيفِ	conjugation	قَلَقٌ	anxiety
مَنَعَ	to prevent	جَانِبٌ	side
زَائِر	a visitor (3rd Person sing. Masc.)		
قَرَّرَ	to decide	أَطَاعَ	to obey
حَمَلَ	to carry	ثَقِيلٌ	heavy
لأَنَّ	because	مُتْعَبٌ/تَعْبَانٌ	tired
الصَّالِحَةُ	good (pl. الصَّالِحَاتِ)	دَخَلَ	to enter
سَعَى	to make an effort, to strive		
تَاللهِ	by Allah	كُفْرَانٌ	rejection
يُصِيبُ	to befall (of evil) (Imper., 3rd Pers. sing. Masc.)		
كَيدَ	artful plot, trick (لأَكِيدَنَّ I shall outwit certainly)		
أَصْنَام	idols (sing. صَنَم)	مَوْلَى	Lord
الظُّلُمَاتِ	the darkness	تَوَكَّل	to trust
إِذْنٌ	permission	تَوَلَّى	to turn away

العَزيز	The Powerful One		
الحَميد	The Praised One	Allah's name of tributes.	
غَيَبَتِ آلجُبِّ	The bottom of the well		
يَلْتَقِطْهُ	Imperfect, perfect إِلْتَقَطَ to pick up		
أَخَافُ (خَوْفٌ)	to frighten (fear)	مُدْبِرينَ	showing back
غَافِلُونَ	heedless (pl.)	النُّور	The light
الصَّمَدُ	One on Whom all depend		
يُولَدُ	Begotten	صِراطُ	path
نَاصِحُونَ	well-wishers	السَّيَّارَةُ	travellers
يَرْتَعُ ، رَتَعَ	enjoy	الذِّئْبُ	wolf
يَحْزُنُ ، حَزِنَ	to grieve	أَحَدُ	One
ذَهَبَ بِهِ	to take some one with		
يَلِدُ وَلَدَ	begets	غَـدًا	tomorrow
كَفُوءُ	similar	يَلْعَبُ ، لَعِبَ	to play

Verb Chart : Imperfect Jussive*

(الفِعْلُ المُضارِعُ المَجْزُومُ)

Corresponding Pronoun	Mood Marker	Subject Marker Suffix	Subject Marker Prefix	Verb Form
		Singular Forms		
هُوَ	above the last letter	ــْ	يَـ	يَفْعَلْ / يَكْتُبْ
هِيَ	above the last letter	ــْ	تَـ	تَكْتُبْ
أَنْتَ	above the last letter	ــْ	تَـ	تَكْتُبْ
أَنْتِ	absence of the final نَ of the indicative mood	ـِي	تَـ	تَكْتُبِي
أَنا	above the last letter	ــْ	ـَ	أَكْتُبْ
		Plural Forms		
هُمْ	absence of the final نَ of the indicative mood	ـُوا	يَـ	يَكْتُبُوا
هُنَّ	No mood marker; identical in jussive, indicative & subjunctive	ـْنَ	يَـ	يَكْتُبْنَ
أَنْتُمْ	absence of the final نَ of the indicative mood	ـُوا	تَـ	تَكْتُبُوا
أَنْتُنَّ	No mood marker; identical in jussive, indicative & subjunctive	ـْنَ	تَـ	تَكْتُبْنَ
نَحْنُ	above the last letter	ــْ	نَـ	نَكْتُبْ

Corresponding Pronoun	Mood Marker	Subject Marker Suffix	Subject Marker Prefix	Verb Form
Dual Forms				
(m) هُمَا	absence of the final ن of the indicative mood	ـَا	ﻳَـ	يَفْعَلَا / ﻳَـ...
(f) هُمَا	absence of the final ن of the indicative mood	ـَا	ﺗَـ	تَفْعَلَا
(m + f) أَنْتُمَا	absence of the final ن of the indicative mood	ـَا	ﺗَـ	تَفْعَلَا

* **Note :** Jussive verbs must be preceded by jussive particles, the most common of which is لَمْ ; there are, of course, other jussive particles.

CHAPTER 10

THE PASSIVE VOICE

1. The Active voice of the verb is called مَعْلُومٌ "known" while
    the Passive is termed مَجْهُولٌ "unknown". The passive is
    formed by changing the vowels of the active. It is charac-
    terized by *dammah* ُ on the first letter of the active follow-
    ing *kasrah* ِ in the perfect and *fathah* َ in the imperfect,
    e.g. :

Perfect

Active		Passive	
فَتَحَ	he opened.	فُتِحَ	it was opened.
فَتَحَ بَابًا	he opened a door.	فُتِحَ بَابٌ	a door was opened
كَتَبَ رِسَالَةً	he wrote a letter.	كُتِبَتْ رِسَالَةٌ	a letter was written
نَصَرَنِي	he helped me.	نُصِرْتُ	I was helped.

Imperfect

Active		Passive	
يَفْتَحُ	he opens.	يُفْتَحُ	It is (being) opened
يَكْتُبُ	he writes.	يُكْتَبُ	It is (being) written
يَنْصُرُكَ	he helps you.	تُنْصَرُ	you are (will be) helped.

The following conjugation will show you the places of vowels :

Perfect

sing. 3rd Pers. Masc.	نُصِرَ *nuṣira*	he was helped.
sing. 3rd Pers. Fem.	نُصِرَتْ *nuṣirat*	she was helped.
sing. 2nd Pers. Masc.	نُصِرْتَ *nuṣirta*	You were helped.
sing. 2nd Pers. Fem.	نُصِرْتِ *nuṣirti*	You were helped.
sing. 1st Pers. Masc. & Fem.	نُصِرْتُ *nuṣirtu*	I was helped.

Imperfect

sing. 3rd Pers. Masc.	يُنْصَرُ *yunṣaru*	he is helped.
sing. 3rd Pers. Fem.	تُنْصَرُ *tunṣaru*	she is helped.
sing. 2nd Pers. Masc.	تُنْصَرُ *tunṣaru*	You are helped.
sing. 2nd Pers. Fem.	تُنْصَرِينَ *tunṣarīna*	You are helped.
sing. 1st Pers. Masc. & Fem.	أُنْصَرُ *'unṣaru*	I was helped.

2. In case of the imperfect subjunctive and jussive the conjugation will be as follows :

Subjunctive		Jussive	
يُكْتَبَ yuktaba		يُكْتَبْ yuktab	
تُكْتَبَ tuktaba		تُكْتَبْ tuktab	
تُكْتَبِي tuktabī		تُكْتَبِي tuktabī	
أُكْتَبَ 'uktaba		أُكْتَبْ 'uktab	

3. The passive voice of perfect from weak verbs is given below :

Perfect

Active		Passive	
قَالَ qāla	he said.	قِيلَ qīla	it was said.
دَعَىٰ da‘ā	he called.	دُعِيَ du‘iya	he was called
بَاعَ bā‘a	he sold.	بِيعَ bī‘a	it was sold.

The passive voice of imperfect from weak verbs will be as follows :

Imperfect

Active		Passive	
يَقُولُ yaqūlu	he says.	يُقَالُ yuqālu	it is said.
يَدْعُو yad‘ū	he calls.	يُدْعَىٰ yud‘ā	he is called
يَبِيعُ yabī‘u	he sells.	يُبَاعُ yubā‘u	it is sold.

4. The subject of a passive verb is called نَائِبُ ٱلْفَاعِل i.e. 'representative of the doer'. The Arabic passive is not like English in which the doer is mentioned with particle 'by' e.g. 'The glass was broken by the maid'. In Arabic for this purpose, an active voice will be used e.g. كَسَرَت ٱلْخَادِمَةُ ٱلْكَأَس. This is the reason why this form in Arabic is termed by ٱلْمَجْهُول i.e. the doer of that act is unknown.

5. **The Participle** (Active and Passive)

The Active participle (from the triliteral verb) is formed by adding an 'alif after the first radical and vowelling the second radical with kasarah, thus :

فَاعِـلٌ	fāʿilun	a doer	Masc. Sing.
فَاعِـلَانِ	fāʿilāni	two doers	Masc. Dual
فَاعِلُونَ	fāʿilūna	doers	Masc. Pl.
فَاعِلَـةٌ	fāʿilatun	a doer	Fem. Sing.
فَاعِلَتَانِ	fāʿilatāni	two doers	Fem. Dual
فَاعِلَاتٌ	fāʿilātun	doers	Fem. Pl.

The Passive Participle (that is not English Past Participle) is formed on the measure مَفْعُولٌ for the simple triliteral verb. The following conjugation will illustrate the prefixed letters and vowelling :

"mafʿūlun" 'which is done', one on whom an action is be fallen.

مَكْتُوبٌ	*Maktūbun*	written.
مَفْتُوحٌ	*Maftūḥun*	opened.
مَضْرُوبٌ	*Maḍrūbun*	struck.

Dual Masc.	مَفْعُولَان مَفْعُولَيْن	*Maf'ūlāni* *Maf'ūlaini*	(Nominative) (Accusative & Genative)
Sing. Fem.	مَفْعُولَةٌ	*Maf'ūlatun*	(Acc. & Gen.)
Dual Fem.	مَفْعُولَتَان مَفْعُولَتَيْن	*Maf'ūlatāni* *Maf'ūlataini*	(Nominative) (Acc. & Gen.)
Pl. Masc.	مَفْعُولُونَ مَفْعُولِينَ	*Maf'ūlūna* *Maf'ūlīna*	(Nominative) (Acc. & Gen.)
Pl. Fem.	مَفْعُولَاتٌ مَفْعُولَاتٍ	*Maf'ūlātun* *Maf'ūlātin*	(Nominative) (Acc. & Gen.)

Examples from The Holy Qur'ān :

3rd Pers. Sing. Masc.	فُعِلَ

يَا أَيُّهَا ٱلَّذِينَ آمَنُوا كُتِبَ عَلَيْكُمُ ٱلصِّيَامُ كَمَا كُتِبَ عَلَى ٱلَّذِينَ مِنْ قَبْلِكُمْ .	2-183 O' you who believe, fasting is prescribed for you (lit. written upon you) as it was prescribed (was written) for those before you.
وَحُشِرَ لِسُلَيْمَانَ جُنُودُهُ	27-17 And there were gathered together unto Solomon his armies.

وَجُمِعَ ٱلشَّمْسُ وَٱلْقَمَرُ	75-9 And the sun and moon are brought together.
أَفَإِن مَاتَ أَوْ قُتِلَ	3-144 If then he dies or is killed.

مَا مَاتُوا وَمَا قُتِلُوا	3-156 They did not die and have not been killed.
أَمْ خُلِقُوا مِنْ غَيْرِ شَيْءٍ	52-35 Or were they created without a (creative) thing?
أُذِنَ لِلَّذِينَ يُقَاتِلُونَ بِأَنَّهُمْ ظُلِمُوا	22-39 Permission (to fight) is given to those who are fought because they have been wronged.

أَفَلَا يَنْظُرُونَ إِلَى ٱلْإِبِلِ كَيْفَ خُلِقَتْ	88-17 Will they not regard the camels, how they are created?
بِأَيِّ ذَنْبٍ قُتِلَتْ	81-9 For what sin she was killed.
وَإِذَا ٱلصُّحُفُ نُشِرَتْ	81-10 And when the leafs (of book records) are spread.

	2nd Pers. Pl. Masc.	فُعِلْتُمْ

وَلَئِنْ قُتِلْتُمْ فِي سَبِيلِ اللهِ أَوْ مُتُّمْ	3-157 And what though you be slain in Allah's way or die.
وَلَئِنْ مُتُّمْ أَوْ قُتِلْتُمْ لَإِلَى اللهِ تُحْشَرُونَ	3-158 And what though you die or be slain, when unto Allah you are gathered.

	1st Pers. Sing. Masc. & Fem.	فُعِلْتُ

وَلَئِنْ رُجِعْتُ إِلَى رَبِّي إِنَّ لِي عِنْدَهُ لَلْحُسْنَى	41-50 And if I am sent back to my Lord I shall have sure good with Him.
وَلَئِنْ رُدِدْتُ إِلَى رَبِّي لَأَجِدَنَّ خَيْراً مِنْهَا مُنْقَلَبَا	18-36 If I am returned to my Lord I will certainly find a returning place better than this.

	1st Pers. Pl. Masc. & Fem.	فُعِلْنَا

يَقُولُونَ لَوْ كَانَ لَنَا مِنَ الأَمْرِ شَيْءٌ مَا قُتِلْنَا ههُنَا	3-154 They say : Had we any hand in the affairs, we should not have been slain here.

3rd Pers. Sing. Masc.	جِيءَ *jī'a* (active: جَاءَ *jā'a*)
	قُضِيَ *quḍiya* (active: قَضَى *qaḍā*)

وَجِيءَ بِالنَّبِيِّينَ وَالشُّهَدَاء وَقُضِيَ بَيْنَهُمْ بِالْحَقِّ	39-69 ...And the prophets and witnesses are brought up and judgement is given between them with justice.

	قِيلَ *qīla* (active: قَالَ *qāla*)

وَقِيلَ بُعْدًا لِلْقَوْمِ الظَّالِمِينَ	11-44 And it was said, away with the iniquitous people.

3rd Pers. Pl. Masc.	سُقُوا *suqū* (active: سَقَى *saqā*)

وَسُقُوا مَاءً حَمِيمًا	47-15 And (who) are given boiling water to drink.

1st Pers. Sing. Masc.	نُهِيتُ *nuhītu* (active: نَهَى *nahā*)

قُلْ : إِنِّي نُهِيتُ أَنْ أَعْبُدَ الَّذِينَ تَدْعُونَ مِنْ دُونِ اللهِ	6-56 Say (O' Muhammad) : I am forbidden to worship those whom you call upon besides Allah.

Imperfect

3rd Pers. Sing. Masc.   يُفْعَلُ

وَمَا أَدْرِى مَا يُـفْـعَـلُ بِي	47-15 And I know not what will be done with me.
لَمْ يُخْلَقْ مِثْلُهَا فِي ٱلْبِـلَاد	89-8 The like of which was not created in the lands.
يُعْرَفُ ٱلْمُجْرِمُونَ بِسِيمَاهُمْ	55-41 The guilty will be known by their marks.

3rd Pers. Pl. Masc.   يُفْعَلُونَ

أَيُشْرِكُونَ مَا لَا يُخْلُقُ شَيْئًا وَهُمْ يُخْلَـقُونَ	7-191 Attribute they as partners to Allah those who created naught, but are themselves created ?
ثُمَّ إِلَيْـهِ يُرْجَعُونَ	6-36 Then to Him they will be returned.
يُـقَاتِـلُونَ فِي سَبِـيلِ اللهِ فَـيَقْتُلُونَ وَيُـقْتَـلُونَ	9-111 They fight in the way of Allah and slay and be slain.

3rd Pers. Sing. Fem.   تُفْعَلُ

وَإِلَى اللهِ تُـرْجَعُ ٱلْأُمُورُ	2-210 And all affairs are returned to Allah.
سَتُكْتَبُ شَهَادَتُهُمْ وَيُسْئَلُونَ	43-19 Their testimony will be recorded and they will be questioned.

3rd Pers. Pl. Fem.	يُفْعَلْنَ

ذَلِكَ أَدْنَى أَنْ يُعْرَفْنَ فَلَا يُؤْذَيْنِ	33-59 That will be better, so that they may be recognized and not annoyed.

2nd Pers. Sing. Masc.	تُفْعَلُ

وَلَا تُسْئَلُ عَنْ أَصْحَابِ الْجَحِيمِ	2-119 And thou will not be asked about dwellers of the hell-fire.

2nd Pers. Dual Masc.	تُفْعَلَانِ

قَالَ : لَا يَأْتِيكُمَا طَعَامٌ تُرْزَقَانِهِ إِلَّا نَبَّأْتُكُمَا بِتَأْوِيلِهِ	12-37 He said : The food which you (two) are given, shall not come unto you but I shall tell you its interpretation.

2nd Pers. Pl. Masc.	تُفْعَلُونَ

ادْخُلُوا الْجَنَّةَ أَنْتُمْ وَأَزْوَاجُكُمْ تُحْبَرُونَ	43-70 Enter the garden, you and your wives, to be made glad.
إِنْ تَجْتَنِبُوا كَبَائِرَ مَا تُنْهَوْنَ عَنْهُ نُكَفِّرْ عَنْكُمْ سَيِّئَاتِكُمْ	4-31 If you avoid the great things which you are forbidden, We will remit from you your evil deeds.

	اسم الفاعـــــل	Active Participle

Sing. Masc.

إِنِّي لَا أُضِيعُ عَمَلَ عَامِلٍ مِنْكُمْ	3-195 Lo! I suffer not the work of any worker.
بَلْ هُوَ شَاعِــرٌ	21-5 Nay, he is but a poet.
فَلَعَلَّكَ بَاخِعٌ نَفْسَكَ	18-6 Yet it may be, (that) thou will torment thy soul.

Dual Masc.

قَالُوا : إِنْ هٰذَانِ لَسَاحِرَانِ	20-63 They said : These are two wizards.

Plural Masc.

وَالَّذِينَ هُمْ لِلزَّكَاةِ فَاعِلُونَ	23-4 And who are payers of Zakat (poordue).

Sing. Fem.

وُجُوهٌ يَوْمَئِذٍ نَاعِمَةٌ لِسَعْيِهَا رَاضِيَةٌ فِي جَنَّةٍ عَالِيَةٍ لَا تَسْمَعُ فِيهَا لَاغِيَةً	88-8/11 In that day other faces will be calm, glad for their past effort. In a high garden, where they hear no idle speech.

	اسم المفعـــول	Passive Participle

Sing. Masc.

أُولَٰئِكَ لَهُمْ رِزْقٌ مَعْلُومٌ	37-41 For them there is a known provision.
كِتَابٌ مَرْقُومٌ	83-20 A written record (book).

Sing. Fem.	
فِيهَا سُرُرٌ مَرْفُوعَةٌ وَأَكْوَابٌ مَوْضُوعَةٌ وَنَمَارِقُ مَصْفُوفَةٌ وَزَرَابِيُّ مَبْثُوثَةٌ	88-13/16 Wherein are couches raised, and goblets set at hand, and cushions ranged, and silken carpets spread.

EXERCISE

A. Translate into Arabic :

The doors of the mosque were opened, and the prayers were offered with (خُشُوعٌ) humility. She did not know that her brother was given a prize yesterday. I know that the Arabs are conquerors and the enemies the conquered. The men mentioned are (some) of (بَعْضَ) my friends. His courage has been mentioned in the history books. He was killed with (السَّيْفُ) the sword because the madmen were angry with him. You have been (كُنْتَ) here for a long time (period). Perhaps you will go now. The prince attended the first session of the Islamic Solidarity Conference. It was inaugurated by the royal speech. King Faisal entered the history through (خِلَالَ) its widest gate. The Qur'an is the widely read book in the world. It is recited in the morning and evening. The Muslim is he who discharges his duties and obey his Lord and benefits to the humanbeing.

B. Translate into English :

بِسْمِ اللهِ ٱلـرَّحْمٰنِ ٱلرَّحِيْمِ . قَـدْ أَفْـلَـحَ ٱلْمُؤْمِنُـوْنَ . الَّـذِيْنَ هُمْ فِي صَلَاتِهِمْ خَاشِعُونَ . وَٱلَّذِيْنَ هُمْ عَنِ ٱللَّغْوِ مُعْرِضُوْنَ . وَٱلَّذِيْنَ هُمْ لِلزَّكَاةِ فَاعِلُوْنَ . وَٱلَّذِيْنَ هُمْ لِفُرُوْجِهِمْ حَافِظُوْنَ . إِلَّا عَلَىٰ أَزْوَاجِهِمْ أَوْ مَا مَلَكَتْ أَيْمَـانُهُمْ فَإِنَّهُمْ غَيْرُ مَلُوْمِيْنَ . فَمَنِ ٱبْتَغَىٰ وَرَاءَ ذٰلِكَ فَأُوْلٰئِكَ هُمُ ٱلْعَادُوْنَ . وَٱلَّـذِيْنَ هُمْ لِأَمَانَاتِهِمْ وَعَهْدِهِمْ رَاعُوْنَ . وَٱلَّذِيْنَ هُمْ عَلَىٰ صَلَوَاتِهِمْ يُحَافِظُوْنَ . أُولٰئِكَ هُمُ ٱلْوَارِثُوْنَ . الَّذِيْنَ يَرِثُوْنَ ٱلْفِرْدَوْسَ هُمْ فِيهَا خَالِدُوْنَ .

VOCABULARY

humility	خُشُوْعٌ	the sword	السَّيْفُ
yesterday	أَمْسِ	angry	غَضْبَانُ
conquered	مَفْتُوْحٍ / مَفْتُوْحُوْنَ .pl – مَفْتُوْحٌ		
madmen	مَجْنُوْنٌ .sing – مَجَانِيْنَ		
period	فَـتْرَةٌ	the prince	الأَمِيْر
attended	إِشْـتَرَكَ	inaugurated	أَفْـتَـتَحَ
entered	دَخَـلَ	widest gate	أَوْسَعُ ٱلْأَبْـوَابِ
to be recited	تَـلَا / يُتْلَىٰ	to be discharged	أَدَّىٰ / يُؤَدَّىٰ
his duties	وَاجِبَاتِـهِ	benefit	يَـنْـفَعُ
prize	جَوَائِرُ .pl – جَائِزَةٌ	human being	الإِنْسَانُ
conqueror	فَاتِحِيْنَ / فَاتِحُوْنَ .pl – فَاتِحٌ		

(الَّذِي .sing) الَّذِينَ	who, that, which (a relative pronoun).
(هُوَ .they (sing هُمْ	pronoun (will be dealt with seperately in coming chapter).
صَلَاةٌ	prayer.
اللَّغْوَ	vain conversation.
(فَرْجٌ .sing) فُرُوجٌ	pudendums.
(زَوْجٌ .sing) أَزْوَاجٌ	wife or husband (spouse).
مَلُومٌ	blameworthy.
وَرَاءَ ذَلَكَ	beyond that.
(عَادٍ .sing) عَادُونَ	transgressor.
(أَمَانَة .sing) أَمَانَات	pledge, trustworthiness, trusteeship.
يُحَافِظُونَ	pay heed to protect.
يَرِثُ	will inherit.
خَالِدُونَ	will abide eternally.
خَاشِعٌ	state of humbleness.
مُعْرِضٌ	shun, avoid.
إِلَّا	except (a particle).
ابْتَغَى	sought, wished.
أُولَئِكَ	such people or such thing (those).
رَاعِي (رَاعٍ) ، رَاعُونْ	shephered, protector.
عَهْدٌ	covenant.
وَارِثٌ	heir.
الْفِرْدَوْسُ	paradise.

CHAPTER 11

THE ADJECTIVES

1. A noun qualified with an adjective is called (in Arabic
اَلْمُـرَكَّبُ ٱلتَّـوْصِيفِي (The Adjectival Compound). The noun
which is to be qualified is termed as مَوْصُوفٌ *mawṣūfun* and the
adjective is صِفَـةٌ *sifatun*. The English simple adjectives such
as 'the long way', 'the white shirt' is translated into Arabic by
placing the noun first, then the adjective. Thus 'the white
shirt' will become 'the shirt white'; 'the long way' will be read
'the way long' and so on, thus :

The long way	الطَّرِيقُ ٱلطَّـوِيـلُ
The white shirt	القَمِيصُ ٱلْأَبْـيَضُ

2. An Arabic adjectival phrase (that is not English adjective
pharse') is formed by an agreement of noun with the adjective, in case ending, definiteness and indefiniteness, number
and gender. e.g. رَجُلٌ كَبِيرٌ 'a big man', ٱلرَّجُلُ ٱلْكَبِيرُ 'the big man'.
Likewise, if the noun is dual or plural, the adjective will take
the same, e.g. رَجُلَانِ كَبِيرَانِ 'two big men', ٱلرَّجُلَانِ الكَبِيرَانِ 'the
two big men', رِجَالٌ كِبَارٌ 'big men' (plural, without an article),
ٱلرِّجَالُ الْكَبَارُ 'the big men' (plural, with an article).

A feminine noun will have an adjective feminised with " ة " أَلـتَّاءُ ٱلْمَرْبُوطَةِ *'at-tā' ul-marbūṭah,* thus :

بِنْتٌ صَغِيرَةٌ	a young girl	ٱلْبِنْتُ ٱلصَّغِيرَةُ	The young girl
بِنْتَانِ صَغِيرَتَانِ	two young girls	ٱلْبِنْتَانِ ٱلصَّغِيرَتَانِ	The two young girls
بَنَاتٌ صَغِيرَاتٌ	young girls	ٱلْبَنَاتُ ٱلصَّغِيرَاتُ	The young girls

The adjectives too will be in full agreement with the nouns in case ending, e.g.

رَجُلٌ كَبِيرٌ	in nominative case	(مَرْفُوعًا)
رَجُلاً كَبِيرًا	in accusative case	(مَنْصُوبًا)
رَجُلٍ كَبِيرٍ	in genetive case	(مَجْرُورًا)

3. If an *"iḍāfah"* phrase takes the place of a noun it will be regarded as a proper noun. Therefore, the adjective will be par-
ticularised with the definite article أَلْ e.g.

بَيْتُ ٱلله ٱلْحَرَامُ	The Holy House of Allah.
مَسْجِدُ ٱلْمَدِينَةِ ٱلْكَبِيرُ	The big mosque of the city.

Note : An alternative of the vowelling can change the type of
the phrase and give quite a different meaning, e.g.

بَيْتُ ٱلله ٱلْعَظِيمُ	*baitullāhil 'aẓīmu*	The great House of Allah
بَيْتُ ٱلله ٱلْعَظِيمِ	*baitullāhil 'aẓīmi*	The House of great Allah

in the first phrase ٱلْعَظِيم "the great" is qualifying بَيْتُ *bait*
"House" and in the latter it is qualifying Allah.

Adjective patterns

1. There are certain paterns for denoting an adjective, the first is the active participle which has already been dealt with in previous lesson. The rest are forms which give the meaning of the active participle with some intensification in meaning. They are derived from what might be termed as 'stative verbs' that is, verbs which denote a state or condition rather than an act.

(a) | فَاعِلٌ fā'ilun, e.g.

صَادِقٌ	ṣādiqun	upright.
عَادِلٌ	'ādilun	just.
جَاهِلٌ	jāhilun	ignorant.

(b) | فَعِيلٌ fa'īlun, e.g.

قَدِيرٌ	qadīrun	powerful.
كَبِيرٌ	kabīrun	big.
عَظِيمٌ	'aẓīmun.	great.

(c) | فَعُولٌ fa'ūlun, e.g.

ظَلُومٌ	ẓalūmun	very oppressor.
جَهُولٌ	jahūlun	very ignorant.

(d) | فَعْلَانُ fa'lān, e.g.

رَحْمَانُ	Raḥmānu	Very Kind, Merciful.
غَضْبَانُ	ghaḍbānu	angry.

عَطْشَانُ	'aṭshānu	thirsty.
زَعْلَانُ	za'lānu	annoyed.

2. Another intensive form of the active participle is فَعَّال fa''āl, e.g. (from The Holy Qur'ān) :

فَعَّالٌ لِمَا يُرِيدُ	85-16 Doer (with all might) of what He intends.
جَبَّار	Jabbār	Compeller.

This pattern is also used to denote occupations, e.g.

خَبَّازٌ	khabbāzun	baker.
خَيَّاطٌ	khayyāṭun	tailor.
جَزَّارٌ	jazzārun	butcher.
طَبَّاخٌ	.ṭabbākhun	cook.
بَقَّالٌ	baqqālun	green grocer.

3. Another common form of adjective is that used for colours and defects. Their form for the masculine singular is أَفْعَلُ 'af'alu and the feminine singular is فَعْلَاءُ fa'lā'u. The plural is فُعْلٌ fu'lun. That is used for both genders. The following table will illustrate all forms of this pattern.

Sing. Masc.	Dual Masc.	Pl. Masc.
أَسْوَدُ 'aswadu	أَسْوَدَانِ 'aswadāni	سُودٌ sūdun
أَبْيَضُ 'abyaḍu	أَبْيَضَانِ 'abyaḍāni	بِيضٌ bīdun

أَحْمَرُ 'aḥmaru	أَحْمَرَانِ 'aḥmarāni	حُمْرٌ .ḥumrun
أَبْكَمُ 'abkamu	أَبْكَمَانِ 'abkamāni	بُكْمٌ bukmun
أَعْرَجُ 'a‘raju	أَعْرَجَانِ 'a‘rajāni	عُرْجٌ ‘urjun
أَعْمَى 'a‘mā	أَعْمَيَانِ 'a‘mayāni	عُمْيٌ ‘umyun
أَصَمُّ 'aṣammu	أَصَمَّانِ 'aṣammāni	صُمٌّ .ṣummun

Sing. Fem.	Dual Fem.	Pl. Fem.
سَوْدَاءُ sawdā'u	سَوْدَاوَانِ sawdāwāni	سُودٌ sūdun
بَيْضَاءُ baiḍā'u	بَيْضَاوَانِ baiḍāwāni	بِيضٌ bīḍun
حَمْرَاءُ .ḥamrā'u	حَمْرَاوَانِ .ḥamrāwāni	حُمْرٌ ḥumrun

Sing. Fem.	Pl. Fem.
خَرْسَاءُ kharsā'u	خُرْسٌ khursun
بَكْمَاءُ bakmā'u	بُكْمٌ bukmun
عَرْجَاءُ ‘arjā'u	عُرْجٌ ‘urjun
عَمْيَاءُ ‘amyā'u	عُمْيٌ ‘umyun
صَمَّاءُ ṣammā'u	صُمٌّ ṣmmun

Note : Except plurals of the pattern, other forms (sing., dual) can neither be nunized with (تَنْوِين) nor can they receive *kasrah* (ـِ)

4. Pattern for the comparative and superlative of adjective is called إِسْمُ ٱلتَّفْضِيل *ismut-tafḍīl*, that is :

Sing. Masc.	أَفْعَلُ *'af'alu*	(The same form as that for colours and defects).
Pl. Masc.	أَفَاعِلُ *'afā'ilu*	
Sing. Fem.	فُعْلَى *fu'lā*	
Pl. Fem.	فُعْلَيَاتُ *fu'layātun*	

Though the grammarians have mentioned dual forms for masculine and feminine, these are in little use.

The singular masculine form has more frequent use than other forms because it denotes both comparative and superlative or elative meanings e.g. ٱلله أَكْبَرُ "Allah is the Greatest".

5. If the root has a doubled consonant as جَدِيدٌ *jadīdun* "new", the superlative form is أَجَدُّ *'ajaddu*, (not أَجْدَدُ *'ajdadu*, أَفْعَلُ). From قَلِيلٌ *qalīlun* "little; few", comes أَقَلُّ *'aqallu* "less; fewer" (not أَقْلَلُ *'aqlalu*).

6. The Arabic preposition for "than" such as in English phrase "smaller than.." is مِنْ *min*, e.g. أَصْغَرُ مِنْ .

عَلِيٌّ أَصْغَرُ مِنْ أَخِيهِ	Ali is smaller (younger) than his brother.
ٱلْبِنْتُ أَصْغَرُ مِنْ أَخِيهَا	The girl is younger than her brother.
ٱلطَّلَبَةُ فِي ٱلْمَدَارِسِ ٱلدِّينِيَّةِ أَقَلُّ عَدَدًا مِنَ ٱلْجَامِعَاتِ	Students in the religious schools are less in number than in the universities.

7. Sometimes, the elative is used as a noun, followed by a gene-tive, e.g. هُوَ أَكْبَرُ رَجُلٍ فِي ٱلْمَدِينَةِ "He is the greatest man in the city". (Also see chapter 29).

Examples from the Holy Qur'ān :

I.	المُذَكَّر مَرْفُوعًا	**Masculine Nominative**

خُلُقٌ عَظِيمٌ	68-4	A sublime manner.
كِتَابٌ مَرْقُومٌ	83-20	A written book.
عَجُوزٌ عَقِيمٌ	51-29	A barren old woman. (both masc. and fem.)
شَيْطَانٌ رَجِيمٌ	81-25	An accursed devil.
كِتَابٌ كَرِيمٌ	27-29	An honourable book.
رَبٌّ غَفُورٌ	34-15	A Forgiving Lord.

II.	المُذَكَّر مَنْصُوبًا	**Masculine Accusative**

مَالًا مَمْدُودًا	74-12	Vast riches.
سِرَاجًا وَهَّاجًا	78-13	A shining lamp.
سَبْعًا شِدَادًا	78-12	Seven strong (ones).
قَوْلًا مَيْسُورًا	17-28	A gentle word.
مَاءً غَدَقًا	72-16	Abundant water.
لَحْمًا طَرِيًّا	16-14	Tender meat flesh.

مَاءً ثَجَّاجًا	78-14	Clouds' water.
كَأْسًا دِهَاقًا	78-34	A pure cup.

III.	المُذَكَّر مَجْرُورًا	Masculine Genetive
ظِلٍّ مَمْدُودٍ	56-30	An extensive shade.
كَفَّارٍ عَنِيدٍ	50-24	A rebellious ungrateful.
سِدْرٍ مَخْضُودٍ	56-28	Thornless Lote-tree.
كِتَابٍ مَكْنُونٍ	56-78	A protected book.
يَوْمٍ مَعْلُومٍ	56-50	An appointed day.
مَاءٍ مَهِينٍ	77-20	Ordinary water.
مَاءٍ مَسْكُوبٍ	56-31	Gushing water.
لَوْحٍ مَحْفُوظٍ	85-22	A guarded tablet.

IV.	المُذَكَّر مَعَ الأَلِف وَاللام	Masc. with the definite article
الفَوْزُ الكَبِيرُ	85-11	The great achievement.
اليَوْمُ المَوْعُودُ	85-2	The promised day.
العِهْنُ المَنْفُوشُ	101-5	The carded wool.
الشَّجَرُ الأَخْضَرُ	36-80	The green tree.
النَّجْمُ الثَّاقِبُ	86-3	The star of piercing brightness.

V.	المُؤَنَّث مَعَ الأَلِف وَاللامْ		Fem. with the definite article
	أَلآيَةُ ٱلْكُبْرَىٰ	79-20	The mighty sign.
	الطَّامَّةُ ٱلْكُبْرَىٰ	79-34	The great calamity.
	النَّفْسُ ٱلْمُطْمَئِنَّةُ	89-27	The soul which is in rest.
	الدَّارُ ٱلآخِرَةُ	29-64	The home of the hereafter.

VI.	الأَلْوَان وَالعَاهَات		Colours and defects
	حَتَّىٰ يَتَبَيَّنَ لَكُمُ ٱلْخَيْطُ ٱلأَبْيَضُ مِنَ ٱلْخَيْطِ ٱلأَسْوَدِ	2-187	...until the white thread becomes distinct to you from the black thread.
	وَأَضْمُمْ يَدَكَ إِلَىٰ جَنَاحِكَ تَخْرُجْ بَيْضَاءَ مِنْ غَيْرِ سُوءٍ آيَةً أُخْرَىٰ	20-22	And thrust thy hand within thy armpit, it will come forth white without hurt (as) another token.
	إِنَّهَا بَقَرَةٌ صَفْرَاءُ	2-69	It is a yellow cow.
	وَمِنَ ٱلْجِبَالِ جُدَدٌ بِيضٌ وَحُمْرٌ مُخْتَلِفٌ أَلْوَانُهَا وَغَرَابِيبُ سُودٌ	35-27	And among the hills are streaks white and red of divers hues, and (others) raven-black.

Some Examples of Adjective Forms : Simple & Comparatives.

إِنَّهُ لَكَبِيرُكُمُ ٱلَّذِي عَلَّمَكُمُ ٱلسِّحْرَ	20-71	Lo! He is your chief who taught you magic.

مَا لِ هَـٰذَا ٱلْكِتَابِ لَا يُغَادِرُ صَغِيرَةً وَلَا كَبِيرَةً إِلَّا أَحْصَاهَا	18-49 What kind of a book is this that leaves not a small thing nor a great thing, without counting it.
أَطَعْنَا سَادَتَنَا وَكُبَرَاءَنَا	33-67 We obeyed our masters and great men.
وَٱلَّذِينَ يَجْتَنِبُونَ كَبَائِرَ ٱلْإِثْمِ وَٱلْفَوَاحِشِ	42-37 And those who shun the worst of sins and indecencies.
وَٱلْفِتْنَةُ أَكْبَرُ مِنَ ٱلْقَتْلِ	2-217 And intrigue (discord) is worse than killing.
وَإِثْمُهُمَا أَكْبَرُ مِنْ نَفْعِهِمَا	2-219 And the sin of them (wine and game) is greater than their usefulness.

EXERCISE

1.   Translate into Arabic :

A Muslim wishes to follow the straight path. I love a red flower, white tea and the green light. Both of them are tall men, but Nadiya and Samira are tiny ones. Girls are hard workers. Boys are good players. The big men and the big women of the world admire good civilization. The Prophet's mosque in Madinah is a beautiful mosque but the mosque of Holy Ka'ba is greater than others. There in Makkah is a good centre of education for blind boys, called the Institution of the

Light. Ali is more clever than his elder brother Hasan. English people have blue eyes, golden hair and white skin. Muslims do not hate any colour. They believe in brotherhood among entire human-beings. The Red Sea is the boundry of Arabia in the West and in the South Arabian Sea. The teacher is angry with them. We are happier than lazy men.

2. Translate into English :

١ – إِنَّ ٱلْمُسْلِمِينَ وَٱلْمُسْلِمَاتِ أَعَدَّ اللهُ لَهُمْ مَغْفِرَةً وَأَجْرًا عَظِيمًا

٢ – هُمُ ٱلتَّائِبُونَ ٱلْعَابِدُونَ ٱلْحَامِدُونَ ٱلسَّائِحُونَ

٣ – يَلْبَسُونَ ثِيَابًا خُضْرًا

٤ – مَنْ تَابَ وَآمَنَ وَعَمِلَ عَمَلًا صَالِحًا

٥ – فَأَنْجَيْنَاهُ وَمَنْ مَعَهُ فِي ٱلْفُلْكِ ٱلْمَشْحُونِ

٦ – إِنَّ رَبَّكَ لَهُوَ ٱلْعَزِيزُ ٱلرَّحِيمُ

٧ – صُمٌّ بُكْمٌ عُمْيٌ فَهُمْ لَا يَرْجِعُونَ

٨ – هٰذَا لِسَانٌ عَرَبِيٌّ مُبِينٌ

٩ – الزَّوْجَةُ ٱلصَّالِحَةُ نِعْمَةٌ مِنَ اللهِ

١٠ – الصَّدِيقُ ٱلْوَفِيُّ أَحَبُّ إِلَى ٱلنَّفْسِ مِنَ ٱلْقَرِيبِ ٱلظَّالِمِ

١١ – كِتَابُ اللهِ ٱلْعَظِيمُ

١٢ – كِتَابُ اللهِ ٱلْعَظِيمِ

١٣ – أَكْبَرُ شُعَرَاءِ ٱلْبَلَدِ قَادِمٌ

VOCABULARY

To follow	أَنْ يَتْبَعَ or أَنْ يَسْلُكَ
The Path	الصِّرَاطُ
Short (Masc.)	قَصِيرٌ (قَصِيرَةٌ .Fem) (قِصَارٌ .Pl. Masc)
Admires	يُحِبُّ (use plural)
Clever	عَاقِلٌ
The Centre	الْمَرْكَزُ
No cleverer than	لَيْسَ أَعْقَلُ مِنْ
People	النَّاسُ
English people	الشَّعْبُ الإِنْجِلِيزِيُّ
Love	الْحُبُّ
Golden	ذَهَبِيٌّ (not on the forms of colours)
Blue	الأَزْرَقُ (use Fem. & Pl.)
Red Sea	الْبَحْرُ الأَحْمَرُ
Happier than	أَفْرَحُ مِنْ or أَكْثَرُ فَرَحًا مِنْ
Straight	الْمُسْتَقِيمُ
Tall (Masc.)	طَوِيلٌ (طَوِيلَةٌ .Fem) (طِوَالٌ .Pl)
The civilization	التَّمَدُّنُ
The Institute of the Light	مَعْهَدُ النُّورِ

Elder	أَكْبَرُ عُمْرًا or أَكْبَرُ مِنْ
Angry	غَضْبَانَ
Lazy	كَسْلَانَ

الْقَانِتُ	the one who obeys. (from ق ن ت)
الْخَاشِعُ	the one who bows in humbleness.
أَعَدَّ	prepared. (3rd Pers. Masc.)
الْمَغْفِرَةُ	the forgiveness.
الْأَجْرُ	the reward.
التَّائِبُ	the one who turns repentant.
الْعَابِدُ	the one who serves Allah.
الصَّائِمُ	the one who fasts.
الرَّاكِعُ	the one who bows down.
السَّاجِدُ	the prostrator (in worship).
الآمِرُ	the orderer, the master.
النَّاهِي	forbider. / الآمِرُ النَّاهِي the absolute master.
لَبِسَ	to wear.
الثِّيَابُ	clothings.

الْفُـلْكُ	the ark.
الْمَشْحُونُ	the laden.
الـرَّحِيمُ	The Merciful.
الْعَزِيـزُ	The Almighty.
الْغَـفُورُ	The Forgiver.
الْحَامِـدُ	the one who praises Allah.
الْلِسَانُ	the tongue, the language.
رَجَعَ	to return. (3rd Pers. Masc. Sing.)

CHAPTER 12

THE PRONOUNS

The Pronouns in Arabic are divided into two forms : detached
and attached.

1. The detached pronouns الضَّمَائِرُ ٱلْمُنْفَصِلَةُ are :

Singular		Dual		Plural	
أَنَا	'anā, I	نَحْنُ	naḥnu, We	نَحْنُ	naḥnu, We
أَنْتَ	'anta, thou (you) (masc.)	أَنْتُمَا	'antumā, You (two) (masc. / fem.)	أَنْتُمْ	'antum, You (masc.)
أَنْتِ	'anti, thou (you) (fem.)			أَنْتُنَّ	'antunna, You (fem.)
هُوَ	huwa, He, It	هُمَا	humā They (two) (masc. / fem.)	هُمْ	hum They (masc.)
هِيَ	hiya, She, It			هُنَّ	hunna They (fem.)

Examples from the Holy Qur'ān :

أَنَا 'anā, I	

وَأَنَـا رَبُّكُمْ فَأَعْبُدُونِ	21-92 ...and I am your Lord, so worship Me.
وَلَا أَنَـا عَابِدٌ مَا عَبَدْتُمْ	109-4 ...and I shall not worship that which ye worship.

أَنْتَ 'anta, thou (you) (sing. masc.)	

فَلَمَّا تَوَفَّيْتَنِي كُنْتَ أَنْتَ الرَّقِيبَ عَلَيْهِمْ	5-117 (Jesus said) "and when Thou tookest me Thou wast (كُنْتَ) the watcher over them".
أَ أَنْتَ قُلْتَ لِلنَّاسِ	5-116 Didst thou say into mankind.

هُـوَ huwa, He, It	

قُلْ : هُـوَ اللهُ أَحَـدٌ	112-1 Say : He is Allah, The One.
هُـوَ اللهُ ٱلَّذِي لَا إِلَـهَ إِلَّا هُـوَ	59-23 He is Allah with Whom, there is no other god.
هُـوَ خَيـرٌ ثَـوَابًا	18-44 He is best to reward.
بَـلْ هُـوَ خَيـرٌ لَكُمْ	24-11 Nay, it is good for you.

هِيَ hiya, She, It		

إِنَّ هِيَ إِلاَّ حَيَاتُنَا ٱلدُّنْيَا	23-37	It is not but our worldly life.
وَهِيَ تَجْرِي بِهِمْ	11-42	And it moves on with them.

نَحْنُ naḥnu, We		

نَحْنُ نَرْزُقُكَ	20-132	We provide for thee.
نَحْنُ أَوْلِيَاؤُكُمْ فِي ٱلْحَيَاةِ ٱلدُّنْيَا وَفِي ٱلآخِرَةِ	41-31	We are your friends in this world's life and in the hereafter.

أَنْتُمْ 'antum, You (pl. masc.)		

قَالَ : أَنْتُمْ شَرٌّ مَكَانًا	12-77	He said : You are in an evil condition.
ثُمَّ أَنْتُمْ تُشْرِكُونَ	6-64	Then you associate others (with Him).

هُمْ hum, They (pl. masc.)		

هُمْ لِلْكُفْرِ يَوْمَئِذٍ أَقْرَبُ مِنْهُمْ لِلإِيمَانِ	3-167	They were on that day nearer to disbelief than to belief.

وَمَا هُـمْ بِخَارِجِينَ مِنْهَا	5-37 And they are not coming forth from it.

هُنَّ hunna, They (pl. fem.)

هُنَّ لِبَاسٌ لَكُمْ وَأَنْتُمْ لِبَاسٌ لَهُـنَّ	2-187 They (wives) are apparel for you and you (men) are apparel for them (wives).

The Pronouns هُمَا *humā* (3rd Pers. Masc. & Fem.) and أَنْتُمَا *'antumā* (2nd Pers. Masc. & Fem.) have rare use in the Holy Qur'ān in their absolute forms. But they are in common use in the language.

هُمَا *humā*, They (two) (masc. & fem.)

ثَانِي إِثْنَيْنِ إِذْ هُمَا فِي ٱلْغَارِ	9-40 He being the second of the two when they (two men) both were in the cave.

ذَاهِبَتَانِ إِلَى ٱلْبَيْتِ	هُمَا	They (two fem.) are going home.
تَسْتَحِقَّانِ ٱلْجَائِزَةَ	أَنْتُمَا	You (two masc. & Fem.) deserve the prize.
طَالِبَانِ فِي ٱلْمَدْرَسَةِ	أَنْتُمَا	You (two masc.) are students in the school.
ذَاهِبَتَانِ إِلَى ٱلْبَيْتِ	أَنْتُمَا	You (two fem.) are going home.

2. The attached Pronouns الضَّمَائِرُ ٱلْمُتَّصِلَةُ are as following :

Third Person		
Singular	**Dual**	**Plural**
هُ *hu,* his, him (Masc.)	هُمَا *humā,* their, them (two) (Masc. or Fem.)	هُمْ *hum,* their them (Masc.)
هَا *hā,* her		هُنَّ *hunna,* their them (Fem.)

Atteched to a noun :

كِتَابُهُ *kitābuhu,* his book.	كِتَابُهُمَا *kitābuhumā,* thier (two Masc. or Fem.) book.	كِتَابُهُمْ *kitābuhum,* their (Masc.) book.
كِتَابُهَا *kitābuhā,* her book.		كِتَابُهُنَّ *kitābuhunna,* their (Fem.) book.

Attached to a Verb : (A pronoun suffixed to a verb functions as the object of that verb).

نَصَرَهُ *naṣarahu,* he helped him.	نَصَرَهُمَا *naṣarahumā,* he helped them (two Masc. or Fem.).	نَصَرَهُمْ *naṣarahum,* he helped them (Masc.).
نَصَرَهَا *naṣarahā,* he helped her.		نَصَرَهُنَّ *naṣarahunna,* he helped them (Fem.).

Second Person		
Singular	**Dual**	**Plural**
كَ *ka,* thee, thy (Masc.)	كُمَا *kumā,* yours, you (two) (Masc. or Fem.)	كُمْ *kum,* yours, you (Masc.)
كِ *ki,* thee, thy (Fem.).		كُنَّ *kunna,* yours, you (Fem.)

Attached to a Noun :

كِتَابُكَ *kitābuka,* thy (Masc.) book.	كِتَابُكُمَا *kitābukumā,* your (two Masc. or Fem.) book.	كِتَابُكُمْ *kitābukum,* your (Masc.) book.
كِتَابُكِ *kitābuki,* thy (Fem.) book.		كِتَابُكُنَّ *kitābukunna,* your (Fem.) book.

Attached to a Verb :

نَصَرَكَ *naṣaraka,* he helped thee (Masc.).	نَصَرَكُمَا *naṣarakumā,* he helped you (two Masc. or Fem.).	نَصَرَكُمْ *naṣarakum,* he helped you (Masc.).
نَصَرَكِ *naṣaraki,* he helped thee (Fem.).		نَصَرَكُنَّ *naṣarakunna,* he helped you (Fem.).

First Person	(Masc. & Fem.)
Singular	**Dual or Plural**
ي *ī*, my	نَا *nā*, our

Attached to a Noun :

كِتَابِي *kitābī*, my book.	كِتَابُـنَا *kitābunā*, our book.

Attached to a Verb :

نَصَرَنِي *naṣaranī*, he helped me.	نَصَرَنَا *naṣaranā*, he helped us.

Note : The Pronouns of 3rd person هُ *hu* is read ه *hi*, هُمَـا *humā* becomes هِمَـا *himā*, and هُمْ *hum* and هُنَّ *hunna* turns to هِمْ *him* and هِنَّ *hinna* sounds when the noun to which the pronoun is suffixed is preceded by a preposition :

كِتَابُـهُ	*kitābuhu*, his book.
فِي كِتَابِـهِ	*fī kitābihi*, in his book.
نَصَرَهُـمْ	*naṣarahum*, he helped them.
هُوَ عَلَىٰ نَصْرِهِمْ قَدِير	*huwa 'alā naṣrihim qadīr*, He is most powerful on their help.
نَصَرَهُنَّ	*naṣarahunna*, he helped them (fem.).
هُوَ عَلَىٰ نَصْرِهِنَّ قَدِير	*huwa 'alā naṣrihinna qadīr*, He is most powerful on their help.

these differences should be noted in the examples from the Holy Qur'ān.

Examples from the Holy Qur'ān :

	3rd Pers. (Masc.) Sing. : ـهُ / هُ *hu.*

وَقَلْبُهُ مُطْمَئِنٌّ بِالْإِيمَانِ	16-106　And his heart is content with faith.
هُـنَالِكَ دَعَا زَكَرِيَّا رَبَّـهُ	3-38　There did Zachariah pray to his Lord.
مَنْ جَاءَ بِالْحَسَنَةِ فَلَهُ خَيْرٌ مِنْهَا	28-84　Whoever brings a good-deed for him is better than its worth.
فَإِذَا خِفْتِ عَلَيْهِ فَأَلْقِيهِ فِي الْيَمِّ	28-7　And when thou fearest for him then cast him into the river.
فَلَمَّا جَاءَهُ وَقَصَّ عَلَيْهِ الْقَصَصَ	28-25　and when he came to him and told him the (whole) story.

	3rd Pers. (Fem.) Sing. : ـهَا / هَا *hā*

كُلَّمَا دَخَلَ عَلَيْهَا زَكَرِيَّا الْمِحْرَابَ وَجَدَ عِنْدَهَا رِزْقًا	3-37　Whenever Zachariah went in the sanctuary where she was, he found that she had food.

	3rd Pers. (Masc. & Fem.) Dual : ـهُمَا / هُمَا *humā*

فَأَكَلَا مِنْهَا فَبَدَتْ لَهُمَا سَوْآتُهُمَا وَطَفِقَا يَخْصِفَانِ عَلَيْهِمَا مِنْ وَرَقِ الْجَنَّةِ	20-121　Then they (two) ate therefore, so their shame became apparent upon them and they began to hide them by the leaves of the Garden.
يَنْزِعُ عَنْهُمَا لِبَاسَهُمَا	7-27　Pulling off from them their clothing.

3rd Pers. (Masc.) Plural : هُمْ / ـهُمْ *hum.*	

أَفَأَمِنُوا أَنْ تَأْتِيَهُمْ غَاشِيَةٌ مِنْ عَذَابِ اللهِ أَوْ تَأْتِيَهُمُ ٱلسَّاعَةُ بَغْتَةً وَهُمْ لَا يَشْعُرُونَ	12-107 Deem they themselves secure from comming on them of a pall of Allah's punishment or comming of The Hour suddenly while they are unaware.
صِرَاطَ ٱلَّذِينَ أَنْعَمْتَ عَلَيْهِمْ غَيْرِ ٱلْمَغْضُوبِ عَلَيْهِمْ	1-7 The path of those whom Thou hast favoured; Not (the path) of those against whom Thou art wrathful.

3rd Pers. (Fem.) Plural : هُنَّ / ـهُنَّ *hunna*	

وَبُعُولَتُهُنَّ أَحَقُّ بِرَدِّهِنَّ	2-228 And their husbands would do better to take them back.
وَعَلَى ٱلْمَوْلُودِ لَهُ رِزْقُهُنَّ وَكِسْوَتُهُنَّ بِٱلْمَعْرُوفِ	2-233 and it is for the fathers to provide them and clothe them honourably.

2nd Pers. (Masc.) Sing. : كَ / ـكَ *ka*	

وَقُلْنَا يَا آدَمُ ٱسْكُنْ أَنْتَ وَزَوْجُكَ ٱلْجَنَّةَ	2-35 And We said: O' Adam, dwell thou and thy wife in the Garden.
قَالُوا ٱدْعُ لَنَا رَبَّكَ	2-69 They said, pray for us unto thy Lord.
وَلَنْ تَرْضَىٰ عَنْكَ ٱلْيَهُودُ	2-120 And the Jews will not be pleased with thee.

إِذْ قَالَ اللهُ يَاعِيسَىٰ إِنِّي مُتَوَفِّيكَ وَرَافِعُكَ إِلَيَّ وَمُطَهِّرُكَ مِنَ ٱلَّذِينَ كَفَرُوا	3-55 And (Remember) when Allah said: O' Jesus! Lo! I am causing thee to die and causing thee to ascend unto Me and cleansing thee of those who disbelieve.

2nd Pers. (Fem.) Sing. : كِ / ـكِ   *ki*

قَالَ يَا مَرْيَمُ أَنَّىٰ لَكِ هَٰذَا	3-37 He said: O' Mary, whence cometh into thee this ?
قَالَ إِنَّمَا أَنَا رَسُولُ رَبِّكِ لِأَهَبَ لَكِ غُلَامًا زَكِيًّا	19-19 He said: I am only a messenger of thy Lord that I may bestow on thee a faultless son.
يَا أُخْتَ هَارُونَ مَا كَانَ أَبُوكِ آمْرَأَ سَوْءٍ وَمَا كَانَتْ أُمُّكِ بَغِيًّا	19-28 O' Sister of Aaron! Thy father was not a wicked man nor was thy mother a harlot.

2nd Pers. (Masc. & Fem.) Dual : كُمَا / ـكُمَا   *kumā*

وَقَالَ مَا نَهَاكُمَا رَبُّكُمَا عَنْ هٰذِهِ ٱلشَّجَرَةِ إِلَّا أَنْ تَكُونَا مَلَكَيْنِ أَوْ تَكُونَا مِنَ ٱلْخَالِدِينَ . وَقَاسَمَهُمَا إِنِّي لَكُمَا لَمِنَ ٱلنَّاصِحِينَ	7-20,21 And said: Your Lord has forbidden you this tree lest you become angels or become of the immortals and he swore to them both. Surely I am a sincere advisor to you.
إِنْ تَتُوبَا إِلَى اللهِ فَقَدْ صَغَتْ قُلُوبُكُمَا	66-4 If you turn to Allah in repentance, then indeed your hearts are inclined (to Him).

يَا بَنِي إِسْرَائِيلَ اذْكُرُوا نِعْمَتِيَ الَّتِي أَنْعَمْتُ عَلَيْكُمْ وَأَنِّي فَضَّلْتُكُمْ عَلَى الْعَالَمِينَ	2-47 O' children of Israel, call to mind My favour which I bestowed on you and that I made you excel the nations.
وَإِذْ نَجَّيْنَاكُمْ مِنْ آلِ فِرْعَوْنَ يَسُومُونَكُمْ سُوءَ الْعَذَابِ يُذَبِّحُونَ أَبْنَاءَكُمْ وَيَسْتَحْيُونَ نِسَاءَكُمْ وَفِي ذَلِكُمْ بَلَاءٌ مِنْ رَبِّكُمْ عَظِيمٌ	2-49 And when We delivered you from Pharoh's people, killing your sons, and sparing your women and in this there was a great trial from your Lord.

يَا أَيُّهَا النَّبِيُّ قُلْ لِأَزْوَاجِكَ إِنْ كُنْتُنَّ تُرِدْنَ الْحَيَاةَ الدُّنْيَا وَزِينَتَهَا فَتَعَالَيْنَ أُمَتِّعْكُنَّ وَأُسَرِّحْكُنَّ سَرَاحًا جَمِيلًا	33-28 O' Prophet, say to thy wives: if you desire this world's life and its adornment, come, I will give you a provision and allow you to depart a goodly departing.
عَسَى رَبُّهُ إِنْ طَلَّقَكُنَّ أَنْ يُبْدِلَهُ أَزْوَاجًا خَيْرًا مِنْكُنَّ	66-5 May be, his Lord, if he divorces you will give him in your place wives better than you.

اذْهَبْ بِكِتَابِي هَذَا	27-28 Take this my letter, or go with this letter of mine.

قَالَ رَبِّ آشْرَحْ لِي صَدْرِي وَيَسِّرْ لِي أَمْرِي وَآحْلُلْ عُقْدَةً مِنْ لِسَانِي يَفْقَهُوا قَوْلِي وَآجْعَلْ لِي وَزِيرًا مِنْ أَهْلِي هَارُونَ أَخِي آشْدُدْ بِهِ أَزْرِي وَأَشْرِكْهُ فِي أَمْرِي	20-25/32 He said: My Lord! expand my breast for me, and loose the knot from my tongue, that they may understand my word and give to me a helper from my family, Aaron my brother. Add to my strength by him and make him share my task.

Attached to a Verb : نِي / ـنِي *nī*

مَا قُلْتُ لَهُمْ إِلَّا مَا أَمَرْتَنِي بِهِ	5-117 I said to them naught save as thou didst command me.
أَيُّكُمْ يَأْتِينِي بِعَرْشِهَا	27-38 Which of you can bring me her throne ?
لَئِنْ بَسَطْتَ إِلَيَّ يَدَكَ لِتَقْتُلَنِي مَا أَنَا بِبَاسِطٍ يَدِي إِلَيْكَ لِأَقْتُلَكَ	5-28 If thou stretch out thy hand against me to kill me I shall not stretch my hand against thee to kill thee.

1st Pers. (Masc. & Fem.) Dual & Plural : نَا / ـنَا *nā*

قَالَا رَبَّنَا ظَلَمْنَا أَنْفُسَنَا وَإِنْ لَمْ تَغْفِرْ لَنَا وَتَرْحَمْنَا لَنَكُونَنَّ مِنَ آلْخَاسِرِينَ	7-23 They (two) said: Our Lord, we have wronged ourselves; and if Thou forgiveth us not, and hast no mercy on us, we shall certainly be of the losers.
وَاللهُ أَمَرَنَا بِهَا	7-28 And Allah has enjoined it upon us.

هٰذَا كِتَابُنَا يَنْطِقُ عَلَيْكُمْ بِالْحَقِّ	45-29 This is Our Book that speaks against you with truth.

Note : For easy and convenient reference, see the chart of Pronouns (Independent and Suffixed) at the end of this chapter.

EXERCISE

1. Translate into Arabic :

For the first three years, or rather less of his mission, the Prophet preached only to his family and to his intimate friends, while the people of Makkah as a whole regarded him as one who had become (مَعْتُوه) a little mad. First of all his converts was his wife Khadija, the second his cousin Ali, whom he had adopted, the third was his servant Zaid. His old friend Abu Bakr was among those early converts with some of his slaves and dependents.

2. Translate into English :

أَوْ كَالَّذِي مَرَّ عَلَىٰ قَرْيَةٍ وَهِيَ خَاوِيَةٌ عَلَىٰ عُرُوشِهَا قَالَ أَنَّىٰ يُحْيِي هٰذِهِ اللَّهُ بَعْدَ مَوْتِهَا فَأَمَاتَهُ اللَّهُ مِائَةَ عَامٍ ثُمَّ بَعَثَهُ قَالَ كَمْ لَبِثْتَ قَالَ لَبِثْتُ يَوْمًا أَوْ بَعْضَ يَوْمٍ قَالَ بَلْ لَبِثْتَ مِائَةَ عَامٍ فَانْظُرْ إِلَىٰ طَعَامِكَ وَشَرَابِكَ لَمْ يَتَسَنَّهْ وَانْظُرْ إِلَىٰ حِمَارِكَ وَلِنَجْعَلَكَ آيَةً لِلنَّاسِ وَانْظُرْ إِلَى الْعِظَامِ كَيْفَ نُنْشِزُهَا ثُمَّ نَكْسُوهَا لَحْمًا . فَلَمَّا تَبَيَّنَ لَهُ قَالَ أَعْلَمُ أَنَّ اللَّهَ عَلَىٰ كُلِّ شَيْءٍ قَدِيرٌ .

VOCABULARY

the first three years	(an adjective phrase) السَّنَوَاتُ ٱلثَّلَاثُ ٱلأولَىٰ
rather	غَالِبًا
less	أَقَلُّ (مِنْهَا)
the mission	المُهِمَّةُ ، الرِّسَالَةُ
to preach	بَلَّـغَ
the family	الأسْرَةُ
the intimate	الأقـربـون
(they) regarded	اعتــبروا
mad	معتــوه
he who converted to Islam	الَّذي أَسْلَم Pl. الَّذينَ أَسْلَمُوا
the slave	الْعَبْدُ Pl. الْعِبَادُ
dependent	تَابِعُ Pl. أتباع

أَوْ	or
كَالَّذي	كَ like, & الذي which, who, that (like of him who...)
قَـرْيَـةٌ	township.
خَاوِيَـةٌ	fallen, empty, in ruins.
عُـرُوشٌ	roofs, Sing. عَرْشٌ
أَنَّـىٰ	how !

170

أَمَـاتَ	caused to die, made (someone die).
أَمَاتَـهُ	made him die.
مَائَـة	hundred.
ثُـمَّ	then
بَعَثَ	to bring back to life.
كَمْ	how long.
لَبِثَ	he tarried, he lingered (3rd person Masc.).
بَـلْ	but, rather.
أُنْـظُرْ	see, look! (Imperative).
لَمْ يَتَسَنَّـهْ	did not get spoiled.
حِمَارُ	ass.
العِظَامُ	the bones. Sing. العَظْمُ
نُـنْشِزُ	We adjust (1st person Imperative Plural).
نَكْسُو	We cover (1st person Imperfect Plural).
فَلَمَّا	thus, then.
تَبَـيَّنَ	(the matter) has been cleared.
قَدِيـرُ	powerful, able.

Pronouns : Independent and Suffix

Person / Gender	Suffixed to a Noun	Independent
Singular Forms		
3rd person / M	كِتَابُهُ / ـهُ	هُوَ
3rd person / F	كِتَابُهَا / ـهَا	هِيَ
2nd person / M	كِتَابُكَ / ـكَ	أَنْتَ
2nd person / F	كِتَابُكِ / ـكِ	أَنْتِ
1st person / M + F	كِتَابِي / ـِي	أَنَا
Plural Forms		
3rd person / M	كِتَابُهُمْ / ـهُمْ	هُمْ
3rd person / F	كِتَابُهُنَّ / ـهُنَّ	هُنَّ
2nd person / M	كِتَابُكُمْ / ـكُمْ	أَنْتُمْ
2nd person / F	كِتَابُكُنَّ / ـكُنَّ	أَنْتُنَّ
1st person / M + F	كِتَابُنَا / ـنَا	نَحْنُ
Dual Forms		
3rd person / M + F	كِتَابُهُمَا / ـهُمَا	هُمَا
2nd person / M + F	كِتَابُكُمَا / ـكُمَا	أَنْتُمَا

M = Masculine.   F = Feminine.

CHAPTER 13

THE PLURAL

The patterns of Arabic roots have been dealt with in chapter 3 and 7. The Noun patterns are also trileteral with exception of few that are supposed to be bilateral. The Flurals are divided into two categories : (a) Solid or Sound, (b) Broken.

A. 1. The Solid Plurals are those formed adding ون in nominative case and by ين in case of accusative or genitive, e.g. مُسْـلِـمُـونَ *Muslimūna* or مُسْـلِمِينَ *Muslimīna* from مُسْـلِمٌ *Muslimun*, فَاعِـلُونَ *fāʻilūna* or فَاعِـلِينَ *fāʻilīna* from فَاعِـلٌ *fāʻilun*. We have a few examples in the following (verses) of the Holy Qur'ān :

قَدْ أَفْلَحَ ٱلْمُؤْمِنُونَ	23-1 Successful indeed are the believers.
ٱلَّذِينَ هُمْ فِي صَلَاتِهِمْ خَاشِعُونَ	23-2 Who are humble in their prayers.
وَٱلَّذِينَ هُمْ عَنِ ٱللَّغْوِ مُعْرِضُونَ	23-3 and who shun what is vain.
وَٱلَّذِينَ هُمْ لِلزَّكَاةِ فَاعِلُونَ	23-4 And who act for the sake of purity.

وَٱلَّذِينَ هُمْ لِفُرُوجِهِمْ حَافِظُونَ	23-5 And who restrain their sexual passions.
إِلَّا عَلَىٰ أَزْوَاجِهِمْ أَوْ مَا مَلَكَتْ أَيْمَانُهُمْ فَإِنَّهُمْ غَيْرُ مَلُومِينَ	23-6 Except in the presence of their mates or those whom their right hands possess, for such surely are not blameable.
فَمَنِ ٱبْتَغَىٰ وَرَاءَ ذَٰلِكَ فَأُولَٰئِكَ هُمُ ٱلْعَادُونَ	23-7 But whoever seeks to go beyond that, such are transgressors.
وَٱلَّذِينَ هُمْ لِأَمَانَاتِهِمْ وَعَهْدِهِمْ رَاعُونَ	23-8 And those who are keepers of their trusts and their covenants.
وَٱلَّذِينَ هُمْ عَلَىٰ صَلَوَاتِهِمْ يُحَافِظُونَ	23-9 And those who keep a guard on their prayers.
أُولَٰئِكَ هُمُ ٱلْوَارِثُونَ	23-10 Those are the heirs,
الَّذِينَ يَرِثُونَ ٱلْفِرْدَوْسَ هُمْ فِيهَا خَالِدُونَ	23-11 Who inherit Paradise, therein they will eternally abide.

A. 2. The solid plural of the feminine is made by adding ات 'āt' after the noun, such as مُسْلِمَاتٌ *Muslimātun* from مُسْلِمَةٌ *Muslimatun*, e.g. (from the Holy Qur'ān) :

	11-11 Surely the men who submit and the women who submit, and the believing men and the believing women, and the obeying men and the obeying women, and the truthful men and the truthful women, and the patient men and the patient women, and the humble men and the humble women, and the charitable men and the charitable women, and the fasting men and the fasting women, and the men who guard their chastity and the women who guard their chastity, and the men who remember Allah much and the women who remember Allah much; Allah has prepared for them forgiveness and a mighty reward.
إِنَّ ٱلْمُسْلِمِينَ وَٱلْمُسْلِمَاتِ وَٱلْمُؤْمِنِينَ وَٱلْمُؤْمِنَاتِ وَٱلْقَانِتِينَ وَٱلْقَانِتَاتِ وَٱلصَّادِقِينَ وَٱلصَّادِقَاتِ وَٱلصَّابِرِينَ وَٱلصَّابِرَاتِ وَٱلْخَاشِعِينَ وَٱلْخَاشِعَاتِ وَٱلْمُتَصَدِّقِينَ وَٱلْمُتَصَدِّقَاتِ وَٱلصَّائِمِينَ وَٱلصَّائِمَاتِ وَٱلْحَافِظِينَ فُرُوجَهُمْ وَٱلْحَافِظَاتِ وَٱلذَّاكِرِينَ ٱللهَ كَثِيرًا وَٱلذَّاكِرَاتِ أَعَدَّ ٱللهُ لَهُمْ مَغْفِرَةً وَأَجْرًا عَظِيمًا	

B. 1. The solid plural is formed by a noun (derived from a triletral root) plus a suffix ـُونَ 'ūna' or ـِينَ 'īna' in case of masculine and ات 'āt' in case of feminine, as seen in above examples. The broken plural is that in which a noun has a prefix or an infix or both of them. To illustrate the difference between solid and broken plurals the following example will be self-explanatory :

طَالِبٌ 'ṭālibun' (a student, a demander, a wisher) is a noun, its plural is طَالِبُونَ 'ṭālibūna' or طَالِبِينَ 'ṭālibīna' or طَالِبَاتٌ 'ṭālibātun', this is called a solid plural as you can see the original word طَالِبٌ 'ṭālibun' is existing in its solid shape. There are some other forms of plural such as طُلَّابٌ 'ṭullābun' in which an أَلِف 'alif is fixed between second and third radicals and the second radical ل lām is duplicated with Shaddah mark. Thus it becomes a broken plural, because the word طَالِب 'ṭālib' is broken by duplicating the second radical ل lām and adding an أَلِف 'alif after ل lām as well as omitting ألف 'alif (or long vowel) after the first radical.

B. 2. The broken plural has many Patterns. Grammarians divide them into two categories : جَمْعُ ٱلْقِلَّة jam'ul-qillati and جَمْعُ ٱلْكَثْرَة jam'ul-kathrati. جَمْعُ ٱلْقِلَّة jam'ul-qillati has four patterns and is grammatically used for a number of more than two and less than ten. These patterns are as follow :

I	أَفْعُلُ 'af'ulu,	e.g.

أَنْهُرٌ 'anhurun, plural of نَهْرٌ nahrun – river.

Examples from the Holy Qur'ān :

أَرْجُلٌ 'arjulun, plural of رِجْلٌ rijlun – leg.

وَتَشْهَدُ أَرْجُلُهُمْ	36-65 And their legs will bear witness.

أَعْيُنٌ *a'yunun*, plural of عَيْنٌ *'ainun* – eye.

وَلَهُمْ أَعْيُنٌ لَا يُبْصِرُونَ بِهَا	7-179 And they have eyes where with they see not.

أَنْفُسٌ *'anfusun*, plural of نَفْسٌ *nafsun* – soul.

مِنَ الْأَمْوَالِ وَالْأَنْفُسِ وَالثَّمَرَاتِ	2-155 (and they may have lose) of property, lives and fruits.

أَشْهُرٌ *'ashhurun*, plural of شَهْرٌ *shahrun* – month.

فَإِذَا انْسَلَخَ الْأَشْهُرُ الْحُرُمُ	9-5 So when the sacred months have passed.

II	أَفْعِلَةٌ *af'ilatun*,	e.g.

أَنْدِيَةٌ *'andiyatun*, plural of نَادِي *nādī* – club.

Examples from the Holy Qur'ān :

أَسْلِحَةٌ *aslihatun*, plural of سِلَاحٌ *silāhun* – arms (weapons).

وَلِيَأْخُذُوا أَسْلِحَتَهُمْ	4-102 and let them take their arms.

أَجْنِحَةٌ *'ajnihatun*, plural of جَنَاحٌ *janāhun* – wing.

جَاعِلِ الْمَلَائِكَةِ رُسُلًا أُولِي أَجْنِحَةٍ	35-1 The Maker of the angels, messengers flying on wings.

أَفْئِدَةٌ *'af'idatun*, plural of فُؤَادٌ *fu'ādun* – heart.

فَاجْعَلْ أَفْئِدَةً مِنَ النَّاسِ تَهْوِي إِلَيْهِمْ	14-37 so make the hearts of some people yearn towards them.

| III | فِعْلَةٌ   *fi'latun*, | e.g. |

صِبْيَةٌ *ṣibyatun*, plural of صَبِيٌّ *ṣabiyyun* – a child,

عِلْيَةٌ *'ilyatun*, plural of عَالِي *'ālī* – high.

Examples from the Holy Qur'ān :

فِتْيَةٌ *fityatun*, plural of فَتًى *fatan* – youth, young man.

| إِنَّهُمْ فِتْيَةٌ آمَنُوا بِرَبِّهِمْ | 18-13 Surely, they are youth who believed in their Lord. |

| IV | أَفْعَالٌ   *'af'ālun*, | e.g. |

أَهْدَافٌ *'ahdāfun*, plural of هَدَفٌ *hadafun* – target. This form of plural is very often used to denote meaning of a plural in a common sense, not for limited numbers, though it is one of the four patterns known as أَوْزَانُ جَمْعِ ٱلْقِلَّةِ (forms of those plurals that point to a number ranging between three to ten).

Some examples from the Holy Qur'ān :

أَنْصَارٌ *'anṣārun*, plural of نَاصِرٌ *nāṣirun* – helper.

| كُونُوا أَنْصَارَ اَللهِ | 61-14 be helpers (in the cause) of Allah. |

أَخْبَارٌ *'akhbārun*, plural of خَبَرٌ *khabarun* – news.

| يَوْمَئِذٍ تُحَدِّثُ أَخْبَارَهَا | 99-4 on the day she will tell her news. |

أَقْفَالٌ 'aqfālun, plural of قُفْلٌ quflun – lock.

| أَمْ عَلَىٰ قُلُوبٍ أَقْفَالُهَا | 47-24   or, are there locks on the hearts. |

أَصْحَابٌ 'aṣḥābun, plural of صَاحِبٌ ṣāḥibun – owner.

| أُولَٰئِكَ أَصْحَابُ ٱلْجَنَّةِ | 2-82   These are the dwellers (owners) of the Garden. |

B. 3. The following are among the more common patterns of the broken plurals :

| I | فُعُولٌ fu'ūlun, | e.g. |

حُرُوفٌ ḥurūfun, plural of حَرْفٌ ḥarfun – letter,

عُلُومٌ 'ulūmun, plural of عِلْمٌ 'ilmun – knowledge.

دُرُوسٌ durūsun, plural of دَرْسٌ darsun – lesson, study

Examples from the Holy Qur'ān :

مُلُوكٌ mulūkun, plural of مَلِكٌ malikun – king.

| قَالَتْ إِنَّ ٱلْمُلُوكَ إِذَا دَخَلُوا قَرْيَةً أَفْسَدُوهَا | 27-34   She said : surely the kings, when they enter a town, ruin it. |

قُلُوبٌ qulūbun, plural of قَلْبٌ qalbun – heart.

| أَلَا بِذِكْرِ اللهِ تَطْمَئِنُّ ٱلْقُلُوبُ | 13-28   Surely! in Allah's remembrance do hearts find rest. |

| II | فِعَالٌ fi'ālun, | e.g. |

كِبَارٌ *kibārun*, plural of كَبِيرٌ *kabīrun* – big.

صِعَابٌ *si'ābun*, plural of صَعْبٌ *sa'bun* – difficult.

كِلَابٌ *kilābun*, plural of كَلْبٌ *kalbun* – dog.

Examples from the Holy Qur'ān :

رِجَالٌ *rijālun*, plural of رَجُلٌ *rajulun* – man.

| رِجَالٌ لَا تُلْهِيهِمْ تِجَارَةٌ وَلَا بِيعٌ عَنْ ذِكْرِ اللهِ | 24-37 Men whom neither merchandise nor selling diverts from the remembrance of Allah. |

بِحَارٌ *bihārun*, plural of بَحْرٌ *bahrun* – sea.

| وَإِذَا ٱلْبِحَارُ سُجِّرَتْ | 81-6   And when the seas rise. |

غِلَاظٌ *ghilāzun*, plural of غَلِيظٌ *ghalīzun* – stern.

شِدَادٌ *shidādun*, plural of شَدِيدٌ *shadīdun* – strong.

| عَلَيْهَا مَلَائِكَةٌ غِلَاظٌ شِدَادٌ لَا يَعْصُونَ اللهَ | 66-6   Over it (i.e. fire) are angels, stern and strong who do not disobey Allah. |

بِغَالٌ *bighālun*, plural of بَغْلٌ *baghlun* – mule.

| وَٱلْخَيْلَ وَٱلْبِغَالَ وَٱلْحَمِيرَ لِتَرْكَبُوهَا وَزِينَةً | 16-8   ..and (He made) horses and mules and asses that you might ride upon them and and as an ornament. |

III	فُعُلٌ *fu'ulun*,	e.g.

كُتُبٌ *kutubun*, plural of كِتَابٌ *kitābun* – book.

سُفُنٌ *sufunun*, plural of سَفِينَةٌ *safīnatun* – ship.

مُدُنٌ *mudunun*, plural of مَدِينَةٌ *madīnatun* – city.

Examples from the Holy Qur'ān :

كُتُبٌ *kutubun*, plural of كِتَابٌ *kitābun* – book.

فِيهَا كُتُبٌ قَيِّمَةٌ	98-3 Wherein are valuable books.

سُبُلٌ *subulun*, plural of سَبِيلٌ *sabīlun* – way.

وَجَعَلَ لَكُمْ فِيهَا سُبُلاً	43-10 and made in it ways for you.

حُرُمٌ *hurumun*, plural of حَرَامٌ *harāmun* – sacred.

مِنْهَا أَرْبَعَةٌ حُرُمٌ	9-36 of these (12 months) four are sacred.

فُرُشٌ *furushun*, plural of فِرَاشٌ *firāshun* – couch.

وَفُرُشٌ مَرْفُوعَةٍ	56-34 and exalted couches.

IV	فُعَلاَءُ *fu'alā'u*,	e.g.

وُزَرَاءُ *wuzarā'u*, plural of وَزِيرٌ *wazīrun* – minister.

أُمَرَاءُ *'umarā'u*, plural of أَمِيرٌ *'amīrun* – prince.

Examples from the Holy Qur'ān :

كُبَرَاءُ kubarā'u, plural of كَبِيرٌ kabīrun – big.

وَقَالُوا رَبَّنَا إِنَّا أَطَعْنَا سَادَتَنَا وَكُبَرَائَنَا فَأَضَلُّونَا ٱلسَّبِيلَ	33-67 and they said : Our Lord, we only obeyed our leaders and our great men, so they led us astray from the path.

شُعَرَاءُ shu'arā'u, plural of شَاعِرٌ shā'irun – poet.

وَٱلشُّعَرَاءُ يَتَّبِعُهُمُ ٱلْغَاوُونَ	26-142 and the poets - the deviators follow them.

سُفَهَاءُ sufahā'u, plural of سَفِيهٌ safīhun – fool.

سَيَقُولُ ٱلسُّفَهَاءُ مِنَ ٱلنَّاسِ	2-142 the fools among the people will say ...

شُفَعَاءُ shufa'ā'u, plural of شَفِيعٌ shafī'un – intercessor.

فَهَلْ لَنَا مِنْ شُفَعَاءَ فَيَشْفَعُوا لَنَا	7-53 are there any inter-cessors on our behalf so that they intercede for us ?

V	أَفْعِلَاءُ 'af'ilā'u,	e.g.

أَصْدِقَاءُ 'aṣdiqā'u, plural of صَدِيقٌ sadīqun – friend.

أَذْكِيَاءُ 'adhkiyā'u, plural of ذَكِيٌّ dhakiyyun – intelligent.

أَصْفِيَاءُ 'aṣfiyā'u, plural of صَفِيٌّ safiyyun – pure, sincere friend.

Examples from the Holy Qur'ān :

أَنْبِيَاءُ *'anbiyā'u,* plural of نَبِيٌّ *nabiyyun* – prophet.

| إِذْ جَعَلَ فِيكُمْ أَنْبِيَاءَ | 5-20   Remember when He raised prophets among you. |

أَغْنِيَاءُ *'aghniyā'u,* plural of غَنِيٌّ *ghaniyyun* – rich.

| لَقَدْ سَمِعَ اللهُ قَوْلَ ٱلَّذِينَ قَالُوا إِنَّ اللهَ فَقِيرٌ وَنَحْنُ أَغْنِيَاءُ | 3-181   Allah has certainly heard the saying of those who said : Allah is poor and we are rich. |

أَدْعِيَاءُ *'ad'iyā'u,* plural of دَعِيٌّ *da'iyyun* – adopted or one taken as son.

| وَمَا جَعَلَ أَدْعِيَاءَكُمْ أَبْنَاءَكُمْ | 33-4   and He did not make whom you assert (to be) your sons (as actual sons). |

| VI | فِعْلَانٌ | *fi'lānun,* | e.g. |

وِلْدَانٌ *wildānun,* plural of وَلَدٌ *waladun* – child.

صِبْيَانٌ *ṣibyānun,* plural of صَبِيٌّ *ṣabiyyun* – young boy.

Examples from the Holy Qur'ān :

| يَجْعَلُ ٱلْوِلْدَانَ شِيبًا | 73-17   (the day) which will make children grey-headed. |

| VII | فُعْلَانٌ | *fu'lānun,* | e.g. |

بُلْدَانٌ *buldānun,* plural of بَلَدٌ *baladun* – city.

قُضْبَانٌ *quḍbānun,* plural of قَضِيبٌ *qaḍībun* – a rod.

C. Forms of the broken plural derived from a quadriliteral (four consonants) noun are as below :

I	فَعَالِلُ *fa'ālilu,*	e.g.

مَجَالِسُ *majālisu,* plural of مَجْلِسٌ *majlisun* – seat, a council.

تَجَارِبُ *tajāribu,* plural of تَجْرِبَةٌ *tajribatun* – an experiment, trial.

Examples from the Holy Qur'ān :

مَسَاجِدُ *masājidu,* plural of مَسْجِدٌ *masjidun* – mosque.

وَمَسَاجِدُ يُذْكَرُ فِيهَا اسْمُ اللهِ كَثِيرًا	22-40 and mosques in wich Allah's name is much remembered.

مَسَاكِنُ *masākinu,* plural of مَسْكَنٌ *maskanun* – dwelling.

وَمَسَاكِنُ تَرْضَوْنَهَا	9-24 ...and dwellings you love ...

مَنَازِلُ *manāzilu,* plural of مَنْزِلٌ *manzilun* – dwelling, stage.

وَالْقَمَر قَدَّرْنَاه مَنَازِلَ	36-39 and the moon, we have ordained for it stages.

مَجَالِسُ *majālisu,* plural of مَجْلِسٌ *majlisun* – a seat, seating place, assembly, council.

إِذَا قِيـلَ لَكُمْ تَفَسَّحُوا فِي الْمَجَالِس فَافْسَحُوا	58-11 When it is said to you, make room in assemblies, make room.

II	فَعَالِـيلُ *fa'ālīlu,* e.g.

سَلَاطِينُ *salāṭīnu,* plural of سُلْطَانٌ *sulṭānun* – sultan, king.

مَكَاتِيبُ *makātību,* plural of مَكْتُوبٌ *maktūbun* – a letter.

Examples from the Holy Qur'ān :

مَحَارِيبُ *maḥārību,* plural of مِحْـرَابٌ *miḥrābun* – prayer niche, mihrab.

تَمَاثِيلُ *tamāthīlu,* plural of تِمْثَالٌ *timthālun* – image, statue.

يَعْمَلُونَ لَهُ مَايَشَاءُ مِنْ مَحَارِيبَ وَتَمَاثِيلَ وَجِفَانٍ كَالْجَوَابِ وَقُـدُورٍ رَاسِيَاتٍ	34-13 They made for him what he pleased, of prayer niches, and images, and bowls (large) as waterring-troughs, and fixed cooking-pots.

Note : The above verse consists of four other plurals besides the first two plural nouns which are shown in examples of the undermentioned examples. The other forms have already been discussed. The last one represents the form of a solid plural for active participle feminine رَاسِيَةٌ *rāsiyatun* (a fixed one).

Caution :

Most of the forms for the broken plural are similar to the verbal nouns such as فُعُلٌ *fu'ulun,* e.g. كُتُبٌ *kutubun,* plural of كِـتَابٌ *kitābun* – a book, and meantime it is a verbal patern as نُزُلٌ (what a guest is offered) or as فِعْلَةٌ *fi'latun,* e.g. فِتْيَـةٌ *fityatun* – youth. Also it stands as a verbal noun as فِتْنَـةٌ *fitnatun.* This form is also confused with forms indicating singularity of a noun, as مِرْيَةٌ

miryatun – doubt. Students are advised to be careful while study-
ing the Holy Qur'ān. The only rule that may help them to distinguish the plural from verbal noun or other forms, is to see either
the word has its singular from the same root or not; if there is a singular it means that the word is a plural, otherwise it is either a verbal noun or an exceptional form of a singular.

EXERCISE

1. Transcribe the following words and write down their forms in
   measuring letters (ف ع ل) :

قُضَاةٌ – قُدُورٌ – جِفَانٍ – قَنَادِيلُ – مَكَاتِيبُ .

2. Pick up forms of the broken plural among the following
   words :

أَنْصَارٌ – نَاصِرِينَ – نَاشِفٌ – مَخَابِزُ – تَلَامِيذُ – قُرْبَانٌ – نُزُلٌ .

3. Translate into English the following verses and sentences :

(١) جَاءَ إِخْوَةُ يُوسُفَ فَدَخَلُوا عَلَيه فَعَرَفَهُم وَهُم لَهُ مُنْكِرُونَ

(٢) قَالُوا قُلوبُنَا غُلْفٌ بَلْ لَعَنَهُم اللهُ بِكُفْرِهِمْ

(٣) تِلْكَ ٱلْأَمْثَالُ نَضْرِبُهَا لِلنَّاسِ

(٤) إِنَّا عَرَضْنَا ٱلْأَمَانَةَ عَلَى ٱلسَّمَوَاتِ وَٱلْأَرْضِ وَٱلْجِبَالِ فَأَبَيْنَ أَنْ يَحْمِلْنَهَا
وَأَشْفَقْنَ مِنْهَا وَحَمَلَهَا ٱلْإِنْسَانُ

(٥) يُخْرِجُهُمْ مِنَ ٱلظُّلُمَاتِ إِلَى ٱلنُّورِ

(٦) إِنَّمَا يَعْمُرُ مَسَاجِدَ اللهِ مَنْ آمَنَ بِاللهِ

(٧) رِجَالٌ لَا تُلْهِيهِم تِجَارَةً وَلَا بَيْعٌ عَنْ ذِكْرِ اللهِ

(٨) وَبُعُولَتُهُنَّ أَحَقُّ بِرَدِّهِنَّ

(٩) وَاخْتِلَافُ أَلْسِنَتِكُمْ وَأَلْوَانِكُمْ

(١٠) ذَهَبَ الْأَغْنِيَاء إِلَىٰ الْمَصَايِف فِي بُلْدَانِ الْغَرْب

(١١) ظَهَرَتْ نَتَائِجُ الْإِمْتِحَانِ السَّنَوِي فَفَرِحَ الطَّلَبَةُ النَّاجِحُونَ ، وَوَضَعُوا
كُتُبَهُم الْقَدِيمَة فِي الصَّنَادِيق وَحَمَلُوا الْكُتُبَ الجَدِيدَةَ فِي الْحَقَائِب
الْيَدَوِيَّة . رَجَعَ الْأَسَاتِذَةُ إِلَىٰ الْمَدْرَسَةِ بَعد قَضَاءِ الْأَجَازَةِ فِي
أَوْطَانِهِم .

4. **Translate into Arabic :**

News about the gathering of pilgrims reached the Council of
Ministers. New arrangements for Hajj affairs are under the
consideration of the council. During the early centuries of the
Islamic history the mosques were the centres of Islamic activities. Today mosques are used for the prayers. Prayers in
Islam have their own significance. They are not like worship-
ping in other religions.

Paradise is meant for further advancement. Muhammad was
sent to the entire world, not for Arabs only. The Holy Qur'ān
has described him as a prophet for all human beings what-
soever be their colour, race, place and time.

VOCABULARY

إِخْوَةٌ plural of أَخٌ	brother.
مُنْكِرُون plural of مُنْكِرٌ	one who does not recognize someone (Act. participle, male, singular).
قُلُوبٌ plural of قَلْبٌ	heart.
غُلْفٌ verbal noun of غَلَفَ also plural of غِلَافٌ	closed, covered, wrap.
الأَمْثَالُ plural of مَثَلٌ	example.
عَرَضَ (Perf. 3rd Person Masc.)	offered.
السَّمٰوَات plural of السَّمَاء	heaven.
الأَمَانَةُ	The trust.
الأَرْضُ	The earth.
أَبَيْنَ (Perf. 3rd Person Fem.)	derived from أَبَىٰ abā – refused.
يَحْمِلْنَ (Imper. Fem. 3rd Person, plural)	derived from حَمَلَ ḥamala – to bear.
أَشْفَقْنَ (Imper. Fem. 3rd Person, plural)	derived from أَشْفَقَ ʾashfaq – to be frightened.
الظُّلُمَاتُ plural of ظُلْمَةٌ zulmatun	darkness.

يَعْمُرُ	(Imp. 3rd Person Masc. sing.)	inhabit, to build.
تَلَهَّىٰ	(Imp. 3rd Person Masc. sing.)	distract.
بُعُولٌ	plural of بَعْل *ba'l*	husband.
أَلْسِنَةٌ	plural of لِسَانٌ *lisānun*	tongue.
أَلْوَانٌ	plural of لَوْنٌ *lawnun*	colour.
مَصَايِفُ	plural of مَصِيفٌ *maṣīfun*	summer place, resort.
بُلْدَانٌ	plural of بِلَادٌ *bilādun*	country.
نَتَائِجُ	plural of نَتِيجَةٌ *natījatun*	result.
صَنَادِيقُ	plural of صُنْدُوقٌ *ṣundūqun*	box.
شُنَطٌ	plural of شَنْطَةٌ *shanṭatun*	hand bag.
أَسَاتِذَةٌ	plural of أُسْتَاذٌ *'ustādhun*	teacher.
أَوْطَانٌ	plural of وَطَنٌ *waṭanun*	homeland.
gathering	جُمُوعٌ	
pilgrims	حُجَّاجٌ	
arrangements	تَدَابِيرُ plural of تَدْبِيرٌ	
consideration	إِعْتِبَارٌ/فِكْرَةٌ	
to advance	تَقَدَّمَ (Perf. 3rd Person Masc.)	
advancement	تَقَدُّمٌ (verbal noun)	

CHAPTER 14

THE PREPOSITIONS

1. The Arabic حَرْفُ ٱلْجَرّ. *harful jarr* is similar to the English preposition. A word followed by an Arabic preposition is taken in the genetive. Consequently its last letter will be vowelled with a *kasrah* e.g. فِي *fī;* "in" فِي كِتَابٍ *fī kitābin;* "in a book" فِي ٱلْكِتَابِ *filkitābi;* "in the book" فِي دِينٍ *fī dīnin;* "in a religion" فِي ٱلدِّينِ *fiddīni;* "in the Religion" and so on.

2. Prepositions are either (a) Inseparable; consisting of one letter always attached to the following word; or (b) separate, which stand alone and are either particles or invariable adverbs of time or place.

(a) Inseparable Prepositions :

I. ب "in, by, with" etc. verbs denoting 'to begin, adhere, seize, attach' are constructed with ب , e.g. اتَّصَلَ بِهِ "he got in contact with him". أَبْدَأُ بِاسْمِ ٱلله. بَدَأَ بِهِ "he began with him". "I start with the name of Allah"; often the verb is omitted: بِسْمِ ٱلله أَمَنَ ب "with the name of Allah". "To believe in" is آمَنَ بِٱلله. e.g. "He believed in Allah". "To swear by" is أُقْسِمُ ب أُقْسِمُ بِيَوْمِ ٱلدِّينِ. e.g. "I swear by the Day of Judgement".

In negative sentences if the predicate is a noun, بِ is often prefixed, e.g. مَا هُوَ بِشَاعِرٍ "He is not a poet". Also without بِ is used as مَا هُوَ شَاعِرٌ or هُوَ لَيْسَ شَاعِراً , but when a negative particle such as مَا or لَيْسَ is followed by an interrogative «أ» 'a' the noun must be prefixed with بِ e.g. :

(95-8) أَلَيْسَ الله بِأَحْكَمِ ٱلْحَاكِمِينَ "Is not Allah the Best of the Judges ?" أَلَسْتُ بِرَبِّكُم "Am I not your Lord ?"

II. تَ 'by' in an oath only : by the name of the Almighty Allah. e.g. (from the Holy Qur'ān)

| وَتَالله لَأَكِيدَنَّ أَصْنَامَكُمْ | 21-57   And, by Allah! I will certainly plan against your idols. |
| تَالله لَقَدْ آثَرَكَ الله عَلَيْنَا | 12-91   They said : By Allah ! Allah has indeed chosen thee over us. |

III. وَ 'by' in an oath. e.g. وَرَبِّ ٱلْبَيْتِ "By the Lord of the (Sacred) House".

| وَٱلسَّمَاءِ ذَاتِ ٱلْبُرُوجِ | By the heaven full of the stars! |
| وَٱلسَّمَاءِ وَٱلطَّارِقِ | By the heaven and the commenly night! |

IV. لِ "for, to, because of". It is used to express the Dative and denotes possession. (= "have") e.g. هٰذَا ٱلْقَـلَمُ لِي "This pen is mine". لَكَ هٰذِهِ ٱلدَّارُ "To you belongs this house".

It denotes the English "of" when it follows an indeterminate noun, e.g. كِتَابٌ لِزَيْدٍ "a book of (belonging to) Zayd". صَاحِبٌ لِي "a friend of me" i.e. "one of my friends".

Examples from the Holy Qur'ān :

لله مَا فِي ٱلسَّمَوَاتِ وَٱلْأَرْضِ	2-284 To Allah belongs whatever is in heavens and whatever is in earth.
لِمَنِ ٱلْمُلْكُ ٱلْيَـوْمَ لله ٱلْوَاحِـدِ ٱلْقَهَّـارِ	40-16 To Whom belongs the kingdom this day ? To Allah, The One, The Subduer (of all).

It is used also for the writer of a book, e.g.
قِصَصُ ٱلنَّبِيِّينَ لِأَبِي الْحَسَن النَّدْوِي   The Stories of the Prophets of (i.e. written by) Abul Ḥasan Al-Nadwi.

It also denotes 'for the benefit of' e.g. (from The Holy Qur'ān) :

مَنْ جَاءَ بِالْحَسَنَةِ فَـلَهُ عَشْرُ أَمْثَالِهَا	6-160 whoever brings a good deed will have tenfold like it.

Often it is used to denote 'the benefit of' (opposite of عَلَى) e.g. (from The Holy Qur'ān) :

قَالُوا أَنَّى يَكُونُ لَهُ ٱلْمُلْكُ عَلَيْنَا	2-247 They said: how can he have a greater right to kingdom over us ?

It is also used to denote the purpose and the cause, e.g.
قَامَ لِنُصْرَتِـهِ "He rose for his help".

وَمَا أَرْسَلْـنَا مِنْ رَسُولٍ إِلَّا بِلِسَانِ قَوْمِـهِ لِيُـبَـيِّنَ لَهُمْ	14-4 And we sent no messenger but with the language of his people, so that he might explain to them.
قَدْ أَنْزَلَ اللهُ إِلَيْكُمْ ذِكْراً . رَسُولاً يَتْلُوا عَلَيْكُمْ آيَاتِ اللهِ مُبَيِّـنَاتٍ لِيُخْرِجَ ٱلَّذِينَ آمَنُوا . . .	65-10,11 Allah has sent down to you a Reminder; a Messenger who recites to you the clear messages of Allah, so that he may bring forth those who believe...
لِيَعْلَمُوا أَنَّ اللهَ عَلَىٰ كُلِّ شَيْءٍ قَدِيرٌ	65-12 that they may know that Allah is Possessor of Power over all things.

لِهَذَا / لِذَلِكَ / لِأَجْلِ هَذَا / لِأَجْلِ ذَلِكَ "for this reason".

Note 1: قَالَ لِـ "to say to" often means (especially in passive), to call, name, e.g. (from The Holy Qur'ān) :

قَالُوا سَمِعْنَا فَتًى يَذْكُرُهُمْ يُقَالُ لَهُ إِبْرَاهِيمُ	21-60 They said: we heard a youth who is called Abraham, speak of them.

Note 2: لِ *li* is changed to لَ *la* before pronominal suffixes (except with the first person), e.g. لَكُمْ / لَهَا / لَهُ

V. كَ as 'like' e.g. (from The Holy Qur'ān) :

وَلَيْسَ ٱلذَّكَرُ كَٱلْأُنْثَى	3-36 And the male is not like the female.
أَوْ كَٱلَّذِي مَرَّ عَلَى قَرْيَةٍ	2-259 Or like him who passed by a town...

(b) Separate Prepositions

I. إِلَى ʾilā "until', e.g. (from The Holy Qur'ān):

ثُمَّ أَتِمُّوا ٱلصِّيَامَ إِلَى ٱللَّيْلِ	2-187 Then complete the fast until the nightfall.

إِلَى ʾilā "to", e.g. (from The Holy Qur'ān):

سُبْحَانَ ٱلَّذِي أَسْرَى بِعَبْدِهِ لَيْلًا مِنَ ٱلْمَسْجِدِ ٱلْحَرَامِ إِلَى ٱلْمَسْجِدِ ٱلْأَقْصَى	17-1 Glory to Him Who carried His servant by night from the Sacred Mosque unto the Remote (Al-Aqṣā) Mosque.

With suffixes إِلَيْهِ 'to him', إِلَيَّ 'to me', e.g. (from The Holy Qur'ān) :

إِلَيْهِ يَصْعَدُ ٱلْكَلِمُ ٱلطَّيِّبُ	35-10 To Him does ascend the goodly word.
ثُمَّ إِلَيَّ مَرْجِعُكُمْ	3-55 Then to Me is your return.

II. حَتَّى ḥattā "until, as far as'' e.g. (from The Holy Qur'ān) :

حَتَّى إِذَا ٱسْتَيْأَسَ ٱلرُّسُلُ	12-110 until, when the messengers despair.

حَتَّى إِذَا جَاءُوهَا فُتِحَتْ أَبْوَابُهَا	39-71 until, when they come to it, its doors are opened.

It is not used with suffixes. Sometimes it is used to mean 'even'
e.g. سَأَلْتُ كُلَّ شَخْصٍ حَتَّى ٱلطِّفْلَ 'I asked everybody, even the
child'. But in this case it has no influence of genetives.

III. عَلَى 'alā, 'over, upon, against, through', e.g. (from The
Holy Qur'ān) :

إِنَّ ٱللهَ عَلَى كُلِّ شَيْءٍ قَـدِيرٌ	2-109 surely Allah is Possessor over all things.
صِرَاطَ ٱلَّذِينَ أَنْعَمْتَ عَلَيْهِمْ	1-7 The path of those upon whom Thou hast bestowed favours.
إِنَّ ٱللهَ وَمَلَائِكَتَهُ يُصَلُّونَ عَلَى ٱلنَّبِيِّ يَا أَيُّهَا ٱلَّذِينَ آمَنُوا صَلُّوا عَلَيْهِ وَسَلِّمُوا تَسْلِيمَا	33-56 Surely, Allah and His angels bless the Prophet. O' you who believe call for blessings on him and salute him (as salute is performed).
سَلَامٌ عَلَيْـكُمْ	13-24 Peace be on you.
وَعَـلَى ٱلَّذِينَ يُطِيقُونَهُ فِدْيَةٌ طَعَامُ مِسْكِينٍ	2-184 And on those who can afford, is redemption by feeding a poor man.

عَلَى is used with suffixes as عَلَيَّ , عَلَيْهِ etc. to denote places :
جَلَسَ عَلَى ٱلْمَائِدَةِ 'he sat at the table'. عَلَى ٱلطَّرِيقِ 'on the way'.
Sometimes it is used in the hostile sense, e.g. : خَـرَجَ عَـلَيْهِ
'he went out, against him'.

Examples from The Holy Qur'ān :

فَأَرْسَلْنَا عَلَيهِم ريحاً وَجُنُوداً لَم تَرَوْهَا	33-9 so we sent against them a strong wind and hosts that you saw not.

IV. عَنْ 'an, 'from, about, concerning, with'.

Examples from The Holy Qur'ān :

وَيَسْئَلُونَكَ عَنِ ٱلرُّوحِ	17-85 And they ask thee about the soul.
ٱلَّذِينَ يَصُدُّونَ عَن سَبِيلِ اللهِ	11-19 those who hinder (men) from the path of Allah.
وَإِذَا سَأَلَكَ عِبَادِى عَنِّي فَإِنِّي قَرِيبٌ	2-186 And when My servants ask thee concerning Me, surely I am nigh.
رَضِيَ اللهُ عَنْهُمْ وَرَضُوا عَنْهُ	5-119 Allah is well pleased with them and they are well pleased with Him.

It is used in place of "away from" and so is used with verbs denoting, "avoid, restrain oneself, forbid, defend" etc.

Examples from The Holy Qur'ān :
(To forbid)

يَأْمُرُونَ بِٱلْمَعْرُوفِ وَيَنْهَوْنَ عَنِ ٱلْمُنْكَرِ	9-71 They enjoin good and forbid evil.

(To defend)

إِنَّ اللهَ يُدَافِعُ عَنِ ٱلَّذِينَ آمَنُوا	22-38 surely Allah defends those who believe.

(To uncover)

وَكَشَفَتْ عَنْ سَاقَيْهَا	27-44 and she bared her legs.

V. فِي *fī,* 'in' with suffixes : فِيهِ 'in him or in it', فِيَّ 'in me', فِيكُمْ 'in you or among you'.

Examples from the Holy Qur'ān :

لَقَدْ كَانَ لَكُمْ فِي رَسُولِ اللهِ أُسْوَةٌ حَسَنَةٌ	33-21 Surely you have in the Messenger of Allah an excellent exemplar.
فِيهِ رِجَالٌ يُحِبُّونَ أَن يَتَطَهَّرُوا	9-108 In it (the mosque) are men who love to purify themselves.
لَقَدْ مَنَّ اللهُ عَلَى ٱلْمُؤْمِنِينَ إِذْ بَعَثَ فِيهِمْ رَسُولاً	3-164 Certainly, Allah conferred a favour on the believers when He raised among them a messenger.

VI. مِنْ *min,* 'from'. It is often interchangeable with عَنْ and used with suffixes such as مِنْهُ 'from him or from it', مِنِّي 'from me', مِنَّا 'from us', etc.

Examples from The Holy Qur'ān :

يُخْرِجُهُمْ مِنَ ٱلظُّلُمَاتِ إِلَى ٱلنُّورِ	2-257 He brings them out of darkness into light.

It is sometimes used to complete the sense of قَبْلُ 'before', and بَعْدُ 'after'. According to the grammarians this kind of (مِنْ) is called 'an additional (مِنْ)' e.g. (from The Holy

Qur'ān) :

لِلّٰهِ الأَمْـرُ مِنْ قَـبْلُ وَمِنْ بَعْـدُ	30-4 Allah's is the Command before and after.

It is also used partitively (للتبعيض) followed by a definite noun in the plural to indicate an indefinite number or quantity, e.g. (from The Holy Qur'ān) :

وَلَٰكِنَّ اللّٰهَ يَجْتَبِي مِنْ رُسُلِهِ مَن يَشَاءُ	3-179 But Allah chooses for His Messenger whom He pleases.
لِـنُرِيَكَ مِن آيَاتِـنَا ٱلْكُبْـرَىٰ	20-23 that We may show thee of Our greater signs.

and to indicate materials e.g. كُرْسِيٌّ مِنْ خَشَبٍ 'a chair of wood'.

Examples from The Holy Qur'ān :

وَيُطَافُ عَلَيْهِمْ بِآنِيَـةٍ مِنْ فِضَّةٍ	76-15 goblets of silver are served round for them.

It is very often used after مَا mā, to explain (للتـبيين) what is intended by the particle, e.g. أَنْـفَـقْتُ مَا كَانَ عِنْـدِي مِنَ ٱلْمَـالِ 'I spent of what was with me in the way of wealth'.

Examples from the Holy Qur'ān :

وَمَا تُنْفِقُوا مِنْ خَيرٍ فَإِنَّ اللّٰهَ بِهِ عَلِيمٌ	2-273 And whatever good thing you spend surely Allah is knower of it.
وَمَا أَصَابَكُمْ مِنْ مُصِيبَةٍ فَبِمَا كَسَبَتْ أَيْدِيكُمْ وَيَعْفُوا عَن كَثِيرٍ	42-30 And whatever misfortune befell you it is on account of what your hands have earned and He pardons much.

VII. مُذْ *mudh*, مُنْذُ *mundhu*, 'since'.

It is not used with suffixes, it is sometimes followed by the nominal, e.g. مَا رَأَيْتُكَ مُنْذُ (مُذْ) يَوْمِ ٱلْجُمْعَةِ "I have not seen you since Friday".

3.   There are a number of nouns used as prepositions, though not endorsed by Arab grammarians, some Western authors listed them as real prepositions, however, these particles are useful for learners as they are in accordance with The Holy Qur'ān :

(a) لَدَى , لَدُنْ , لَدَيَّ *ladā, ladun, ladayya*, "with" (Latin 'apad') with suffixes لَدَيْهِمْ "with them", لَدَيَّ "with me", لَدَيْهِ "with him", لَدُنِّي "with me, to me".

Examples from The Holy Qur'ān :

لَا يَخَافُ لَدَيَّ ٱلْمُرْسَلُونَ	27-10 surely, the Massengers fear not in My presence.
وَإِنَّهُ فِي أُمِّ ٱلْكِتَابِ لَدَيْنَا لَعَلِيٌّ حَكِيمٌ	43-4 And it is in the Original of the Book with Us, truly elevated, full of wisdom.
الَر! كِتَابٌ أُحْكِمَتْ آيَاتُهُ ثُمَّ فُصِّلَتْ مِن لَدُنْ حَكِيمٍ خَبِيرٍ	11-1 A book whose verses are characterized by wisdom, then they are made plain from One, Wise, Aware.
وَمَا كُنْتَ لَدَيْهِمْ إِذْ يُلْقُونَ أَقْلَامَهُمْ	3-44 And thou wast not with them when they cast their pens

(b) مَعَ *ma'a*, "with", e.g. (from The Holy Qur'ān) :

إِنَّ اللهَ مَعَ ٱلصَّابِرِينَ	2-153 Allah is with the patients.

(c) عِنْدَ ‘inda, "with, at", used for place : جَلَسْتُ عِنْدَهُ ‘I sat with (beside) him'.

Examples from The Holy Qur'ān :

وَلاَ تُقَاتِلُوهُمْ عِنْدَ ٱلْمَسْجِدِ ٱلْحَرَامِ	2-191 and fight not with them at the Sacred Mosque.

Use of time : جَاءَ عِنْدَ طُلُوعِ ٱلشَّمْسِ "he came at sunrise". It is often used to denote the meaning "for, to, near, presence".

Examples from The Holy Qur'ān :

وَتَحْسَبُونَهُ هَيِّنًا وَهُوَ عِنْدَ اللهِ عَظِيمٌ	24-15 You counted it a trifle, and in the sight of Allah it is very great.
آذْكُرْنِي عِنْدَ رَبِّكَ	12-42 Remember me in presence of thy Lord.

It is also used with the meaning 'to have'.

Examples from The Holy Qur'ān :

مَا عِنْدَكُمْ يَنْفَدُ وَمَا عِنْدَ اللهِ بَاقٍ	16-96 whatever you possess will pass away and what Allah has, will remain.

EXERCISE

1. **Translate into Arabic :**

... in short, a life which fully represents all aspects of human existence and combines all that is best.and noblest in terms of sentiments and behaviour is the life of Prophet Muhammad (Peace be upon him). This is the highest standard of perfection for every body, in every respect and for all places and times. Supposing you are a rich man you have an ideal to follow in the person of the merchant of Makkah and the treasurer of Bahrain. If you are poor, you must emulate the example of the internee of Shi'b Abi Talib and (later) the guest of the people of Madinah.

2. **Translate into English :**

١ - لَمْ يَكُنْ بَطَلُ الأَبْطَالِ وَخَاتَمُ ٱلنَّبِيِّينَ صَلَّى الله عَلَيْهِ وَسَلَّمْ إِلَّا بَشَراً يُوحَىٰ إِلَيْهِ وَمَا أُوتِيَ عَنْ طَرِيقِ ٱلْوَحْى قَدْ فُصِّلَتْ آيَاتُهُ فِي ٱلْكِتَابِ وَفِيمَا عَدا ذَلِكَ مِنَ ٱلأَقْوَالِ وَٱلأَعْمَالِ فَإِنَّمَا هِيَ ثَمَرَةُ عَقْلٍ رَاجِحٍ وَلِسَانٍ فَصِيحٍ فِي ذَاتٍ فَذَّةٍ .

٢ - إِنَّ أَوَّلَ شَرْطٍ لِنَجَاحِ ٱلْبَائِعِ أَنْ يُحِبَّ عَمَلَهُ وَأَنْ يُوَجَّهَ إِلَيْهِ كُلُّ اهْتِمَامِهِ حَتَّىٰ يُؤَدِّيَهُ فِي سُهُولَةٍ وَيُسْرٍ وَعَنْ رِضَا وَٱرْتِيَاحٍ عَلَى أَنْ يَكُونَ ٱلْبَائِعُ بِجَانِبِ ذَلِكَ مُتَفَائِلاً . وَٱلإِبْتِسَامَةُ عَلَى وَجْهِ ٱلْبَائِعِ ضَرُورَةٌ مِن ضَرُورَاتِ هَذِهِ ٱلمَهْنَةِ وَبِدُونِهَا لَا يَسْتَقِيمُ لَهُ عَمَلٌ .

٣ - أَهَمُّ شَيْءٍ عِنْدَ عَالِمٍ كِتَابُهُ ، وَعِنْدَ أَصْحَابِ ٱلمِهَنِ ٱلْيَدَوِيَّةِ عُدَّتُهُمْ ، وَعِنْدَ ٱلْجُنْدِيِّ سِلاحُهُ .

VOCABULARY	
Hero of Heroes	بَطَلُ ٱلأَبْطَالِ
The Last Prophet	خَاتَمُ ٱلنَّبِيِّينَ
human being	البَشَر / الإِنْسَانُ
revealed	أُوحِيَ
way	طَرِيق / سَبِيل
stated clearly	المُصَرَّح بِهِ
the sign	الآيَة

among the sayings	مِنَ الأَقْوَال
deeds	الأَعْمَال
front	الأَمَام
wisdom, intellect	العَقْل
matured	الرَّاجِح / النَّاضِج
apart from that	فضلاً عن . . .
frank talk	القَوْلُ ٱلصَّرِيح
condition	الشَّرطُ
success	النَّجاح
the merchant	التَّاجِر
to love	Perf. أَحَبَّ Imperf. يُحِبُّ
to direct	يُوَجِّه Imperf. وَجَّه Perf. توجيه
attention to	الاهْتَمَامُ بِـ
in order to	لِ / لأَجْلِ
to do, perform, discharge (duty)	Perf. أَدَّى Imperf. يُؤَدِي
easiness	السُّهُولَةُ / اليُسْرُ
delightfully	ابْتَهَاجاً
aside from this	مَاعَدا ذَلِكَ
optimistic / optimism	متفائل / التفاؤل
smiling	التَّبَسُّم / الابْتِسَامُ
necessity	الضَّرُورَة

profession	المِهْنَـةُ
does not stand	لَا يَسْتَقِـيـمُ
the most important thing	أَهَـمُّ شَيءٍ
tool	العُـدَّةُ
soldier	الْجُنْـدِيُّ
arms	السِّـلَاحُ
personal	الـذَّات
unique	الفَـذَّةُ
represents	يُمَثِّـلُ
aspects	الظَّـوَاهِرَ plural of ظَاهِرَةٌ
existence	الوجُـود - البَقَاء
sentiments	العَــوَاطف
behaviour	السُّـلُوكُ
perfection	التَـوَافُـق
respect	الإِجْـلَال
supposing	عَلى فرضٍ
rich	الغَنِـيُّ
idol	الصَّـنَمُ
treasurer	الخَـازن
internee	الدَاخِـلُ

CHAPTER 15

THE IMPERATIVE

1. The Imperative فِعْلُ آلأَمْرِ is a modification of the Imperfect. It is formed by :
   (a) Taking away the vowel of the final radical as in case of the jussive.
   (b) Dropping the pronominal prefix.
   (c) Replacing it by an أَلِف 'alif, e.g.

   كَتَبَ "to write". Imperfect يَكْتُبُ "he writes".

   Imperative أُكْتُبْ "write!"

2. This أ 'alif may be vowelled with *dammah* or *kasrah*. If the second radical of the imperfect has *dammah*, the prefixed 'alif will take *dammah* otherwise it will be vowelled with *kasrah*.

   Thus from يَنْصُرُ , the imperative will be أُنْصُرْ , and from يَضْرِبُ and يَفْتَحُ , the imperatives will be إِفْتَحْ and إِضْرِبْ respectively.

3. In case of a weak letter in the middle radical of the imperfect such as يَقُولُ and يَبِيعُ , no 'alif is prefixed; the first radical will receive the vowel that will agree with the vowel of the middle radical, thus: قَال "to say", Imperfect يَقُول "he says", Imperative قُلْ "say!". بَاعَ "to sell", Imperfect يَبِيعُ "he sells", Imperative بِعْ "sell!".

4. The prefixing *'alif* of the imperative is applied at the beginning of a statement, otherwise this *'alif* will be considered silent. Consequently, the second radical will determine the pattern of the imperative, e.g.:

كُلُوا وَاشْرَبُوا "eat and drink!" إِجْلِسْ وَاكْتُبْ "sit and write!".

Example from the Holy Qur'ān :

| اعْمَلُوا آلَ دَاوُودَ شُكْراً | O' children of David, work hard in thanks. |

5. The following conjugation of the imperative represents its common pattern :

	from يَكْتُبُ = يَفْعُلُ	from يَفْتَحُ = يَفْعَلُ	from يَضْرِبُ = يَفْعِلُ
Sing. 2nd pers. Masc.	أُكْتُبْ	إِفْتَحْ	إِضْرِبْ
Sing. 2nd pers. Fem.	أُكْتُبِي	إِفْتَحِي	إِضْرِبِي
Dual 2nd pers. Masc. & Fem.	أُكْتُبَا	إِفْتَحَا	إِضْرِبَا
Plural 2nd pers. Masc.	أُكْتُبُوا	إِفْتَحُوا	إِضْرِبُوا
Plural 2nd pers. Fem.	أُكْتُبْنَ	إِفْتَحْنَ	إِضْرِبْنَ

	from يَقُولُ	from يَبِيعُ
Sing. 2nd pers. Masc.	قُــلْ	بِــعْ
Sing. 2nd pers. Fem.	قُــولِي	بِــيعِي

Dual 2nd pers. Masc. & Fem.	قُولَا	بِيعَا
Plural 2nd pers. Masc.	قُولُوا	بِيعُوا
Plural 2nd pers. Fem.	قُلْنَ	بِعْنَ

The negative imperative فِعْــل النــهي is formed by the 2nd person, Imperfect (Jussive) preceded by لَا thus:

لَا تَكْتُبْ	لَا تَقُلْ	لَا تَبِعْ
لَا تَكْتُبِي	لَا تَقُولِي	لَا تَبِيعِي
لَا تَكْتُبَا	لَا تَقُولَا	لَا تَبِيعَا
لَا تَكْتُبُوا	لَا تَقُولُوا	لَا تَبِيعُوا
لَا تَكْتُبْنَ	لَا تَقُلْنَ	لَا تَبِعْنَ

Examples from The Holy Qur'ān :

Pattern I أُكْتُبْ "write",

from كَتَبَ "to write", Imperfect يَكْتُبُ "he writes"

اُرْكُضْ بِـرِجْلِكَ هَـذَا مُغْتَسَلٌ بَـارِدٌ وَشَـرَابٌ	38-42 Urge with thy foot; here is a cool washing-place and drink.

أُكْتُبِي Sing. Fem.

يَا مَرْيَمُ اقْـنُتِي لِرَبِّكِ وَاسْجُدِي	3-43 O' Mary, be obedient to thy Lord and do "Sajdah".

أُكْتُبُوا Plural Masc.

| وَاسْجُدُوا وَاعْبُدُوا رَبَّكُمْ | 22-77 And do 'sajdah' and serve your Lord. |

أُكْتُبْنَ Plural Fem.

| وَاذْكُرْنَ مَا يُتْلَى فِي بُيُوتِكُنَّ | 33-34 And remember that which is recited in your houses. |

Pattern II إِفْتَحْ "open",

from فَتَحَ "to open", Imperfect يَفْتَحُ "he opens"

| يَا أَبَتِ افْعَلْ مَا تُؤْمَرُ | 37-102 O' my father, do as those art commanded. |

إِفْتَحِي Sing. Fem.

| وَارْكَعِي مَعَ الرَّاكِعِينَ | 3-43 and bow thyself with whom who bow themselves. |
| وَقِيلَ يَا أَرْضُ ابْلَعِي مَاءَكَ | 11-44 and it was said : O' earth swallow thy water. |

إِفْتَحُوا Plural Masc.

| وَافْعَلُوا الخَيْرَ لَعَلَّكُمْ تُفْلِحُون | 22-77 and do good that you may succeed. |

Pattern III إِضْرِبْ "strike", Sing. Masc.

from ضَرَبَ "to strike", Imperfect يَضْرِبُ "he strikes"

| فَقُلْنَا اضْرِبْ بِعَصَاكَ الْحَجَرَ | 2-60 We said: strike on the rock with thy staff. |

Plural Masc. إِضْرِبُوا

فَقُلْنَا اضْرِبُوهُ بِبَعْضِهَا	2-73 so We said: strike him with it partially.

From Weak Verbs : قُـلْ **Sing. Masc.**

وَقُـلْ لَهُمَا قَوْلاً كَرِيماً	17-23 and speak to them a generous word.

Plural Masc. قُـولُـوا

قُلْ مُوتُوا بِغَيْـظِكُمْ	3-119 Say: Die in your rage.

Plural Fem. قُـلْنَ

وَقُـلْنَ قَـوْلاً مَعْـرُوفاً ٭ وَقَـرْنَ فِي بُـيُوتِكُنَّ	33-32,33 and speak a word of goodness and stay in your houses.

6. Imperative from Hamzated verbs

Verbs of which the first radical is *hamzah* such as أَكَلَ "to eat" Imperfect يَأْكُل "he eats", have their imperative without an *'alif*, e.g. :

Sing. 2nd pers. Masc. كُلْ "eat", as خُذْ "take", e.g.

خُـذْ مِنْ أَمْـوَالِهِمْ صَدَقَـةً	9-103 take alms out of their property.

Sing. 2nd pers. Fem. كُلِي "eat", e.g.

فَكُلِي وَاشْرَبِي وَقَـرِّي عَيْـناً	19-26 eat and, drink and be delighted.

Dual 2nd pers. Masc. & Fem. كُلَا "eat", e.g.

وَكُلَا مِنْهَا رَغَـدا	2-35 and eat from it in plenty.

Plural 2nd pers. Fem. as قَرْنَ ، قُلْنَ of weak verb's imperative.
Verbs hamzated in their middle radical such as سَأَلَ "to ask";
Imperfect يَسْأَلُ. The Imperative will be سَلْ "ask", e.g. (from
The Holy Qur'ān) :

سَـلْ بَنِي إِسْرَائِيـل	2-211 Ask the children of Israel.

also إِسْأَلْ with 'alif vowelled with *kasrah,* e.g. (from The
Holy Qur'ān) :

وَإِسْـأَلِ الْقَـرْيَـةَ الَّتِي كُـنَّا فِيهَا	12-82 and ask the town where we were.

If *hamzah* occurs in the third radical such as قَـرَأَ, the imperative will be إِقْـرَأْ "Read!", e.g. (from The Holy Qur'ān) :

إِقْـرَأْ بِاسْمِ رَبِّكَ الَّذِي خَلَقَ	96-1 Read in the name of thy Lord.

**Some Examples of the negative imperative from the Holy
Qur'ān :**

يَا أَبَتِ لَا تَعْبُـدِ الشَّيْطَانَ	19-44 O my father, serve not Satan.
لَا تَـقُمْ فِيـهِ أَبَـداً	9-108 Never stand in it.
فَلَا تَـقُل لَهُمَا أُفٍّ وَلَا تَنْهَرْهُمَا	17-23 Say not "Fie" to them nor chide them.

فَلَا تَدْعُ مَعَ اللهِ إِلٰهاً آخَرَ	26-213 so call not upon another God with Allah.
وَلَا تَقْبَلُوا لَهُم شَهَادَةً أَبَداً	24-4 Never accept their evidence.
وَلَا تَـقُولُوا لِمَنْ يُـقْتَلُ فِي سَبِيلِ اللهِ أَمْــوَاتٌ	2-154 and call them not dead those who are killed in the way of Allah.

7. The "Emphatic Nūn"

To emphasize the meaning of a verb, the imperfect has some-times, emphatic *nūn* which is suffixed without any other alter-nation. This type of *nūn* is called نُونُ ٱلتَّوْكِيد "nūnut-tawkīd". It has two kinds : a duplicated on with *shaddah,* and another with *sukūn,* i.e. vowelless.

The former is termed نُون ثَقِيلَة *nūn thaqilah* and the latter is نُون خَفِيفَة *nūn khafīfah,* e.g. (from The Holy Qur'ān) :

nūn thaqilah	
تَاللهِ لَأَكِيدَنَّ أَصْنَامَكُم	21-57 And by Allah I will certainly plan against your idols.

nūn khafīfah	
لَنَسْفَعاً بِالنَّاصِيَةِ	96-15 We will seize him by the forelock.

It is also used with imperative to denote 'strict command'.
Compare :

إِذْهَبْ	go!
إِذْهَـبَنْ	you should go.
إِذْهَـبَنَّ	you must go.

لَا تَـذْهَبْ	Do not go!
لَا تَـذْهَـبَنْ	Never go.
لَا تَـذْهَـبَنَّ	You musn't go.

The 'emphatic nūn' can be suffixed with all parts of imperfect,
while the imperative is made by the parts of 2nd person only.
The following conjugation will show the modification of imperfect and imperative with 'emphatic nūns' :

3rd pers. Sing. Masc.	لِيَذْهَبَنَّ	He should go.
3rd pers. Sing. Fem.	لِتَذْهَبَنَّ	She should go.
2nd pers. Sing. Masc.	لِتَذْهَبَنَّ	You should go.
2nd pers. Sing. Fem.	لِتَذْهَبَنَّ	You should go.
First person Sing.	لأَذْهَبَنَّ	I should go.
3rd pers. Dual Masc.	لِيَذْهَبَانَّ	They (two) should go.
3rd pers. Dual Fem.	لِتَذْهَبَانَّ	They (two) should go.

2nd pers. Dual Masc.	لِتَذْهَبَانِّ	You (two) should go.
2nd pers. Dual Fem.	لِتَذْهَبَانِّ	You (two) should go.
3rd pers. Plural Masc.	لِتَذْهَبُنَّ	You (all) should go.
3rd pers. Plural Fem.	لِتَذْهَبْنَّ	You (all) should go.
First person Plural	لِنَذْهَبَنَّ	We should go.

It is often used in the negative cases and rarely in other forms.

Examples from The Holy Qur'ān :

وَلَا يَحْسَبَنَّ ٱلَّذِينَ كَفَرُوا أَنَّمَا نُمْلِى لَهُمْ خَيْرٌ لِأَنْفُسِهِمْ	3-178 And let not those who disbelieve think that Our granting them respite is good for themselves.
وَلَا تَحْسَبَنَّ اللهَ غَافِلًا عَمَّا يَعْمَلُ ٱلظَّالِمُونَ	14-42 And think not Allah to be heedless of what the unjust do.
وَلَا تَقُولَنَّ لِشَيْءٍ إِنِّي فَاعِلٌ ذٰلِكَ غَداً إِلَّا أَنْ يَشَاءَ اللهُ	18-23,24 And say not of anything: I will do that tomorrow ... unless Allah wills.
فَلَا تَمُوتُنَّ إِلَّا وَأَنْتُمْ مُسْلِمُونَ	2-132 So die not unless you are Muslims (submitting ones).

Note : For easy and convenient reference, see the "Imperative Verb Conjugation Chart" at the end of this chapter.

EXERCISE

1. Distinguish difference patterns of the imperatives given below :

   إِبْلِعِى ، أُقْصِرِى ، قُولوا ، إسْألُوا ، سَلْ ، قُم ، خُذْنَ ، قُولا ، إِجْمَعِى ،
   إضْرِبُوا ، لاَ تَحْسَبْ ، لاَ تَحْسَبَنَّ .

2. Is there any difference between :

   إفْعَلوا ، وَافْعَلُوا ، قال : اذهَبوا ، وَقَالَ اذْهَبُوا ، اذْهَبْ وَافْتَحِ آلبَابَ ،
   إذهَبْ يَا وَلَدُ ، إفْتح آلبَابَ .

3. Make imperatives from the following verbs :

   نَصَرَ يَنْصُرُ ، كَرُمَ يَكْرُمُ ، حَسِبَ يَحْسَبُ ، قَتَلَ يَقْتُلُ ، بَلَغَ يَبْلُغُ ،
   جَعَلَ يَجْعَلُ .

4. **Translate into Arabic :**

   1. Look! O' friends, what you have done.
   2. O' boys, enter and sit by my side.
   3. O' believer, open your heart for good advice.
   4. O' Men, do not think Allah is heedless of your doing.
   5. Never go to evil places.
   6. Do whatever you are commanded.
   7. Recite the Holy Qur'ān every morning.
   8. Say not what is unjust. Do pray for your parents and relatives.

5. Translate into English :

وَقُلْ جَاءَ ٱلْحَقُّ وَزَهَقَ ٱلْبَاطِلُ إِنَّ ٱلْبَاطِلَ كَانَ زَهُوقاً ، خُذْ مِنْ أَمْوَالِهِمْ صَدَقَةً تُطَهِّرُهُمْ ، يَا بُنَيَّ لَا تُشْرِكْ بِالله ، لَا تَجْعَلُوا مَعَ اللهِ إِلَـهًا آخَرَ ، إِعْمَلُوا آلَ دَاوُودَ شُكْراً ، جَاهِدِ ٱلْكُفَّارَ وَاغْلُظْ عَلَيهِم ، طَهِّرْ بَـيْتِيَ لِلطَّائِفِينَ وَٱلْعَاكِفِينَ وَٱلرُّكَّعِ ٱلسُّجُودِ .

VOCABULARY

look	اُنْظُرْ	from	نَظَرَ يَـنْظُرُ
enter	ادْخُلْ	from	دَخَلَ يَدْخُـلُ
open	إِفْتَحْ	from	فَتَحَ يَـفْتَحُ
think	فَكِّرْ	from	فَكَّرَ يُفَكِّرُ (derived form)
heedless	غَافِلٌ	Active participle from	غَفَلَ يَغْفَلُ
command	أَمْـرٌ		
recite	اتْلُ	from	تَلَا يَـتْلُو (weak verb)
unjust	ظُـلْمٌ		
parents	الوَالِدَيْنِ	Dual of	وَالِـدٌ
relatives	الأقرِبَاء	Plural of	قَرِيبٌ

الحَقُّ	the truth.
بَاطِل	falsehood
زَهَقَ	vanished (3rd person).
زَهُوقٌ	bound to vanish (verbal noun).
صَدَقَةٌ	alm, charity.
تُطَهِّرُ	make clear, pure (from derived form).
لَا تَرْكَنُوا	do not incline (imperative Plural, Masc. 3rd pers.).
القَبْرُ	the tomb.
جَاهِدْ	struggle.
اغْلُظْ	be firm against someone.
المُنَافِقِينَ	hypocrites, plural of المُنَافِق hypocrite.
الطَّائِفِينَ	plural of طَائِف who gets round the Holy Ka'bah.

The Imperative Verb Conjugation Chart

جدول تصريف فعل الأمر

					Verb Type	
تَدَحْرَجْ	اسْعَ	ادْعُ	ارْمِ	اقْضِ		تَدَحْرَجْ
تَسَلَّمْ						تَسَلَّمْ
اسْتَقْبِلْ / اسْتَقْبِلَا					اسْتَقْبِلْ – اسْتَقْبِلَا	
					اِفْعَلْ	
					فَعِّلْ	
						Corres-ponding Pronoun
أَنْتَ					أَنْتَ	

CHAPTER 16

THE DERIVED FORMS OF THE VERBS - I, II, III

Forms derived from the triliteral roots are made by the addition of prefixes, suffixes and infixes. Through these modifications the variations in the shade of meaning are obtained.

Arabic roots are formed into words by addition of vowels; these added vowels and consonants make certain STOCK PATTERNS or FORMS. Each particular form produces its own particular modification of the basic meaning of the root. For instance meaning of the verb قَتَلَ *qatala* is "to kill", thus a long vowel after the first radical ق makes it قَاتَلَ *qātala*, that means "to fight another person". If the second radical of this verb قـتـل is duplicated to become قَتَّلَ *qattala*, which means "he (3rd person Sing. Masc.) massacred" (the action was intensified).

The total number of these derived forms is 15 and they are referred to by their serial number such as form I, II, III and so on. The important ones which are used in the Qur'ān are given below:

I. *fa'ala*, e.g. ضَرَبَ. *ḍaraba*, 'to give parable'.

كَيْفَ ضَرَبَ اللهُ مَثَلاً	14-24 How Allah sets forth a parable.

II. *fa''ala*, e.g. صَدَّقَ. *ṣaddaqa*, 'to believe'.

بَلْ جَاءَ بِٱلْحَقِّ وَصَدَّقَ ٱلْمُرْسَلِينَ	37-37 Nay, he has brought the Truth and gave credence to the messengers.

III. *fā'ala*, e.g. قَاتَلَ *qātala*, 'to fight with'.

قَاتَلَ مَعَهُ رِبِّيُّونَ كَثِيرٌ	3-146 Many godly men have fought with him.

IV. *'af'ala*, e.g. أَحْسَنَ *'aḥsana*, 'to do good to someone else'.

قَدْ أَحْسَنَ اللهُ لَهُ رِزْقاً	65-11 Allah has indeed given him a good sustenance.

V. *tafa''ala*, e.g. تَقَبَّلَ *taqabbala*, 'to accept'.

فَتَقَبَّلَهَا رَبُّهَا بِقَبُولٍ حَسَنٍ	3-37 so her Lord accepted her with a goodly acceptance.

VI. *tafā'ala*, e.g. تَقَاتَلَ *taqātala*, 'to fight'.

وَمَا لَكُمْ لَا تُقَاتِلُونَ فِي سَبِيلِ اللهِ	4-75 and what reason have you not to fight in the way of Allah.

VII. *'infa'ala*, e.g. إِنْطَلَقَ *'inṭalaqa*, 'to set out'.

وَإِنْطَلَقَ ٱلْمَلَأُ مِنْهُمْ . . .	38-6 and chief of them started saying…

VIII. *'ifta'ala*, e.g. إِقْتَرَبَ *'iqtaraba*, 'to get high, to draw near'.

اقْتَرَبَ لِلنَّاسِ حِسَابُهُمْ	21-1 Their reckoning has drawn near to the people.

IX. *'if'alla*, e.g. إِسْوَدَّ *'iswadda*, 'to turn black'.

فَأَمَّا ٱلَّذِينَ إِسْوَدَّتْ وُجُوهُهُمْ	3-106 then so to those whose faces became black.

X. *'istaf'alla*, e.g. إِسْتَغْفَرَ *'istaghfara*, 'to seek forgiveness'.

وَٱسْتَغْفَرَ لَهُمُ الرَّسُولُ	4-64 And the Messenger asked forgiveness of Allah.

The Verb Form II *(fa''ala)*

1. The first stem is the absolute form of triliteral verb which stands as root-form for all described stems as dealt within Chapter 4.

2. The second stem is formed from the triliteral root by duplicating the second radical that is ع in فَعَلَ , e.g. كَسَّرَ from كَسَرَ. This form or stem denotes a causative meaning, e.g. عَلِمَ "to know", عَلَّمَ "to teach" (to cause some one to know).

Example from The Holy Qur'ān :

عَلَّمَ الإِنْسَانَ مَا لَمْ يَعْلَمْ	96-5 He (i.e. Allah) taught man what he did not know.

حَمَلَ "to carry", حَمَّلَ "to load" (to make someone to carry).

Example from The Holy Qur'ān :

رَبَّنَا! وَلَا تُحَمِّلْنَا مَا لَا طَاقَةَ لَنَا بِهِ	2-286 Our Lord, impose not on us that which we have not the strength to bear.

Note : "Impose not on us" is the rendering of لَا تُحَمِّلْنَا ; its literal translation is "do not burden us".

3. If the verb is Intransitive in the first form, it becomes transitive in this form, e.g. فَرِحَ 'to be glad', and فَرَّحَ 'to gladden'; ضَعُفَ 'to be weak', and ضَعَّفَ 'to weaken'.

Intransitive : حَكَمَ 'to judge'.

Example from The Holy Qur'ān :

إِنَّا أَنْزَلْنَا إِلَيْكَ ٱلْكِتَابَ بِالْحَقِّ لِتَحْكُمَ بَـيْنَ ٱلـنَّاسِ	4-105 We revealed to you the Book that you may judge between mankind.

Transitive : حَكَّمَ 'to make some one a judge'.

Example from The Holy Qur'ān :

فَلَا وَرَبِّكَ لَا يُؤْمِنُونَ حَتَّى يُحَكِّمُوكَ فِيمَا شَجَرَ بَـيْنَهُمْ	4-65 But no, by Thy Lord, they will not believe until they make you the judge in all disputes among them.

4. Intensive meaning i.e. an act is done with great violence or continued for a long time e.g. كَسَرَ 'to break' كَسَّرَ 'to break in pieces, to smash', قَطَعَ 'to cut', قَطَّعَ 'to cut to pieces', قَتَلَ 'to kill', قَتَّلَ 'to massacre'.

Examples from The Holy Qur'ān :

وَقَتَـلَ دَاوُودُ جَالُوتَ	2-251 and David killed Goliath.
وَقُتِّلُوا تَـقْتِيلًا	33-61 They were massacred.

5. Declarative or Stimative : e.g. صَدَقَ 'to tell the truth', صَدَّقَ 'to declare that one speaks the truth', 'to believe'.

Examples from The Holy Qur'ān :

قُـلْ : صَدَقَ الله	3-95 Say : Allah told the truth.
وَصَـدَّقَ ٱلْمُرْسَـلِـينَ	37-37 And He affirmed the truth of the Messengers.
فَـلَا صَدَّقَ وَلَا صَلَّىٰ وَلَكِنْ كَذَّبَ وَتَـوَلَّىٰ	75-31,32 So he accepted not the Truth nor prayed but denied and turned back.
وَرَتِّـلِ ٱلْقُـرْآنَ تَـرْتِيلاً	73-4 and recite the Qur'ān in chanting manner.
وَكَبِّرْهُ تَكْبِـيرا	17-111 and proclaim His greatness magnifying (Him).
وَٱلَّذِي جَاءَ بِالصِّدْقِ وَصَدَّقَ بِـهِ أُولَئِكَ هُمُ ٱلْمُتَّـقُونَ	39-33 and he who brings the truth and accepts the truth - such are the dutiful.
كَذٰلِكَ زَيَّنَّا لِكُلِّ أُمَّـةٍ عَمَلَهُم	6-108 thus to every people have we made their deeds fair-looking.
وَلَكِنَّ الله حَبَّبَ إِلَيْكُمُ ٱلإِيمَانَ وَزَيَّـنَـهُ فِي قُـلُوبِكُم	49-7 But Allah has endeared the faith to you and made it seemly to you.
وَلَا نُكَذِّبَ بِآيَاتِ رَبِّـنَا	6-27 and we would not reject the message of our Lord.

The Verb Form III   *(fāʿala = qātala)*

This stem is formed by inserting an *'alif* between first and second radicals of the root-form فَعَلَ *faʿala*, and it means "to do something with another person". Thus from root forms :

فَعَلَ *faʿala*, "he did", will be فَاعَلَ *fāʿala*, "They did something with another".

كَتَبَ *kataba*, "he wrote", will be كَاتَبَ *kātaba*, "he corresponded with".

قَتَلَ *qatala*, "he killed", will be قَاتَلَ *qātala*, "he faught with".

سَبَقَ *sabaqa*, "he preceded", will be سَابَقَ *sābaqa*, "he ran a race with".

This stem is sometimes denominative, e.g. ضَاعَفَ *ḍāʿafa*, "to make something double", from ضِعْف *ḍiʿf*. سَافَرَ *sāfara*, "to go on a journey", from سَفَرَ *safara*, "journey". قَابَلَ *qābala*, "to be in front of, to compare one thing with another, to interview".

The Passive Perfect is قُوتِلَ *qūtila*, and passive imperfect : يُقَاتَلُ *yuqātalu*.

The conjugation of this stem كَاتَبَ "to write to, to correspond with" is as below :

Perfect	Passive Perfect	Passive Imperfect
كَاتَبَ	كُوتِبَ	يُكَاتَبُ
قَاتَلَ	قُوتِلَ	يُقَاتَلُ
سَابَقَ	سُوبِقَ	يُسَابَقُ
جَاهَدَ	جُوهِدَ	يُجَاهَدُ

Imperative	Active Part.	Passive Part.
كَاتِبْ	مُكَاتِبٌ	مُكَاتَبٌ
قَاتِلْ	مُقَاتِلٌ	مُقَاتَلٌ
سَابِقْ	مُسَابِقٌ	مُسَابَقٌ
جَاهِدْ	مُجَاهِدٌ	مُجَاهَدٌ

The verbal noun has two alternative forms :

1. مُكَاتَبَةٌ *mukātabat(un)*, signifying the act of writing to, or corresponding with, anyone.

2. كِتَابٌ *kitāb(un)*, this is used as a simple nounn to mean a book or a letter.

Examples from The Holy Qur'ān :

يُقَاتِلُونَ فِي سَبِيلِ اللهِ فَيَقْتُلُونَ وَيُقْتَلُونَ	9-111 They fight in Allah's way so they slay and are sain.
وَمَا أُرِيدُ أَنْ أُخَالِفَكُمْ إِلَى مَا أَنْهَاكُمْ عَنْهُ	11-88 and I desire not to act in opposition to you in which I forbid you.
وَمَنْ جَاهَدَ فَإِنَّمَا يُجَاهِدُ لِنَفْسِهِ	29-6 And whoever strives hard, strives for himself.
إِنَّمَا جَزَاءُ ٱلَّذِينَ يُحَارِبُونَ اللهَ وَرَسُولَهُ	5-33 The only punishment of those who wage war against Allah and His Messenger...

وَٱلَّذِينَ ٱتَّخَذُوا مَسْجِداً ضِرَاراً وَكُفْراً وَتَفْرِيقاً بَيْنَ ٱلْمُؤْمِنِينَ وَإِرْصَاداً لِمَنْ حَارَبَ اللهَ وَرَسُولَه	9-107 And they who built a mosque to cause harm (to Islam) and to help (disbelief) and to cause division among the believers and refuge for him who made war against Allah and His Messenger before.
فَحَاسَبْنَاهَا حِسَاباً شَدِيداً	65-8 so We called it to severe account.

Note : For easy reference, see Derived Forms Conjugation Charts II and III at the end of this Chapter.

EXERCISE

1. Translate into Arabic :

(a) Say: This is my way; I call on Allah with sure knowledge. I and whoever follow me glory be to Allah! and I am not of the idolaters.

We did not send before thee (any messenger) save men whom we inspired from among the folk of the twonships – have they not travelled in the land and seen the nature of the consequence for those who were before them ? And verily, the abode of the Hereafter, for those who ward off (evil), is best. Have ye then no sense ?

(b) As you know, when the war broke out last year between our Arab brothers and their Zionist enemies, our brothers advanced to the battle-field hailing the Name of God Almighty, saying: *Allāh-u-Akbar, Allāh-u-Akbar,* (God is greatest, God is greatest), There is no deity but God. The result was they routed their enemies in the canal zone, in the Golan Heights, which proves to the Muslims that holding firmly to their religion, ideology, faith in God and dedication to Him will bring them victory in various fields, God willing.

(c) 1. Brother, bring us fresh (new) coffee at once from the kitchen.
2. The minister commanded them to bring forward the robber.
3. I ordered them to tell their friends about this affair, but they did not believe me.
4. Man proposes, but God disposes.
5. Send that man to me, so that I may supervise his work. He has disobeyed my orders many times.
6. Bring in the doctor so that we can consult him about the prince's condition.
7. Do not mix with the people next door.
8. The government inspectors travelled to the village, greeted the shaikh, and witnessed the horse races. Then they inspected the new houses.
9. During the journey, we saw from a distance the bedouins, round the well.

2. **Translate into English :**

يَا أَخِي الْمُسْلِمُ إِنَّ اللهَ كَتَبَ عَلَيكَ الصِّيَامَ كَمَا كَتَبَهُ عَلَى الَّذِينَ سَبَقُوكَ ، وَهُوَ اللهُ الَّذِي خَلَقَكَ وَأَرْسَلَ إِلَيْكَ رَسُولاً وَأَنْزَلَ عَلَيكَ كِتَاباً يُصَدِّقُ كُتُبَ الأَوَّلِينَ ، وَالأَنْبِيَاءَ الْمُرْسَلِينَ ، فَجَاهِدْ فِي سَبِيلِهِ ، وَلاَ تُخَالِفْ أَمْرَهُ وَسَاعِدْ أَخَاكَ الْمُسْلِمَ ، وَلاَ تَكُنْ مُسْرِفاً فِي النَّفَقَاتِ ، وَالَّذِي يَعْصِي اللهَ وَرَسُولَهُ كَأَنَّهُ يُحَارِبُ اللهَ الَّذِي جَاءَ بِالصِّدْقِ وَصَدَّقَ بِهِ فَهُوَ مُؤْمِنٌ ، أَحْسِنْ إِلَى النَّاسِ كَمَا أَحْسَنَ اللهُ إِلَيْكَ .

VOCABULARY

To call	call on دَعَا imperf. يَدعُو – دَعَا إِلَى
sure knowledge, insight	بَصِيرَةٌ
folk	أَهْـلٌ
township	قَـرْيَـةٌ
to travel	يَسِيرُ / يُسَافِرُ سَارَ / سَافَرَ
consequence	(عَاقَبَ / يُعَاقِبُ verb III) عَوَاقِب .Pl عَاقِبَةٌ
abode	حَيَاةٌ
ward off	يُعْرِضُ verb IV أَعْـرَضَ
to have sense, to feel	يَشْعُرُ شَعَرَ
broke out / VII	إِنْفَجَرَ
enemies	عَـدُوٌّ of .Pl أَعْـدَاء
to advance / V	يَتَقَدَّمُ تَـقَـدَّمَ
battlefield	مَيْدَانُ الْحَرْب
to hail / II	تَكْبِيرٌ verbal noun يُكَبِّرُ / كَبَّرَ
diety	إِلـهٌ
to rout out	يَسْتَأْصِلُ / اسْتَأْصَلَ
canal	قَنَـوَات .Pl قَنَاة

zone	مِنْطَقَـة
ideology	عَقـيدَةٌ Pl. عَقَائِدُ
faith	الإيمَـان
dedication / VIII	الالتجاء (التجأ / يَلتَجِيءُ)
victory	الفَـتح
various	مُتَنَوّعٌ - مُخْتَلِفٌ
God willing	إنْ شَاءَ آللّه
fresh	طَـازِجٌ
kitchen	مَطْبَـخٌ
propose	يَقْتَرِحُ يُصَمِّمُ يَقْصِدُ
dispose / IV	يُـبْطِـلُ
'so that' use preposition	لِ
disobey	يَعْصِي
condition	الحَـالُ
attack (imperative)	هَاجِمْ verbal noun الهُجُومُ
mix	اخْتَلَطَ يَخْتَلِطُ
government	الحُكُومَـة
inspector	مُرَاقِبٌ ، مُفَتِّشٌ

village	قَرْيَـــةٌ
to greet	يُحَيِّي حَيَّا
race	مُسَابَـقَـــةٌ
bedouins	البَـــدْوُ
well	بِئْـــرٌ
distance	بُعْـــدُ

كَتَبَ	to write (here use prescribed).
سَبَقَ	to pass before.
جَاهَدَ	to strive.
خَالَفَ	to oppose
المُسرفُ	he who exceeds the limits (especially in expenditures).
كَأَنَّـهُ	as he
الصِّدقُ	the truth.
صَدَّقَ	to believe.
أَحْسِنْ	(Imperative); do the good, behave nicely.

DERIVED FORMS CONJUGATION CHART II

Verb : قَرَّرَ / يُقَرِّرُ   Verb Form : II

Imperative	Imperfect Subjunctive	Imperfect Jussive	Imperfect Indicative	Perfect	Pronoun
	when the verb is preceded by a subjunctive particle such as	when the verb is preceded by a jussive particle such as			
	(لَنْ) يُقَرِّرَ	(لَمْ) يُقَرِّرْ	يُقَرِّرُ	قَرَّرَ	هُوَ
	تُقَرِّرَ	تُقَرِّرْ	تُقَرِّرُ	قَرَّرَتْ	هِيَ
	يُقَرِّرُوا	يُقَرِّرُوا	يُقَرِّرُونَ	قَرَّرُوا	هُمْ
	يُقَرِّرْنَ	يُقَرِّرْنَ	يُقَرِّرْنَ	قَرَّرْنَ	هُنَّ
	يُقَرِّرَا	يُقَرِّرَا	يُقَرِّرَانِ	قَرَّرَا	هُمَا (M)
	تُقَرِّرَا	تُقَرِّرَا	تُقَرِّرَانِ	قَرَّرَتَا	هُمَا (F)
قَرِّرْ	تُقَرِّرَ	تُقَرِّرْ	تُقَرِّرُ	قَرَّرْتَ	أَنْتَ
قَرِّري	تُقَرِّري	تُقَرِّري	تُقَرِّرِينَ	قَرَّرْتِ	أَنْتِ
قَرِّرُوا	تُقَرِّرُوا	تُقَرِّرُوا	تُقَرِّرُونَ	قَرَّرْتُمْ	أَنْتُمْ
قَرِّرْنَ	تُقَرِّرْنَ	تُقَرِّرْنَ	تُقَرِّرْنَ	قَرَّرْتُنَّ	أَنْتُنَّ
قَرِّرَا	تُقَرِّرَا	تُقَرِّرَا	تُقَرِّرَانِ	قَرَّرْتُمَا	أَنْتُمَا (M+F)
	أُقَرِّرَ	أُقَرِّرْ	أُقَرِّرُ	قَرَّرْتُ	أَنَا
	نُقَرِّرَ	نُقَرِّرْ	نُقَرِّرُ	قَرَّرْنَا	نَحْنُ

Verbal Noun : (تَفْعِيلٌ) تَقْرِيرٌ   Active Participle : مُقَرِّرٌ   Passive Participle : مُقَرَّرٌ

Verb Characteristics :
* It has a stem with a double middle radical.
* In the perfect form of the verb both first and second radicals have the vowel a (ﹷ).
* In the imperfect form, the first radical has the vowel a (ﹷ), and the second radical has the vowel i (ﹻ).
* The vowel of the subject-marker prefixes is u (ﹹ).

DERIVED FORMS CONJUGATION CHART III

Verb : شَارَكَ / يُشَارِكُ   Verb Form : III

Imperative	Imperfect Subjunctive	Imperfect Jussive	Imperfect Indicative	Perfect	Pronoun
	when the verb is preceded by a subjunctive particle such as	when the verb is preceded by a jussive particle such as			
	(لَنْ) يُشَارِكَ	(لَمْ) يُشَارِكْ	يُشَارِكُ	شَارَكَ	هُوَ
	تُشَارِكَ	تُشَارِكْ	تُشَارِكُ	شَارَكَتْ	هِيَ
	يُشَارِكُوا	يُشَارِكُوا	يُشَارِكُونَ	شَارَكُوا	هُمْ
	يُشَارِكْنَ	يُشَارِكْنَ	يُشَارِكْنَ	شَارَكْنَ	هُنَّ
	يُشَارِكَا	يُشَارِكَا	يُشَارِكَانِ	شَارَكَا	هُمَا (M)
	تُشَارِكَا	تُشَارِكَا	تُشَارِكَانِ	شَارَكَتَا	هُمَا (F)
شَارِكْ	تُشَارِكَ	تُشَارِكْ	تُشَارِكُ	شَارَكْتَ	أَنْتَ
شَارِكِي	تُشَارِكِي	تُشَارِكِي	تُشَارِكِينَ	شَارَكْتِ	أَنْتِ
شَارِكُوا	تُشَارِكُوا	تُشَارِكُوا	تُشَارِكُونَ	شَارَكْتُمْ	أَنْتُمْ
شَارِكْنَ	تُشَارِكْنَ	تُشَارِكْنَ	تُشَارِكْنَ	شَارَكْتُنَّ	أَنْتُنَّ
شَارِكَا	تُشَارِكَا	تُشَارِكَا	تُشَارِكَانِ	شَارَكْتُمَا	أَنْتُمَا (M+F)
	أُشَارِكَ	أُشَارِكْ	أُشَارِكُ	شَارَكْتُ	أَنَا
	نُشَارِكَ	نُشَارِكْ	نُشَارِكُ	شَارَكْنَا	نَحْنُ

Verbal Noun : مُشَارَكَةٌ (مُفَاعَلَةٌ)   Active Participle : مُشَارِكٌ   Passive Participle : مُشَارَكٌ

Verb Characteristics :
* It has a stem with a long vowel $\bar{a}$ (ا) after the first radical.
* In the perfect form of the verb both first and second radicals have the vowel a (ﹷ).
* In the imperfect form, the first radical has the vowel a (ﹷ), and the second radical has the vowel i (ﹺ).
* The vowel of the subject-marker prefixes is u (ﹹ).

CHAPTER 17

DERIVED FORMS - IV, V, VI

The Verb Form IV : أَفْعَلَ 'af'ala = أَخْرَجَ 'akhraja

This stem is formed by prefixing an 'alif vocalized with fatḥah to the root-form. Thus فَعَلَ fa'ala becomes أَفْعَلَ 'af'ala, and خَرَجَ kharaja becomes أَخْرَجَ 'akhraja.

1.   The meaning of the fourth form is 'causative', e.g. if kharaja "to go out" is diverted to أَخْرَجَ 'akhraja, will mean: "to take out, to drive out".

Examples from The Holy Qur'ān :

كَمَا أَخْرَجَكَ رَبُّكَ مِنْ بَيْتِكَ بِالْحَـــقِّ	8-5 Just as thy Lord took thee out of thy house, in truth.

From the root-form ذَهَبَ dhahaba, "to go", أَذْهَبَ 'adh haba "to take out", e.g. :

وَقَالُوا : الحَمْدُ لله الَّذِي أَذْهَبَ عَنَّا الْحَـزَنَ	35-34 And they said : Praise be to Allah Who removed from us (all sorrow).

From the root-form نَزَلَ nazala, "to descend", أَنْزَلَ 'anzala "to take or bring down", e.g. :

وَبِالْحَقِّ أَنْزَلْنَاهُ وَبِالْحَقِّ نَزَلَ	17-105 We sent down the (Qur'ān) in truth and in truth had it descended.

2. With a slight difference, often this stem has the meaning of the root-form e.g. خَبَرَ *khabara* means "to inform" as does أَخْبَرَ *'akhbara* of stem IV. Likewise صَلَحَ. *ṣallaha*, "to repair" أَصْلَحَ *'aṣlaha*, "to rectify, reform". عَلِمَ *'alima* "to know" أَعْلَمَ *'a'lama*, "to inform".

3. There are a few intransitives of this stem, e.g. أَسْلَمَ *'aslama*, "to surrender to the will of Allah", (or to become a Muslim). In Qur'ānic words :

قَالَ أَسْلَمْتُ لِرَبِّ ٱلْعَالَمِينَ	2-131 He said! I surrendered to the Lord of the Worlds.

أَرْسَلَ *'arsala*, "to send", e.g.

هُوَ ٱلَّذِي أَرْسَلَ رَسُولَهُ بِالْهُدَى	9-33 It is He Who sent His Messenger with the guidance.

أَقْبَلَ *'aqbala*, "to approach, to come forward", e.g.

قَالُوا وَأَقْبَلُوا عَلَيْهِم : مَاذَا تَفْقِدُونَ	12-71 They came forward and said: what are you seeking for?

The conjugation of this stem will be as below. The verb of example is أَخْرَجَ *'akhraja*, that is derived from خَرَجَ *kharaja*.

	Perfect	Passive Perfect	Imperfect	Passive Imperfect	Impera-tive
3rd pers. Masc.	أَخْرَجَ	أُخْرِجَ	يُخْرِجُ	يُخْرَجُ	
3rd pers. Fem.	أَخْرَجَتْ	أُخْرِجَتْ	تُخْرِجُ	تُخْرَجُ	

	Perfect	Passive Perfect	Imperfect	Passive Imperfect	Imperative
2nd pers. Masc.	أَخْرَجْتَ	أُخْرِجْتَ	تُخْرِجُ	تُخْرَجُ	أَخْرِجْ
2nd pers. Fem.	أَخْرَجْتِ	أُخْرِجْتِ	تُخْرِجِينَ	تُخْرَجِينَ	أَخْرِجِي
1st pers.	أَخْرَجْتُ	أُخْرِجْتُ	أُخْرِجُ	أُخْرَجُ	

Active particle : مُخْرِجٌ *mukhrijun.*

Passive particle : مُخْرَجٌ *mukhrajun.*

Verbal noun is : إِخْرَاجٌ *'ikhrājun.*

The Verb Form V : تَفَعَّلَ *tafaʿʿala* – تَقَبَّلَ *taqabbala.*

This form is formed from the second stem: فَعَّلَ = صَدَّقَ by prefixing the syallable تـ ; thus صَدَّقَ will become تَصَدَّقَ . The meaning of this form is most frequently the reflexing of II form, e.g. فَرَّقَ "to separate", تَفَرَّقَ (to separate oneself, to scatter), عَلَّمَ "to teach", تَعَلَّمَ (to teach oneself, to learn), ذَكَّرَ "to remind", تَذَكَّرَ (to recall, remember).

Examples from The Holy Qur'ān :

Verbs of Form II : فَعَّلَ *faʿʿala*

مَا يُفَرِّقُونَ بِهِ بَيْنَ ٱلْمَرْءِ وَزَوْجِهِ	2-102 They cause division between man and his wife.
عَلَّمَ الإِنْسَانَ مَا لَمْ يَعْلَمْ	96-5 He taught man what he did not know.
وَذَكِّرْ (Imperative) فَإِنَّ الذِّكْرَى تَنْفَعُ الْمُؤْمِنِينَ	51-5 Remind! For remembrance benefits the believers.

Verbs of Form V : تَفَعَّلَ *tafaʿʿala*

وَمَا تَفَرَّقَ الَّذِينَ أُوتُوا الْكِتَابَ إِلَّا مِنْ بَعْدِ مَا جَاءَتْهُمُ الْبَيِّنَةُ	98-4 The people of the Scripture did not divide until the clear proof came unto them.
وَيَتَعَلَّمُونَ مَا يَضُرُّهُمْ وَلَا يَنْفَعُهُمْ	2-102 And they learn what harms them and profits them not.
وَمَا يَتَذَكَّرُ إِلَّا مَنْ يُنِيبُ	40-13 The ones who remember are only those who turn (to Allah).

1. This form is also used to form verbs from nouns, especially nouns of quality or status, e.g. :

   From نَصْرَانِيٌّ "a Christian", تَنَصَّرَ "to become a Christian",

   From يَهُودِيٌّ "a Jew", تَهَوَّدَ "to become a Jew".

2. It also means thinking or representing oneself to have certain quality or status which he/she does not actually possess, e.g. :

   كَبِير "great", تَكَبَّرَ "to think oneself great, to be proud",

   نَبِيٌّ "prophet", تَنَبَّأَ "to claim to be a Prophet".

   Conjugation of تَعَلَّمَ "to learn", is as below :

	Perfect	Imperfect	Impera-tive	Active particle	Passive particle
3rd pers. Masc.	تَعَلَّمَ	يَتَعَلَّمُ		مُتَعَلِّمٌ	مُتَعَلَّمٌ
3rd pers. Fem.	تَعَلَّمَتْ	تَتَعَلَّمُ			
2nd pers. Masc.	تَعَلَّمْتَ	تَتَعَلَّمُ	تَعَلَّمْ		
2nd pers. Fem.	تَعَلَّمْتِ	تَتَعَلَّمِينَ	تَعَلَّمِي		
1st pers.	تَعَلَّمْتُ	أَتَعَلَّمُ			

Verbal noun : تَعَلُّمٌ

رَبَّنَا! تَقَبَّلْ مِنَّا	2-127 (Imperative) Our Lord! accept from us.
وَلَكِن مَا تَعَمَّدَتْ قُلُوبُكُمْ	33-5 and but what your hearts intended.
وَتَقَطَّعَتْ بِهِمُ الأَسْبَابُ	2-166 and their ties are cut as under.
قَدْ نَرَى تَقَلُّبَ وَجْهِكَ فِي السَّمَاءِ	2-144 Indeed We see the turning of thy face to heaven.
إِذْ تَسَوَّرُوا الْمِحْرَابَ	38-21 When they climbed the wall to the chamber.
تُكَلِّمُ النَّاسَ فِي الْمَهْدِ	5-110 Thou spokest to people in the cardle.

The Verb Form VI : تَفَاعَلَ *tafā'ala*

تَجَاوَبَ *tajāwaba*, "to respond to one another".

This form is formed from form III فَاعَلَ *fā'ala*, by prefixing a
ت *ta*, before the first radical. Thus, فَاعَلَ *fā'ala*, becomes تَفَاعَلَ
tafā'ala, e.g. قَاتَلَ "to fight" becomes تَقَاتَلَ "to fight each other".
In relation to meaning, this form tends to be reflexive of form III.

Examples :

قَاتَلَ	to fight	تَقَاتَلَ	to fight each other.
حَارَبَ	to fight	تَحَارَبَ	to fight each other.
عَاوَنَ	to help	تَعَاوَنَ	to cooperate together.
وَافَقَ	to agree with	تَوَافَقَ	to agree together.

Examples from The Holy Qur'ān :

وَتَعَاوَنُوا عَلَى البِرِّ وَالتَّقْوَىٰ وَلاَ تَعَاوَنُوا عَلَى الإِثْمِ وَالعُدْوَانِ	5-2 Help ye one another in right-eousness and piety and help ye not one another in sin and rancour.
وَلَوْ تَوَاعَدتُّمْ لاخْتَلَفْتُمْ فِي المِيعَادِ	8-42 Even if ye had promised each other (to meet) ye would certainly have failed in the appointment.
وَلَوْ أَرَاكَهُمْ كَثِيراً لَفَشِلْتُمْ وَلَتَنَازَعْتُمْ فِي الأَمْرِ	8-43 If he had shown them to thee as many, ye would surely, have been discouraged and ye would have disputed with each other in decision.
فَلَمَّا تَرَاءَتِ الفِئَتَانِ نَكَصَ عَلَى عَقِبَيْهِ	8-48 But when the two forces came in sight of each other, he turned on his heels.
فَليُقَاتِلْ فِي سَبِيلِ اللهِ الَّذِينَ يَشْرُونَ الحَيَاةَ الدُّنْيَا بالآخِرَةِ وَمَن يُقَاتِلْ فِي سَبِيلِ اللهِ فَيُقْتَلْ أَوْ يَغْلِبْ فَسَوْفَ نُؤْتِيهِ أَجْراً عَظِيماً	4/74 Let those who fight in the cause of Allah sell the life of this world for the hereafter. To him who fights in the cause of God, whether he is slain or gets victory, We shall give him very soon a re-ward of great value.
مَا لَكُمْ لَا تَنَاصَرُونَ	37-25 What is the matter with you that ye help not each other.
إِلاَّ الَّذِينَ آمَنُوا وَعَمِلُوا الصَّالِحَاتِ وَتَوَاصَوْا بالحَقِّ وَتَوَاصَوْا بالصَّبْرِ	103-3 Except such as have faith and do righteous deeds and join together in the mutual teaching of truth, and of patience and constancy.

Some Verbs of Form VI :

تَـعَاوَنَ	to cooperate together.
تَـفَارَقَ	to disperse, to depart from each other.
تَـوَاعَـدَ	to promise each other.
تَظَـاهَـرَ	to show, to demonstrate, to pretend.
تَـوَافَـقَ	to agree together.
تَحَادَثَ	to converse together.
تَـقَابَـلَ	to meet each other.

Note : For easy reference, see Derived Forms Conjugation Charts IV, V, and VI at the end of this chapter.

EXERCISE

1. Translate into Arabic :

(a) We conversed about this matter this evening, but did not agree. The Muslims and Christians fought each other a long time ago, but they agree today on many things. The learned ones were talking together about Islam. They expect our advance from this side.

(b) 1. These countries had only one system of education and that was the purely religious Islamic system.

   2. But the religious schools retained their old method and curriculum and did not catch up with the demands of the time.

3. When English domination was fully established in the nineteenth century, the rulers introduced modern schools and started English and modern branches of learning as required subjects in schools.

4. People got more interested in modern schools, because those who graduated from them and received academic certificates, were appointed as officials and given government jobs.

5. The certificates which are given to the graduates of religions are not accepted either in offices or in modern schools or government agencies.

6. They were not able to preserve the old standard because the old subjects which were taught in traditional schools did not leave any time for other subjects.

7. Thus it was necessary to reduce the number of traditional subjects so that modern subjects could be accommodated.

2. **Translate into English :**

أَمَرَنَا رَبُّنَا أَنْ نَتَعَاوَنَ عَلَى البِرِّ وَآلتَّقْوَى .

المُسْلِمُونَ لاَ يَتَقَاتَلُونَ فِيمَا بَيْنَهُمْ .

أَيُّهَا آلمُسْلِمُونَ ، مَا لَكُمْ لاَ تَنَاصَرُونَ ، تَعَاوَنوا فِي أَدَاءِ آلوَاجِبِ .

اللُّغَةُ العَرَبِيَّةُ سَهْلَةٌ غَنِيَّةٌ بِالْكَلِمَاتِ وَالمَعَاني ، إنَّ أَعْدَاءَ اللُّغَةِ العَرَبِيَّةِ يُظْهِرُونَ صُعُوبَاتٍ كَثِيرَةً فِي تَعَلُّمِهَا لِغَرَضٍ فِي أَنْفُسِهِمْ .

تَرَكْنَا أَصْدِقَاءَنَا فِي الحَدِيقَةِ وَهُمْ يَتَحَادَثُونَ .

* * *

قُـلْ مَن يَـرْزُقُكُم مِنَ السَّمَاءِ وَالأَرْض ، أَمَّن يَملِكُ السَّمْعَ وَالأَبْصَارَ وَمِنْ
يُخْرِجُ الْحَيَّ مِنَ المَيِّتِ وَيُخْرِجُ الْمَيِّتَ مِنَ الْحَيِّ وَمَنْ يُـدَبِّـرُ الأَمْرَ فَسَيَقُولُونَ
اللهُ فَقُلْ أَفَلاَ تَعْقِلُونَ .

وَمِنْهُمْ مَن يُـؤْمِنُ بِـهِ وَمِنهُمْ مَن لاَ يُؤْمِنُ بِـهِ وَرَبُّكَ أَعْلَمُ بِالمُفْسِدِين .

VOCABULARY

to converse / V	تَحَادَثَ also / VI يَتَحَدَّثُ تَحَدَّثَ
to agree / III	وَافَـقَ
system	مَـنْـهَـجٌ
to retain / V	يَـتَـمَسَّكُ تَمَسَّكَ بِهِ
curriculum	أَلْـمَـنَاهِجُ آلـدِّرَاسِيَّةُ
to catch up	أَدْرَكَ بِـهِ الإِدْرَاكُ أَخَذَ بِـهِ
domination	أَلإِسْتِعْمَارُ
branches	فَرْعٌ plural of فُرُوعٌ
required / VII	إِحْتَـاجَ إِلَى
graduated (verb) / V	يَـتَخَرَّجُ تَخَرَّجَ
certificate	شَهَادَاتٌ : plural شَهَادَةٌ
to appoint	عُيِّنَ , use passive case عَيَّنَ
to be accommodated	يَضَعُ passive of يُوضَعُ

البِـرُّ	good deeds
التَّـقْـوَىٰ	God-fearing
تَـقَاتَـلَ	VI / to fight each other
تَـنَاصَرَ	VI / to help each other (against enemies)
سَهْـلَـةٌ	easy
غَنِيٌّ ـ غَنِيَّـةٌ.	rich ـ (Fem.)
صُعُوبَاتٌ	plural of صُعُوبَةٌ , hardship, difficulty
تَـرَكَ	(he) left
تَحَادَثَ يَتَحَادَثُونَ	to converse
أَمْ ـ مَنْ	or who is .. ?
أَلسَّمْعَ	the sense of hearing
يَمْلِكُ	possess
أَلْـبَصَرَ	the sense of seeing
يُـخْرِجُ	brings forth
يُـدَبِّـرُ	plans, proposes, decides, etc.

DERIVED FORMS CONJUGATION CHART IV

Verb : أَخْبَرَ / يُخْبِرُ   Verb Form : IV

Imperative	Imperfect Subjunctive	Imperfect Jussive	Imperfect Indicative	Perfect	Pronoun
	when the verb is preceded by a subjunctive particle such as	when the verb is preceded by a jussive particle such as			
	(لَنْ) يُخْبِرَ	(لَمْ) يُخْبِرْ	يُخْبِرُ	أَخْبَرَ	هُوَ
	تُخْبِرَ	تُخْبِرْ	تُخْبِرُ	أَخْبَرَتْ	هِيَ
	يُخْبِرُوا	يُخْبِرُوا	يُخْبِرُونَ	أَخْبَرُوا	هُمْ
	يُخْبِرْنَ	يُخْبِرْنَ	يُخْبِرْنَ	أَخْبَرْنَ	هُنَّ
	يُخْبِرَا	يُخْبِرَا	يُخْبِرَانِ	أَخْبَرَا	هُمَا (M)
	تُخْبِرَا	تُخْبِرَا	تُخْبِرَانِ	أَخْبَرَتَا	هُمَا (F)
أَخْبِرْ	تُخْبِرَ	تُخْبِرْ	تُخْبِرُ	أَخْبَرْتَ	أَنْتَ
أَخْبِري	تُخْبِري	تُخْبِري	تُخْبِرِينَ	أَخْبَرْتِ	أَنْتِ
أَخْبِرُوا	تُخْبِرُوا	تُخْبِرُوا	تُخْبِرُونَ	أَخْبَرْتُمْ	أَنْتُمْ
أَخْبِرْنَ	تُخْبِرْنَ	تُخْبِرْنَ	تُخْبِرْنَ	أَخْبَرْتُنَّ	أَنْتُنَّ
أَخْبِرَا	تُخْبِرَا	تُخْبِرَا	تُخْبِرَانِ	أَخْبَرْتُمَا	أَنْتُمَا (M+F)
	أُخْبِرَ	أُخْبِرْ	أُخْبِرُ	أَخْبَرْتُ	أَنَا
	نُخْبِرَ	نُخْبِرْ	نُخْبِرُ	أَخْبَرْنَا	نَحْنُ

Verbal Noun : إِخْبَارٌ (إِفْعَالٌ)   Active Participle : مُخْبِرٌ   Passive Participle : مُخْبَرٌ

Verb Characteristics :
* It has a perfect stem beginning with the prefix 'a (أ) which is not present in the imperfect. * In the perfect form of the verb there is zero vowel (ـْ) on the first radical, and the second radical has an a (ـَ) vowel. * In the imperfect form of the verb, the first radical remains with zero vowel (ـْ), and the second radical receives an i (ـِ) vowel. * The vowel of the subject-marker prefixes is u (ـُ).

DERIVED FORMS CONJUGATION CHART V

Verb : تَقَدَّمَ / يَتَقَدَّمُ   Verb Form : V

Imperative	Imperfect Subjunctive	Imperfect Jussive	Imperfect Indicative	Perfect	Pronoun
	when the verb is preceded by a subjunctive particle such as	when the verb is preceded by a jussive particle such as			
	(لَنْ) يَتَقَدَّمَ	(لَمْ) يَتَقَدَّمْ	يَتَقَدَّمُ	تَقَدَّمَ	هُوَ
	تَتَقَدَّمَ	تَتَقَدَّمْ	تَتَقَدَّمُ	تَقَدَّمَتْ	هِيَ
	يَتَقَدَّمُوا	يَتَقَدَّمُوا	يَتَقَدَّمُونَ	تَقَدَّمُوا	هُمْ
	يَتَقَدَّمْنَ	يَتَقَدَّمْنَ	يَتَقَدَّمْنَ	تَقَدَّمْنَ	هُنَّ
	يَتَقَدَّمَا	يَتَقَدَّمَا	يَتَقَدَّمَانِ	تَقَدَّمَا	هُمَا (M)
	تَتَقَدَّمَا	تَتَقَدَّمَا	تَتَقَدَّمَانِ	تَقَدَّمَتَا	هُمَا (F)
تَقَدَّمْ	تَتَقَدَّمَ	تَتَقَدَّمْ	تَتَقَدَّمُ	تَقَدَّمْتَ	أَنْتَ
تَقَدَّمِي	تَتَقَدَّمِي	تَتَقَدَّمِي	تَتَقَدَّمِينَ	تَقَدَّمْتِ	أَنْتِ
تَقَدَّمُوا	تَتَقَدَّمُوا	تَتَقَدَّمُوا	تَتَقَدَّمُونَ	تَقَدَّمْتُمْ	أَنْتُمْ
تَقَدَّمْنَ	تَتَقَدَّمْنَ	تَتَقَدَّمْنَ	تَتَقَدَّمْنَ	تَقَدَّمْتُنَّ	أَنْتُنَّ
تَقَدَّمَا	تَتَقَدَّمَا	تَتَقَدَّمَا	تَتَقَدَّمَانِ	تَقَدَّمْتُمَا	أَنْتُمَا (M+F)
	أَتَقَدَّمَ	أَتَقَدَّمْ	أَتَقَدَّمُ	تَقَدَّمْتُ	أَنَا
	نَتَقَدَّمَ	نَتَقَدَّمْ	نَتَقَدَّمُ	تَقَدَّمْنَا	نَحْنُ

Verbal Noun : تَقَدُّم (تَفَعُّلٌ)   Active Participle : مُتَقَدِّم   Passive Participle : مُتَقَدَّم

Verb Characteristics :
* It has a stem with a prefix *ta* (تَ) and a double middle radical.
* The stem vowel & the preceding vowel are both *a* (ـَ) in both the perfect & the imperfect forms.
* The vowel of the subject-marker prefixes is *a* (ـَ).

DERIVED FORMS CONJUGATION CHART VI

Verb : تَنَاوَلَ / يَتَنَاوَلُ   Verb Form : VI

Imperative	Imperfect Subjunctive	Imperfect Jussive	Imperfect Indicative	Perfect	Pronoun
	when the verb is preceded by a subjunctive particle such as	when the verb is preceded by a jussive particle such as			
	(لَنْ) يَتَنَاوَلَ	(لَمْ) يَتَنَاوَلْ	يَتَنَاوَلُ	تَنَاوَلَ	هُوَ
	تَتَنَاوَلَ	تَتَنَاوَلْ	تَتَنَاوَلُ	تَنَاوَلَتْ	هِيَ
	يَتَنَاوَلُوا	يَتَنَاوَلُوا	يَتَنَاوَلُونَ	تَنَاوَلُوا	هُمْ
	يَتَنَاوَلْنَ	يَتَنَاوَلْنَ	يَتَنَاوَلْنَ	تَنَاوَلْنَ	هُنَّ
	يَتَنَاوَلَا	يَتَنَاوَلَا	يَتَنَاوَلَانِ	تَنَاوَلَا	(M) هُمَا
	تَتَنَاوَلَا	تَتَنَاوَلَا	تَتَنَاوَلَانِ	تَنَاوَلَتَا	(F) هُمَا
تَنَاوَلْ	تَتَنَاوَلَ	تَتَنَاوَلْ	تَتَنَاوَلُ	تَنَاوَلْتَ	أَنْتَ
تَنَاوَلِي	تَتَنَاوَلِي	تَتَنَاوَلِي	تَتَنَاوَلِينَ	تَنَاوَلْتِ	أَنْتِ
تَنَاوَلُوا	تَتَنَاوَلُوا	تَتَنَاوَلُوا	تَتَنَاوَلُونَ	تَنَاوَلْتُمْ	أَنْتُمْ
تَنَاوَلْنَ	تَتَنَاوَلْنَ	تَتَنَاوَلْنَ	تَتَنَاوَلْنَ	تَنَاوَلْتُنَّ	أَنْتُنَّ
تَنَاوَلَا	تَتَنَاوَلَا	تَتَنَاوَلَا	تَتَنَاوَلَانِ	تَنَاوَلْتُمَا	(M+F) أَنْتُمَا
	أَتَنَاوَلَ	أَتَنَاوَلْ	أَتَنَاوَلُ	تَنَاوَلْتُ	أَنَا
	نَتَنَاوَلَ	نَتَنَاوَلْ	نَتَنَاوَلُ	تَنَاوَلْنَا	نَحْنُ

Verbal Noun : تَنَاوُلٌ (تَفَاعُلٌ)   Active Participle : مُتَنَاوِلٌ   Passive Participle : مُتَنَاوَلٌ

Verb Characteristics :
* It has a stem with a prefix *ta* (تَ) and a long vowel *ā* (ا) after the first radical.
* The stem vowel is *a* (ـَ) in both the perfect & the imperfect forms of the verb.
* The vowel of the subject-marker prefixes is *a* (ـَ).

CHAPTER 18

DERIVED FORMS – VII TO X

The Verb Form VII : إِنْـفَعَلَ *’infa‘ala*

This form is formed from the first form فَعَلَ *fa‘ala*, by prefixing the syllable إِنْ *in*. Thus كَسَرَ *kasara*, becomes إِنْكَسَرَ *’inkasara*.

Form VII verbs combine the meanings of reflexive of form I and passive of form I. For example, the form I verbصَرَفَ *.ṣarafa*, may mean (a) "to send away"(someone) or (b) "to spend" (money). The form VII إِنْصَرَفَ *’inṣarafa*, may be reflexive of (a), i.e. "to send oneself away" = "to go away, depart", if the subject is a person, or it may be the equivalent of a passive of (b), "to be spent", if speaking of money.

The verbs فَعَلَ "to do", كَسَرَ "to break", and قَطَعَ "to cut" when altered to form VII, become إِنْـفَعَـلَ "to be done", إِنْـكَسَـرَ "to be broken", and إِنْقَطَعَ "to be cut off, to come to an end".

It is also important to note that form VII is the intransitive counterpart of a transitive form I verb. Examine the following examples :

I	سَحَبَ	"to withdraw (something)".
VII	إِنْسَحَبَ	"to withdraw, retreat" – (intransitive).

I	كَسَرَ	"to break (something)".
VII	إنْكَسَرَ	"to get broken" – (intransitive).
I	فَتَحَ	"to open (something)".
VII	إنْفَتَحَ	"to open up, unfold" – (intransitive).

There is certainly a difference between the passive verb, which is formed from the changing of vowels, e.g. كُسِرَ *kusira*, "to be broken", and verb of this form (*'inkasara*) which is translated in the same way; "to be broken". In fact the passive verb indicates that the act has taken place by someone discoverable, while in the verb of this form the act is done either through a human agency or automatically or through an unknown inner cause. To understand the difference the following example should be carefully observed :

$$
\left.\begin{array}{r}
\text{انْقَطَعَتِ الأَسْبَابُ} \\
\text{قُطِعَتِ الأَسْبَابُ}
\end{array}\right\}
\text{"The means were cut off (eliminated)"}
$$

In first form, the verb suggests no reason or hidden hand behind the cutting of the means, while the second form shows involvement of some reason or hand though it is not discoverable. Take another example :

$$
\left.\begin{array}{r}
\text{انْكَسَرَ الْبَابُ} \\
\text{كُسِرَ الْبَابُ}
\end{array}\right\}
\text{"The door was broken"}
$$

In first form, the verb suggests that the door was broken by any undiscoverable way, say it might have happened by itself, due to being very old or by wind, etc., while the second form indicates that there was some one who had broken the door, but his name was not mentioned here.

Examples from The Holy Qur'ān :

3rd pers. Masc.	
وَانْطَلَقَ الْمَلَأُ مِنْهُمْ أَنِ امْشُوا وَاصْبِرُوا عَلَى آلِهَتِكُمْ ، إِنَّ هَذَا لَشَيْءٌ يُرَادُ	38-6 The chiefs among them go about exhorting : Go and be staunch to your gods. Lo! this is a thing designed.

3rd pers. Dual Masc.	
فَانْطَلَقَا حَتَّى إِذَا رَكِبَا فِي السَّفِينَةِ خَرَقَهَا	18-72 So the two of them set out, till when they were in the ship, he made a hole therein.

3rd pers. Pl. Masc.	
وَإِذَا انْقَلَبُوا إِلَى أَهْلِهِمُ انْقَلَبُوا فَكِهِينَ	83-31 And when they returned to their own folk they returned jesting.

3rd pers. Fem.	
فَانْبَجَسَتْ مِنْهُ اثْنَتَا عَشْرَةَ عَيْنًا	7-160 And there gushed forth therefrom twelve springs.

3rd pers. Masc.	
ثُمَّ ٱرْجِعِ ٱلْبَصَرَ كَرَّتَيْنِ يَنْقَلِبْ إِلَيْكَ ٱلْبَصَرُ خَاسِئاً وَهُوَ حَسِيرٌ	67-4 Then look again and yet again, thy sight will return into thee weakened and made dim.

3rd pers. Fem. Verbal noun	
إِذَا ٱلسَّمَاءُ ٱنْفَطَرَتْ	82-1 When the heaven is cleft asunder.
فَمَنْ يَكْفُرْ بِٱلطَّاغُوتِ وَيُؤْمِنْ بِٱللهِ فَقَدِ ٱسْتَمْسَكَ بِٱلْعُرْوَةِ ٱلْوُثْقَىٰ . لَا ٱنْفِصَامَ لَهَــا	2-256 And he who rejects false dieties and believes in Allah has grasped the most trust-worthy handhold with no breakdown.

Imperative : 2nd pers. Pl. Masc.	
ٱنْطَلِقُوا إِلَىٰ مَا كُنْتُمْ بِهِ تُكَذِّبُونَ	77-29 Depart unto that which you used to reject.

Active particle : Plural Masc.	
وَٱلْمُشْرِكِينَ مُنْفَكِّينَ	98-1 and … the polytheists were not going to depart.

Passive particle : Singular Fem.	
وَٱلْمُنْخَنِقَةُ وَٱلْمَوْقُوذَةُ	5-3 That which has been killed by strangulating or killed by a violent blow.

	Perfect	**Imperfect**	**Imperative**	**Verbal Noun**
Masc.	إِنْكَسَرَ	يَنْكَسِرُ	إِنْكَسِرْ	إِنْكِسَارُ
Fem.	إِنْكَسَرَتْ	تَنْكَسِرُ	إِنْكَسِري	
Active Participle: مُنْكَسِرُ				

Note : The variation of vowel in the second radical, that is س, in the verb.

Passive Participle: Can not be formed because this stem denotes that the work is done by itself, while passive indicates that some-one caused the action to happen.

Some other verbs of this stem :

إِنْقِطَاعٌ	to be cut off.	إِنْبِعَاثٌ	to march.
إِنْصِرَافٌ	to get away.	إِنْحِصَارٌ	to surround.
إِنْقِلَابٌ	to get turned up side down.		

The Verb Form VIII : إِفْتَعَلَ *'ifta'ala*

1. This form is formed from the first form *fa'ala* by prefixing a *hamzah* vowelled with *kasarah* and infixing a ت *ta*, after the first radical. Thus فَعَلَ will be shaped in this form as إِفْتَعَلَ *'ifta'ala*, and جَمَعَ *jama'a* إِجْتَمَعَ *'ijtama'a*, خَبَرَ *khabara* إِخْتَبَرَ *'ikhtabara*, نَصَرَ *nasara* إِنْتَصَرَ *'intasara*.

Examples from The Holy Qur'ān :

أَنَّهُ اسْتَمَعَ نَفَرٌ مِنَ ٱلْجِنِّ	72-1 A company of Jinns listened.

(The verb إِسْتَمَعَ *'istama'a* is derived from سَمَعَ "to hear").

| فَاحْتَمَلَ السَّيْلُ زَبَدًا رَابِيًا | 13-17 The torrent bears away the foam that mounts up to the surface. |

(The word إِحْتَمَلَ 3rd pers. Masc. "to bear" is derived from حَمَلَ hamala, "to carry").

| وَإِنَّ الَّذِينَ اخْتَلَفُوا فِي الكِتَابِ لَفِي شِقَاقٍ بَعِيدٍ | 2-176 Those who dispute in the Book are in schism far (from the purpose). |

(The verb اخْتَلَفُوا "to dispute, to disagree or to cause a dispute" is drawn from خَلَفُوا 3rd person Plural Masc. "to succeed someone").

| وَآخَرُونَ اعْتَرَفُوا بِذُنُوبِهم | 9-102 (There are those) who have acknowledged their worng-doings. |

(In this verse the verb اعْتَرَفُوا "they acknowledged", is derived from عَرَفُوا, 3rd person Plural Masc., "to recognize, to distinguish").

| وَاعْتَصِمُوا بِحَبْلِ اللهِ جَمِيعًا | 3-103 hold fast all together by the rope of Allah. |

The verb اعْتَصِمُوا is the imperative form, Plural Masc. that means : "Hold!", is derived from عَصَمُوا "to protect some thing or someone".

2. If the first radical (that is ف in فَعَلَ fa'ala, ج in جَمَعَ jama'a, and ن in نَصَرَ nasara), is one of the emphatic letters (i.e.

ط (ص ، ض ، ط ، ظ). The following additional letter will be
instead of ت, e.g. in The Holy Qur'ān :

فَاعْبُدْهُ وَاصْطَبِرْ لِعِبَادَتِه	19-65 Therefore, worship Him and be steadfast in His service.

Note : The verb اصْطَبِرْ imperative, 2nd person Sing. Masc.,
"be steadfast" was supposed to be اصْتَبِرْ with ت instead of ط
but because of ص , that is the first radical of this verb, and
one of the four emphatic letters, the ت (t) is changed to ط (ṭ).
Likewise, there is in The Holy Qur'ān :

وَاصْطَنَعْتُك لِنَفْسِي	20-41 And I have attached thee to Myself.

(The verb اصْطَنَعْتُ 1st person Sing., which is derived from
صَنَعْتُ "I made". Note the changing of ت to ط).

إِلَّا مَا اضْطُرِرْتُمْ إِلَيْهِ	6-119 Except under compulsion of necessity.

The verb اضْطُرِرْ , passive, 2nd person Plural Masc., is derived
from the root form of ضَرَرْ but in this the infixed ت was
changed to ط to agree with the emphatic letter of the first
radical.

Characteristic of form VIII verbs is that the infixed ت has a
tendency to undergo an *assimilation* process. If the first radical is a dental stop, fricative, or sibilant, the inserted ت is assimilated to it. Involved in the assimilation process are the following consonents :

ت ، ث ، د ، ذ ، ز ، ص ، ض ، ط ، ظ

The following are the rules of assimilation involved :

(1) After the voiced consonants د and ز , the inserted ت becomes voiced and is written as د . Compare the following:

I	زَادَ	"to add, make additions to".
VIII	اِزْدَادَ	"to increase, grow larger" (instead of اِزْتَادَ).

I	دَعَا	"to call, to invite".
VIII	اِدَّعَى	"to claim, allege, maintain" (instead of اِدْتَعَى).

(2) After ذ , the inserted ت becomes د , but ذ itself also becomes د , and both د 's are written دّ (with *shaddah*) :

I	ذَكَرَ	"to mention".
VIII	اِدَّكَرَ	"to remember" (instead of اِذْتَكَرَ).

(3) After a first radical ت , the inserted ت will not assimilate
into another sound, but both letters are combined with
shaddah, thus :

I	تَبِعَ	"to follow, succeed, come after".
VIII	اِتَّبَعَ	"to follow, succeed, come after" (instead of اِتْتَبَعَ).

(4) After the emphatic consonants ص , ض and ط , the
inserted ت becomes the emphatic ط . Examples :

I	صَدَمَ	"to bump, knock".
VIII	اِصْطَدَمَ	"to collide with" (instead of اِصْتَدَمَ).

I	ضَرَّ	"to harm, hurt".
VIII	اِضْطَرَّ	"to force, compel, to be obliged" (instead of اِضْتَرَّ).

I	طَلَعَ	"to rise, come into view".
VIII	اِطَّلَعَ	"to look, to be informed about" (instead of اِطْتَلَعَ).

(5) After the fricatives ث and ظ , the inserted ت is completely assimilated, and the resultant double consonant is written with *shaddah*. Examples :

I	ثَأَرَ	"to avenge".
VIII	اِثَّأَرَ	"to get one's revenge, be avanged" (instead of اِثْتَأَرَ).

I	ظَلَمَ	"to oppress".
VIII	اِظَّلَمَ	"to suffer injustice" (instead of اِظْتَلَمَ).

(6) A special feature of assimilation occurs when a form VIII verb is based on a form I verb whose first radical is و *wāw*. In this case the و itself assimilates to the inserted ت .
Examples :

I	وَصَلَ	"to arrive".
VIII	اِتَّصَلَ	"to get in touch" (instead of اِوْتَصَلَ).

I	وَحَدَ	"to be unique".
VIII	اتَّحَدَ	"to unite" (instead of اوْتَحَدَ).

3. Conjugation of إِفْتَعَلَ = إِجْتَمَعَ "to assemble".

	Perfect	Imperfect	Imperative	Active Participle	Passive Participle
3rd person Sing. Masc.	إِجْتَمَعَ	يَجْتَمِعُ		مُجْتَمِعٌ	مُجْتَمَعٌ
3rd person Sing. Fem.	إِجْتَمَعَتْ	تَجْتَمِعُ		(Note the second radical is vowelled with kasrah).	(Note the second radical is vowelled with fatha).
2nd person Sing. Masc.	إِجْتَمَعْتَ	تَجْتَمِعُ	إِجْتَمِعْ		
2nd person Sing. Fem.	إِجْتَمَعْتِ	تَجْتَمِعِينَ	إِجْتَمِعِي		
1st person Singular	إِجْتَمَعْتُ	أَجْتَمِعُ			
1st person Plural	إِجْتَمَعْنَا	نَجْتَمِعُ			

(a) The meaning of this form is like VII, i.e. reflexive of the simple verb first form, e.g. جَمَعَ *jama'a* "to collect", إِجْتَمَعَ *'ijtama'a* "to collect themselves, assemble" (hence الإِجْتِمَاعُ *'al'ijtimā'u* "the meeting").
سَمِعَ *sami'a* "to hear", إِسْتَمَعَ *'istama'a* "to listen". شَغَلَ *shaghala* "to occupy, keep busy", إِشْتَغَلَ *'ishtaghala* "to be busy, to work".

(b) It also has the sense of doing something for oneself, e.g. كَسَبَ *kasaba* "to acquire", إِكْتَسَبَ *'iktasaba* "to gain". كَشَفَ *kashafa* "to uncover", إِكْتَشَفَ *'iktashafa* "to discover". بَدَعَ *bada'a* "to initiate", اِبْتَدَعَ *ibtada'a* "invent".

(c) Sometimes, it seems to be reserved for odd by way of meaning e.g.: ضَرَبَ. *daraba* "to strike", إِضْطَرَبَ *'idtaraba* "to be disturbed, shaken". حَمَـلَ. *hamala* "to carry" إِحْتَمَلَ *'ihtamala* "to bear, with sense of endurance, to be proble". حَرَمَ. *harama* "to forbid", إِحْـتَـرَمَ *'ihtarama* "to respect".

(d) It often has the same meaning as the root form, e.g.: بَسَمَ *basama,* إِبْـتَسَمَ *'ibtasama* "to smile".

Examples from The Holy Qur'ān :

لَهَا مَا كَسَبَتْ ، وَعَلَيهَا مَا اكْتَسَبَتْ	2-286 For it (any soul) is that which it earns (of good) and against it that it works (of evil).
إِلَّا مَن اغْتَرَفَ غُرْفَةً بِيَـدِه	2-249 except he who takes a handful of (water) with his hand.
اقْتَرَبَتِ السَّاعَةُ وَانْشَقَّ الْقَمَرُ	54-1 The hour (of Judgement) is nigh, and the moon is cleft asunder.
إِنَّ الله اصْطَفَاكِ	3-42 (O Mary!) God hath chosen thee.

The Verb Form IX : إِنْفَعَلَ *'if'alla* = إِحْمَرَّ *'ihmarra*

This form is formed from the first (root) by prefixing a *hamzah* vowelled with *kasrah* and doubling the third radical, e.g.: إِحْمَـرَّ *'ihmarra* "to be, or to become red".

This form is used only to express colours and defects, e.g. :

إخْضَرَّ   'ikhḍarra   "to be, or to become green".

إسْوَدَّ   'iswadda   "to be, or to become black".

إبْـيَـضَّ   'ibyaḍḍah   "to be, or to become white" (see chapter 11).

This conjugation of this form is as following :
(Note : There is no passive form from this verb)

	Perfect	Imperfect	Imperative	Active Part.	Passive Part.
3rd person Sing. Masc.	إحْمَرَّ	يَحْمَرُّ		مُحْمَرٌّ	مُحْمَرٌّ
3rd person Sing. Fem.	إحْمَرَّتْ	تَحْمَرُّ		مُحْمَرَّةٌ	مُحْمَرَّةٌ
2nd person Sing. Masc.	إحْمَرَرْتَ	تَحْمَرُّ	إحْمَرِرْ		
2nd person Sing. Fem.	إحْمَرَرْتِ	تَحْمَرِّينَ	إحْمَرِّي		
1st pers. Sing. Fem. / Masc.	إحْمَرَرْتُ	أَحْمَرُّ			
3rd person Dual Masc.	إحْمَرَّا	يَحْمَرَّانِ		مُحْمَرَّانِ	مُحْمَرَّانِ
3rd person Dual Fem.	إحْمَرَّتَا	تَحْمَرَّانِ		مُحْمَرَّتَانِ	مُحْمَرَّتَانِ
2nd person Dual Masc.	إحْمَرَرْتُمَا				
2nd person Dual Fem.	إحْمَرَرْتُمَا				
3rd person Plural Masc.	إحْمَرُّوا	يَحْمَرُّونَ		مُحْمَرُّونَ	مُحْمَرُّونَ
3rd person Plural Fem.	إحْمَرَرْنَ	يَحْمَرِرْنَ		مُحْمَرَّاتٌ	مُحْمَرَّاتٌ
2nd person Plural Masc.	إحْمَرَرْتُم	تَحْمَرُّونَ			
2nd person Plural Fem.	إحْمَرَرْتُنَّ	تَحْمَرِرْنَ			
1st pers. Pl. Fem. / Masc.	إحْمَرَرْنَا	نَحْمَرُّ			

Examples from The Holy Qur'ān :

يَوْمَ تَبْيَضُّ وُجُوهٌ وَتَسْوَدُّ وُجُوهٌ فَأَمَّا الَّذِينَ اسْوَدَّتْ وُجُوهُهُمْ : أَكَفَرْتُمْ بَعْدَ إِيمَانِكُم فَذُوقُوا العَذَابَ بِمَا كُنْتُمْ تَكْفُرُونَ وَأَمَّا الَّذِينَ ابْيَضَّتْ وُجُوهُهُمْ فَفِي رَحْمَةِ اللهِ هُمْ فِيهَا خَالِدُونَ .	3-106,107 On the day when some faces will be (lit up with) white, and some faces will be (in the gloom of) black. To those whose faces will be black: Did you reject faith after accepting it? Taste then the penalty for rejection of faith. But those whose faces will be (lit with) white they will be in the light of Allah's mercy, therein to dwell (for ever).
وَابْيَضَّتْ عَيْنَاهُ مِنَ الْحُزْنِ فَهُوَ كَظِيمٌ	12-84 And his eyes become white with sorrow.
فَتُصْبِحُ الأَرْضُ مُخْضَرَّةً	22-63 The earth becomes covered with green.
ظَلَّ وَجْهُهُ مُسْوَدًّا	16-58 His face remained darkend.

The Verb Form X : إِسْتَفْعَلَ 'istaf'ala = إِسْتَقْبَلَ 'istaqbala

This form is formed from the root form فَعَلَ by prefixing the syllable of three letter إِسْتَ , e.g. from قَبِلَ , إِسْتَقْبَلَ from نَصَرَ , إِسْتَنْصَرَ etc. The meaning of the verb of this form is :

1. The reflexive of the IV form أَفْعَلَ . Thus, أَخْبَرَ "to inform", إِسْتَخْبَرَ "to be made knwon", أَسْلَمَ "to give up, or to deliver", إِسْتَسْلَمَ "to give onself up, to surrender".

2. This form also indicates that a person thinks that a certain thing possesses the quality expressed by the root form, i.e. (estimative) :

عَظُمَ "to be great"   إِسْتَعْظَمَ "to regard something as great",

حَسُنَ "to be handsome"   إِسْتَحْسَنَ "to regard something as good",

ثَـقُلَ "to be heavy"   إِسْتَـثْـقَلَ "to find something heavy".

3. The form often expresses the seeking, asking, or demanding what is expressed by the root form, e.g. :

رَجَعَ "to return",   إِسْتَـرْجَعَ "to reclaim, to recall",

غَـفَـرَ "to pardon",   إِسْتَغْفَرَ "to ask for pardon",

أَذِنَ "to permit",   إِسْتَأْذَنَ "to ask permission".

4. Sometimes this form gives a causative meaning, e.g. :

خَرَجَ "to get out",   إِسْتَخْرَجَ "to draw out, to extract".

5. This form is also demonative in which case it invites factitive and reflexive, e.g. :

خَلَفَ "to succeed",   إِسْتَخْلَفَ "to appoint one as successor or caliph (خَلِيفَةٌ)".

حَجَرٌ "a stone",   إِسْتَحْجَرَ "to become like stone".

The following are the conjugation of this form :

Verb : إِسْتَقْبَلَ   Verb Form : X   Verbal Noun إِسْتِقْبَالٌ

Verb Meaning :" to welcome, to receive"

Passive Participle	Active Participle	Imperative	Imperfect Indicative	Perfect	Person or Corresponding subject
مُسْتَقْبَلٌ	مُسْتَقْبِلٌ		يَسْتَقْبِلُ	إِسْتَقْبَلَ	هُوَ
مُسْتَقْبَلَةٌ	مُسْتَقْبِلَةٌ		تَسْتَقْبِلُ	إِسْتَقْبَلَتْ	هِيَ
مُسْتَقْبَلُونَ	مُسْتَقْبِلُونَ		يَسْتَقْبِلُونَ	إِسْتَقْبَلُوا	هُمْ
مُسْتَقْبَلَاتٌ	مُسْتَقْبِلَاتٌ		يَسْتَقْبِلْنَ	إِسْتَقْبَلْنَ	هُنَّ
مُسْتَقْبَلَانِ	مُسْتَقْبِلَانِ		يَسْتَقْبِلَانِ	إِسْتَقْبَلَا	هُمَا (M)
مُسْتَقْبَلَتَانِ	مُسْتَقْبِلَتَانِ		تَسْتَقْبِلَانِ	إِسْتَقْبَلَتَا	هُمَا (F)
مُسْتَقْبَلٌ	مُسْتَقْبِلٌ	إِسْتَقْبِلْ	تَسْتَقْبِلُ	إِسْتَقْبَلْتَ	أَنْتَ
مُسْتَقْبَلَةٌ	مُسْتَقْبِلَةٌ	إِسْتَقْبِلِي	تَسْتَقْبِلِينَ	إِسْتَقْبَلْتِ	أَنْتِ
مُسْتَقْبَلُونَ	مُسْتَقْبِلُونَ	إِسْتَقْبِلُوا	تَسْتَقْبِلُونَ	إِسْتَقْبَلْتُمْ	أَنْتُمْ
مُسْتَقْبَلَاتٌ	مُسْتَقْبِلَاتٌ	إِسْتَقْبِلْنَ	تَسْتَقْبِلْنَ	إِسْتَقْبَلْتُنَّ	أَنْتُنَّ
مُسْتَقْبَلَانِ	مُسْتَقْبِلَانِ	إِسْتَقْبِلَا	تَسْتَقْبِلَانِ	إِسْتَقْبَلْتُمَا	أَنْتُمَا (M)
مُسْتَقْبَلَتَانِ	مُسْتَقْبِلَتَانِ	إِسْتَقْبِلَا	تَسْتَقْبِلَانِ	إِسْتَقْبَلْتُمَا	أَنْتُمَا (F)
مُسْتَقْبَلٌ	مُسْتَقْبِلٌ		أَسْتَقْبِلُ	إِسْتَقْبَلْتُ	أَنَا
مُسْتَقْبَلُونَ	مُسْتَقْبِلُونَ		نَسْتَقْبِلُ	إِسْتَقْبَلْنَا	نَحْنُ

Examples from The Holy Qur'ān :

قَالَ : أَتَسْتَبْدِلُونَ الَّذِي هُوَ أَدْنى بِالَّذِي هُوَ خَيْرٌ	2-61 He said: Would you exchange that is higher for which is lower ?
إِذ تَسْتَغِيثُونَ رَبَّكُمْ فَاسْتَجَابَ لَكُمْ	8-9 When you sought help of your Lord and He answered you.
وَيَسْتَخْرِجَا كَنْزَهُمَا رَحْمَةً مِن رَّبِّكَ	18-82 And (they) should bring forth their treasure as a mercy from thy Lord.
يَسْتَبْشِرُونَ بِنِعْمَةٍ مِنَ اللهِ وَفَضْلٍ وَأَنَّ اللهَ لَا يُضِيعُ أَجْرَ ٱلْمُؤْمِنِينَ . الَّذِينَ ٱسْتَجَابُوا للهِ وَٱلرَّسُولِ مِن بَعْدِ مَآ أَصَابَهُمُ ٱلْقَرْحُ لِلَّذِينَ أَحْسَنُوا مِنْهُمْ وَٱتَّقَوْا أَجْرٌ عَظِيمٌ	3-171, 172 They rejoice because of favour from Allah and kindness, and that Allah wastes not the wages of the believers. As for those who heard the call of Allah and the Messenger after what befell them (in the fight); for such of them as do right and ward off (evil) there is great reward.
وَٱسْتَشْهِدُوا شَهِيدَيْنِ مِن رِّجَالِكُمْ	2-282 And call two witnesses from among your men.
وَإِنْ أَرَدتُّمْ أَنْ تَسْتَرْضِعُوا أَوْلَادَكُمْ فَلَا جُنَاحَ عَلَيْكُمْ	2-233 And if you wish to give your children out to nurse, it is no sin for you.
فَٱسْتَبْشِرُوا بِبَيْعِكُمُ ٱلَّذِي بَايَعْتُمْ بِهِ	9-111 (Imperative) Rejoice then in your bargain that you have made.
وَكَانُوا مُسْتَبْصِرِينَ	29-38 And they were keen observers. (Active Part.)

| وُجُوهٌ يَوْمَئِذٍ مُسْفِرَةٌ ضَاحِكَةٌ مُسْتَبْشِرَةٌ | 80-38, 39   On that day faces will be bright as dawn, laughing, rejoicing at good news. (Active Part.) |

Note : For easy reference, see Derived Forms Conjugation Charts VII, VIII, IX, and X at the end of this chapter.

EXERCISE

1. Translate into Arabic :

(a) It was during that last pilgrimage, that the surah "Succour" was revealed, which he received as an announcement of approaching death. Soon after his return to Al-Madinah he fell ill. The tidings of his illness caused dismay throughout Arabia and anguish to the folk of Al-Madinah, Makkah and Taif, his hometowns. At early dawn on the last day of his earthly life he came out from his room beside the mosque at Al-Madinah and joined the public prayer, which Abu Bakr had been leading since his illness. And there was great relief among the people who supposed him well again. When, later in the day, the rumour grew that he was dead, 'Umar threatened those who spread the rumour with dire punishment, declaring it a crime to think that the messenger of God could die. He was storming at the people in this strain when Abu Bakr came into the mosque and overheard him.

(b) How many hours have you been waiting for your friend ?
Write a letter to your father with due respect.
How do you work in the month of Ramaḍān?
The Government has recognized women's rights in election.

Arabs were victorious in their war against Israel.

Go away, girl, and occupy yourself in the kitchen.

There is a political disturbance in some of the European countries.

The elders think that the youth of today are lazy.

The Western pattern of life is hardly acceptable in the Islamic society.

(c) Two white cars stopped at the traffic light when it was red.
A boy in white pants went to the market along with his sister in a red shirt.

2. Translate into English :

١ - إنْقَلَبَتْ سَيَّارَةٌ فِي الطَّرِيقِ وَلَمْ يَنْكَشِفِ السَّبَبُ الرَّئِيسِيُّ لِهَذَا الحَادِثِ .

٢ - إنْتَحَرَ شَابٌّ فِي لَنْدَن وَلَمْ يُعْلَمْ بَعْدُ سَبَبُ أَنْتِحَارِهِ .

٣ - إسْتَفْسَرَتِ المَحْكَمَةُ العُلْيَا مِنَ الشُّرْطَةِ عَنِ الحَادِثِ .

٤ - تَمَّ إنتِخَابُ عَالِمٍ كَبِيرٍ رَئِيسًا لِمَجْمَعٍ إِسْلَامِيٍّ مَعْرُوفٍ .

٥ - جَاءَ فِي آلْقُرْآنِ الكَرِيمِ : لَوْ كُنْتَ فَظًّا غَلِيظَ القَلْبِ لَانَفَضُّوا مِنْ حَوْلِكَ .

٦ - وَقَّعَ المُوَظَّفُونَ قَبْلَ آنْصِرَافِهِمْ عَلَى سِجِلِّ الحُضُورِ .

٧ - إنْقَطَعَ التَّيَارُ الكَهْرَبَائِيُّ مَسَاءَ أَمْسِ .

٨ - زَارَ المَمْلَكَةَ مَلِكٌ مِن مُلُوكِ العَالَمِ وَاسْتُقْبِلَ إِسْتِقْبَالًا حَافِلًا .

٩ - خَرَجَ الطَّلَبَةُ مُسْتَبْشِرِينَ بِنَتَائِجِ آخْتِبَارِهِمِ السَّنَوِيّ .

١٠ - إسْتَوْضَحَ الطَّالِبُ مِنَ المُدَرِّسِ المَوَاضِعَ الصَّعْبَةَ مِنْ دُرُوسِهِ .

264

إِنْتَحَرَ	(VII) to commit suicide.
إِنْقَلَبَ	(VII) to be overturned.
إِنْكَشَفَ	(VII) to be disclosed.
السَّبَبُ	reason.
الرَّئِيسِي	main.
انْتِخَاب	VII (v.n.) election.
رَئِيسٌ	chief, president.
فَظٌّ	rude.
غَلِيظٌ	anguish, of thick blood.
إِنْفَضَّ	(VII) to disperse.
وَقَّعَ	(II) to sign (signature).
إِنْصِرَاف	VII (v.n.) leaving back.
سِجِلٌّ	register.
إِنْقَطَعَ	(VII) to cut off, to be off.
أُمْس	yesterday.

أُسْتُقْبِلَ	was received (pass. of اسْتَقْبَلَ , (X) 'to receive').
الْمُسْتَبْشِرُ	one who gets good news. (Act. Part. X)
اسْتَفْسَرَ	(X) to inquire.
إسْتَوْضَحَ	(X) to ask for details, to ask clarification.

duration	أَثْنَاء
pilgrimage	الحَجُّ
announcement	الإعْـلَانُ
approaching	قُرْب الوُصُول – القُرْبُ
news, tidings	أَخْبَار
grief	الْحُـزْنُ – الأَسٰى
earthly life	الحَيَاةُ الدُّنْيَوِيَّةُ
relief	الطُّمَأْنِينَةُ

DERIVED FORMS CONJUGATION CHART VII

Verb : اِنْسَحَبَ / يَنْسَحِبُ   Verb Form : VII

Imperative	Imperfect Subjunctive	Imperfect Jussive	Imperfect Indicative	Perfect	Pronoun
	when the verb is preceded by a subjunctive particle such as	when the verb is preceded by a jussive particle such as			
	(لَنْ) يَنْسَحِبْ	(لَمْ) يَنْسَحِبْ	يَنْسَحِبُ	اِنْسَحَبَ	هُـوَ
	تَنْسَحِبْ	تَنْسَحِبْ	تَنْسَحِبُ	اِنْسَحَبَتْ	هِيَ
	يَنْسَحِبُوا	يَنْسَحِبُوا	يَنْسَحِبُونَ	اِنْسَحَبُوا	هُمْ
	يَنْسَحِبْنَ	يَنْسَحِبْنَ	يَنْسَحِبْنَ	اِنْسَحَبْنَ	هُنَّ
	يَنْسَحِبَا	يَنْسَحِبَا	يَنْسَحِبَانِ	اِنْسَحَبَا	هُمَا (M)
	تَنْسَحِبَا	تَنْسَحِبَا	تَنْسَحِبَانِ	اِنْسَحَبَتَا	هُمَا (F)
اِنْسَحِبْ	تَنْسَحِبْ	تَنْسَحِبْ	تَنْسَحِبُ	اِنْسَحَبْتَ	أَنْتَ
إِنْسَحِبِي	تَنْسَحِبِي	تَنْسَحِبِي	تَنْسَحِبِينَ	اِنْسَحَبْتِ	أَنْتِ
اِنْسَحِبُوا	تَنْسَحِبُوا	تَنْسَحِبُوا	تَنْسَحِبُونَ	اِنْسَحَبْتُمْ	أَنْتُمْ
اِنْسَحِبْنَ	تَنْسَحِبْنَ	تَنْسَحِبْنَ	تَنْسَحِبْنَ	اِنْسَحَبْتُنَّ	أَنْتُنَّ
اِنْسَحِبَا	تَنْسَحِبَا	تَنْسَحِبَا	تَنْسَحِبَانِ	اِنْسَحَبْتُمَا	أَنْتُمَا (M+F)
	أَنْسَحِبْ	أَنْسَحِبْ	أَنْسَحِبُ	اِنْسَحَبْتُ	أَنَـا
	نَنْسَحِبْ	نَنْسَحِبْ	نَنْسَحِبُ	اِنْسَحَبْنَا	نَحْنُ

Verbal Noun : (اِنْفِعَـالٌ) اِنْسِحَابٌ   Active Participle : مُنْسَحِبٌ   Passive Participle : مُنْسَحَبٌ

Verb Characteristics :
* It has a stem starting with the prefix *n-* (نْ). The perfect form is written with a *waṣla* (elided hamza) before the *n-* prefix.
* The vowel of the first radical is a *fatḥa* (ـَ) in both the perfect and imperfect forms.
* The stem vowel of the perfect is a *fatḥa* (ـَ), and the stem vowel of the imperfect is a *kasara* (ـِ).   * The vowel of the subject-marker prefixes is *fatḥa* (ـَ).

DERIVED FORMS CONJUGATION CHART VIII

Verb : (إلَى) اِسْتَمَعَ / يَسْتَمِعُ   Verb Form : VIII

Imperative	Imperfect Subjunctive	Imperfect Jussive	Imperfect Indicative	Perfect	Pronoun
	when the verb is preceded by a subjunctive particle such as	when the verb is preceded by a jussive particle such as			
	(لَنْ) يَسْتَمِعَ	(لَمْ) يَسْتَمِعْ	يَسْتَمِعُ	اِسْتَمَعَ	هُوَ
	تَسْتَمِعَ	تَسْتَمِعْ	تَسْتَمِعُ	اِسْتَمَعَتْ	هِيَ
	يَسْتَمِعُوا	يَسْتَمِعُوا	يَسْتَمِعُونَ	اِسْتَمَعُوا	هُمْ
	يَسْتَمِعْنَ	يَسْتَمِعْنَ	يَسْتَمِعْنَ	اِسْتَمَعْنَ	هُنَّ
	يَسْتَمِعَا	يَسْتَمِعَا	يَسْتَمِعَانِ	اِسْتَمَعَا	هُمَا (M)
	تَسْتَمِعَا	تَسْتَمِعَا	تَسْتَمِعَانِ	اِسْتَمَعَتَا	هُمَا (F)
اِسْتَمِعْ	تَسْتَمِعَ	تَسْتَمِعْ	تَسْتَمِعُ	اِسْتَمَعْتَ	أَنْتَ
اِسْتَمِعِي	تَسْتَمِعِي	تَسْتَمِعِي	تَسْتَمِعِينَ	اِسْتَمَعْتِ	أَنْتِ
اِسْتَمِعُوا	تَسْتَمِعُوا	تَسْتَمِعُوا	تَسْتَمِعُونَ	اِسْتَمَعْتُمْ	أَنْتُمْ
اِسْتَمِعْنَ	تَسْتَمِعْنَ	تَسْتَمِعْنَ	تَسْتَمِعْنَ	اِسْتَمَعْتُنَّ	أَنْتُنَّ
اِسْتَمِعَا	تَسْتَمِعَا	تَسْتَمِعَا	تَسْتَمِعَانِ	اِسْتَمَعْتُمَا	أَنْتُمَا (M+F)
	أَسْتَمِعَ	أَسْتَمِعْ	أَسْتَمِعُ	اِسْتَمَعْتُ	أَنَا
	نَسْتَمِعَ	نَسْتَمِعْ	نَسْتَمِعُ	اِسْتَمَعْنَا	نَحْنُ

Verbal Noun : اِسْتِمَاعُ (اِفْتِعَالٌ)   Active Participle : مُسْتَمِعٌ   Passive Participle : مُسْتَمَعٌ

Verb Characteristics :
* It has a stem with the reflexive affix *ta* (تَ) insered after the first radical of the root.
* The perfect form is written with a *waṣla* (elided hamza) before the first radical.
* The first radical has a zero vowel *(sukūn)* in both the perfect and imperfect forms.
* The stem of the perfect is a *fatḥa* (ـَ) , and the stem of the imperfect is a *kasara* (ـِ).
* The subject-marker prefixes vowel is *fatḥa* (ـَ).

DERIVED FORMS CONJUGATION CHART IX

Verb : اِسْوَدَّ / يَسْوَدُّ (to turn black)   Verb Form : IX

Imperative	Imperfect Subjunctive	Imperfect Jussive	Imperfect Indicative	Perfect	Pronoun
	A subjunctive particle such as (لَنْ) is needed	A jussive particle such as (لَمْ) is needed			
	(لَنْ) يَسْوَدَّ	(لَمْ) يَسْوَدَّ	يَسْوَدُّ	اِسْوَدَّ	هُوَ
	تَسْوَدَّ	تَسْوَدَّ	تَسْوَدُّ	اِسْوَدَّتْ	هِيَ
	يَسْوَدُّوا	يَسْوَدُّوا	يَسْوَدُّونَ	اِسْوَدُّوا	هُمْ
	يَسْوَدِدْنَ	يَسْوَدِدْنَ	يَسْوَدِدْنَ	اِسْوَدَدْنَ	هُنَّ
	يَسْوَدَّا	يَسْوَدَّا	يَسْوَدَّانِ	اِسْوَدَّا	هُمَا (M)
	تَسْوَدَّا	تَسْوَدَّا	تَسْوَدَّانِ	اِسْوَدَّتَا	هُمَا (F)
اِسْوَدِدْ	تَسْوَدَّ	تَسْوَدَّ	تَسْوَدُّ	اِسْوَدَدْتَ	أَنْتَ
إِسْوَدِّي	تَسْوَدِّي	تَسْوَدِّي	تَسْوَدِّينَ	اِسْوَدَدْتِ	أَنْتِ
اِسْوَدُّوا	تَسْوَدُّوا	تَسْوَدُّوا	تَسْوَدُّونَ	اِسْوَدَدْتُمْ	أَنْتُمْ
اِسْوَدِدْنَ	تَسْوَدِدْنَ	تَسْوَدِدْنَ	تَسْوَدِدْنَ	اِسْوَدَدْتُنَّ	أَنْتُنَّ
اِسْوَدَّا	تَسْوَدَّا	تَسْوَدَّا	تَسْوَدَّانِ	اِسْوَدَدْتُمَا	أَنْتُمَا (M+F)
	أَسْوَدَّ	أَسْوَدَّ	أَسْوَدُّ	اِسْوَدَدْتُ	أَنَا
	نَسْوَدَّ	نَسْوَدَّ	نَسْوَدُّ	اِسْوَدَدْنَا	نَحْنُ

Verbal Noun : اِسْوِدَادُ (اِفْعِلَالٌ)   Active and/or Passive Participle : مُسْوَدَّةُ / مُسْوَدُّ

Verb Characteristics :

* It has a perfect tense stem with a *hamzah* which is elidable. * It has a stem with the last radical doubled, in both perfect and imperfect tenses. * The vowel of the first radical is a *fatha* (ـَ) in both the perfect and imperfect tenses. * The vowel of the second radical (stem vowel) is a *fatha* (ـَ) in both the perfect and imperfect tenses. * The subject-marker prefixes vowel is *fatha* (ـَ). * Form IX verbs always denote colors or physical and mental defects. * They are the least common of the ten forms of verbs.

DERIVED FORMS CONJUGATION CHART X

Verb : اِسْتَعْمَلَ / يَسْتَعْمِلُ   Verb Form : X

Imperative	Imperfect Subjunctive	Imperfect Jussive	Imperfect Indicative	Perfect	Pronoun
	when the verb is preceded by a subjunctive particle such as	when the verb is preceded by a jussive particle such as			
	(لَنْ) يَسْتَعْمِلَ	(لَمْ) يَسْتَعْمِلْ	يَسْتَعْمِلُ	اِسْتَعْمَلَ	هُوَ
	تَسْتَعْمِلَ	تَسْتَعْمِلْ	تَسْتَعْمِلُ	اِسْتَعْمَلَتْ	هِيَ
	يَسْتَعْمِلُوا	يَسْتَعْمِلُوا	يَسْتَعْمِلُونَ	اِسْتَعْمَلُوا	هُمْ
	يَسْتَعْمِلْنَ	يَسْتَعْمِلْنَ	يَسْتَعْمِلْنَ	اِسْتَعْمَلْنَ	هُنَّ
	يَسْتَعْمِلَا	يَسْتَعْمِلَا	يَسْتَعْمِلَانِ	اِسْتَعْمَلَا	هُمَا (M)
	تَسْتَعْمِلَا	تَسْتَعْمِلَا	تَسْتَعْمِلَانِ	اِسْتَعْمَلَتَا	هُمَا (F)
اِسْتَعْمِلْ	تَسْتَعْمِلَ	تَسْتَعْمِلْ	تَسْتَعْمِلُ	اِسْتَعْمَلْتَ	أَنْتَ
اِسْتَعْمِلِي	تَسْتَعْمِلِي	تَسْتَعْمِلِي	تَسْتَعْمِلِينَ	اِسْتَعْمَلْتِ	أَنْتِ
اِسْتَعْمِلُوا	تَسْتَعْمِلُوا	تَسْتَعْمِلُوا	تَسْتَعْمِلُونَ	اِسْتَعْمَلْتُمْ	أَنْتُمْ
اِسْتَعْمِلْنَ	تَسْتَعْمِلْنَ	تَسْتَعْمِلْنَ	تَسْتَعْمِلْنَ	اِسْتَعْمَلْتُنَّ	أَنْتُنَّ
اِسْتَعْمِلَا	تَسْتَعْمِلَا	تَسْتَعْمِلَا	تَسْتَعْمِلَانِ	إِسْتَعْمَلْتُمَا	أَنْتُمَا (M+F)
	أَسْتَعْمِلَ	أَسْتَعْمِلْ	أَسْتَعْمِلُ	اِسْتَعْمَلْتُ	أَنَا
	نَسْتَعْمِلَ	نَسْتَعْمِلْ	نَسْتَعْمِلُ	اِسْتَعْمَلْنَا	نَحْنُ

Verbal Noun: اِسْتِعْمَالٌ (اِسْتِفْعَالٌ) Active Participle: مُسْتَعْمِلٌ Passive Participle: مُسْتَعْمَلٌ

Verb Characteristics :
* It is characterized by having a stem beginning with -sta- (سْتَ). Besides, the perfect stem has an initial elidable *hamzah.*
* Both the stem vowel and the preceding vowel are always *a* (ـَ) in the perfect.
* In the imperfect, the stem vowel is always *i* (ـِ) and the first vowel is always *a* (ـَ).
* The vowel of the subject-marker prefix is always *a* (ـَ) in the imperfect.

270   ٢٧٠

CHAPTER 19

THE UNSOUND (WEAK) VERBS

Arabic verbs are divided into :

  (a) Sound verbs أَفْعَالٌ صَحِيحَةٌ

  (b) Unsound verbs أَفْعَالٌ مُعْتَلَّةٌ

The forms of the sound verbs have been discussed in previous chapters. Now we start learning the forms of unsound verbs, that is, comprising :

1. Verbs constructed by all consonants but some of them have one of the three radicals duplicated, e.g. مَـدَدَ which is pronounced with assimilation إدغـام , i.e. two radicals are written as one with *shaddah*, e.g. مَدَّ , instead of writing or saying مَدَدَ . Some other forms are those in which a *hamzah* takes place of a radical, e.g.:

In	أَسِفَ	the first radical is a *hamzah*.
In	سَأَلَ	the second radical is a *hamzah*.
In	بَرَأَ	the third radical is a *hamzah*.

Contrasting the consonantal verbs, either hamzited or duplicated radicals, are verbs codified with weak letters (مُعْتَلٌّ). That means either *wāw* (و) or *yā'* (ي) has occurred in place of one of the radicals causing certain changes in all forms and stems of the verbs.

2. The Verbs of duplicated radicals

When a word has a cluster of two consonants, as مَدَ – مَدَدَ , it will be pronounced with *shaddah*, if it has a short vowel, i.e. *fathah, dammah,* or *kasrah.* Otherwise, i.e. in case of ending the word on a *sukūn,* both will be sounded without assimilation e.g. رَدَّ (to restore, to reply) رَدّوا (they replied), but when it is followed by a ت or ن, the assimilation will be left, and will be pronounced as مَدَدْنَ، رَدَدْتُ or مَدَدْتُ، رَدَدْنَ , etc.

In the imperfect, this necessitates shifting the vowel forward from the second radical, e.g. يَمُدُّ (he extends), but in case of jussive يَمْدُدْ *yamdud,* as a rule the assimilation does not take place where the third radical has *sukūn,* e.g. :

مَدَدْنَا	we extended.
مَدَدْنَ	they (Fem.) extended.
لَمْ يَمْدُدْ	he (Masc.) did not extend.
لَمْ نَمْدُدْ	we (Masc. & Fem.) did not extend.
لَمْ أَمْدُدْ	I (Masc. & Fem.) did not extend.

Where the second radical is separated from the third by a long vowel no assimilation can take place, e.g. :

مَرْدُودٌ	Passive Participle	one who was turned out.
إِرْدَادٌ	Verbal noun	turning out.

Conjugation of مَـدَّ

(a) Perfect :

		Dual	Plural
Sing. 3rd Person (M).	مَـدَّ	مَـدَّا	مَـدُّوا
Sing. 3rd Person (F).	مَدَّتْ	مَدَّتَا	مَدَدْنَ
Sing. 2nd Person, (M).	مَدَدْتَ	مَدَدْتُمَا	مَدَدْتُمْ
Sing. 2nd Person, (F).	مَدَدْت		مَدَدْتُنَّ
1st Person, (M & F).	مَدَدْتُ		مَدَدْنَا

(b) Imperfect :

Indicative	Subjunctive	Jussive
يَمُدُّ	يَمُدَّ	يَمْدُدْ
تَمُدُّ	تَمُدَّ	تَمْدُدْ
تَمُدِّينَ	تَمُدِّي	تَمْدُدِي
أَمُدُّ	أَمُدَّ	أَمْدُدْ

	Imperative	Negative Imperative
Masc.	أُمْـدُدْ مُـدَّ	لَا تَمُـدَّ
Fem.	أُمْـدُدِي مُـدِّي	لَا تَمُـدِّي
Part. Active مَادُّ		Part. Passive مَمْدُودُ

Note : For full conjugation of a doubled verb and easy reference, please see the Conjugation Chart at the end of
this chapter.

3. Hamzated verbs

The *hamzah*, which is written on the *'alif* (as أ , إ , أ) or between two letters (as ء) or separately after a final letter as بَاءَ ، نَاءَ etc., is counted in verbs as a consonant, and as such may be the initial, middle or final radicals e.g. The initial: أَجَرَ "to reward, to recompense"; أَكَلَ "to eat"; أَخَذَ "to take". The middle as in سَأَلَ "to ask"; سَئِمَ "to be disgusted at". The final radical as in قَرَأَ "to read"; خَطَأَ "to transgress"; and بَطُؤَ "to be slow".

(a) Hamzah as Initial Radical :

In certain verbs أَخَذَ "to take"; أَمَرَ "to command"; أَكَلَ "to eat", the initial *hamzah* is dropped in the imperative, e.g. :

Imperative

Root form Verb	Masculine Singular	Feminine Singular	Dual	Plural Masc.	Plural Fem.
أَخَذَ	خُذْ	خُذِي	خُذَا	خُذُوا	خُذْنَ
أَمَرَ	مُرْ	مُرِي	مُرَا	مُرُوا	مُرْنَ
أَكَلَ	كُلْ	كُلِي	كُلَا	كُلُوا	كُلْنَ

The conjugation of أَمَرَ "to command" is as below :

	Perf.	Imper. Indic.	Subj.	Juss.
3rd Pers. (M)	أَمَرَ	يَأْمُرُ	يَأْمُرَ	يَأْمُرْ
3rd Pers. (F)	أَمَرَتْ	تَأْمُرُ	تَأْمُرَ	تَأْمُرْ
2nd Pers. (M)	أَمَرْتَ	تَأْمُرُ	تَأْمُرَ	تَأْمُرْ
2nd Pers. (F)	أَمَرْتِ	تَأْمُرِينَ	تَأْمُرِي	تَأْمُرِي
1st Pers. (M & F)	أَمَرْتُ	آمُرُ	آمُرَ	آمُرْ

	Active Part.	Passive Part.
Singular Masc.	آمِـرٌ	مَـأْمُـورٌ
Singular Fem.	آمِـرَةٌ	مَـأْمُـورَةٌ
Plural Masc.	آمِـرُونَ	مَـأْمُـورُونَ
Plural Fem.	آمِـرَاتٌ	مَـأْمُـورَاتٌ

الأَمْـرُ – أَمْـرُ Verbal Noun يُؤْمَـرُ Imperfect أُمِـرَ Passive Perfect

Note : When this initial *hamzah* is followed by an *'alif* the latter is replaced by a prolonged vowel called *maddah*, e.g., in 1st Person Imperfect an *'alif* is prefixed to indicate imperfect as usual. Thus, the *hamzah* of initial radical and this *'alif* got together, and the two were assimilated in one with *maddah* sound as you see in the last row of the above conjugation.

In case of imperative, the conjugation from أَمَـرَ has already been given above. From other roots, such as أَكَلَ , the same rule will apply as:

أَخَـذَ = خُـذْ   أَكَلَ = كُلْ

Examples from The Holy Qur'ān :

1. Verbal Noun: الأَمَـرُ or أَمْـرُ "order, matter, duty, command, plan, task, etc."

Nominative: مَرْفُوعٌ

أَتَاهَا أَمْرُنَا لَـيْلًا أَوْ نَـهَارًا	10-24 There reaches it Our command by night or by day.
حَتَّىٰ إِذَا جَاءَ أَمْـرُنَا	11-40 But when there came Our command.

	Accusative : مَنْصُوبٌ

وَلَا أَعْصِى لَكَ أَمْـرًا	18-69 And I shall not dis-obey thee in aught.
فَأَجْمِعُوا أَمْرَكُمْ وَشُرَكَاءَكُمْ	10-71 Get ye then an agree-ment about your plan and your partners.

	Genetive : مَجْرُورٌ

وَآتَيْنَاهُمْ بَيِّنَاتٍ مِنَ الأَمْرِ	45-17 And We granted them clear signs in affairs.

2. Perfect :

لَا يَعْصُونَ اللهَ مَا أَمَـرَهُمْ	66-6 They flinch not (from executing) what Allah hath commanded them.
أَمَـرَ أَلَّا تَعْبُـدُوا إِلَّا إِيَّـاهُ	12-40 (3rd Pers. Masc.) He hath commanded that ye worship none but He.
مَا قُلْتُ لَهُمْ إِلَّا مَا أَمَرْتَنِي بِـهِ	5-117 (2nd P. Masc.) Never said I to them aught except what Thou commanded me
مَا مَنَعَكَ أَلَّا تَسْجُدَ إِذْ أَمَرْتُكَ	7-12 (Allah said:) what prevented thee from bowing when I commanded thee?

3. Imperfect Indicative :

إِنَّ اللهَ يَأْمُرُ بِالْعَدْلِ وَآلإِحْسَانِ	16-90 Allah commands justice and the doing of good.

وَكَانَ يَأْمُرُ أَهْلَهُ بِالصَّلَاةِ	19-55 And he used to com-mand his people for prayer.
فَانْظُرِي مَاذَا تَأْمُرِينَ	27-33 (2nd Pers. Imperf.) So consider what thou command.
وَيَقْتُلُونَ ٱلَّذِينَ يَأْمُرُونَ بِالْقِسْطِ مِنَ ٱلنَّاسِ	3-21 And they slay those who teach just dealing with mankind.
أَتَأْمُرُونَ ٱلنَّاسَ بِالْبِرِّ وَتَنْسَوْنَ أَنْفُسَكُمْ	2-44 (2nd Pers. Masc. Pl.) Do you command people to right conduct and forget yourselves?

4. Passive Perfect:

قُلْ إِنَّمَا أُمِرْتُ أَنْ أَعْبُدَ اللهَ وَلَا أُشْرِكَ بِهِ	13-36 (1st Pers. Perfect) Say I am commanded to worship Allah and not join partners with Him.

5. Passive Imperfect:

فَٱصْدَعْ بِمَا تُؤْمَرُ	15-94 Therefore, expound openly what you are commanded.
يَا أَبَتِ ٱفْعَلْ مَا تُؤْمَرُ	37-102 O' my father, do as thou art commanded.
فَٱفْعَلُوا مَا تُؤْمَرُونَ	2-68 (Now) do what you (Masc. Pl.) are commanded.

6. Imperfect Assimilated case (with *maddah*) :

وَلَئِن لَّمْ يَفْعَلْ مَا آمُرُهُ	12-32 And if he does not do what I command him…

7. Imperative (with *'alif*) :

وَأْمُـرْ أَهْلَكَ بِالصَّلَـوٰةِ وَآصْطَبِـرْ عَلَيْهَا	20-132 And command your (Masc. sing.) people to pray and be constant therein.

(b) Hamzah as middle radical :

The middle radical may be vowelled with *dammah*, *fatha* or *kasrah*.

In this case a *hamzah* will be written over an *'alif*.

Conjugation of سَأَلَ *sa'ala*, "to ask" :

	Perf.	Imperf. Indic.	Subj.	Jussive
3rd Pers. (M)	سَأَلَ	يَسْأَلُ	يَسْأَلَ	يَسْأَلْ
3rd Pers. (F)	سَأَلَتْ	تَسْأَلُ	تَسْأَلَ	تَسْأَلْ
2nd Pers. (M)	سَأَلْتَ	تَسْأَلُ	تَسْأَلَ	تَسْأَلْ
2nd Pers. (F)	سَأَلْتِ	تَسْأَلِينَ	تَسْأَلِي	تَسْأَلِي
1st Pers. (M & F)	سَأَلْتُ	أَسْأَلُ	أَسْأَلَ	أَسْأَلْ

Imperative :

2nd Pers. Sing. Masculine	سَـلْ or إِسْأَلْ
2nd Pers. Sing. Feminine	سَلِي or إِسْأَلِي

Active Part. سَائِلٌ
Passive Part. مَسْؤُولٌ , مَسْئُولٌ
Perfect Passive سُئِلَ
Imperfect يُسْأَلُ

Examples from The Holy Qur'ān :

Past Perfect :

3rd Person Singular Masculine

سَأَلَ سَائِلٌ بِعَذَابٍ وَاقِعٍ	70-1 A questioner has asked about the chastisement to befall.
سَأَلَهُمْ خَزَنَتُهَا: أَلَمْ يَأْتِكُمْ نَذِيرٌ	67-8 Its keepers asked them, did not come to you a warner?
اليَومَ يَئِسَ الَّذِينَ كَفَرُوا مِنْ دِينِكُمْ	5-3 This day have those who disbelieve despaired of your Religion.
كَمَا يَئِسَ الْكُفَّارُ مِن أَصْحَابِ الْقُـــبُورِ	60-13 as the disbelievers despaired of those in the graves.

3rd Person Plural Masculine

فَقَدْ سَأَلُوا مُوسَى أَكْبَرَ مِنْ ذَلِكَ	4-153 They demanded of Moses a greater thing than that.
أُولَئِكَ يَـئِسُوا مِن رَّحْمَتِي	29-23 They are who despaired of My Mercy.

2nd Person Singular Masculine

وَلَئِنْ سَأَلْتَهُمْ	29-61 And if thou ask them.

1st Person Singular

إِنْ سَأَلْتُكَ عَن شَيْءٍ بَـعْـدَهَا فَلَا تُصَاحِبْنِي	18-76 He said: if I ask thee about any thing after this, keep not company with me.

Imperfect Indicative :

3rd Person Singular Masculine

يَسْأَلُكَ أَهْلُ ٱلْكِتَابِ	4-153 The people of the Book ask thee.
يَسْأَلُ أَيَّانَ يَوْمُ ٱلْقِيَامَةِ	75-6 He asks: when is the Day of Resurrection?
لَا يَسْأَمُ الْإِنْسَانُ مِن دُعَاءِ ٱلْخَيْرِ	41-49 Man tires not of praying for good.

(From root « س ء م » "to get tired").

3rd Person Plural Masculine

يَسْأَلُونَكَ عَنِ الأهِلَّةِ	2-189 They ask thee of the new moon.
وَهُم لَا يَسْأَمُونَ	41-38 And they tire not.

1st Person Singular Masculine

وَمَا أَسْأَلُكُمْ عَلَيْهِ مِن أَجْرٍ	26-180 And I ask of you no reward for it.

Imperfect Subjunctive

لِيَسْأَلَ ٱلصَّادِقِينَ عَن صِدْقِهِم	33-8 That He may question the truthful of their truth.
قَالَ رَبِّ إِنِّي أَعُوذُ بِكَ أَنْ أَسْأَلَكَ مَا لَيْسَ لِي بِهِ عِلْمٌ	11-47 He said, O' my Lord! lest I may ask Thee that whereof I have no knowledge.
أَم تُرِيدُونَ أَنْ تَسْأَلُوا رَسُولَكُمْ	2-108 Or you wish to interrogate your messenger.

Negative (Jussive)

أَفَلَمْ يَـيْـأَس الَّذِينَ آمَنُوا	13-31 Are not those who believe convince that...

Passive Perfect :

كَمَا سُئِلَ مُـوسَى	2-108 as Moses was questioned.
وَإِذَا ٱلْمَوْءُودَةُ سُئِلَتْ	81-8 and when the one buried alive is asked.

(Root form د / ء / و (وأد) "to bury alive").

Passive Imperfect :

وَلَا تُسْأَلُ عَن أَصْحَابِ ٱلْجَحِيمِ	2-119 And thou will not be called upon to answer for the companions of the flaming fire.
وَلَا تُسْأَلُـونَ عَمَّا كَانُوا يَعْمَلُونَ	2-141 And you (Masc. Pl.) will not be asked of what they did.

Imperfect (with emphatic *nūn*) :

تَا ٱللَّهِ لَـتُسْأَلُـنَّ	16-56 By Allah! you shall certainly be questioned.

Active Part :

Sing. :	وَأَمَّا ٱلسَّائِلَ فَلَا تَنْهَرْ	93-10 And him who asks, chide not.
Plural:	آيَاتٌ لِلسَّائِلِينَ	12-7 Signs for the inquirers.

Passive Part :

Sing.: أُولَئِكَ كَانَ عَنْـهُ مَسْئُولاً	17-36 All of these will be asked.
Plural: وَقِفُوهُمْ إِنَّهُمْ مَسْئُولُونُ	37-24 And stop them, for they will be questioned.

Verbal Noun :

قَالَ لَقَدْ ظَلَمَكَ بِسُؤَالِ نَعْجَتِكَ	38-25 He said, surely he wronged thee in demanding thy ewe.
وَأَنْزَلْـنَا آلحَدِيدَ فِيـهِ بَأْسٌ شَدِيدٌ	57-25 And We sent down iron wherein is a great violence.

(c) Hamzah as Final Radical :

Conjugation of قَـرَأَ *qara'a*, "to read" :

	Perfect	Imperf. Indic.	Subj.	Jussive
3rd Person Masc.	قَـرَأَ	يَـقْرَأُ	يَـقْرَأَ	يَـقْرَأْ
3rd Person Fem.	قَـرَأَتْ	تَـقْرَأُ	تَـقْرَأَ	تَـقْرَأْ
2nd Person Masc.	قَـرَأَتَ	تَـقْرَأُ	تَـقْرَأَ	تَـقْرَأْ
2nd Person Fem.	قَـرَأَتِ	تَـقْرَئِينَ	تَـقْرَئِي	تَـقْرَئِي
1st Person Common	قَـرَأْتُ	أَقْـرَأُ	أَقْـرَأَ	أَقْـرَأْ

Imperative :

2nd Pers. Sing. Masc. إِقْـرَأْ	2nd Pers. Sing. Fem. إِقْـرَئِي
Active Part: قَارِئٌ *qāri'un*, or قَارِي *qāri*	Passive Part: مَقْـرُوءٌ
Passive Imperfect: يُـقْرَأُ ، يُـقْرَأَ ، يُـقْرَأْ	Passive Perfect: قُرِئَ

Examples from The Holy Qur'ān :

Perfect :

3rd Person Singular Masculine :

كَيْفَ بَدَأَ ٱلْخَلْقَ	29-20 How He made the first creation.
فَقَرَأَهُ عَلَيْهِمْ	26-199 And he had read it to them.

2nd Person Singular Masculine :

فَإِذَا قَرَأْتَ ٱلْقُرْآنَ	16-98 So when thou recitest the Qur'ān

1st Person Plural Common

كَمَا بَدَأْنَا أَوَّلَ خَلْقٍ نُعِيدُهُ	21-104 As We began the first creation We shall reproduce it.
فَإِذَا قَرَأْنَاهُ فَٱتَّبِعْ قُرْآنَهُ	75-18 So when We recite it, follow its recitation.

Imperfect :

3rd Person Singular Masculine :

إِنَّهُ يَبْدَأُ ٱلْخَلْقَ	10-4 He starts creation.

3rd Person Plural Masculine :

يَقْرَأُونَ ٱلْكِتَابَ	10-94 They read The Book.

2nd Person Masculine (Subjunctive) :

وَقُرْآنًا فَرَقْنَاهُ لِتَقْرَأَهُ عَلَى ٱلنَّاسِ	17-106 And it is a Qur'ān We have made distinct so that thou mayest read it to the people.

Imperative :

إِقْرَأْ بِاسْمِ رَبِّكَ ٱلَّذِي خَلَقَ	96-1 Read in the name of Thy Lord, Who creates...

Verbal Noun : القُرآن Qur'ān

فَٱتَّبِعْ قُرْآنَهُ	75-18 follow thou its reading.
وَقُرْآناً فَرَقْنَاهُ	17-106 and (it is) a Qur'ān that We have divided.

EXERCISE

1. **Translate into English :**

١ - قَالَ رَبِّ اشْرَحْ لِي صَدْرِي وَيَسِّرْ لِي أَمْرِي وَاحْلُلْ عُقْدَةً مِنْ لِسَانِي يَفْقَهُوا قَوْلِي وَاجْعَلْ لِي وَزِيرًا مِنْ أَهْلِي هَارُونَ أَخِي اشْدُدْ بِهِ أَزْرِي وَأَشْرِكْهُ فِي أَمْرِي كَيْ نُسَبِّحَكَ كَثِيرًا وَنَذْكُرَكَ كَثِيرًا إِنَّكَ كُنْتَ بِنَا بَصِيرًا ، قَالَ قَدْ أُوتِيتَ سُؤْلَكَ يَا مُوسَىٰ .

٢ - يَجِبُ أَنْ نَقْرَأَ ٱلْقُرْآنَ ، وَنَتَدَبَّرَ مَعَانِيهِ ، وَنَعْمَلَ بِأَوَامِرِ ٱلدِّينِ ٱلإِسْلَامِي ، حَتَّىٰ نَفُوزَ بِالسَّعَادَةِ فِي ٱلدُّنْيَا وَٱلآخِرَةِ .

٣ - إِتَّصِفْ بِالأَمَانَةِ وَٱلصِّدْقِ فِي مُعَامَلَتِكَ لِلنَّاسِ ، فَلَقَدْ عُرِفَ ٱلرَّسُولُ صَلَّى الله عَلَيْهِ وَسَلَّم بِهَاتَيْنِ ٱلصِّفَتَيْنِ ، وَنُودِيَ بَيْنَ قَوْمِهِ بِٱلصَّادِقِ ٱلأَمِينِ .

2. **Translate into Arabic :**

1. The teacher has explained the lesson to the students.
2. The Minister has written long reports on the matter.

284   ٢٨٤

3. Al-Mu'tamar al-Islami resolved (قَرَّرَ) to establish a Department for Islamic Jurisprudence.

4. The government has been requested to do something for the deserving officials.

5. Help your friend in time of anxiety. (الشِّدة)

6. I passed (مَررتُ بـ) by many fine buildings during my visit to Riyadh.

7. Affairs have settled down in the foreign companies.

8. It pleased me (أعْجَبني) very much to see you here this morning.

9. The Holy Qur'ān says : "Allah has not made two hearts in one body", which means one can not love two things equally. When the love of wealth occupies the heart of man, it does not leave enough space for the love of anything else. All considerations other than wealth become submerged and subservient to love of wealth. A great preacher of Islam is quoted saying: "It is not a sin to keep wealth at home, it is not sin to keep wealth in the hand but it is sin to keep wealth in the heart".

VOCABULARY

إشْرَحْ	(Imperative of) شَرَحَ - يَشْرَحُ to lay open.
صَدْرٌ	breast, heart, (Plural : صُدُورٌ).
يَسِّرْ	(Imperative of) يَسَّرَ II يُيَسِّرُ to make easy.
أَمْرٌ	matter, affair (Plural : أُمُورٌ).
أُحْلُلْ	(Imperative of) حَلَّ - يَحُلُّ to loose.
عُقْدَةٌ	knot (Plural : عُقَدٌ).
يَفْقَهُ	to understand.

إجْعَلْ	(Imperative of) جَعَلَ – يَجْعَلُ to make.
وَزِيرٌ	Aider, supporter.
أَشْـدُدْ	(Imperative of) شَـدَّ – يَشُدُّ to support.
أَزْرُ	arm.
أَشْرِكُ	(Imperfect 1st Pers. Sing.) أَشْرَكَ – يُشْرِكُ to make as partner.
كَيْ	in order to, so that.
نُسَبِّحَ	(Imperfect 1st Pers. Plural) سَبَّحَ to glorify.
أُوتِيتَ	(IV Passive case of) أَتَى – يُؤْتِي to be given.
سُؤْلٌ	demand, request, need.
نَذْكُرَ	(from ذَكَرَ – يَذْكُرُ) we remember.
يَجِبُ	to owe يَجِبُ أَنْ (subjunctive)
تُدَبِّرُ	to think over.
أَوَامِرُ	Plural of أَمْرٌ order, command.
حَتَّى	in order to.
فَـوْزٌ	success.
سَعَادَةٌ	Prosperity, happiness.
إتَّصَفَ	from وَصَفَ – يَصِفُ to be described by.
الأَمَانَةُ	trustworthiness, trust.
مُعَامَلَةٌ	dealings, treatment.

عُرِفَ	Passive of عَرَفَ to know.
نُودِيَ	Passive of نَادَى to be called, to be announced.
قَوْمٌ	folk, people.
صَادِقٌ	Truthful.
الأمِين	Trustworthy.

report	تَقْرِير (Plural تَقَارِير)
to establish	يُقِيمُ - أَقَامُ ، يُؤَسِّسُ - أَسَّسَ
Jurisprudence	الفِقْهُ
deserving	الْمُسْتَحَقُّ
companies	الشَّرِكَاتُ (Plural شَرِكَة)
equally	بِالْمُسَاوَاةِ
wealth	الْمَالُ
to occupy	يَشْغَلُ - شَغَلَ
place	مَكَانٌ
consideration	الإِعْتِبَارُ VIII إِعْتَبَرَ
to submerge	يَحْجُبُ
subservient	تَابِعٌ
to explain	شَرَحَ - يَشْرَحُ

CONJUGATION CHART

Verb : عَدَّ – يَعُدُّ (to count, to consider)   Verb Form : Doubled (I)

Imperative	Imperfect Subjunctive	Imperfect Jussive	Imperfect Indicative	Perfect	Pronoun
	A subjunctive particle such as (لَنْ) is needed	A jussive particle such as (لَمْ) is needed			Person or corresponding subject
	يَعُدَّ	يَعُدَّ / يَعْدُدْ	يَعُدُّ	عَدَّ	هُوَ
	تَعُدَّ	تَعُدَّ / تَعْدُدْ	تَعُدُّ	عَدَّتْ	هِيَ
	يَعُدُّوا	يَعُدُّوا	يَعُدُّونَ	عَدُّوا	هُمْ
	يَعْدُدْنَ	يَعْدُدْنَ	يَعْدُدْنَ	عَدَدْنَ	هُنَّ
	يَعُدَّا	يَعُدَّا	يَعُدَّانِ	عَدَّا	هُمَا (M)
	تَعُدَّا	تَعُدَّا	تَعُدَّانِ	عَدَّتَا	هُمَا (F)
عُدَّ / أُعْدُدْ	تَعُدَّ	تَعُدَّ / تَعْدُدْ	تَعُدُّ	عَدَدْتَ	أَنْتَ
عُدِّي	تَعُدِّي	تَعُدِّي	تَعُدِّينَ	عَدَدْتِ	أَنْتِ
عُدُّوا	تَعُدُّوا	تَعُدُّوا	تَعُدُّونَ	عَدَدْتُمْ	أَنْتُمْ
أُعْدُدْنَ	تَعْدُدْنَ	تَعْدُدْنَ	تَعْدُدْنَ	عَدَدْتُنَّ	أَنْتُنَّ
عُدَّا	تَعُدَّا	تَعُدَّا	تَعُدَّانِ	عَدَدْتُمَا	أَنْتُمَا (M+F)
	أَعُدَّ	أَعُدَّ / أَعْدُدْ	أَعُدُّ	عَدَدْتُ	أَنَا
	نَعُدَّ	نَعُدَّ / نَعْدُدْ	نَعُدُّ	عَدَدْنَا	نَحْنُ

Verbal Noun : عَدٌّ   Active Participle : عَادٌّ   Passive Participle : مَعْدُودٌ

Verb Characteristics :

* It has identical second and third radicals, written once with a *shaddah* on top of it.
* It has two stems, a regular one if the inflectional suffix begins with a consonant (-t or -n), and a doubled stem if the suffix begins with a vowel (-a, -ā, -u, -ū).
* If there is no inflectional suffix (i.e. *sukūn*) there is a choice of using either of the two stems.

CHAPTER 20

THE NUMERALS

The Cardinal Numbers

All numerals are not governed by a single rule, but in general terms they are treated as the declinable nouns; as their ending vowels are changed according to their cases, thus :

1. وَاحِدٌ "one" (in Nominative مَرْفُوعٌ case)
   Examples from The Holy Qur'ān :

| أَنَّمَا إِلَـهُكُمْ إِلَـهٌ وَاحِدٌ | 18-110 ...that your God is One God. |

(in Accusative مَنْصُوبٌ case) :

| وَمَا أُمِرُوا إِلَّا لِيَعْبُدُوا إِلَـهًا وَاحِدًا | 9-31 And they are enjoined that they should serve One God only. |

(in the Genitive مَجْرُورٌ case) :

| وَإِذْ قُلْتُمْ يَا مُوسَى لَنْ نَصْبِرَ عَلَى طَعَامٍ وَاحِدٍ | 2-61 And when you said : O' Musa (Moses) we can not bear with one food. |

The feminine form of وَاحِدٌ is وَاحِدَةٌ , i.e. with a feminine ending, e.g. :

| Nom. فَإِنَّمَا هِيَ زَجْرَةٌ وَاحِدَةٌ | 37-19 so it shall only be a single chiding. |

Acc.	كَانَ ٱلنَّاسُ أُمَّةً وَاحِدَةً	2-213	(all) People were a single nation.
Gen.	مِنْ نَفْسٍ وَاحِدَةٍ	4-1	...from a single being.

There is another form for "one" that is read أَحَدٌ , e.g. :

Nom.	قُلْ هُوَ اللهُ أَحَدٌ	112-1	say He, God, is One.
Acc.	وَلَا يُشْرِكُ فِي حُكْمِهِ أَحَدًا	18-26	And He does not make anyone His associate in His Judgement.
Gen.	هَلْ يَرَاكُمْ مِنْ أَحَدٍ	9-127	Does anyone see you?

إِحْدَى (with 'alif maqṣūrah) is feminine of أَحَدٌ , e.g.

وَإِذْ يَعِدُكُمُ اللهُ إِحْدَى الطَّائِفَتَيْنِ	8-7	And when Allah promised you one of two parties.

It is written with normal أَلِف as إِحْدَا when a pronoun is attached to it, e.g.

قَالَتْ إِحْدَاهُمَا : يَا أَبَتِ . . .	28-26	said one of the two girls : O' my father...

2. Two (masc.) : Nominative : إِثْنَانِ   Acc. & Gen. : إِثْنَيْنِ

   Two (fem.) : Nominative : إِثْنَيْنِ   Acc. & Gen. : إِثْنَتَيْنِ

   Examples from the Holy Qur'ān :

إِثْنَانِ ذَوَا عَدْلٍ مِنْكُمْ	5-106	two just persons from among you.

مِنَ ٱلضَّأْنِ ٱثْنَيْنِ وَمِنَ ٱلْمَعْزِ ٱثْنَيْنِ	6-143 two of sheep and two of goats.
فَإِنْ كُنَّ نِسَاءً فَوْقَ ٱثْنَتَيْنِ	4-11 But if there are more than two females...

3.   From 3 to 10 :

	Masc.	Fem.	
3	ثَلَاثٌ	ثَلَاثَةٌ	(also writen as ثَلَثٌ and ثَلَثَةٌ).
4	أَرْبَعُ	أَرْبَعَةٌ	
5	خَمْسُ	خَمْسَةٌ	
6	سِتٌّ	سِتَّةٌ	
7	سَبْعُ	سَبْعَةٌ	
8	ثَمَانٍ	ثَمَانِيَةٌ	(also writen as ثَمْنٍ and ثَمْنِيَةٌ).
9	تِسْعُ	تِسْعَةٌ	
10	عَشَرُ	عَشَرَةٌ	

The Arabic equivalent of phrases like "three books" or "five women", where the numeral is one of those from "three" to "ten" inclusive, is an 'iḍāfah construction. The numeral serves as the first term of the 'iḍāfah and thus has no "nunation", and takes whatever case its function in the sentence requires; the counted noun serves as the second term of the 'iḍāfah and is always **genitive, plural** and **indefinite** :

Nom.	حَضَرَ ثَلَاثَةُ رِجَالٍ	"Three men came".
	حَضَرَتْ ثَلَاثُ نِسَاءٍ	"Three women came".
Acc.	قَابَلْتُ ثَلَاثَةَ رِجَالٍ	"I met three men".
	قَابَلْتُ ثَلَاثَ نِسَاءٍ	"I met three women".
Gen.	تَحَدَّثْتُ إِلَى ثَلَاثَةِ رِجَالٍ	"I talked to three man".
	تَحَدَّثْتُ إِلَى ثَلَاثِ نِسَاءٍ	"I talked to three women".

In construction of this type, each number has two forms: one with final ـة tā' marbūṭah (the feminine form) and one without it (the masculine form). It is important to not that there is a rule of **reversed agreement of genders** for these numerals in relation to the counted nouns associated with them. This means that if the counted noun is masculine, the feminine form of the numerals is used with it, and vice versa.

Note : The masculine form ثَمَانٍ "eight" belongs to a group of nouns called **defective**. When followed by a noun, the missing ي yā' is restored, and thus it will assume the following forms :

Nom. and/or Gen.	حَضَرَتْ ثَمَانِي طَالِبَاتٍ	'Eight (female) students came'.
	سَلَّمْتُ عَلَى ثَمَانِي طَالِبَاتٍ	I saluted eight (female) students'.
Acc.	قَابَلْتُ ثَمَانِيَ مُدَرِّسَاتٍ	'I met eight (female) students'.

Examples from The Holy Qur'ān :

ثَلَاثَ لَيَالٍ	19-10	three nights
ثَلَاثَةِ أَيَّامٍ	2-196	three days
أَرْبَعُ شَهَادَاتٍ	24-6	four witnesses
أَرْبَعَةِ أَيَّامٍ	41-10	four days

(Not from the Holy Qur'ān) خَمْسَ مَرَّاتٍ five times.

خَمْسَةٌ ، سَادِسُهُمْ كَلْبُهُمْ	18-22	(they are) five, the sixth is their dog.
سِتَّةِ أَيَّامٍ	7-53	(in) six days.

(Not from the Holy Qur'ān) سِتَّ لَيَالٍ six nights.

سَبْعَ بَقَرَاتٍ	12-43	seven cows.
سَبْعَةُ أَبْوَابٍ	15-44	seven doors.
ثَمَانِيَ حِجَجٍ	6-143	eight pilgrimages.
ثَمَانِيَةَ أَيَّامٍ	69-7	eight days.
تِسْعَ آيَاتٍ	17-101	nine signs.
تِسْعَةُ رَهْطٍ	27-48	nine persons.
عَشْرُ أَمْثَالِهَا	6-160	ten likt it.
عَشَرَةِ مَسَاكِينَ	5-89	ten poor men.

Note : The gender of the numerals depends on the singular form of the noun and not on its plural form.

4. 11 and 12

	Masc.	Fem.	
11	أَحَدَ عَشَرَ	إِحْدَىٰ عَشْرَةَ	
12	إِثْنَا عَشَرَ	إِثْنَتَا عَشْرَةَ	in the Nominative case.
	إِثْنَيْ عَشَرَ	إِثْنَتَيْ عَشْرَةَ	in the Accusative case.

Examples from The Holy Qur'ān :

Nom.	Masc.	أَحَدَ عَشَرَ كَوْكَبًا	12-4	eleven stars.
	Masc.	إِثْنَا عَشَرَ شَهْرًا	9-36	twelve months.
	Fem.	إِثْنَتَا عَشْرَةَ عَيْنًا	2-60	twelve springs.
Acc. Masc.		وَبَعَثْنَا مِنْهُمُ إِثْنَيْ عَشَرَ نَقِيبًا	5-12	and We raised up among them twelve chieftains.
Acc. Fem.		وَقَطَّعْنَاهُمُ اثْنَتَيْ عَشْرَةَ أَسْبَاطًا	7-160	And We divided them into twelve tribes.

5. From 13 to 19

	with Masc. nouns	with Fem. nouns		with Masc. nouns	with Fem. nouns
13	ثَلَاثَةَ عَشَرَ	ثَلَاثَ عَشْرَةَ	17	سَبْعَةَ عَشَرَ	سَبْعَ عَشْرَةَ
14	أَرْبَعَةَ عَشَرَ	أَرْبَعَ عَشْرَةَ	18	ثَمَانِيَةَ عَشَرَ	ثَمَانِي عَشْرَةَ
15	خَمْسَةَ عَشَرَ	خَمْسَ عَشْرَةَ	19	تِسْعَةَ عَشَرَ	تِسْعَ عَشْرَةَ
16	سِتَّةَ عَشَرَ	سِتَّ عَشْرَةَ			

All the numerals from 11 to 99 are followed by a **singular noun in the Accusative** as they are تَمْيِيز *tamyīz* "nouns of specification", e.g. :

ثَلَاثَ عَشْرَةَ طَالِبَةً	13 female students.
أَرْبَعَ عَشْرَةَ بِنْتًا	14 girls.
ثَلَاثَةَ عَشَرَ طَالِبًا	13 male students.
أَرْبَعَةَ عَشَرَ وَلَدًا	14 boys.

Note : All these are indeclinable, i.e. their ending vowels can not be changed due to their preceding elements. Thus

قَرَأْتُ ثَلَاثَةَ عَشَرَ كِتَابًا	I read 13 books.
وَجَدْتُ فِي ثَلَاثَةَ عَشَرَ كِتَابًا	I found in 13 books.

6. From 20 to 90

The multiples of ten, 20 to 90 are common to masculine and feminine:

	Nominative	Accusative and Genetive		Nominative	Accusative and Genetive
20	عِشْرُونَ	عِشْرِينَ	60	سِتُّونَ	سِتِّينَ
30	ثَلَاثُونَ	ثَلَاثِينَ	70	سَبْعُونَ	سَبْعِينَ
40	أَرْبَعُونَ	أَرْبَعِينَ	80	ثَمَانُونَ	ثَمَانِينَ
50	خَمْسُونَ	خَمْسِينَ	90	تِسْعُونَ	تِسْعِينَ

All these numbers from 20 to 99, like these from 11 to 19, are followed by a noun of *tamyīz* (noun of specification) in the accusative singular form.

Examples from The Holy Qur'ān :

وَفِصَالُهُ ثَلَاثُونَ شَهْرًا	46-15 And his weaning is thirty months.
وَوَاعَدْنَا مُوسَىٰ ثَلَاثِينَ لَيْلَةً	7-142 And we appointed with Musa (Moses) a time of thirty nights.
وَإِذْ وَاعَدْنَا مُوسَىٰ أَرْبَعِينَ لَيْلَةً	2-51 And when we appointed with Musa (Moses) a time of forty nights.
وَبَلَغَ أَرْبَعِينَ سَنَةً	46-15 ...and reached 40 years.
إِلَّا خَمْسِينَ عَامًا	29-14 excluding 50 years.
فَإِطْعَامُ سِتِّينَ مِسْكِينًا	58-4 so feeding of 60 poors.
ذَرْعُهَا سَبْعُونَ ذِرَاعًا	69-32 The length of which is seventy cubits.
وَاخْتَارَ مُوسَىٰ قَوْمَهُ سَبْعِينَ رَجُلًا	7-155 And Musa (Moses) chose out of his people seventy men...

7.   From 21 to 99

	Masculine	Feminine
21	وَاحِدٌ وَعِشْرُونَ	وَاحِدَةٌ وَعِشْرُونَ / إِحْدَىٰ وَعِشْرُونَ
22	إِثْنَانِ وَعِشْرُونَ	إِثْنَتَانِ وَعِشْرُونَ

... and so on.

8. From 100 upwards

100	مِئَةٌ	Also written مَائَةٌ
200	مِئَتَانِ	Also written مَائَتَانِ
300	ثَلَاثُ مِئَةٍ	
400	أَرْبَعُ مِئَةٍ	
500	خَمْسُ مِئَةٍ	
600	سِتُّ مِئَةٍ	
700	سَبْعُ مِئَةٍ	
800	ثَمَانِي مِئَةٍ	
900	تِسْعُ مِئَةٍ	
1000	أَلْفٌ	
2000	أَلْفَانِ	
3000	ثَلَاثَةُ آلَافٍ	

etc. to 10,000

100,000	مِئَةُ أَلْفٍ
Million	مِلْيُون Plural: مَلَايِين

Note : These numerals from 100 are nouns and take their following noun in the Genetive Singular.

In compound numerals over 100 the noun follows the rule governing its relation to the last element and the number.

Thus "103 men" the rule for 3 must be followed. Therefore the noun must be in the Genitive plural, e.g.:

103 boys.   مَائَةٌ وَثَلَاثَةُ أَوْلَادٍ

The Ordinal Numbers

1. The ordinal numbers from 1 to 10 are formed on the pattern of the active participle، فَاعِلٌ ، derived from cardinals; except الأَوَّلُ - الأُولَىٰ "the first" which has a special form.

Masculine	Feminine	
الأَوَّلُ	الأُولَىٰ	the first
الثَّاني	الثَّانِيَةُ	the second (without article ثانٍ)
الثَّالِثُ	الثَّالِثَةُ	the third
الرَّابِعُ	الرَّابِعَةُ	the fourth
الخَامِسُ	الخَامِسَةُ	the fifth
السَّادِسُ	السَّادِسَةُ	the sixth
السَّابِعُ	السَّابِعَةُ	the seventh
الثَّامِنُ	الثَّامِنَةُ	the eighth
التَّاسِعُ	التَّاسِعَةُ	the ninth
العَاشِرُ	العَاشِرَةُ	the tenth

The ending vowels of the above change according to their declension.

Examples from The Holy Qur'ān :

هُوَ ٱلأَوَّلُ وَٱلآخِرُ	57-3 He is the First and the Last.
ثَانِيَ ٱثْنَيْنِ إِذْ هُمَا فِي ٱلْغَارِ	9-40 the second of the two when they were in the cave.

فَعَزَّزْنَا بِثَالِثٍ	36-14 then We strengthened them with a third.
ثَلَاثَةٌ رَابِعُهُمْ كَلْبُهُمْ	18-22 (they are) Three, the fourth of them is their dog.
وَالْخَامِسَةُ أَنَّ لَعْنَةَ اللهِ عَلَيْهِ إِنْ كَانَ مِنَ ٱلْكَاذِبِينَ	24-7 And the fifth (time) that the curse of Allah be on him if he is one of the liars.
سَادِسُهُمْ كَلْبُهُمْ	1822 Their sixth is their dog.

After 10, the cardinal numbers are used as Ordinals, so far as the above numbers are included in them.

Masculine	Feminine	
الْحَادِيَ عَشَرَ	الْحَادِيَةَ عَشْرَةَ	the eleventh
الثَّانِيَ عَشَرَ	الثَّانِيَةَ عَشْرَةَ	the twelth
الثَّالِثَ عَشَرَ	الثَّالِثَةَ عَشْرَةَ	the thirteenth
الرَّابِعَ عَشَرَ	الرَّابِعَةَ عَشْرَةَ	the fourteenth

Higher numbers run as follows :
"The twentieth" الْعِشْرُونَ for both Masculine and Feminine.

Masculine	Feminine	
الْحَادِيَ وَٱلْعِشْرُونَ	الْحَادِيَةُ وَٱلْعِشْرُونَ	the twenty first
الثَّانِيَ وَٱلْعِشْرُونَ	الثَّانِيَةُ وَٱلْعِشْرُونَ	the twenty second
الثَّالِثَ وَٱلْعِشْرُونَ	الثَّالِثَةُ وَٱلْعِشْرُونَ	the twenty third

"The hundredth" أَلْمِئَةُ for both Masculine and Feminine.

$$\boxed{\textbf{EXERCISE}}$$

1. **Translate into Arabic :**

The Holy Qur'ān is divided into one hundred fourteen chapters; each of which is called a *sūrah* سُورَة . These chapters or
suwar سُوَر (plural of سُورَة) are not of equal length. The
highest number of verses in a chapter is two hundred eighty six
and the smallest only three verses. The total number of verses
in the Holy Qur'ān is six thousand four hundred and forty
seven. For the purpose of recitation the Holy Qur'ān is also
divided into thirty parts of equal length, called a جُـزْء ; every
part being again subdivided into four quarters. But these divi-
sions have nothing to do with the subject-matter of the Holy
Qur'ān, and so also the division into seven *manāzil* or por-
tions, which is meant only for the completion of the recital of
the Holy Qur'ān in seven days. The Qur'ān was revealed
piecemeal during a period of twenty three years. The First
Chapter of the Holy Qur'ān is سُورَةُ ٱلْفَاتِحَـة *Sūrat-ul-Fātiḥah*
that means "The Opening Chapter". It consists of seven verses.

The second chapter is known as سُورَةُ ٱلْبَقَـرَة *Sūrat-ul-Baqarah*
(The Cow). *Sūrat-ul-'Anfāl* سُورَةُ الأَنْـفَال (The Accession) is
the eight, and سُورَةُ ٱلتَّوَبَـة *Sūrat-tu-Tawbah* (The Immunity)
is the ninth among the chapters of the Holy Qur'ān.

300   ٣٠٠

2. Translate into English :

وُلِدَ مُحَمَّدٌ صَلَّى اللهُ عَلَيْهِ وَسَلَّمَ يَتِيمًا وَمَاتَتْ أُمُّهُ وَهُوَ ابْنُ ثَلَاثِ سَنَوَاتٍ
وَكَفِلَهُ عَمُّهُ أَبُوطَالِبٍ . تَزَوَّجَ السَّيِّدَةَ خَدِيجَةَ بِنْتِ خُوَيْلِدٍ عِنْدَمَا بَلَغَ
الْخَامِسَةَ وَالْعِشْرِينَ مِنْ عُمْرِهِ . وَكَانَ عُمْرُ السَّيِّدَةِ خَدِيجَةَ آنَذَاكَ أَرْبَعِينَ
عَامًا . وَبَعَثَهُ اللهُ نَبِيًّا وَأَنْزَلَ عَلَيْهِ أَوَّلَ وَحْيٍ عِنْدَمَا بَلَغَ أَرْبَعِينَ عَامًا مِنْ
عُمْرِهِ . وَبَقِيَ بِمَكَّةَ الْمُكَرَّمَةَ ثَلَاثَ عَشْرَةَ سَنَةً . ثُمَّ هَاجَرَ إِلَى الْمَدِينَةِ
الْمُنَوَّرَةِ حَيْثُ عَاشَ عَشَرَ سَنَوَاتٍ . وَقَبْلَ أَنْ يُهَاجِرَ إِلَى الْمَدِينَةِ عَاشَ ثَلَاثَ
سَنَوَاتٍ فِي شِعْبِ أَبِي طَالِبٍ ، عِنْدَمَا قَاطَعَتْهُ قُرَيْشٌ .

قَدْ فَرَضَ اللهُ عَلَى الْمُسْلِمِينَ الصَّوْمَ فِي الْعَامِ الثَّانِي لِلْهِجْرَةِ ، وَ
وَقَعَتْ مَعْرَكَةُ « بَدْرٍ » فِي الْعَامِ نَفْسِهِ . وَبَعْدَ سَنَةٍ وَاحِدَةٍ وَقَعَتْ مَعْرَكَةُ
أُحُدٍ .

وَتَمَّ فَتْحُ مَكَّةَ الْمُكَرَّمَةِ فِي الْعَامِ الْعَاشِرِ مِنَ الْهِجْرَةِ ، وَتُوُفِّيَ رَسُولُ اللهِ
صَلَّى اللهُ عَلَيْهِ وَسَلَّمَ فِي الثَّالِثَةِ وَالسِّتِّينَ مِنْ عُمْرِهِ ، وَقَدْ أَكْمَلَ اللهُ لَهُ
الدِّينَ وَأَتَمَّ عَلَيْهِ نِعْمَتَهُ وَرَضِيَ لَهُ الْإِسْلَامَ دِينًا .

VOCABULARY

divided	مُوَزَّعٌ Passive Participle of وَزَّع II, also تُقْسَمُ
the division	التَّوْزِيعُ - التَّقْسِيمُ
equal	مُتَسَاوٍ Active Participle of تَسَاوى VI to be equal سَوَّى
length	الطُّولُ
the highest number	أَكْبَرُ عَدَدٍ
the smallest number	أَصْغَرُ عَدَدٍ
total	المَجْمُوع
nothing to do with	لَا صِلَةَ لَهُ بِـ - عَدِيمُ الصِّلَةِ بِـ
portions	حِصَصٌ Plural of حِصَّةُ
completion	تَكْمِلَةُ (v.n.) or إِتْمَامٌ (v.n.) of IV
piecemeals	نُجُوما نَجْمَ or قِطْعَةُ Plural of

orphan	يَتِيمٌ
birthday, time of birth	مَوْلِدٌ
took him in his guardianship	كَفِلَهُ
married	تَزَوَّجَ

302   ٣٠٢

then	آنَذَاك
sent as a messenger	بَعَثَ
Revelation	الْـوَحْيُ
immigrated	هَاجَرَ
lived	عَاشَ
to boycott	قَاطَعَ
battle	مَعْرَكَةٌ
conquest	فَتْحٌ
died	تُـوُفِّيَ
completed	أَكْـمَلَ
fulfilled	أَتَـمَّ
agreed, confirmed upon	رَضِيَ لـ

CHAPTER 21

PRONOUNS : DEMONSTRATIVE, RELATIVE AND INTERROGATIVE

A. Demonstrative Pronouns : إِسْمُ ٱلْإِشَارَة *'ismu-l-'ishārah* have two forms, one for near distance and another for far-distance.

1. Demonstrative Pronouns for near distance إِسْمُ ٱلْإِشَارَة لِلْقَرِيب are as below :

	Masculine		Feminine		
Singular, all cases	هٰذَا	*hādhā*	هٰذه	*hādhihi*	this
Dual, Nominative	هٰذَان	*hādhāni*	هَاتَان	*hātāni*	these
Dual, Accusative, Dual, Genitive	هٰذَيْن	*hādhayni*	هَاتَـيْن	*hātayni*	these
Plural, all cases	هـٰؤُلَاء		*hā'ulā'i*		these

It is to be noted that *hādhā* هٰذَا is not written with a full *'alif* after ـهـ as it was supposed to, but instead of هَاذَا it is written with a short vertical stroke above the letter : هٰذَا = هـ .

We have a plural form common to both genders that is هُؤُلَاء but it is used only for human beings. Otherwise, هٰذه singular form of the feminine, is enough to refer to the collective or plural non-human nouns. The following examples from the Holy Qur'ān will illustrate the rules :

هٰـذَا	

وَهٰـذَا كِتَابٌ مُصَدِّقٌ	46-12 And, this is a Book that verifies (previous divine books).
وَهٰـذَا بَعْلِي شَيْخًا	11-72 And this is my husband, an old man.
أَنَا يُوسُفُ وَهٰـذَا أَخِي	12-90 I am Joseph and this is my brother.

هٰـذَانِ	

قَالُوا إِنْ هٰـذَانِ لَسَاحِرَانِ	20-63 They said: These are two enchanters.

هٰـذِهِ	

قُلْ هٰـذِهِ سَبِيلِي	12-108 Say: This is my way.
إِنَّ هٰـذِهِ أُمَّتُكُمْ أُمَّةً وَاحِدَةً	21-92 Surely, This your community is a single community.
مَا هٰـذِهِ التَّمَاثِيلُ ٱلَّتِي أَنْـتُمْ لَـهَا عَاكِفُونَ	21-52 What are these images to whose worship you cleave.

Note : سَبِيلٌ "way" is a feminine noun.

أُمَّةٌ "community" is a collective noun.

تَمَاثِيلُ plural of تِمْثَالٌ "image".

Dual Feminine for the accusative and genitive cases.

Examples from the Holy Qur'ān :

	هَاتَيْنِ

إِحْدَى ٱبْنَتَيَّ هَاتَيْنِ	28-27 One of these two daughters.

	هَـٰؤُلَاءِ

كُلًّا نُمِدُّ هَـٰؤُلَاءِ وَهَـٰؤُلَاءِ مِنْ عَطَاءِ رَبِّكَ	17-20 All do We aid-these as well as those out of the bounty of thy Lord.
يَا قَوْمِ هَـٰؤُلَاءِ بَنَاتِي هُنَّ أَطْهَرُ لَكُمْ	11-78 O' my people! these are my daughters, they are purer for you.

2. Demonstrative pronouns for a far distance إِسْمُ ٱلْإِشَارَةِ لِلْبَعِيدِ are as following :

Masc. Sing. ذٰلِكَ, also written as ذَالِكَ *dhālika,* "that", e.g. (from the Holy Qur'ān) :

ذٰلِكَ ٱلْكِتَابُ لَا رَيْبَ فِيهِ	2-2 That is The Book; No doubt in it.

It is also used for things of the near distance in order to emphasise the greatness or seriousness of the object pointed at, e.g. (from the Holy Qur'ān) :

ذٰلِكَ مَا كُنَّا نَبْغِ	18-64 This was what we wanted.

Further this pronoun is basically a combination of ذَا *dhā* that is real pronoun and لَكَ "for you". Consequently if the address is more than one, it could be changed from ذَالِكَ to ذَالِكُمْ *dhālikum*, i.e. 'This is to be demonstrated for you people', e.g. (from the Holy Qur'ān :

ذلِكُمْ وَصَّاكُمْ بِهِ	6-151 That is what He enjoins you.

Feminine Singular تِلْكَ *tilka*, "that, this", e.g. (from the Holy Qur'ān):

تِلْكَ أُمَّةٌ قَدْ خَلَتْ	2-134 That is a nation who have passed away.
تِلْكَ ٱلرُّسُلُ فَضَّلْنَا بَعْضَهُمْ عَلَىٰ بَعْضٍ	2-253 Those are the messengers, We made some of them excel others.
وَمَا تِلْكَ بِيَمِينِكَ يَا مُوسَىٰ	20-17 and what is this in thy right hand, O' Moses?

In the Arabic usage there are forms for duals such as ذَانِكَ *dhānika*, ذَيْنِكَ *dhainika*, for masculine and تَانِكَ *tānika* and تَيْنِكَ *tainaka*, for feminine, but these forms neither have occured in the Holy Qur'ān nor in the modern use.

The plural form common to the masculine and feminine is أُولَئِكَ *'ulā'ika*, that is written as أُولَٰئِكَ , e.g. (from the Holy Qur'ān) :

أُولَٰئِكَ عَلَىٰ هُدًى مِن رَّبِّهِمْ وَأُولَٰئِكَ هُمُ ٱلْمُفْلِحُونَ	2-5 These are on a right course from their Lord and these are successful.

B. The Relative Pronoun الإِسْمُ ٱلْمَوْصُولُ *'al-'ismu-l-mawṣūlu*, is expressed by ٱلَّذِي *'alladhī*, that has a defined form as follows:

	Sing.	Dual	Plural
Masc. Nominative	ٱلَّذِي	ٱللَّذَانِ	ٱلَّذِينَ
Masc. Accusative and Genetive	ٱلَّذِي	ٱللَّذَيْنِ	ٱلَّذِينَ
Fem. Nominative	ٱلَّتِي	ٱللَّتَانِ	ٱلَّئِي or ٱلَّتِي
Fem. Accusative and Genetive	ٱلَّتِي	ٱللَّتَيْنِ	ٱلَّئِي

Examples from the Holy Qur'ān :

ٱلَّذِي (Masc. singular, in all case) :

هُوَ ٱلَّذِي أَرْسَلَ رَسُولَهُ بِٱلْهُدَى	48-28 He is Who hath sent His messenger with the guidance.
وَٱلَّذِي جَاءَ بِٱلصِّدْقِ وَصَدَّقَ بِهِ أُولَئِكَ هُمُ ٱلْمُتَّقُونَ	39-33 And who so bringeth the truth and believeth therein, such are the dutiful.
ٱلله ٱلَّذِي لَا إِلَهَ إِلَّا هُوَ	59-22 He is Allah, beside Him there is no other god.

ٱلَّذَانِ (Masc. dual, nominative case) :

وَٱلَّذَانِ يَأْتِيَانِهَا مِنْكُمْ فَآذُوهُمَا	4-16 And as for two of you who are guilty of it, give them both a slight punishment.

ٱلَّذَيْنِ (Masc. dual, accusative and genitive case) :

رَبَّنَا أَرِنَا ٱلَّذَيْنِ أَضَلَّانَا	41-29 Our Lord! show us those (two) who led us astray.

ٱلَّـذِينَ (Masc. plural, in all cases) :

وَٱلَّـذِينَ آمَنُوا أَشَدُّ حُبًّا لله	2-165 and those who believe, are stronger in their love for Allah.
وَلَوْ يَـرَى ٱلَّذِينَ ظَلَمُوا إِذْ يَـرَوْنَ ٱلْعَذَابَ أَنَّ ٱلْقُوَّةَ لله جَمِيعًا	2-165 ...and O' that the wrongdoers had seen, when they see the chastisement, that power is wholly Allah's.
إِذْ تَـبَرَّأَ ٱلَّذِينَ ٱتُّبِعُوا مِـنَ ٱلَّذِينَ ٱتَّـبَعُوا	2-166 When those who were followed denounce those who followed.
وَقَالَ ٱلَّذِينَ ٱتَّـبَعُوا لَوْ أَنَّ لَـنَا كَرَّةً	2-167 And those who followed will say: If we could have our return.

ٱلَّـتِي (Fem. singular, for all cases) :

ٱدْفَعْ بِٱلَّـتِي هِيَ أَحْسَنُ	41-34 Repel (evil) with what is best.
وَٱلَّـتِي لَمْ تَمُتْ فِي مَـنَامِهَا	39-42 and that (soul) which dieth not (yet) in its sleep.

ٱللَّاتِي *'allātī* and ٱلَّـئِي *'allā'ī* (Fem. plural of ٱلَّـتِي) :

وَٱلَّـتِي يَـأْتِـيْنَ ٱلْـفَاحِشَةَ مِنْ نِسَائِكُمْ	4-15 and as for those of your women who are guilty of indecency.
وَٱللَّـئِي يَـئِسْنَ مِنَ ٱلْمَحِيضِ	65-4 and those (women) who despair of a menstruation.
وَٱللَّـئِي لَمْ يَحِضْنَ	65-4 and those who have not (yet) manstruation.

C. Interrogative Pronouns اِسْمُ ٱلْإِسْتِفْهَام 'ismu-l-'istifhām, are :

I. مَنْ man, "who"

Examples from the Holy Qur'ān :

مَنْ خَلَقَ ٱلسَّمَـٰوَاتِ وَٱلْأَرْضَ	29-61 Who created the heavens and the earth?
مَنْ فَعَلَ هَـٰذَا بِآلِـهَتِـنَا	21-59 Who has done this to our gods?
قُـلْ فَمَنْ يَمْلِكُ مِنَ اللهِ شَيْئًا	5-17 Say: Who then can control anything against Allah?

Sometimes a demonstrative pronoun ذَا dhā, is attached after مَنْ man, to denote implied negative meaning, e.g. (from the Holy Qur'ān) :

مَنْ ذَا ٱلَّذِي يَشْفَعُ عِنْدَهُ إِلَّا بِإِذْنِـه	2-255 Who is he that can intercede with Him but by His permission?

It is also sometimes, preceded by a particle of preposition or conjunction and in this case the مِنْ min of مَنْ man, is assimilated with a final letter of that particle thus :

The combination of عَنْ and مِنْ is عَمَّنْ 'amman, "from whom", or it is combined with أَمْ of conjunction, "or" as أَمَّنْ 'amman "or how?", e.g. (from the Holy Qur'ān) :

أَمَّـنْ هُوَ قَانِتٌ أَنَاءَ ٱلَّـيْلِ	39-9 or is he who is obedient during hours of the night?

| قُـلْ مَنْ يَـرْزُقُكُـم مِنَ ٱلسَّـمَـاءِ وَٱلْأَرْضِ أَمَّـنْ يَمْـلِكُ ٱلسَّـمْـعَ وَٱلْأبْصَـارَ وَمَنْ يُخْـرِجُ ٱلْحَيَّ مِنَ ٱلْمَيِّتِ وَيُخْـرِجُ ٱلْمَيِّتَ مِنَ ٱلْحَيِّ وَمَنْ يُـدَبِّـرُ ٱلْأَمْـرَ | 10-31 Say : Who gives you sustenance from the heaven and the earth, or Who controls the hearing and the sight, and Who brings forth the living from the dead and brings forth the dead from the living and Who regulates the affairs? |

Besides denoting the meaning of an interrogative pronoun مَـنْ is also a particle of the relative noun, that gives the meaning of "who, that" or "which", e.g. (from the Holy Qur'ān) :

وَقَـدْ خَابَ مَـنِ ٱفْـتَـرَىٰ	20-61 And he fails indeed who forges (a lie).
مَنْ خَشِيَ ٱلرَّحْمَـٰنَ بِٱلْغَيْبِ وَجَآءَ بِقَلْبٍ مُنِيبٍ	50-33 Who fears Ar-Raḥmān in secret and comes with a contrite heart.
فَمَنْ شَرِبَ مِنْـهُ فَلَيْسَ مِنِّي وَمَنْ لَمْ يَطْعَمْـهُ فَإِنَّـهُ مِنِّي إِلَّا مَنِ ٱغْتَـرَفَ غُـرْفَـةً بِـيَدِهِ	2-249 Whoever drinks from it he is not of me and whoever taste it not, he is surely of me except who he takes handful with his hand.

II. مَا "what", e.g. (from the Holy Qur'ān) :

| قَالُوا وَمَا ٱلرَّحْمَـٰنُ | 25-60 ... they say : what is Ar-Raḥmān ? |
| مَا هَـٰذِهِ ٱلتَّمَاثِيلُ | 21-52 What are these images? |

A particle of the demonstrative ذَا *dhā* is placed after مَا, if the interrogative sentence begins with a verb e.g. (from the Holy Qur'ān) :

فَأَرُونِي مَاذَا خَلَقَ	31-11 then show me what he has created.
مَاذَا أَرَادَ اللهُ بِهَـذَا مَثَلًا	2-26 what is it that Allah means by this parable !
أَرُونِي مَاذَا خَلَقُوا مِنَ الْأَرْضِ	35-40 Show me what they created from the earth.

After some preposition it is sometimes written مَ (i.e. with a short vowel *fatḥah* instead of a long vowel 'alif أَلِفْ) as لِمَ "for what, why?" (For لِمَا *lima* or لِمَاذَا *limādhā*), likewise, after عَنْ as عَمَّ i.e. عَنْ + مَا = عَمَّا shortened to عَمَّ "of what, what about", but only in case of a question, e.g. (from the Holy Qur'ān) :

لِمَ أَذِنْتَ لَهُم	9-43 Why didst thou permit them?
عَمَّ يَـتَسَاءَلُونَ	78-1 Of what they ask one another?

Otherwise, the أَلِفْ of مَا remains even after prefixing عَنْ or لِ .

Students may note that there are three usages of (مَا) :

1. as negative particle as :

مَا فَعَلْتُ هٰذَا بِأَمْرِي	I did not do it with my own decision.

2. as interrogative particle as :

مَا تِلْكَ بَيَمِينِكَ	What is this in thy right hand?

3. as a relative pronoun as :

هَـٰذَا مَا وَعَدَ ٱلرَّحْمَـٰنُ   This is what Ar-Raḥmān had promised.

Apart from the contents, the meaning of مَا can be known by its place with a noun or verb : if it is placed before past tense it will denote a negative as مَا فَعَلَ "he did not do", if it is before a noun, then it means an interrogation as مَا هُوَ "what is he?" or before an imperfect verb مَا يَفْعَلُ ٱللهُ بِعَذَابِكُمْ "what shall Allah do by giving you punishment?" As a relative pronoun it is always placed before a verb, thus : (from the Holy Qur'ān)

لَهَا مَا كَسَبَتْ وَعَلَيْهَا مَا ٱكْتَسَبَتْ	2-286 For it is that which it earns (of good) and against it that it works (of evil).
أَفَرَأَيْـتُم مَّا تُمْنُونَ	56-58 See you that which you emit?
أَفَرَأَيْـتُم مَّا تَحْرُثُونَ	56-63 See you what you sow?
هَـٰذَا مَا وَعَدَ ٱلرَّحْمَـٰنُ وَصَدَقَ ٱلْمُرْسَلُونَ	36-52 This is what Allah (Ar-Raḥmān) promised and the messengers told the truth.

III. أَيٌّ 'ayyun, Fem. أَيَّةٌ 'ayyatun, "which", is declinable (مُعْرَب) and is treated as a noun so takes a following noun in genitive, e.g. أَيُّ رَجُلٍ "which man?", أَيَّةُ بِنْتٍ "which girl?".

Examples from the Holy Qur'ān :

وَسَيَعْلَمُ ٱلَّذِينَ ظَـلَمُوا أَيَّ مُنْقَلَبٍ يَنْقَلِبُونَ	26-227 And they who do wrong, will know to what final place of turning they will turn back.

بِأَيِّكُمُ ٱلْمَفْتُونُ	68-6 Which of you is mad?
أَيُّكُمْ زَادَتْهُ هَـٰذِهِ إِيمَانًا	9-124 Which of you has it strengthened in faith?

IV. هَلْ *hal*. It forms an interrogative sentence with a verb or pronoun. It is equivalent to an English question with an auxiliary verb 'to do' or a question with a verb 'to be', e.g. :

– هَـلْ رَأَيْتَ أَحَـدًا ؟   Did you see anyone?

– هَـلْ أَنْتَ طَالِبُ عِلْمٍ ؟   Are you a student (seeker of knowledge)?

Examples from the Holy Qur'ān :

قُلْ هَلْ تَرَبَّصُونَ بِنَآ إِلَّا إِحْـدَى ٱلْحُسْنَيَيْـنِ	9-52 Say : Do you wait for us but one of two most excellent things ?
وَهَـلْ أَتَـاكَ نَبَؤُاْ ٱلْخَصْمِ	38-21 and has the story of the adversaries came to thee?
هَـلْ أَتَـاكَ حَـدِيثُ ٱلْـغَاشِيَـةِ	88-1 Has there come to thee the news of the overwhelming events?

EXERCISE

1. Translate into Arabic :

1. Did you know that famous poet? Yes I know his name; he is Iqbal of Pakistan.
2. This is a good man and that (Fem.) is his sister.
3. The tree has good shade.
4. These Arabs are nice persons.
5. Those men have not arrived so far.
6. This woman returned from England yesterday.
7. Which men killed a dog yesterday?
8. How many persons attended the Jum'ah prayer in that village?
9. What did you demand of (مِنْ) your student in the university?
10. This is the great mosque of the city.
11. I found these books in Maktabah of Ḥaramain at Makkah.
12. This is a great building of a merchant.
13. Whose son is 'Abdul Ḥamīd?
14. Is he a minister's son?
15. These two men are friends and those two are enemies.
16. The daughter of a teacher has memorized the Holy Qur'ān by heart.
17. This is the man who won the 1st prize.
18. This is that girl who failed in the examination.
19. This is that boy who got first position in the examination.
20. This is the girl who arrived yesterday from Baghdad.

2. Translate into English :

مَنْ جَاءَ بِٱلْحَسَنَةِ فَلَهُ عَشْرُ أَمْثَالِهَا . مَنْ قَالَ لَا إِلَهَ إِلَّا اللهُ دَخَلَ ٱلْجَنَّةَ . مَنْ صَلَّىٰ صَلَاتَنَا وَأَكَلَ ذَبِيحَتَنَا فَهُوَ مِنَّا . مَنْ لَمْ يَرْحَمْ صَغِيرَنَا وَلَمْ يُوَقِّرْ كَبِيرَنَا فَلَيْسَ مِنَّا . مَنْ جَاءَ مِنَ ٱلْمَدِينَةِ ٱلْمُنَوَّرَةِ أَمْسِ ؟ مَاذَا تُرِيدُ مِنَ ٱلْمُعَلِّمِ أَكْثَرَ مِنَ ٱلتَّعْلِيمِ ؟ مَنْ هُوَ وَرَاءَكَ ؟ هَلْ أَنْتَ شَاعِرٌ ؟ مَنْ فَعَلَ هَـذَا ؟ مَنْ دَخَلَ ٱلْبَيْتَ فَهُوَ آمِنٌ . هَـذَا هُـوَ ٱلْكَلْبُ ٱلَّذِي أَكَلَ ٱلْقِطَّ ٱلَّذِي أَكَلَ ٱلْـفَأْرَ ٱلَّذِي قَـتَلْـتُهُ أَمْسِ . هَـلْ هِيَ أُخْتُكَ ٱلَّتِي حَفِظَتِ ٱلْقُرْآنَ ٱلْكَرِيمَ وَفَازَتْ بِٱلْجَائِـزَةِ ؟

<table>
<tr><td colspan="2" align="center">**VOCABULARY**</td></tr>
<tr><td>the famous</td><td>المَعْرُوفُ</td></tr>
<tr><td>the tree</td><td>الشَّجَرَةُ</td></tr>
<tr><td>the shade</td><td>الظِّلُّ</td></tr>
<tr><td>nice, good hearted</td><td>طَيِّبٌ</td></tr>
<tr><td>arrived (he)</td><td>وَصَلَ</td></tr>
<tr><td>demanded (he)</td><td>طَالَبَ</td></tr>
<tr><td>the building</td><td>العِمَارَةُ</td></tr>
<tr><td>the merchant</td><td>التَّاجِرُ</td></tr>
</table>

the enemy	العَــدُوُّ
memorization (v.n.)	الحِفْـظُ
by heart	عَنْ ظَهْرِ قَلْبٍ
the prize	الجَائِـزَةُ
won (he)	فَــازَ بِ
the examination	الإِخْتِبَـارُ
the position	أَلْمَكَانَةُ ، أَلْمَرْكِـزُ ، الدَّرَجَـةُ

الحَسَنَةُ	the good deed.
أَمْثَـالٌ	plural of مَثَـلٌ parable.
يَـرْحَمُ - رَحِمَ	to be merciful.
يُـوَقِّرُ	to regard, to respect.
أَمِـنَ	to be safe.

CHAPTER 22

THE DECLENSION

The Noun is generally divided into two groups, those are :

1. **Declinable :** i.e. governed by their preceding elements consequently changing their ending vowels, called مُعْرَب *mu'rab*, e.g. :

Nominative Case:	صَدَقَ ٱلرَّسُولُ	The Messenger spoke the Truth.
Accusative Case:	صَدَّقُوا ٱلرَّسُولَ	They believed in the Messenger.
Genitive Case:	صَحَابَةُ ٱلرَّسُولِ	The companions of the Messenger.

2. Those which have stationary state of their ending vowels and do not accept any influence of عَوَامِل (elements) are called : مَبْنِي *mabnī*, e.g. :

Nominative Case:	صَدَقَ مُوسَىٰ	Moses spoke the Truth.
Accusative Case:	صَدَّقُوا مُوسَىٰ	They believed in Moses.
Genitive Case:	صَحَابَةُ مُوسَىٰ	The companions of Moses.

There are certain classes of nouns that are not fully declined. This class of noun is called غَيْرُ مُنْصَرِف "*ghair munṣarif*".

According to European grammarians, it may be termed as 'Diptotes' that opposes triptotes. However, the declination of this class would be as following :

قَالَ فِرْعَوْنُ	Pharaoh said.
كَذَّبُوا فِرْعَوْنَ	They denied Pharaoh.
أَصْحَابُ فِرْعَوْنَ	The companions of Pharaoh.

It is to be noted that Diptotes differ from other declinable nouns in two respects; First: there is no Nunization (i.e. a sound of "an", "un", or "in"). Second: there are only two different vowel endings; the accusative and genitive both having (فَتْحَة) *fathah*.

As most Arabic nounds are declinable and they have several types and classes, they will be dealt with separately in the following chapters.

Indeclinable Nouns : Nouns of indeclinable groups are as following :

(a) All forms of pronouns, whether independent or suffixed, such as : سَمِعْتُ , شَرِبْتَ , هُمْ , هِيَ , هُوَ.

(b) Particles like : مَتَى , قَدْ , مَنْ , عَلَى etc.

(c) Nouns ending in *'alif* but spelled with ending ى as : مُوسَى *Mūsā*, عِيسَى *'Isā*, etc. This type of *'alif* is called أَلِفْ مَقْصُورَة *'alif maqsūrah*, likewise : كُبْرَى *kubrā*, fem., elative of أَكْبَر "biggest one", e.g. (from the Holy Qur'ān) :

لَقَدْ رَأَى مِنْ آيَاتِ رَبِّهِ ٱلْكُبْرَى	53-18 Certainly he saw the greatest signs of his Lord.

ذِكْرَىٰ dhikrā, "recollection", e.g. :

فَلاَ تَقْعُدْ بَعْدَ ٱلذِّكْرَىٰ مَعَ ٱلْقَوْمِ ٱلظَّالِمِينَ	6-68 Then sit not after recollection with the unjust people.

هُدَىٰ hudā, "guide", e.g. :

هُدًى لِلْمُتَّقِينَ	2-2 (This book is) a guide to those who fear (Allah).

عَصَا 'aṣā, "stick", e.g. :

أَضْرِبْ بِعَصَاكَ ٱلْحَجَرَ	2-60 strike the rock with thy stick (staff).

(d) The masculine singular, elative and colour-defect nouns of the form أَفْعَلَ, e.g. أَحْسَنَ "the most beautiful", e.g. (from the Holy Qur'ān) :

فَحَيُّوا بِأَحْسَنَ مِنْهَا	4-86 greet with better than it.

(e) Adjective of the pattern فَعْلَان as غَضْبَان ghaḍbān, "angry", e.g. (from the Holy Qur'ān) :

وَلَمَّا رَجَعَ مُوسَىٰ إِلَىٰ قَوْمِهِ غَضْبَانَ أَسِفًا	7-150 and when Moses returned to his people wrathful, grieved.

Diptotes غَيْرُ مُنْصَرِف

(a) Most proper names of non-Arabic origin whether personal or geographical are diptotes as : فِرْعَوْنَ

قَالَ ٱلْمَلأُ مِنْ قَوْمِ فِرْعَوْنَ	7-109 the chief of Pharao's people said...

سُلَيْمَانُ

| إِنَّهُ مِنْ سُلَيْمَانَ | 27-30 It is from Sulaimān (Solomon). |

هَارُوتَ – مَارُوتَ – بَابِلُ

| وَمَا أُنْزِلَ عَلَى ٱلْمَلَكَيْنِ بِبَابِلَ هَارُوتَ وَمَارُوتَ | 2-102 such things that were revealed at Babylon to the two angles Hārūt and Mārūt. |

مَدْيَنَ

| وَإِلَى مَدْيَنَ أَخَاهُمْ شُعَيْبًا | 7-85 And to Madyan (We sent) their brother Shu'aib. |

ثَمُودَ

| وَإِلَى ثَمُودَ أَخَاهُمْ صَلِحًا | 7-73 And to Thamūd (We sent) their brother Ṣāliḥ. |

(b) Broken plurals of the following patterns :

فُعَلَاءُ fu'alā'u, as وُزَرَاءُ wuzarā'u, "ministers", e.g. (from the Holy Qur'ān :   شُفَعَاءُ

| هٰؤُلَاءِ شُفَعَاؤُنَا | 10-18 These are our inter-cessors. |

رُحَمَاءُ

| رُحَمَاءُ بَيْنَهُمْ | 48-29 compassionate among themselves. |

عُلَمَاءُ

| عُلَمَاءُ بَنِي إِسْرَائِيلَ | 26-197 Learned men of the children of Israel. |

فَعْلَى fa‘lā, as مَرْضَى marḍā, plural of مَرِيض marīḍ, "patient", e.g. (from the Holy Qur'ān) :

عَلِمَ أَنْ سَيَكُونُ مِنْكُم مَّرْضَى	73-20 He knew that there will be some sick among you.

فَعَائِلُ fa‘ā'ilu, as مَدَائِنُ madā'inu, plural of مَدِينَة madīnah "city", e.g. (from the Holy Qur'ān) :

وَأَرْسِلْ فِي ٱلْمَدَائِنِ حَاشِرِينَ	7-111 and sent (summoners) to the cities.

فَعَالَى fa‘ālā, as يَتَامَى yatāmā, plural of يَتِيم yatīm, "orphan", e.g. (from the Holy Qur'ān) :

وَيَسْأَلُونَكَ عَنِ ٱلْيَتَامَى	2-220 and they ask thee concerning the orphans.

فَعَالِلُ fa‘ālilu, as دَرَاهِمُ darāhimu, plural of دِرْهَم dirham, "sivler coin", e.g. (from the Holy Qur'ān) :

وَشَرَوْهُ بِثَمَنٍ بَخْسٍ دَرَاهِمَ مَعْدُودَةٍ	12-20 and they sold him for a small price, a few pieces of silver.

فَعَالِيلُ fa‘ālīlu, as خَنَازِيرُ khanāzīru, plural of خِنْزِير khinzīr, "pig", e.g. (from the Holy Qur'ān) :

وَجَعَلَ مِنْهُمُ ٱلْقِرْدَةَ وَٱلْخَنَازِيرَ	5-60 (and of whom) He made apes and pigs.

Diptotes are treated as triptote (مُنْصَرِف) when they are made definite in any way, e.g. :

- فِي ٱلْمَدَائِنِ ٱلَّتِي سَكَنُوهَا   -   in the cities where they dwelled.
- مِنْ مَدَائِنِ ٱلْعَرَب   -   from the cities of Arabia.

EXERCISE

1. **Translate into Arabic :**

   1. Islam orders its followers to look after widows and orphans.

   2. When our Prophet was six years old his mother died.

   3. His father died before he was born.

   4. We see in big cities of the world people travelling by underground trains.

   5. The helping and guidance of blind men is among the duties recommended to Muslims.

   6. He had many pigs, apart from his cows and sheep.

   7. He met a white girl, so he took her into employment as a servant girl in a black man's house. But she deserted him suddenly, without permission two days later.

   8. They followed the enemy and found them hesitating in the sand. So they destroyed them straight away.

   9. England had many colonies in the past and her sailors were famous.

   10. I saw you in my right hand and Lozely on my left.

   11. I knew from the perspiration flowing on his forehead that his endeavors had tired him.

   12. I met a lame man and a tall Muslim in the street and I did not know when they had come.

2. Translate into English :

لَيْسَ عَلَى آلأَعْمَى حَرَجٌ وَلَا عَلَى آلأَعْرَجِ حَرَجٌ – الشُّعَرَاءُ يَتَّبِعُهُمْ الْغَاوُونَ ، أَلَمْ تَرَ أَنَّهُمْ فِي كُلِّ وَادٍ يَهِيمُونَ – قَالَتْ كُبْرَى آلْبَنَاتِ لِأُخْتِهَا الصَّغِيرَةِ لَا تَتْرُكِي عَمَلَ آلْيَوْمِ لِلْغَدِ – سَمِعْتُ آلْعَصَافِيرَ تُغَرِّدُ عَلَى آلْأَغْصَانِ – كَمْ أَخًا لَكَ وَكَمْ أُخْتًا؟ – كَمْ مِنْ قَرْيَةٍ أَهْلَكَهَا اللهُ – كُلًّا نُمِدُّ هَـؤُلَاءِ وَهَـؤُلَاءِ مِنْ عَطَاءِ رَبِّكَ – إِرْحَمُوا آلْيَتَامَى فَإِنَّهُمْ فَقَدُوا آبَاءَهُمْ – إِعْمَلُوا آلْمَعْرُوفَ نَحْوَ الأَرَامِل ، الأَرْمَلَةُ وَآلْمَرِيضُ وَآلْفَقِيرُ أَحَقُّ بِالإِحْسَانِ مِنْ غَيْرِهِمْ – القُرآنُ يَهْدِي لِلَّتِي هِيَ أَقْوَمُ – رَسُولُ الله صَادِقٌ أَمِينٌ ، بُعِثَ لِلْبَشَرِيَّةِ جَمْعَاءَ – الأَبْيَضُ وَآلأَسْوَدُ عِنْدَ اللهِ سَوَاءٌ ، إِنَّ اللهَ لَا يَنْظُرُ إِلَى صُوَرِكُمْ وَأَلْوَانِكُمْ ، إِنَّ اللهَ يَنْظُرُ إِلَى قُلُوبِكُمْ وَأَعْمَالِكُمْ .

VOCABULARY

to look after	رَعَى – يَرْعَى *ra'ā – yar'ā*
under-ground	تَحْتَ آلأَرْضِ النَّفَقُ
the train	القِطَار
to intercede	شَفَعَ – يَشْفَعُ
the pig	الخِنْزِيرُ
the cow	البَقَرَة

the sheep	الغَنَمُ (collective noun)
employment	الوَظِيفَةُ - الخِدْمَةُ
the servant girl	الخَادِمَةُ
to desert, to flee	أَبَقَ - يَأْبَقُ or هَرَبَ - يَهْرُبُ
suddenly	فَجْأَةً
permission	الإذْنُ
to follow	أَتْبَعَ - يُتْبِعُ (IV)
the colonies	المُسْتَعْمَرَاتُ plural of مُسْتَعْمَرَةٌ colony (X)
perspiration	التَعَرُّقُ (V verbal noun)
the forehead	الجَبِينُ
the endeavours	الجُهُودُ
to tire	أَتْعَبَ - يُتْعِبُ (form IV verb)

الأَعْرَج	the lame.
الأَعْمَى	the blind man.
حَرَجٌ	harm, objection.
الغَاوُون	Act. Part. plural of غَاوٍ - mislead.
وَادٍ	field, valley.

هَامَ – يَهِيمُ	to wonder.
كُبْرَى الـبَنَاتِ	the elder daughter.
الْعُصْفُورَةُ	the bird.
يُـغَـرِّدُ	to sing. (imp. indicative verb)
الْيَـوْمَ	today.
الغَـدُ	tomorrow.
مَدَّ – يَمُـدُّ	to extend, to help. (he) (double radicals).
أَرَامِـلُ	widows. plural of أَرْمَلَـةٌ widow.
أَقْـوَمُ	(elative) straighter, sounder, more adequate.
صَادِقٌ	truthful.
الأَمِـينُ	the trustworthy.
جَمْعَاء	all of them. (feminine)
صُـوَرٌ	plural of صُورَةٌ face, picture.
أَلْـوَانٌ	plural of لَـوْنٌ colour.

CHAPTER 23

NOUNS : DECLINABLE الأَسْمَاء المعربة

As already stated, the noun is either declinable or indeclinable. In the previous chapter the indeclinable nouns were treated. In chapter 8 we have mentioned that the imperfect has three moods which are distinguished through the declension. Again the declension is the result of the preceding letters or nouns which are placed for modification of the forms.

Let us recollect here once again that a noun has three cases :

Nominative	indicated by	ضَمَّة ـُ dammah
Accusative	indicated by	فَتْحَة ـَ fathah
Genitive	indicated by	كَسَرَة ـِ kasarah

1. The nominative is used :

(a) For the subject of a verbal sentence, e.g.

خَلَقَ اللهُ السَّمٰوَاتِ وَالأَرْضَ	Allah has created the heavens and the earth.

(b) For the subject of a nominal sentence, (termed مُبْتَدَأ mubtada', see chapter 2), e.g. :

الرَّسُولُ صَادِقٌ	The Messenger is true (man).

(c) As the predicate of a nominal sentence. صَادِقٌ ṣādiqun is predicate; it is termed as خَبَرٌ khabarun.

(d) As the predicate of إِنَّ , أَنَّ , لَعَلَّ , لَيْتَ, e.g. :

إِنَّ رَبَّكَ كَرِيمٌ	Verily your Lord is Kind (God)
أَلَمْ أَقُلْ لَكَ أَنَّ اللهَ عَلَى كُلِّ شَيْءٍ قَـدِيـرٌ	Did not I say to you that Allah is Most Powerful over every-thing ?

Is is important for students to note that إِنَّ and أَنَّ both are used to emphasise the meaning of the predicate, but إِنَّ is used only in the beginning of a sentence, while أَنَّ indicates to the statement, e.g. :

قُلْتُ لَكَ أَنَّ صَدِيقَكَ قَادِمٌ	I told you that your friend is coming.

لَيْتَ "would that", e.g. (from the Holy Qur'ān) :

يَا لَيْتَنِي كُنْتُ تُرَابًا	7840 O'! would that I were dust.

لَعَلَّ la'alla, "may, perhaps", e.g. (from the Holy Qur'ān) :

لَا تَدْرِي لَعَلَّ اللهَ يُحْدِثُ بَعْدَ ذٰلِكَ أَمْـرًا	65-1 Thou knowest not that Allah mey after that bring an event to pass.

The above particles are termed as حُرُوفٌ مُشَبَّهَةٌ بِالْفِعْل "letters resembling verbs" and referred to as: (إِنَّ and sisters).

(e) After the vocative particle أَيُّهَا (always used with the ar-ticle), e.g. أَيُّهَا ٱلنَّاسُ "O' people!" also after يَا in the singular without nunaiton, e.g. يَا رَجُلُ "O' man". يَا عَلِيُّ "O' 'Alī".

(f) For a noun in apposition to another nominative, e.g. :

قَالَ اللهُ ٱلْعَظِيمُ	said Allah, the Great.

(g) A noun connected to a nominative preceding noun by means of a connecting particle (حَرْف عَطْف) , such as, وَ "and" or أوْ "or". This noun is known in Arabic as ٱلْمَعْطُوف , e.g. :

صَدَقَ اللهُ وَرَسُولُهُ	Allah and His Messenger told the truth.
سَيَحْضُرُ أَحْمَدُ أوْ عَلِيٌّ	Aḥmad or 'Alī will come.

(h) A noun that functions as the subject of an equational sentence prededed by كَانَ or one of its sisters (كَانَ وَأَخْوَاتُهَا) ; these are a special group of irregular verbs which have the tendency to introduce and precede equational sentences to actualize special meanings. The most common of them are :
كَانَ , أَصْبَحَ , أَمْسَىٰ , أَضْحَىٰ , ظَلَّ , بَاتَ , مَازَالَ , مَادَامَ .

Examples from the Holy Qur'ān :

مَـا كَانَ إِبْـرَاهِيمُ يَـهُودِيًـا وَلاَ نَصْـرَانِيـًّا	3-67 Abraham was not a Jew nor yet a Christian.
وَأَصْبَحَ فُؤَادُ أُمِّ مُوسَىٰ فَارِغًا	28-10 There came to be a void in the heart of Moses' mother.
وَإِذَا بُشِّرَ أَحَدُهُم بِٱلأُنْثَىٰ ظَلَّ وَجْهُهُ مُسْوَدًّا	16-58 When news is brought to one of them of (the birth of) a female child his face remained darkened...

2. Arab Grammarians divide the declension into two types, one is by vowels that is الإِعْرَابُ بِٱلْحَرَكَاتِ and another is declension by letters الإِعْرَابُ بِٱلْحُرُوفِ . Here are letters or dipthongs that take place for the vowels :

– In case of nominative, و wāw will take place of *dammah*.
– In case of accusative, ألف 'alif will take place of *fathah*.
– In case of genitive, ي yā' will take place of *kasrah*.

These declensions are traditionally represented in 'The five nouns' (الأَسْمَاءُ ٱلْخَمْسَةُ), which are : ذُو , فُو , حَمٌ , أَخٌ , أَبٌ .

Examples from the Holy Qur'ān :

Nominative :

أَبُـو	'abū

أَبُـونَا شَيْخٌ كَبِيرٌ	28-23 Our father is a very old man.

أَخُـو	'akhū

أَنَا أَخُـوكَ	12-69 I am thy brother.

ذُو	dhū

وَرَبُّـكَ ٱلْغَفُـورُ ذُو ٱلـرَّحْمَةِ	18-58 And thy Lord is Forgiving, Full of Mercy.

Accusative :

	أَبَا	'abā

وَجَاءُوا أَبَاهُمْ	12-16 They came to their father.

	أَخَا	'akhā

نَحْفَظُ أَخَانَا	12-65 We protect our brother

	ذَا	dhā

حَتَّى إِذَا فَتَحْنَا عَلَيْهِم بَابًا ذَا عَذَابٍ	23-77 Until when we opened a door of chastisement.

Genitive :

	أَبِي	'abī

قَالَ يُوسُفُ لِأَبِيهِ	12-4 Joseph said to his father.

	أَخِي	'akhī

أَنَا يُوسُفُ وَهَـٰذَا أَخِي	12-90 I am Joseph and he is my brother.

	ذِي	dhī

يَسْئَلُونَكَ عَنْ ذِي ٱلْقَرْنَيْنِ	18-83 They ask thee about Dhilqarnain.

EXERCISE

1. Translate into Arabic :

Among (بَيْنَ) all the religious books of the world, the Holy
Qur'ān is the only book which has the pure text. Every word
and letter of the Holy Book is revealed. There is only one
Qur'ān that is read in the East and West. There is no different
texts of the Holy Book. This is learnt by heart. Thousands of
Muslims read its text every day. They try to comprehend the
meaning of the Qur'ān. They know that the Qur'ān was revealed to Sayyidinā Muḥammad, may peace and blessing of
Allah be upon him (صَلَّى الله عَلَيْهِ وَسَلَّم). The Qur'ān has told
us the real story of Joseph; when he said to his father, "I saw
eleven stars and the sun and the moon bowing to me".

2. Translate into English :

أَذِنَ لَهُ ٱلرَّحْمَنُ . لَنْ تُغْنِيَ عَنْهُمْ أَمْوَالُهُمْ . لَنْ يَقْدِرَ عَلَيْهِ أَحَدٌ . لَنْ تُغْنِيَ

عَنْكُمْ فِئَتُكُمْ . أَحَاطَ بِهِم سُرَادِقُهَا . كَبُرَ عَلَيكَ إِعْرَاضُهُمْ . يَطُوفُ

عَلَيهِم غِلْمَانٌ . طَالَ عَلَيْهُمُ ٱلْأَمَدُ . كَبُرَ عَلَيكُمْ مَقَامِي . لَا يَحُضُّ عَلَى

طَعَامِ ٱلْمِسْكِينِ . صَدُّوا عَنْ سَبِيلِ اللهِ . أَتَمَّهَا عَلَى أَبَوَيكَ . تَبَّتْ يَدَا

أَبِي لَهَبٍ . جَاءَ إِخْوَةُ يُوسُفَ . إِنَّمَا ٱلْمُؤْمِنُونَ إِخْوَةٌ . أَخَذَ بِرَأْسِ

أَخِيهِ . قَدْ سَرَقَ أَخٌ لَهُ مِنْ قَبْلُ .

3. Identify the subjects of the sentences in the following verses :

سَوفَ يُؤتي اللهُ أَجرَ ٱلمُؤمِنينَ . لَقَدْ نادانَا نُوحٌ . لَمْ يَطْمِثْهُنَّ إِنسٌ . لَنْ تَنْفَعَكُمْ أَرْحامُكُمْ . لَنْ تَمَسَّنا ٱلنّارُ . أَخَذَهُ اللهُ . كَذَّبَتْ قَومُ نُوحٍ المُرْسَلينَ . يمحُ اللهُ ٱلبَاطِلَ .

<table>
<tr><td colspan="3" align="center">**VOCABULARY**</td></tr>
</table>

religion	دِيـن	religious books الكُتُبُ الدِّيـنِـيَّـةُ
the text	النَّصُّ	
the pure	الخَالِصُ	
revealed	أُوحِيَ	(passive case for the perfect form IV)
... is read	يُـقْرَأُ	(passive case for imperfect «hamzated»)
to memorize	حَفِظَ - يَحْفَظُ	
thousands	آلَافٌ	
comprehend	وَعَى - يَعِي	
the real story	القِصَّةُ ٱلْوَاقِـعِـيَّـةُ	

أَذِنَ	to permit.
لَنْ تُغْنِيَ	will never avail (form V) ought against ...
لَنْ يَقْدِرَ	will never have power upon.
أَحَاطَ	surrounded. (IV)
سُرَادِقٌ	chambers.
كَبُرَ	it was hard to ...
إِعْرَاضٌ	turning away, shunning. (v.n. of form IV)
يَطُوفُ	to circulate, walk about, to make rounds.
غِلْمَانٌ	boys. (plural of غُلَامٌ boy).
الْأَمَدُ	limited time.
الْمُقَامُ	end, place.
كَذَّبَ	to deny. (II)
الْحَقُّ	the truth.

CHAPTER 24

DECLENSION OF THE NOUN

Accusative Case = Objects

The Accusative mark نَصْبُ is used for the objects of a verb.
There are five kinds of objects :

1. Direct object مَفْعُولُ بِهِ , e.g. :

خَلَقَ اللهُ ٱلأَرْضَ	Allah has created the eath.
قَرَأْتُ كِتَابًا	I read a book.

Some verbs take two objects, e.g. :

أَرْسَلَ اللهُ مُحَمَّدًا رَسُولًا	Allah has sent Muḥammad (as a) Messenger.

Examples from the Holy Qur'ān :

فَقَدَرَ عَلَيْهِ رِزْقَهُ	89-16 Then restricting for him his subsistence.
ٱبْتَلَاهُ رَبُّهُ	89-15 His Lord tried him.
وَسَوْفَ يُؤْتِ اللهُ ٱلْمُؤْمِنِينَ أَجْرًا عَظِيمًا	4-146 And Allah will soon grant the believers a mighty reward.
قَدْ فَرَضَ اللهُ لَكُمْ تَحِلَّةَ أَيْمَانِكُمْ	66-2 Allah has indeed sanctioned for you the expiation of your oaths.

لَقَـدْ جِئْتِ شَيْئًا فَرِيًّا	19-27 (O' Mary) thou hast indeed brought a strange thing.
خَلَقَـكَ فَسَوَّاكَ فَعَـدَلَكَ	82-7 (Who) created thee, then made thee complete, then made thee in a right good state.
لَقَدْ أَضَلَّ مِنْكُمْ جِبِلًّا كَثِيرًا	36-62 He hath led astray of you a great multitude.
وَلِمَنْ خَافَ مَقَامَ رَبِّـهِ	55-46 And for him who fears to stand before his Lord.
وَنَهَى ٱلنَّفْسَ عَنِ ٱلْهَوَىٰ	79-40 And restrains himself from low designs.

2. As the absolute object المَفْـعُولُ ٱلْمُطْـلَـقُ

The verbal noun is placed in the accusative after its own verb as a sort of adverb to describe the manner, time, and sometimes to denote that the verb of the sentence is meant by speaker in its real and complete sense, e.g. (from the Holy Qur'ān) :

فَصَّلْنَاهُ تَفْصِيلًا	17-12 We have explained it completely.
فَسَوْفَ يُحَاسَبُ حِسَابًا يَسِيرًا	84-8 His account will be taken by an easy reckoning.

It sometimes confuses students to see the verbal noun repeated in accusative without any change in the meaning, thus to them :

فَرِحَ فَـرْحًا	he was glad.
ضَرَبَ ضَرْبًا	he struck

have same meaning as فَرِحَ and ضَرَبَ . Some European authors like Harywood/Nahmad observed that the absolute object serves "to balance the sentence from the musical point of view".

This type of confusion could be raised if the correct sense of this type of object is not known. The real sense of فَرِحَ فَرَحًا is "he was really glad" and likewise ضَرَبَ ضَرْبًا means that someone has physically struck.

Examples from the Holy Qur'ān :

وَمَهَّدتُّ لَـهُ تَمْهِيدًا	74-14 And I made (life) smooth.
يَـنْسِفُهَا رَبِّي نَسْـفًا	20-105 Say: My Lord will scatter them as scattered dust.
يُـفَجِّـرُونَـهَا تَـفْجِيرًا	76-6 They will make it flow in abundance.
أَنَّا صَبَـبْنَا ٱلْمَاءَ صَبًّا	80-25 We have poured down abundant water.

It is qualified by an adjective to specify the type of action, e.g. (from the Holy Qur'ān) :

وَتُحِبُّونَ ٱلْمَالَ حُبًّا جَمًّا	89-20 And you love wealth with exceeding love.
وَلِيُبْلِيَ ٱلْمُؤْمِـنِينَ مِنْـهُ بَلَاءً حَسَنًا	8-17 He might test the believers by a fair test.
إِنَّا فَتَحْنَـا لَكَ فَتْحًا مُبِـينًا	48-1 Surely We have granted thee a clear victory.
وَأُسَرِّحْكُنَّ سَرَاحًا جَمِـيلًا	33-28 And will release you a fair release.

أَقْرَضْتُمُ اللهَ قَرْضًا حَسَنًا	5-12 Lend unto Allah a kindly loan.
فَيَمِيلُونَ عَلَيْكُمْ مَيْلَةً وَاحِدَةً	4-102 That they may attack you once for all.

Sometimes it comes after a verb of passive case, e.g. :

زُلْزِلَتِ الْأَرْضُ زِلْزَالَهَا	99-1 When earth is shaken with her (final) earthquake.
كَلَّا إِذَا دُكَّتِ الْأَرْضُ دَكًّا دَكًّا	89-21 Nay! But when the earth is ground to atoms, grinding, grinding.
وَبُسَّتِ الْجِبَالُ بَسًّا	56-5 And the hills are ground to powder.
وَذُلِّلَتْ قُطُوفُهَا تَذْلِيلًا	76-14 And the clustered fruits thereof bow down.

3. Object for Time and Place المَفْعُولُ فِيهِ , e.g. (from the Holy Qur'ān) :

سَيَعْلَمُونَ غَدًا	54-26 They will know tomorrow.
وَنُدْخِلْكُمْ مُدْخَلًا كَرِيمًا	4-31 and we cause you to enter an honourable place of eternity.
انْتَبَذَتْ مِنْ أَهْلِهَا مَكَانًا شَرْقِيًّا	19-16 She drew aside from her family to an eastern place.
قَالَ لَبِثْتُ يَوْمًا أَوْ بَعْضَ يَوْمٍ	2-259 He said I have tarried a day or a part of a day.

فَاللهُ يَحْكُمُ بَيْنَكُمْ يَوْمَ ٱلْقِيَامَةِ	4-141 And Allah will judge between you on the day of Resurrection.

Such accusatives may be expressed by prepositional phrases. Examples (from the Holy Qur'ān) :

وَتَرَكْنَا يُوسُفَ عِنْدَ مَتَاعِنَا	12-17 And left Joseph by our goods.
وَأَلْفَيَا سَيِّدَهَا لَدَى ٱلْبَابِ	12-25 and they met her husband at the door.
لِيُحَاجُّوكُمْ بِهِ عِنْدَ رَبِّكُمْ	2-76 that they may contend with you by this before your Lord.
عَاهَدتُّمْ عِنْدَ ٱلْمَسْجِدِ ٱلْحَرَامِ	9-7 You made an agreement at the sacred mosque.

They also are placed by particles denoting meaning of place; they are actually called 'adverbs of place' in Arabic, e.g. (from the Holy Qur'ān) :

خَلْفٌ   behind

وَمِنْ خَلْفِهِمْ سَدًّا	36-9 and a barrier behind them.

فَوْقَ   above

وَفَوْقَ كُلِّ ذِي عِلْمٍ عَلِيمٌ	12-76 and above every possessor of knowledge is the All-knowing One.

تَحْتَ   beneath, under

قَدْ جَعَلَ رَبُّكِ تَحْتَكِ سَرِيًّا	19-24 Surely thy Lord has provided a stream beneath thee.

أَسْفَلَ   lower

وَٱلرَّكْبُ أَسْفَلَ مِنْكُمْ	8-42 While the caravan was in a lower place than you.

الْيَمِين   right hand

الشِّمَال   left hand

وَتَرَى ٱلشَّمْسَ إِذَا طَلَعَتْ تَزَاوَرُ عَنْ كَهْفِهِمْ ذَاتَ ٱلْيَمِينِ وَإِذَا غَرَبَتْ تَقْرِضُهُمْ ذَاتَ ٱلشِّمَالِ	18-17 and thou mightest see the sun, when it rose, decline from their cave to the right, and when it go past them behind on the left.

وَرَاءَ   behind

وَكَانَ وَرَاءَهُمْ مَلِكٌ	18-79 and there was behind them a king.

4. Object for expressing 'aim' and 'purpose' الْمَفْعُولُ لَهُ. This is expressed by a verbal noun in the accusative, e.g. قُمْتُ إِكْرَامًا لَهُ "I rose to honour him (in a gesture of honour for him)".

Examples from the Holy Qur'ān :

فَأَتْبَعَهُمْ فِرْعَوْنُ وَجُنُودُهُ بَغْيًا وَعَدْوًا	10-90 Then Pharaoh and his hosts followed them for oppression and tyranny.

بَدَّلُوا نِعْمَةَ اللهِ كُفْرًا	14-28 (who) exchanged Allah's favour for disbelief.
وَأَعْيُنُهُمْ تَفِيضُ مِنَ ٱلدَّمْعِ حَزَنًا	9-92 and their eyes over-flowed with tears of grief.

Sometimes, a phrase or clause is placed with a verbal noun in the accusative, e.g. (from the Holy Qur'ān) :

وَٱلَّذِينَ يُنْفِقُونَ أَمْوَالَهُمْ رِئَاءَ ٱلنَّاسِ	4-38 and those who spend their wealth to be seen by men.
يَجْعَلُونَ أَصَابِعَهُمْ فِي آذَانِهِمْ مِّنَ ٱلصَّوَاعِقِ حَذَرَ ٱلْمَوْتِ	2-19 they put their fingers into their ears because of the thunder-peal, for fear of death.

5. Object for denoting meaning of 'with', 'by' or 'during', المَفْعُولُ مَعَهُ .

Examples from the Holy Qur'ān :

فَأَجْمِعُوا أَمْرَكُمْ وَشُرَكَاءَكُمْ	10-71 So decide upon your course of action, you and your partners.
قُوا أَنْفُسَكُمْ وَأَهْلِيكُمْ نَارًا	66-6 Ward off from your-selves and your families a fire…

EXERCISE

1. **Translate into Arabic :**

Allah has revealed this Book to Sayyidinā (سَيِّـدِنَـا) Muḥammad, may peace and blessing of Allah be upon him. A Muslim recites the Holy Qur'ān every morning. They fast during the month of Ramaḍān, pay poor-due (زَكَاة) and perform Hajj to the sacred House of Allah.

Islamic Law abolishes the criminal activities of evil-doers. My friend came to see me last night. They went along with their families. Arabic is the richest language from the vocabulary point of view, every verb has tens of modifications. We love Arabic as it is the language of the Holy Qur'ān, traditions of the Prophet (Ṣ) and it will be the language of Paradise. Your father has brought a good pen for you.

2. **Translate into English :**

أَرْسَلَ اللهُ نُوحًا إِلَىٰ قَوْمِهِ ، فَدَعَا نُوحٌ قَوْمَهُ إِلَىٰ عِبَـادَةِ اللهِ وَتَقْـوَاهُ
وَطَـاعَتِـهِ ، فَـلَمْ يُـؤْمِنْ إِلَّا عَـدَدٌ قَلِيلٌ مِنْهُمْ وَعَصَىٰ ٱلْبَـاقِي وَازْدَادُوا
عِصْيَـانًا ، وَلَمَّا يَـئِسَ مِنْهُمْ دَعَا عَلَيْهِم وَقَـالَ :

« رَبِّ لَا تَـذَرْ عَلَىٰ ٱلْأَرْضِ مِنَ ٱلْكَافِرِينَ دَيَّارًا ، إِنَّكَ إِن تَـذَرْهُمْ يُضِلُّوا
عِبَادَكَ وَلَا يَـلِدُوا إِلَّا فَاجِـرًا كَفَّارًا » .

344   ٣٤٤

to recite (he)	يَتْـلُوا - تَـلَا
to fast (he)	يَصُومُ - صَـامَ
to perform (he)	يُـؤَدِّي - أَدَّىٰ
to cut off	يَقْطَعُ - قَطَعَ (Use passive case)
criminal	المُجْرِمَـةُ - الإِجْرَامِيَّـةُ
activity	النَّشَاطُ
rich	غَنِيٌّ Richest أَغْـنَىٰ
point of view	مِنْ نَاحِيَةٍ
vocabulary	الكَلِمَاتُ - المُفْرَداتُ
modification	الأَنْـوَاعُ - وَآلأَشْـكَالُ
for the sake of	لِأَجْـلِ

أَرْسَلَ	to send. أَرْسَلَ - يُـرْسِلُ (IV)	
قَـوْمٌ	nation, people.	
عِـبَادَةٌ	worship, service.	

تَـقْـوَىٰ	God fearing.
طَاعَـةٌ	obedience. أَطَاعَ - يُـطِـيعُ (IV)
عَصَىٰ	to disobey. عَصَىٰ - يَـعْصِي
إِزْدَاد	increased.
عِصْـيَان	disobedience.
يَـئِسَ	to despair. يَـئِسَ - يَـيْـئَسُ
دَعَا عَلَيْـه	cursed him.
لَا تَـذَر	do not leave (May thou leave not).
دَيَّـارٌ	inhabitant.
يُضِـلُّ	to mislead.
فَـاجِرٌ	sin-doer (sinner).
كَـفَّارٌ	disbeliever.

CHAPTER 25

الحَــالُ *AL-ḤĀL*

Some other accusative cases :

1. حَال (ḥāl) is an Arabic grammatical term that means the circumstances obtaining at the time when the action of the main verb takes place. It is expressed by an accusative or by a finite verb, e.g. :

    جَاءَ رَجُلٌ سَاعِيًا or جَاءَ رَجُلٌ يَسْعَىٰ "A man came running".

    Such a ḥāl accusative is usually placed after a direct object, e.g. (from the Holy Qur'ān) :

تَـرَكُوكَ قَـائِـمًا	62-11 ...leave thee standing.
سَخَّرَ لَكُمُ ٱلشَّمْسَ وَٱلْقَمَرَ دَائِبَيْن	121-33 He has made subservient to you the sun and the moon, pursuing their courses.
أَفَمَنْ يَمْشِي مُكِبًّا عَلَىٰ وَجْهِهِ أَهْـدَىٰ أَمَّنْ يَمْشِي سَوِيًّا عَلَىٰ صِرَاطٍ مُّسْتَقِيمٍ	67-22 Is he who goes prone upon his face, better guided or he who walks upright on a straight path ?
قُومُـوا لله قَانِـتِـيـنَ	2-238 Stand up truly obedient to Allah.
يَمُرُّونَ عَلَـيْهَا وَهُمْ عَنْهَا مُعْرِضُونَ	12-105 Do they pass by! yet they turn away from it.

It often refers to the subject of the sentence as :

يَذْكُرُونَ اللّٰهَ قِيَامًا وَقُعُودًا , but it could refer to object as: تَرَكُوكَ قَائِمًا
or to some genitive as (from the Holy Qur'ān) :

وَنَزَعْنَا مَا فِي صُدُورِهِمْ مِّنْ غِلٍّ إِخْوَانًا	15-47 And We rooted out whatever of rancour is in their breasts as brethren.
فَخَرَجَ مِنْهَا خَائِفًا يَتَرَقَّبُ	28-21 He went forth there – from fearing, awaiting.
سِيقَ ٱلَّذِينَ ٱتَّقَوْا رَبَّهُمْ إِلَى ٱلْجَنَّةِ زُمَرًا	39-73 Those who keep their duty to their Lord are conveyed to the garden in companies.
وَلَّى مُدْبِرًا وَلَمْ يُعَقِّبْ	27-10 He turned back retreating and did not return.

The accusative *ḥāl* is nearly always an active participle, but it may also be a passive participle, e.g. (from the Holy Qur'ān) :

يَنْقَلِبُ إِلَى أَهْلِهِ مَسْرُورًا	84-9 He will go back to his people rejoicing.
يَصْلَاهَا مَذْمُومًا مَّدْحُورًا	17-18 He will enter it (Hell) despised, driven away.
يَجِدُونَهُ مَكْتُوبًا	7-157 They find him mentioned.

Also a verbal noun may replace the active participle, e.g. (from the Holy Qur'ān) :

وَلَّوْا عَلَى أَدْبَارِهِمْ نُفُورًا	17-46 They turn their backs in aversion.

يَـذْكُـرُونَ اللهَ قِيَامًا وَقُـعُودًا	3-191 Those who remember Allah standing and sitting.
وَعِبَادُ ٱلرَّحْمٰنِ ٱلَّذِينَ يَمْشُونَ عَلَى ٱلأَرْضِ هَـوْنًا	25-63 And the servants of the Bneficient are they who walk on the earth in humility.

The verbal *ḥāl* occasionally refers, not to any specific part of previous sentence (i.e. subject, object, etc.), but to the whole statement, e.g. (from the Holy Qur'ān) :

أَوَلَـمْ يَـرَوْا إِلَى مَا خَلَقَ اللهُ مِنْ شَيْءٍ يَتَفَيَّؤُا ظِلاَلُهُ عَـن ٱلْيَـمِين وَٱلشَّمَـائِـل سُجَّدًا لله وَهُمْ دَاخِرُونَ	16-48 Have they not observed all things that Allah hath created, how their shadows incline to the right and to the left, making prostration unto Allah, and they are lowly.
وَلِلهِ يَسْجُدُ مَا فِي ٱلسَّمٰوَاتِ وَمَا فِي ٱلأَرْضِ مِنْ دَابَّةٍ وَٱلْمَلاَئِكَةُ وَهُمْ لاَ يَسْتَكْبِرُونَ	16-49 And unto Allah maketh prostration whatsoever is in the heavens and whatsoever is in the earth of living creatures, and the angles (also), and they are not proud..
يَخَـافُونَ رَبَّـهُـمْ مِّنْ فَوْقِهِـمْ وَيَـفْـعَلُونَ مَا يُـؤْمَـرُونَ	16-50 They fear their Lord above them, and do what they are bidden.

2. The specification   التميــيز

It is expressed by an accusative and is resembling to *ḥāl* in having a finite verb, but it is used to clarify what is less clear by the verb of the sentence. In English it may be translated sometimes by "in regard to" but is not true in all cases, i.e. : نَفْسًا (طِبْ) be good in regard to soul (i.e. rejoice heartily).

Examples from the Holy Qur'ān :

لَنْ تَبْلُغَ ٱلْجِبَالَ طُـولًا	17-37 Nor canst thou reach the mountains in regard to height.

But most often it is used only to explain the verb as :

كَبُرَ مَقْتًا عِنْدَ الله	61-3 It is most hateful in the sight of Allah.
كَبُرَتْ كَلِمَةً تَخْرُجُ مِنْ أَفْوَاهِهِمْ	18-5 Dreadful is the word that cometh out of their mouths.
لَا يُظْلَمُونَ فَتِيـلًا	17-71 They will not be dealt with a whit unjustly.
يَدْخُلُونَ فِي دِينِ اللهِ أَفْوَاجًا	110-2 (and thou seest) men entering the religion of Allah in companies.

After كَمْ "how much, how many", the noun will be singular accusative, e.g. كَمْ أَخًا لَكَ ، وَكَمْ أُخْـتًا ؟ "How many brother have you and how many sisters?". If (كَمْ) is also used to show that the object has a large number, in this case it is not used for questioning about the number and takes the following noun in genitive.

Examples from the Holy Qur'ān :

كَمْ مِنْ قَرْيَةٍ أَهْلَكْنَاهَا	7-4 How many a township have we destroyed!
وَكَمْ قَصَمْنَا مِنْ قَرْيَةٍ	21-11 How many a community that dealt unjustly have we shattered.

The numerals take the following noun in *tamyīz*. Thus plurals of them are taken in genitive with *'iḍāfah*, e.g. :

خَمْسَةُ كُتُبٍ "five books",   عَشَرَةُ أَقْلَامٍ "ten pens"

The noun counted after numbers 13 to 99 are expressed in singular as accusative, e.g. :

تِسْعَةَ عَشَرَ كِتَابًا "19 books",   خَمْسَةَ عَشَرَ قَلَمًا "15 pens",

From hundred onwards the counted object *(tamyīz)* is treated as genitive singular, e.g. : مَائَةُ حَبَّةٍ "hundred grains".

3.   The Predicate of كَانَ and its sisters.

Examples from the Holy Qur'ān :

كَانَ مِزَاجُهَا كَافُورًا	76-5 It was tempered with camphore.
كَانَ شَرُّهُ مُسْتَطِيرًا	76-7 (A day) the evil of which was widespread.
مَا كَانَتْ أُمُّكِ بَغِيًّا	19-28 Thy mother was not an unchaste woman.
كَانَتِ آمْرَأَتِي عَاقِرًا	19-5 My wife was barren.
وَكَانَ أَمْرُ اللهِ مَفْعُولًا	4-47 And the command of Allah was (and is) always excecuted.

وَكَانَ اللّٰهُ غَفُورًا رَحِيمًا	4-96 And Allah was (and is) ever Forgiving, Merciful.

4. For the subject of إِنَّ and its sisters.

Examples from the Holy Qur'ān :

وَ إِنَّ ٱلـدِّيـنَ لَـوَاقِـعٌ	51-6 And the judgement will surely come to pass.
إِنَّ ٱلظَّنَّ لَا يُغْنِي مِنَ ٱلْحَقِّ شَيْئًا	10-36 Surely conjecture will not avail aught against the truth.
إِنَّ ٱلْمُتَّقِينَ فِي جَنَّاتٍ وَنَهَرٍ	54-54 Surely the God-fearers will be among gardens and rivers.
لَعَلَّ اللّٰهَ يُحْدِثُ بَعْدَ ذٰلِكَ أَمْرًا	65-1 Allah may, after that, bring about an event.
كَأَنَّـهُنَّ ٱلْيَاقُـوتُ وَٱلْـمَرْجَانُ	55-58 As though they are rubies and pearls.
لَعَلَّهُ يَـزَّكَّىٰ	80-3 He might purify himself.

5. In the construction of لَا لِنَفِي ٱلْـجِنْسِ , that is, after the لَا , which denies absolutely the class or species in the place or circumstances defined in the sentence. This accusative has no nunization, e.g. (from the Holy Qur'ān) :

لَا رَيْبَ فِيهِ	2-2 There is no doubt in it.
لَا أَصْغَرَ مِنْ ذٰلِكَ وَلَا أَكْبَرَ	10-61 Nor anything less than that nor larger.

لَا خَلَاقَ لَهُمْ فِي ٱلْآخِرَةِ	3-77 They have no portion in the Hereafter.

The negative مَا is used for the same purpose. They are termed as 'negative particles resembling verbs', (مَا وَ لَا الْمُشَبِّهة بِلَـيْسَ).

Examples from the Holy Qur'ān :

وَمَا هُمْ عَنْهَا بِغَائِبِـينَ	82-16 And they will not be absent from it.
وَمَا لَهُمْ مِّنْ دُونِـهِ مِنْ وَالٍ	13-11 And besides Him they have no protector.
وَمَا أَنْتَ عَلَيْهِمْ بِجَبَّارٍ	50-45 And thou art not one to compel them.
وَمَا رَبُّكَ بِظَلَّامٍ لِلْعَبِـيدِ	41-46 And thy Lord is not in the least unjust to the servants.
مَا هَـذَا بَشَـرًا	12-31 This is not a human being.

6. When the noun after the vocative particle حَرْفُ ٱلنَّـدَاء is the first term of an 'iḍāfah, called in Arabic مُضَاف, e.g. :

يَا عَبْدَ اللهِ – "O' 'Abdullah",

يَا عَبْدَ ٱلرَّحْمٰنِ – "O' 'Abdar-Raḥmān",

يَا أَمِـيرَ ٱلْمُـؤْمِـنِـينَ – "O' Prince of the believers".

7. **Exception** الإِسْتِـثْـنَاءُ

The exception is expressed by the particle إِلَّا that generally takes the accusative in its following noun. A 'sentence of an exception' has two parts, the 'excepted' and the 'generality', for example, if we say: "The pilgrims came from all parts of the world apart from Muslims in occupied Palestine", 'The Muslims of the world' is the generality, and 'Muslims in occupied Palestine' is the exception.

Examples from the Holy Qur'ân :

كُلُّ شَيْءٍ هَالِكٌ إِلَّا وَجْهَهُ	28-88 Everything will perish save His countenance.

كُلُّ شَيْءٍ هَالِكٌ – generality

إِلَّا – particle of exception

وَجْهَهُ – excepted.

Most often the generality is not mentioned at all, e.g. :

لَا يَخْرُجُ إِلَّا نَكِدًا	7-58 Only evil cometh forth (from it).
مَا يَعْلَمُ جُنُودَ رَبِّكَ إِلَّا هُوَ	74-31 None knoweth the hosts of thy Lord save Him.

The noun after إِلَّا may occur in nominative, e.g. :

هَلْ جَزَاءُ آلْإِحْسَانِ إِلَّا آلْإِحْسَانُ	55-60 Is the reward of goodness aught save goodness.
مَا يَعْلَمُهُمْ إِلَّا قَلِيلٌ	18-22 · None knoweth them save a few.
إِنْ هُوَ إِلَّا ذِكْرٌ لِلْعَالَمِينَ	12-104 It is not else than a reminder unto the people.

8. For any adjective modifying an accusative noun, or any noun in opposition to another accusative noun.

Examples from the Holy Qur'ān :

وَقُولُـوا لَـهُمْ قَـوْلاً مَعْـرُوفًـا	4-5	and speak kindly to them.
إِنَّا أَرْسَلْـنَاكَ شَاهِدًا وَمُـبَشِّـرًا	33-45	(O' Prophet) Lo! We have sent thee a witness and a bearer of good tidings.

9. In certain exclamations the usual explanation being that there is a suppressed verb فعل محذوف .

Examples from the Holy Qur'ān :

طُـوبَـىٰ لَـهُمْ	13-29	Joy is for them.
لَا مَـرْحَبَا بِـهِـمْ	38-59	No word of welcome for them.

The genitive case has already been dealt with in chapters three and fourteen.

EXERCISE

1. **Translate into Arabic :**

I found Aḥmad sleeping when I went to see him. Muslims were offering prayers in a straight row like a solid wall. They spent their nights reciting the Holy Qur'ān during the month of Ramaḍān. He came back from the school in a jolly mood. He was caught by surprise when he saw the manner of sacrifice done by Muslims for the sake of their religion. It is most hateful in the sight of Allah to say much and do nothing. People entered the fold of Islam in group after group. How much is the price of the book ?

How many boys are in your class? So many townships were destroyed by enemies. He got five books, ten pens, 15 pencils and one hundred pieces of paper sheets. His mother was a very noble lady and his father a minister of state, but his companions were evil doers. Surely, Islam is the righteous way of life.

Perhaps people may realize this fact in which there is no doubt. Our Lord is not unjust to the human beings. All teachers have arrived except Mr. George. Indeed the reward of kindness is not but kindness.

2. Translate into English :

بَيْنَمَا كَانَ ٱلْخَلِيفَةُ عُمَرُ بْنُ ٱلْخَطَّابِ جَالِسًا يَقْضِي بَيْنَ ٱلنَّاسِ ، وَكَانَ كِبَارُ ٱلصَّحَابَةِ جَالِسِينَ حَوْلَهُ ، أَقْبَلَ غُلَامٌ بَاكِيًا صَائِحًا وَهُوَ يَقُولُ : قُتِلَ وَالِدِي مَظْلُومًا ، قَتَلَهُ أَحَدُ رُعَاةِ ٱلْإِبِلِ بِغَيْرِ ٱلْحَقِّ ، فَسَأَلَهُ سَيِّدُنَا عُمَرُ : كَيْفَ كَانَ ذٰلِكَ ، وَمَنْ هُوَ ٱلْقَاتِلُ ؟ فَقَالَ ٱلْغُلَامُ : إِنِّي لَا أَعْرِفُ ٱلْقَاتِلَ ، إِنَّمَا وَجَدْتُ وَالِدِي مَقْتُولًا فِي بُسْتَانِهِ . وَبَيْنَمَا كَانَ ٱلْغُلَامُ يَتَحَدَّثُ إِلَى ٱلْخَلِيفَةِ ، رَأَى ٱلنَّاسُ فَتًى يَسْعَى إِلَى مَجْلِسِ ٱلْخَلِيفَةِ عُمَرَ ، وَٱلْعَرَقُ يَتَصَبَّبُ مِنْ جَبِينِهِ ، فَقَالَ عُمَرُ : مَا وَرَاءَكَ ؟ قَالَ ٱلْفَتَى : إِنِّي أَرْتَكَبْتُ جَرِيمَةً نَكْرَاءَ ، فَقَدْ قَتَلْتُ شَيْخًا كَانَ يَحْرُسُ بُسْتَانَهُ ، لِأَنَّهُ رَمَى نَاقَتِي بِحَجَرٍ فَهَلَكَتْ ، فَلَمْ أَسْتَطِعِ ٱلصَّبْرَ عَلَى هُلْكَةِ نَاقَتِي ، وَرَمَيْتُ بِٱلْحَجَرِ إِلَى رَأْسِ ٱلشَّيْخِ فَأَصْبَحَ جُثَّةً هَامِدَةً . وَجِئْتُ إِلَيْكَ لِتُنَفِّذَ فِيَّ أَمْرَ ٱللهِ ، وَتُطَهِّرَنِي مِنَ ٱلْإِثْمِ ؛ فَإِنِّي أَخَافُ رَبِّيَ يَوْمًا عَسِيرًا ، يَوْمَ لَا يَنْفَعُ مَالٌ وَلَا بَنُونٌ إِلَّا مَنْ أَتَى ٱللهَ بِقَلْبٍ سَلِيمٍ .

sleeping	نَائِمًا (verb : نَامَ - يَـنَامُ)
to offer	أَدَّى - يُـؤَدِّي
the straight	السَّـوِيُّ
the row	الصَـفُّ
the solid	الْمُسْتَحْكَم (Passive part. X)
to recite	تَـلَا - يَـتْلُوا
jolly	فَرِحًا - مُـنْبَسِطًا
to get caught by surprise	(V) تَحَيَّرَ - يَـتَحَيَّرُ
manner	الأَسْلُوبُ - الطَّرِيقَةُ - الأَدَبُ
sacrifice	التَضْحِيَةُ
hateful	مَكْرُوهٌ - بَغِيضٌ
how much, how many	كَمْ
destroyed	خُرِّبَ (passive of II خَرَّبَ - يُخَرِّبُ)
companion	صَاحِبٌ Pl. أَصْحَابٌ or صَحَابَةٌ / صِحَابَةٌ
unjust	ظَـالِمٌ - غَيْـرَ عَادِلٍ

يَقْضِي – قَضَىٰ	to judge.
أَقْبَلَ	came forward.
غُلَامٌ	a lad.
بَاكِيًا	crying (from يَبْكِي – بَكَىٰ to cry).
صَائِحًا	noising, shouting (from يَصِيحُ – صَاحَ to make noise).
رُعَاةً	Plural of رَاعٍ (رَاعِي) tender, shephered.
الإِبْلِ	camels (collective noun).
بِغَيْرِ ٱلْحَقِّ	without any legal right.
فَتَىٰ	a lad, a youth.
يَسْعَىٰ	running (from يَسْعَىٰ – سَعَىٰ to run).
العَرَقُ	perspiration.
يَتَصَبَّبُ	to perspire (V).
مَجْلِسٌ	meeting place.
مَا وَرَاءَكَ؟	what do you want? (Lit: what is behind you).
إِرْتَكَبْتُ	I have committed (a crime) (VIII).
جَرِيمَةٌ	crime.

نَكْرَاءَ	abominable (Lit: unusual).
يَحْرُسُ	to protect, guard (كَانَ يَحْرِس – was protecting).
رَمَىٰ	he stoned (رَمَىٰ - يَـرْمِي – to throw).
نَاقَـةٌ	She – camel.
هُلِكَتْ	was killed (passive of هَـلَكَ - يَـهْلِكُ).
تُـنَفَّـذَ	to execute.
فِيَّ	in me, on me.
تُطَـهَّـرَ	to purify.
عَسِـير	tuff.
يَـنْـفَعُ	to profit, to benefit. (نَـفَـعَ - يَـنْـفَعُ)

CHAPTER 26

CONDITIONAL SENTENCES

1. A conditional sentence is introduced by one of the following particles :

إِنْ "if", e.g. (from the Holy Qur'ān) :

وَإِنْ تُبْدُوا مَا فِي أَنْفُسِكُمْ أَوْ تُخْفُوهُ يُحَاسِبْكُمْ بِهِ اللهُ	2-284 And whether ye make known what is in your minds or hide it, Allah will bring you to account for it.

مَنْ "who, whom, whoever", e.g. (from the Holy Qur'ān) :

مَنْ يَعْمَلْ سُوءًا يُجْزَ بِهِ	4-123 He who doeth wrong will have the recompense thereof.

مَهْمَا "whatever", e.g. (from the Holy Qur'ān) :

وَقَالُوا: مَهْمَا تَأْتِنَا بِهِ مِنْ آيَةٍ لِتَسْحَرَنَا بِهَا فَمَا نَحْنُ لَكَ بِمُؤْمِنِينَ	7-132 and they said: whatever portent thou bringest wherewith to bewitch us we shall not put faith in thee.

أَيُّ "which, whichsoever", e.g. (from the Holy Qur'ān) :

أَيًّا مَا تَدْعُوا ، فَلَهُ ٱلْأَسْمَاءُ ٱلْحُسْنَىٰ	17-110 unto whichsoever ye cry (it is the same), His are the most beautiful names.

لَوْ "if", e.g. (from the Holy Qur'ān) :

| وَلَوْ كُنْتُ أَعْلَمُ ٱلْغَيْبَ لَاسْتَكْثَرْتُ مِنَ ٱلْخَيْرِ | 7-188   Had I knowledge of the unseen I should have much of good. |

إِذَا "when", e.g. (from the Holy Qur'ān) :

| فَإِذَا ذَهَبَ ٱلْخَوْفُ سَلَقُوكُمْ بِأَلْسِنَةٍ حِدَادٍ | 33-19   When the fear departeth they scold you with sharp tongues. |

لَئِنْ "if", e.g. (from the Holy Qur'ān) :

| لَئِنْ لَمْ يَفْعَلْ مَا آمُرُهُ لَيُسْجَنَنَّ | 12-32   But if he does not what I bid him, he verily shall be imprisoned. |
| لَئِنْ شَكَرْتُمْ لَأَزِيدَنَّكُمْ | 14-7   If ye give thanks, I will give you more. |

لَمَّا "when", e.g. (from the Holy Qur'ān) :

| وَلَمَّا دَخَلُوا عَلَىٰ يُوسُفَ آوَىٰ إِلَيْهِ أَخَاهُ | 12-69   And when they went in before Joseph, he took his brother unto himself. |

Some other conjunction followed by a negative particle لَا as لَوْلَا "if not" or "had...not", used for implied meaning, e.g. (from the Holy Qur'ān) :

| وَلَوْلَا إِذْ دَخَلْتَ جَنَّتَكَ قُلْتَ مَا شَاءَ الله' | 18-39   And wherefore didst thou not say, when thou entered the garden: It is as Allah pleased. |

وَلَوْلَا دَفْعُ اللهِ ٱلنَّاسَ بَعْضَهُمْ بِبَعْضٍ لَفَسَدَتِ ٱلْأَرْضُ	2-251 And were it not for Allah's repelling some men by others, the earth would be certainly in a state of disorder.

There are some other conjunctions used in conditional sentences. Though not occuring in the Holy Qur'ān, they are endorsed by grammarians, for example :

مَتَىٰ "whenever", e.g.

مَتَىٰ تَأْتِهِ تَجِدْ عِنْدَهُ خَيْرًا	whenever you come to him, you will find what is good.

أَيَّانَ "whenever", e.g.

أَيَّانَ نُؤْمِنْكَ تَأْمَنْ غَيْرَنَا	whenever we trust in you, you will trust in others besides us.

2.   A conditional sentence consists of two parts : فِعْلُ ٱلشَّرْطِ "the condition (Protasis)", and جَوَابُ ٱلشَّرْطِ or جَزَاءُ ٱلشَّرْطِ "answer of the condition", (i.e. Apodosis).

(a) In Arabic, the condition and its answer, in verbal sentences, are sometimes in the jussive mood, e.g. (from the Holy Qur'ān) :

وَإِنْ تَعُودُوا نَعُدْ	8-19 If ye return, we shall return.
إِنْ يَثْقَفُوكُمْ يَكُونُوا لَكُمْ أَعْدَآءً	60-2 If they have upper hand on you, they will be your foes.

(b) or in the perfect, with ف of conjunction prefixed to the verb of the "answer of the condition" (Apodosis), e.g. (from the Holy Qur'ān) :

فَـإِذَا طَعِمْتُمْ فَـٱنْـتَشِرُوا	33-53 When your meal is finished, then disperse.
فَـإِذَا فَـرَغْتَ فَـٱنْصَبْ	94-7 So when thou art relieved, still toil.

(c) Without ف in the answer, the perfect is used to indicate a habitual happening, e.g. (from the Holy Qur'ān) :

فَـإِذَا ذَهَبَ ٱلْخَوْفُ سَلَـقُوكُمْ بِـأَلْسِنَةٍ حِـدَادٍ	33-19 When the fear departeth, they scold you with sharp tongues.
وَ إِذَا خَاطَـبَـهُمُ ٱلْجَاهِـلُونَ قَـالُوا : سَـلَامًـا	25-63 and when the foolish ones address them, answer : Peace.

(d) The answer (Apodosis) of the لَوْ may be introduced by the attached particle لَ to give stress on the nature of the sentence, e.g. (from the Holy Qur'ān) :

لَوْ شَاءَ رَبُّكَ لَجَعَلَ ٱلنَّـاسَ أُمَّـةً وَاحِـدَةً	11-118 If thy Lord had wished, He would have made men one people.
لَوْ شَاءَ اللهُ لَأَعْنَـتَـكُمْ	2-220 Had Allah willed He could have over-burdened you.

(e) The condition introduced by إِنْ may be used to express the impossibility of the condition, that is called in Arabic term as ٱلتَّعْلِيقُ بِالمُحَال "to hand to the impossible", e.g. (from the

364

٣٦٤

Holy Qur'ān) :

قُـلْ إِنْ كَانَ لِلـرَّحْمٰنِ وَلَـدٌ فَـأَنَا أَوَّلُ ٱلْعَابِـدِينَ	43-81 Say (O' Muḥammad), If the Beneficent hath a son, I am the foremost worshippers.

Note : The Translaters of the Holy Qur'ān take this إِنْ as a negative particle, therefore, exact translation would be :

قُـلْ إِنْ كَانَ لِلـرَّحْمٰنِ وَلَـدٌ فَـأَنَا أَوَّلُ ٱلْعَابِـدِينَ	43-81 Say (O' Muḥammad), The Beneficent One hath no son, I am first among the worshippers.

(f) إِنْ followed by إِلَّا is merely negative particle, e.g. (from the Holy Qur'ān) :

إِنْ كُلُّ مَنْ فِي ٱلسَّمٰوَاتِ وَٱلْأَرْضِ إِلَّا آتِي ٱلرَّحْمٰنِ عَـبْـدًا	19-93 There is none in the heaven and the earth but cometh unto the Beneficent as a slave.

Sometimes without إِلَّا gives the same negative sense, e.g. (from the Holy Qur'ān) :

وَإِنْ أَدْرِي لَعَـلَّـهُ فِـتْـنَةٌ لَّكُمْ وَمَتَاعٌ إِلَىٰ حِيـنٍ	21-111 And I know not if this may be a trial for you and a provision for a fixed time.

EXERCISE

A. Translate into Arabic :

1. If only (use لَوْ أَنَّ) you had helped the Muslim soldiers, they would not have fallen into the hands of that treacherous enemy.

2. If you had seen what happened to the unbelievers who worshipped idols, you would have given up your false ideas, and the teachings of the Porphet (May peace and blessing al Allah be upon him) would have guided you to the right path.

3. If you do the afternoon prayers earlier, we can leave for Madinah before sunset.

4. When you open the door, the sun comes in.

5. If my friend had asked for a proof, I would have told him what was preached in the *Khuṭbah* on Friday.

6. If what was on the table does not please him, let him take what is in the cupboard also.

7. If he acts (use عَمِلَ) according to the Islamic teachings, he will gain good rewards in this world and in the Hereafter.

8. If you see a fire, call the fire brigade; they will come and put it out quickly.

9. If he has faith in Allah, he will not be afraid of the dangers.

9. If he has faith in Allah, he will not be afraid of the dangers.

10. If you do not work hard, you will certainly not succeed.

11. Whatever (use مَهْمَا) the case may be the Muslims throughout the world will realize that their survival depends on their unity.

12. If you do not find a boat on the river, that is not my fault.

B. Translate into English :

لَوْ أَنَّكُمْ صَلَّيْتُمْ صَلَاةَ ٱلْعَصْرِ مُبَكِّرًا كَانَ يُمْكِنُنَا ٱلْخُرُوجُ قَبْلَ ٱلْمَغْرِبِ .

لَوْ أَنَّكُمْ وَافَقْتُمْ عَلَى ٱلْمَشْرُوعِ قَبْلَ هٰذَا ٱلْعَامِ لَكَانَتِ ٱلْمَبَانِي قَدِ

ٱكْتَمَلَتْ ٱلْآنَ . إِنِّي مُسَافِرٌ إِلَى مَدِينَةِ ٱلرَّسُولِ صَلَّى الله عَلَيْهِ وَسَلَّمَ

بَعْدَ ٱنْتِهَاءِ هٰذَا ٱلْأُسْبُوعِ . إِنْ كُنْتَ عَاقِلًا عَمِلْتَ عَلَىٰ نَصِيحَةِ وَالِدِكَ وَمَا

ضَيَّعْتَ ٱلْفُرْصَةَ . مَهْمَا كَانَ بَلَدُكَ وَلَوْنُكَ فَأَنْتَ مُسْلِمٌ وَأَخٌ لِكُلِّ مُسْلِمٍ .

لَوْ دَرَسْتَ ٱلْكُتُبَ ٱلدِّينِيَّةَ لَعَرَفْتَ أَنَّ ٱلْإِسْلَامَ دِينٌ صَالِحٌ لِكُلِّ زَمَانٍ

وَمَكَانٍ . لَوْ قَرَأْتَ ٱلْقُرْآنَ وَحَاوَلْتَ أَنْ تَفْهَمَ مَعَانِيَهُ لَآمَنْتَ بِالله

وَرَسُولِهِ . لَئِنْ لَمْ تَفْعَلْ مَا أَمَرَكَ بِهِ دِينُكَ لَنْ تَجِدَ طَرِيقَ ٱلْحَقِّ . لَوْ

سَلَكْتَ طَرِيقَ ٱلْهُدَى لَنِلْتَ ٱلْخَيْرَ فِي ٱلدُّنْيَا وَٱلْآخِرَةِ .

حَرِيقٌ	Plural : حَرَائِـق fire, conflagration.
إِنْـطَـفَـأَ	to get put out. (VII)
أَطْـفَـأَ	to extinguish, put out. (IV)
فِرْقَـةُ ٱلْمَطَافِئَ	fire brigade.
صَلَّىٰ	to pray. (II)
صَنَـمٌ	Plural : أَصْنَام idol.
عَـبـدَ	to worship.
نَجَـحَ	to succeed.
الوَعْـظُ	preaching.
الخُطْبَـةُ	lecture, Muslim Friday sermon, oration.
دُولَابٌ	Plural : دَوَالِـيب cupboard.
وَافَـقَ	to approve. (III)
إِكْتَمَـلَ	to complete.
تَـعَالِيم	teachings.

unbelievers	Sing. كَافِرٌ كُفَّارٌ
earlier	مُبَكِّرًا
sun	شَمْسٌ
the proof	الدَّلِيل
according to	وِفْقًا لِ
The Hereafter	الآخِرَة
to be afraid	خَافَ (خَافَ - يَخَافُ)
survival	البَقَاء (بَقِي - يَبْقَى)
unity	الوَحْدَةُ
fault	الخَطَأُ
throughout the world	العَالَم بِأَجْمَعِهِ

CHAPTER 27

THE NOUN – DISTINCTION AND PATTERNS

1. Distinction

The noun is distinguished from that of verbs and particles by :

(I) It can be modified by vowels and governed by preceeding elements, e.g. (Nominative) ذٰلِكَ ٱلْكِـتَابُ "This book", (Accusative) قَـرَأْتُ ٱلْكِـتَابَ "I read the book", (Genitive) وَجَدْتُ فِي ٱلْكِـتَابِ "I found in the book".

(II) Its number can be changed from singular to dual and plurals, e.g. :

	Sing.	Dual	Plural
Nominative	كِـتَابٌ	كِـتَابَانِ	كُـتُبٌ
Accusative & Genitive		كِـتَابَـيْنِ	

(III) It accepts أل of the definite article, e.g. كِتَابٌ *kitābun*, الكِـتَابُ *'alkitābu*.

2. Patterns

There are three main patterns of a noun :

(I) Simple nouns.

(II) The nouns derived from verbs or from other nouns.

(III) The verbal nouns.

I. Simple nouns are formed from the root-form of a word by slight changes in the vowelling, e.g. دَارٌ "house", أُذُنٌ "ear", عَيْنٌ "eye", أَرْضٌ "earth", سَمَاءٌ "heaven", جَنَّةٌ "garden", نَارٌ "fire", etc...

II-A. Derived nouns from the verbs are formed by vowels infixed and letters prefixed, or by both, e.g. :

(a) a long vowel infixed after the first radical to form a pattern for an active participle as:

عَامِلٌ "doer", from عَمِلَ "to do",

عَالِمٌ "learned (one)", from عَلِمَ "to know",

شَاعِرٌ "poet", from شَعَرَ "to feel".

(b) a long vowel infixed after the second radical forms a pattern, denotes the meaning of a passive participle from a root which has no pattern of فَاعِلٌ for act. part. as وَزِيرٌ , from وَزَرَ "to support", because وَازِر wāzir is not heard.

– or though the pattern of فَاعِل is found but used in a different meaning, as شَاهِدٌ "observer, witness" but شَهِيدٌ "martyr".

– or describes an adjective possessed by someone as a natural feature, i.e. not gained by himself, as جَمِيلٌ "beautiful", قَبِيحٌ "ugly".

– or derived from the roots of which the third person singular, perfect, has *dammah* in its second radical as عَظُمَ – كَرُمَ – شَرُفَ , thus the act. participle is عَظِيمٌ – شَرِيفٌ – كَرِيمٌ respectively, the plural is usually of the measure فَعْلَى and

. فِعَـالٌ , e.g. جَرْحَىٰ جَرِيحٌ , plural "wounded", from جُرْحٌ
مَرِيضٌ . قَـتْـلٌ from قَـتْـلَىٰ plural ,"murdered" قَـتِـيـلٌ
"ill, sick", plural مَـرْضَىٰ from مَـرَضٌ

Example from the Holy Qur'ān :

عَلِمَ أَنْ سَيَكُونُ مِنْكُمْ مَرْضَىٰ	73-20 He knew that there will be sick ones among you.

and كِـرَامٌ plural of كَـرِيمٌ , عِظَـامٌ plural of عَظِيمٌ , e.g.
كِرَامٌ بَـرَرَةٌ "noble and pious ones".

(c) Pattern for the passive participle is formed by prefixing
a *mīm* and infixing a long (و) vowel after second radical,
e.g. مَفْعُولٌ "done", from فَعَلَ "to do", مَقْبُولٌ "accepted",
from قَبِلَ "to accept". ·

(d) Patterns denoting place and times إِسْمُ الـزَّمَانِ وَالْمَكَانِ .
The noun of place and time expresses the place where the
action of a verb is committed, as the time or occassion of
that verb. Such nouns are measured on the patterns.
مَفْعَلٌ "maf'alun" or مَفْعِلٌ "maf'ilun".

Examples from the Holy Qur'ān :

مَشْرَقٌ – East, from شَرَقَ "to rise",
مَغْرَبٌ – West, from غَـرُبَ "to set".

وَلِلَّهِ الْمَشْرِقُ وَ الْمَغْرِبُ	2-115 For Allah is the East and the West.

مَسْجِدٌ – mosque, from سَجَدَ "to worship".

شَطْرَ ٱلْمَسْجِدِ ٱلْحَرَامِ	2-144 Towards the Sacred Mosque.

مَرْعَىٰ – pasture, from رَعَىٰ "to tend cattles".

وَٱلَّذِي أَخْرَجَ ٱلْمَرْعَىٰ	87-4 And He who brought forth herbage.

مَلْجَأٌ – refuge, from لَجَأَ "to take refuge".

لَا مَلْجَأَ مِنَ اللهِ إِلَّا إِلَيْهِ	9-118 There is no refuge from Allah but in Him.

مَأْوَىٰ – abode, from آوَىٰ إِلَىٰ "to resort to".

فَإِنَّ ٱلْجَنَّةَ هِيَ ٱلْمَأْوَىٰ	79-41 The garden is surely the abode.

مَوْعِدٌ – the place or time of the meeting, from وَعَدَ "to promise".

إِنَّ مَوْعِدَهُمُ ٱلصُّبْحُ	11-81 Their appointed time is the morning.

Note : Words on this and all above given patterns are frequently used in the Holy Qur'ān.

(e) Patterns expressing names of instruments (إِسْمُ ٱلْآلَةِ) are formed by prefixing a *mīm* and infixing a long (الــف) vowel after the second radical on the pattern.

مِفْعَلَةٌ *mif'alatun*, as مِرْوَحَةٌ *mirwaḥatun*, "a fan", from رَوَحَ "to blow".

مِفْعَلٌ *mif'alun*, as مِبْرَدٌ *mibradun*, "a file", from بَرَدَ "to file".

مِفْعَالٌ *mif'ālun*, as مِفْتَاحٌ *miftāḥun*, "a key", from فَتَحَ "to open".

Examples from the Holy Qur'ān :

مِنْسَأَةٌ = مِفْعَلَةٌ , from نَسَأَ "to delay".

تَأْكُلُ مِنْسَأَتَهُ	34-14	Eating his staff.

مِثْقَالٌ = مِفْعَالٌ , from ثَقُلَ "to be heavy, to weigh".

مِثْقَالَ ذَرَّةٍ	99-7	atom's weight.

مِيْزَانٌ = مِفْعَالٌ , from وَزَنَ "to weigh".

وَوَضَعَ ٱلْمِيْزَانَ	55-7	and He hath set the measure.

مِفْتَاحٌ = مِفْعَالٌ , plural مَفَاتِحُ or مَفَاتِيحُ , from فَتَحَ "to open".

وَعِنْدَهُ مَفَاتِحُ ٱلْغَيْبِ	6-59	and with Him are the keys of the invisible.

II-B. Derived nouns from the nouns as حَمِيَّةٌ "zealotry" from الـحِـمَى "enthusiasm"; جَاهِلِيَّةٌ "age of ignorance", from الجَهْلُ "ignorance". Both of these two words occurred in one verse of the Holy Qur'ān :

إِذْ جَعَلَ ٱلَّذِينَ كَفَرُوا فِي قُلُوبِهِمُ ٱلْحَمِيَّةَ حَمِيَّةَ ٱلْجَاهِلِـيَّةِ	48-26	When those who disbelieve had set up in their hearts zealotry, zealotry of the age of ignorance.

1. Name the patterns of the following words :

يَدٌ ، أَنْمُلَةٌ ، رَأْسٌ ، مِرْجَلٌ ، أَرْجُلٌ ، مَسَانِدُ ، مِقْبَضَةٌ ، مِنْقَلَةٌ ،

مِرْصَادٌ ، الوَطَنِيَّةُ ، مَجُوسٌ ، رَاضِيَةٌ ، مَنْظُورَةٌ .

2. **Translate into Arabic :**

Muslims say their prayers inside the mosques, sometimes they offer prayers in their homes, in fields, trains and everywhere because Allah is everywhere. The East and the West belong to Him.

The appointed time for all of us is the Day of Judgement. Makkah is a meeting place for Muslims from every country. Allah is only God who created blacks, whites, reds and people of all colours. Every human being has an equal right of living.

Arabic is the key to the treasures of knowledge. Muslims love their homeland and offer all kinds of sacrifices for their land but, however, they do not worship it. Non-Muslims have a very distorted conception of Islamic Religion. Islam commands you: think only of what is good for all human beings, consider not the wrong that has been done to you, pardon others and do good to all.

3. Translate into English :

أَمَرَ ٱلْمَغْفُورُ لَهُ جَلَالَةُ ٱلْمَلِكِ عَبْدُ ٱلْعَزِيزِ بِتَوْسِعَةِ ٱلْمَسْجِدِ ٱلنَّبَوِيِّ الشَّرِيفِ . وَكَانَ هٰذَا ٱلْأَمْرُ نُقْطَةَ ٱلْبَدْءِ فِي ٱلتَّنْفِيذِ ٱلْفِعْلِيِّ . وَقَدْ تَضَافَرَتِ ٱلْقُوَى عَلَىٰ إِنْجَازِ ٱلْمَشْرُوعِ ٱلْعَظِيمِ بِأَسْرَعِ مَا يُمْكِنُ ، وَلَمْ تَمْضِ إِلَّا سَنَوَاتٌ قَلِيلَةٌ حَتَّىٰ ٱسْتَوَى ٱلْبِنَاءُ قَائِمًا ، يَبْهَرُ ٱلْأَنْظَارَ وَيَسُرُّ ٱلْقُلُوبَ بِمَا ٱحْتَوَى مِنْ آيَاتِ ٱلْفَنِّ وَٱلْجَلَالِ ، مِمَّا يَلِيقُ بِقُدْسِيَّةِ ٱلْمَسْجِدِ ٱلنَّبَوِيِّ ٱلشَّرِيفِ ، وَمَكَانَتِهِ ٱلسَّامِيَةِ فِي قُلُوبِ ٱلْمُسْلِمِينَ . وَفِي حَفْلٍ عَظِيمٍ ، حَضَرَتْهُ وُفُودٌ شَتَّى مِنْ جَمِيعِ أَنْحَاءِ ٱلْعَالَمِ ٱلْإِسْلَامِيِّ ، ٱفْتَتَحَ جَلَالَةُ ٱلْمَلِكِ ٱلتَّوْسِعَةَ الحَدِيثَةَ بَيْنَ التَّهْلِيلِ وَالتَّكْبِيرِ .

to say prayer	(تَـأْدِيَـةٌ) – أَدَّىٰ – يُـؤَدِّي / أَدَّىٰ الصَّلَاةَ
inside the mosque	دَاخِل المَسْجِـد
erverywhere	كُلَّ مَكَان
the appointed time	المَـوْعِـد
The Day of Judgement	يَـوْمَ آلدِّيـن
the Creater	الخَالِـق
the sacrifice	ضَحَّىٰ – يُضَحِّي / الـتَّضْحِيَةُ
the distorted	(ألْبَـتْـرُ) – بَـتَـرَ – يَبْـتُـرُ / المَبْتُور
the conception	الـنَّظَرِيَّـة
the command	الْأَمْـر
the wrong, injustice	الظُّـلْم

مِئْـذَنَـةٌ	a minaret from which call to the prayers is made. Plural مَـآذَن
مِدْخَنَـةٌ	chimney
مَعْمَـلُ	factory

مَصْـدَرٌ	source.
النِّـدَاءُ	the call, from نَادَى – يُنَادِي (النِّدَاء)
الصُّفُوف ، الفُصُول	the classes.
الشَّـرُّ	the evil.
كُـلُّ	all.
السَّهْـلُ	the easy.
المُلْتَـبَسُ	the confused.
المَجْهُـولُ	the unknown.
الحِفْـظُ	the keeping, the protection.
التَّـقْوِيَّـةُ	the strengthening.
المَغْـفُورٌ لَـهُ	the forgiven one.
جَلَالَةُ آلْمَلِـك	his majesty the King.
تَـوْسِعَـةٌ	extension.
نُـقْطَـةٌ	point.
البَـدْءُ	the commencing, the beginning.
التَّـنْفِيـذُ	the executing.

الفِعْلِيُّ	the practical, actual.
تَضَافَرَتْ / تَضَافَرَ - يَتَضَافَرُ	got together.
المَشْرُوع	the project, plan.
أَسْرَع مَا يُمْكن	as soon as possible.
سَنَوَاتٍ	years.
اسْتَوَى	stood (constructed).
يَبْهَرُ	to wander.
الأَنْظَارَ	the sights.
يَسُرُّ	to make happy, to please.
إِحْتَوَى	contained, included.
آيَات	sings, plural of آيَةٌ.
الفَنِّيُّ	the artistic.
وُفُود	deligates.
شَتَّى	different.
أَنْحَاءُ	corners, parts, directions.
إِفْتَتَح	inaugurated.
الجَلَال	mighty, loftiness, splendor.

CHAPTER 28

THE VERBAL NOUN

1. The Arabic root-form is called "مَصْدَرٌ = source" that can be
    seen most clearly in the third person masculine of the perfect
    of a simple verb. Whereas the root-form or مَصْدَر not infre-
    quently includes a letter of increase. For example دُخُولٌ is a
    maṣdar as دَخَلٌ "to enter", but the latter is used to be the
    first entry in an Arabic dictionary while the former is deemed
    to be a derived form from دَخَلَ .

    Therefore, grammarians differentiate between مَصْـدَر that
    expresses the verbal idea and إِسْمُ ٱلْمَصْـدَر ; the verbal noun
    which always stands as a noun.

2. The verbal forms are not governed by a certain rule, as all of
    them are " سَمَاعِي = heard ones". According to Sībawaih
    and Suyūṭi, there are 30 permanent patterns for the verbal
    nouns. Most of them are frequently used in the Holy Qur'ān.
    Here, only one example from each pattern is being men-
    tioned :

Examples from the Holy Qur'ān :

قَتْلٌ : فَعْلٌ

فَطَوَّعَتْ لَـهُ نَفْسُـهُ قَـتْلَ أَخِيـهِ	5-30 His mind made it easy for him; killing his brother.

شِرْكٌ : فِعْلٌ

إِنَّ ٱلشِّرْكَ لَظُلْمٌ عَظِيمٌ	31-13 Surely ascribing partners to Him is a gravious iniquity.

غُلْفٌ : فُعْلٌ

وَقَالُوا قُلُوبُنَا غُلْفٌ	2-88 They said: our hearts are the wrappings (which preserve God's word).

كَبَدٌ : فَعَلٌ

لَقَدْ خَلَقْنَا ٱلْإِنْسَانَ فِي كَبَدٍ	90-4 We have certainly created man to face difficulties.

فَرِحٌ : فَعِلٌ

إِنَّهُ لَفَرِحٌ فَخُورٌ	11-10 He is exultantly, boastful.

قُبُلٌ : فُعُلٌ

إِن كَانَ قَمِيصُهُ قُدَّ مِنْ قُبُلٍ	12-26 If his shirt is rent in front.

رَحْمَةٌ : فَعْلَةٌ

ذِكْرُ رَحْمَةِ رَبِّكَ	19-2 A mention of the mercy of thy Lord.

قِسْمَةٌ : فِعْلَةٌ

تِلْكَ إِذًا قِسْمَةٌ ضِيزَىٰ	53-22 This indeed is an unjust division.

صَدَقَةٌ : فَعَلَةٌ

فَفِدْيَةٌ مِنْ صِيَامٍ أَوْ صَدَقَةٍ	2-196 so a compensation by fasting or alms-giving.

كَلِمَةٌ : فَعِلَةٌ

وَتَمَّتْ كَلِمَةُ رَبِّكَ	6-115 And the word of thy Lord has been accomplished.

ذِكْرَىٰ : فِعْلَىٰ

إِنْ هُوَ إِلَّا ذِكْرَىٰ	6-90 It is not but a reminder.

دَعْوَىٰ : فَعْلَىٰ

فَمَا زَالَتْ تِلْكَ دَعْوَاهُمْ	21-15 And this cry of theirs ceased not.

بُشْرَىٰ : فُعْلَىٰ

يَا بُشْرَىٰ ! هٰذَا غُلَامٌ	12-19 O' good news! This is a youth.

غُفْرَانَ : فُعْلَانَ

غُفْرَانَكَ رَبَّنَا	2-285 Thy forgiveness our Lord!

عِصْيَانَ : فِعْلَانَ

وَٱلْفُسُوقَ وَٱلْعِصْيَانَ	49-7 and transgression and disobedience.

ذَهَابٌ : فَعَالٌ

وَإِنَّا عَلَىٰ ذَهَابٍ بِهِ لَقَادِرُونَ	23-18 and We are indeed able of carrying it away.

خِصَامٌ : فِعَالٌ

| وَهُوَ أَلَدُّ ٱلْخِصَامِ | 2-204   and he is the most violent of adversaries. |

سُؤَالٌ : فُعَالٌ

| ظَلَمَكَ بِسُؤَالِ نَعْجَتِكَ | 38-24   Surely he has wronged thee in demanding thy ewe. |

بَرَاءَةٌ : فَعَالَةٌ

| بَرَاءَةٌ مِّنَ اللهِ | 9-1   A declaration of immunity from Allah. |

سِقَايَةٌ : فِعَالَةٌ

| أَجَعَلْتُمْ سِقَايَةَ ٱلْحَاجِّ | 9-19   Do you hold the giving of water to the pilgrims. |

غُرُوبٌ : فُعُولٌ

| وَقَبْلَ ٱلْغُرُوبِ | 50-39   And before the setting. |

قَبُولٌ : فَعُولٌ

| فَتَقَبَّلَهَا رَبُّهَا بِقَبُولٍ حَسَنٍ | 3-37   so her Lord accepted her with a goodly acceptance. |

فَرِيٌّ : فَعِيْلٌ

| لَقَدْ جِئْتِ شَيْئًا فَرِيًّا | 19-27   O' Mary thou has indeed brought a strange thing. |

حَمُولَةٌ : فَعُولَةٌ

حَمُولَةً وَفَرْشًا	6-142 And of the cattle (He has created) some for burden, some for slaughter.

3. The verbal noun on the pattern of فَعَلَان denotes meaning of something continously flowing and moving without stop as جَرَيَانٌ "to flow the water", سَرَيَانٌ "to infiltrate", but not used in the Holy Book.

4. There is a kind of مَصْدَر called الَمَصْدَر الـمِيمِي in which a *mīm* (م) is prefixed. Its pattern is the same as مَفْعِـلٌ , مَفْعَلٌ; also مُفْعَلٌ . Few examples from of the إِسْمُ آلزَّمَانِ وَآلْـمَكَانِ the Holy Qur'ān are as following :

مُـدْخَـلٌ : مُفْعَلٌ

رَبِّ أَدْخِلْنِي مُـدْخَـلَ صِـدْقٍ	17-80 My Lord! make me enter a truthful entering.

مُـخْرَجٌ : مُفْعَلٌ

وَأَخْرِجْنِي مُخْرَجَ صِـدْقٍ	17-80 and make me go forth a truthful going.

مُـقَامٌ

حَسُنَتْ مُسْتَـقَـرًّا وَمُـقَامًا	25-76 Goodly is the abode and the resting place.

5. Another pattern of the verbal noun فِعْلَةٌ is used to express the kind or type of an act, e.g. يَمْشِي مِشْيَةَ آلْجُنْـدِي "he walks like a soldier" (like the walking of the soldier).

6. There is a pattern فَعْـلَـةٌ among the patterns of the verbal noun called إِسْمُ ٱلْمَرَّةِ to specify the number of time an act is committed.

Example from the Holy Qur'ān :

قَـبَضْتُ قَـبْضَةً مِنْ أَثَرِ ٱلرَّسُولِ	20-96 I took a handful from the footprints of the Messenger.

The pattern فَعْلَةٌ , as قَـبْضَةٌ is used for the single act, and it takes the dual قَـبْضَتَــانِ , and the sound feminine plurals, as قَـبَضَاتٍ .

7. **The Diminutive** إِسْمُ ٱلتَّصْغِـير is formed from a noun of three consonants according to the pattern فُـعَيْلٌ , as فُـلَـيْسٌ , from فِـلْسٌ "money".

From a noun that has more than three consonants, four or five, the patterns of the diminutive would be :

دِرْهَمٌ , from دُرَيْهِمٌ , as فُـعَـيْـعِلٌ

عُصْفُورٌ , from عُصَيْـفِـيرٌ , as فُـعَـيْـعِيلٌ .

8. **The Comparative and Superlative of adjectives** إِسْمُ ٱلتَّـفْضِيلُ , are formed from the three radicals and their pattern is the same as that of colours and defects. Thus from حَبِـيبٌ "beloved" is formed أَحَـبُّ "more beloved, dearer". From كَبِـيرٌ "great" is formed أَكْـبَرُ "greater".

Example from the Holy Qur'ān :

وَإِثْـمُهُمَا أَكْـبَرُ مِنْ نَـفْعِـهِمَا	2-219 and their sin is greater than their advantage.

The feminine of أَفْعَلُ , as أَكْبَرُ , is فُعْلَى , as كُبْرَى , but the form أَفْعَلُ is used for feminine comparative adjectives.

Example from the Holy Qur'ān :

إِلَّا هِيَ أَكْبَرُ مِنْ أُخْتِهَا	43-48 But she is older than her sister.

Though أَفْعَلُ has dual and plural forms: أَفْعَلَانِ as أَكْبَرَانِ and أَفَاعِلُ , as أَكَابِرُ , also the feminine form فُعْلَى as كُبْرَى has its plural form فُعْلَيَاتٌ as كُبْرَيَاتٌ , only أَفْعَلُ is used in all cases, e.g. (from the Holy Qur'ān) for dual :

إِذْ قَالُوا لَيُوسُفُ وَأَخُوهُ أَحَبُّ إِلَى أَبِينَا مِنَّا	12-8 When they said : Certainly Yusuf (Joseph) and his brother are dearer to our father.

Students may note the form أَحَبُّ singular has been used instead of أَحَبَّانِ of dual.

Example from the Holy Qur'ān – For plural :

قُلْ : إِنْ كَانَ آبَاؤُكُمْ وَ أَبْنَاؤُكُمْ وَإِخْوَانُكُمْ وَأَزْوَاجُكُمْ وَعَشِيرَتُكُمْ وَأَمْوَالٌ اقْتَرَفْتُمُوهَا وَتِجَارَةٌ تَخْشَوْنَ كَسَادَهَا وَمَسَاكِنُ تَرْضَوْنَهَا أَحَبَّ إِلَيْكُمْ مِنَ اللهِ وَرَسُولِهِ	9-24 If your father and your sons, and your brothers and your wives and your kinsfolk and the wealth you have acquired and trades whose dullness you fear and dwelling you love are dearer for you than Allah and His Messenger.

But if this type of noun is used in the meaning of elative, the gender and the number will be preserved accordingly, e.g. اللهُ أَكْبَر "Allah is great".

Examples from the Holy Qur'ān :

يَوْمَ نَبْطِشُ ٱلْبَطْشَةَ ٱلْكُبْرَىٰ	44-16 On the day when We seize (them) with the most violent seizing.
وَكَذَلِكَ جَعَلْنَا فِي كُلِّ قَرْيَةٍ أَكَابِرَ مُجْرِمِيهَا	6-123 And thus have We made in every town the greater ones of its guilty.

The comparative and superlative patterns are derived from three radicals. Thus from كَبِير is formed أَكْبَر ; from صَغِير is formed أَصْغَر. In case of participles of the derived forms, words with more than three consonants, and words of the pattern أَفْعَل, the comparative is formed either by أَكْثَر or أَشَدُّ followed by a noun in the accusative (a verbal noun, as a rule), e.g. أَبْيَض "white"; أَشَدُّ بَيَاضًا "whiter".

Examples from the Holy Qur'ān :

وَٱلَّذِينَ آمَنُوا أَشَدُّ حُبًّا لله	2-165 And those who believe are stronger in (their) love for Allah.
أَنَا أَكْثَرُ مِنْكَ مَالًا وَأَعَزُّ نَفَرًا	18-34 I have greater wealth than thou, and am mightier in followers.

EXERCISE

1. Translate into Arabic :

In all systems of education, language is the medium containing the culture as well as the store-house of knowledge. But as far as Islamic culture is concerned, the Arabic language stands for more than that since it is the medium of the Qur'ān which is the source of Islamic culture, its spirit as well as the core of Islamic science, injunctions, laws, principles and ethics. It is, therefore, impossible to speak of Islam, its culture and science separately and away from the Arabic language. This does not mean that Islam has imposed one language on all Muslims since difference of language and speech is a universal law of human nature.

But this does not mean that the language of the Qur'ān is the language of knowledge for all those who believe in the religion of Islam. Every Muslim knows this fact whatever his race, nationality and dialect among Muslims may be. It does not prevent the language of the Qur'ān from being the first and the foremost of the Islamic languages.*

---

* Dr. Tawfiq Mohammad, "The Arabic Language and Islamic Education", a paper submitted to First World Congress on Muslim Education.

2. Translate into English :

طَلَعْتُ جَبَلَ النُّورِ وَ وَقَفْتُ عَلَى غَارِ حِرَاء وَ قُلْتُ لِنَفْسِي : هُنَا أَكْرَمَ اللهُ بِالرِّسَالَةِ مُحَمَّدًا صَلَّى اللهُ عَلَيْهِ وسلَّمَ وَنَزَلَ عَلَيْهِ الوَحْيُ الأَوَّلُ ، فَمِنْ هُنَا طَلَعَتِ الشَّمْسُ الَّتِي أَفَاضَتْ عَلَى العَالَمِ نُوراً جَدِيداً وَمَا أَكْثَرَ مَا اسْتَقْبَلَ العَالَمُ صَبَاحًا لَا جِدَّةَ فِيهِ وَلَا طَرَافَةَ وَلَا خَيْرَ فِيهِ وَلَا سَعَادَةَ ، وَمَا أَكْثَرَ مَا اسْتَقْبَلَ العَالَمُ صَبَاحًا اسْتَيْقَظَ فِيهِ الإِنْسَانُ وَلَمْ تَسْتَيْقِظِ الإِنْسَانِيَّةُ وَاسْتَيْقَظَتْ فِيهِ الأَجْسَامُ وَلَمْ تَسْتَيْقِظْ فِيهِ القُلُوبُ وَالأَرْوَاحُ ، وَمَا أَكْثَرَ النَّهَارُ المُظْلِمُ وَالصُّبْحُ الكَاذِبُ فِي تَارِيخِ العَالَمِ ، وَلَكِنْ مِنْ هُنَا طَلَعَ الصُّبْحُ الصَّادِقُ الَّذِي أَشْرَقَ نُورُهُ عَلَى كُلِّ شَيْءٍ وَاسْتَيْقَظَ فِيهِ الكَوْنُ وَتَغَيَّرَ مَجْرَى التَّارِيخِ . *

VOCABULARY

system	مَنْهَج	Plural مَنَاهِج
education	التَّعْلِيم	(v.n.) II
medium	وَاسِطَة	Plural وَسَائِط
culture	الحَضَارَة	Plural الحَضَارَات
store-house	المَخْزَن	Plural المَخَازِن
stand for	يَقُومُ لِ	
spirit	رُوحٌ	Plural أَرْوَاح

---

* Prof. Sayyid Abul Hasan Ali Nadwi الطريق إلى المدينة , P. 48, Dar Al-Qalam, Cairo, 1974.

core	لُبٌّ Plural أَلْبَابٌ
injuction	الإرشاد IV (v.n.)
principles	المَبَادِئ Plural of المَبْدَأ
impossible	مُسْتَحِيل X (Act. Part.)
ethics (Adj. N.)	الآدَاب Plural of الأدَب
separately	انفصل (Act. Part.) مُنْفَصِلاً VII (Use in accusative).
impose	فَرَضَ – عَلى
since	لَمَا – مُنْذُ – مَا دَامَ (Use any suitable particle).
universal	العَالَمِيُّ
nature	الطَّبِيعَةُ
race	النَّسْلُ
nationality	الوَطَنِيَّةُ – الجِنْسِيَّةُ
dialect	اللَّهْجَةُ
prevent	يَمْنَعُ – مَنَعَ
foremost	قَبْلَ كُلِّ شَيْءٍ – أَهَمُّ شَيْءٍ

طَلَعْتُ	1st Person Singular Perfect طَلَعَ - يَطْلُعُ - to climb, to accend.
وَقَفْتُ	1st Person Singular Perfect وَقَفَ - يَقِفُ - to stop, to stand.
غَــار	cave.
أَكْرَمَ	3rd Person Singular IV - to give honour.
الرِّسَالَةُ	Prophethood (Lit: communication).
نَزَلَ	3rd Person Singular I - came down.
الوَحْي	revelation.
طَلَعَتْ	3rd Person Singular Fem. Perfect - arose.
أَفَاضَتْ	3rd Person Singular Fem. Perfect - bestowed.
يَسْتَقْبِلُ	3rd Person Singular Masc. Imperfect - receives.
مَا أَكْثُرُمَا . . .	so many times.
طَرَافَة	newness, novelty.
اسْتَيْقَظَ	3rd Person Singular Masc. X - woke up.
الأَجْسَام	bodies, Plural of جِسْمٌ
النَّهَارُ	day.

المُظْلِمُ	dark, (Act. Part.) IV.
الكَاذِبُ	the liar.
الصَّادِقُ	the truthful.
أَشْـرَقَ	delighted (IV).
الكَـوْنُ	the universe.
تَـغَـيَّـرُ	changed (V).
مَجْـرَىٰ	current, course.

CHAPTER 29

CONJUNCTION & INTERJECTION

1.   The particles used as conjunctions are :

(a) و *wāw,* "and" – to link a sentence to another one or a noun to another noun, e.g. (from the Holy Qur'ān) :

وَ إِذْ يَرْفَعُ إِبْرَاهِيمُ ٱلْقَوَاعِدَ مِنَ ٱلْبَيْتِ وَ إِسْمَاعِيلُ	2-127 And when Ibrāhīm (Abraham) and Ismā'īl (Ishmael) raised the foundation of The House.
إِذَا زُلْزِلَتِ ٱلْأَرْضُ زِلْزَالَهَا وَ أَخْرَجَتِ ٱلْأَرْضُ أَثْقَالَهَا وَ قَالَ ٱلْإِنْسَانُ مَا لَهَا؟	99-1/3 When the earth is shaken with her shaking and earth brings forth her burdens and man says : What has befallen her ?

و between two sentences, of which the second is a nominal sentence, often means "while"; that forms a structure of *ḥāl,* and this و is called وَاوُ ٱلْحَال , e.g. (from the Holy Qur'ān) :

وَدَخَلَ جَنَّتَهُ وَهُوَ ظَالِمٌ لِنَفْسِهِ	18-35 And he went into his garden while he was unjust to himself.
أَأَلِدُ وَأَنَا عَجُوزٌ	11-72 Shall I bear a child while I am an old woman ?

The و is usually dropped when a verbal *ḥāl* sentence follows, e.g. (from the Holy Qur'ān) :

وَجَاءَ مِنْ أَقْصَا ٱلْمَدِينَةِ رَجُلٌ يَسْعَىٰ	36-20 And from the remote part of the city there came a man running.

(b) ف *fa*, "then" expresses sequence as well as it joins the sentences, e.g. (from the Holy Qur'ān) :

فَتَلَقَّىٰ آدَمُ مِنْ رَّبِّهِ كَلِمَـاتٍ فَتَابَ عَلَيْــهِ	2-37 And Adam received words from his Lord and He forgave him.
ٱلَّذِي خَلَقَ فَسَوَّىٰ ، وَٱلَّذِي قَـدَّرَ فَهَـدَىٰ وَٱلَّـذِي أَخْرَجَ ٱلْمَرْعَىٰ فَجَعَلَهُ غُثَاءً أَحْوَىٰ	87-2/5 Who created then made complete and Who measured then guided and Who brought forth herbage then made it dried up dust-coloured.

(c) أَوْ *'aw*, "or" for one of two or more than two things; to express doubt or give choice of one among few mentioned deeds, e.g. (from the Holy Qur'ān) :

لَبِثْنَا يَوْمًا أَوْ بَعْضَ يَوْمٍ	23-113 We tarried a day or part of day.
فَكَفَّـارَتُهُ إِطْعَـامُ عَشَرَةِ مَسَاكِينَ مِنْ أَوْسَطِ مَا تُطْعِمُونَ أَهْلِيكُمْ أَوْ كِسْوَتُهُمْ أَوْ تَحْرِيرُ رَقَبَةٍ	5-89 So its expiation is the feeding of ten poor men (with average (food) you feed your families with) or their clothings, or the freeing of a neck.

(d) أَمْ *'am*, "whether" for determination of one among few choices. In this case a *hamzah* (ء) is put before one of two equivalents, e.g. (from the Holy Qur'ān) :

أَأَنْـذَرْتَهُمْ أَمْ لَمْ تُـنْذِرْهُمْ	2-6 Alike to them whether thou warnst them or warnst them not.

(e) إِذْ *'idh*, "since, when, after, because" is used with nominal or verbal sentences, such as (from the Holy Qur'ān) :

إِذْ يَـرْفَعُ إِبْـرَاهِيمُ ٱلْقَـوَاعِـدَ	2-127 When Ibrahim used to raise the foundations.
إِذْ قَالَ رَبُّـكَ لِلْمَلَائِـكَةِ	2-30 (Remember) when thy Lord said to the angels...

(f) إِذَا *'idhā*, "when, if", originally used for times, e.g. (from the Holy Qur'ān) :

وَإِذَا قِـيلَ لَـهُمْ آمِـنُوا . . .	2-13 and when it is said to them believe !
وَإِذَا لَقُوا ٱلَّذِينَ آمَـنُوا قَالُوا : آمَـنَّا	2-14 And when met those who believed they said we believe.

The difference between إِذْ and إِذَا is that the former refers to something that happened in the past while the latter indicates to a time related to the present or future; thus a sentence such: . . . . إِذْ قَـالَ رَبُّـكَ "when thy Lord said" recalls a happening of the past; but, إِذَا جَـاءَ نَصْـرُ الله "when Allah's help has come" (has appeared), denotes the then situation of the Islamic call and response of people. Yet, the sentence

إِذَا زُلْزِلَتِ ٱلْأَرْضُ زِلْزَالَهَا "when the earth is shaken its shaking", informs about a situation relating to the future.

(g) ثُمَّ *thumma,* "after that, then, thereupon", e.g. (from the Holy Qur'ān) :

وَلَقَدْ خَلَقْنَاكُمْ ثُمَّ صَوَّرْنَاكُمْ ، ثُمَّ قُلْنَا لِلْمَلَائِكَةِ...	7-11 And We indeed created you then We fashioned you, then We said to the angels...

(h) حَتَّى *ḥatta,* "until, even, up to", to indicate the termination of an object, e.g. أَكَلْتُ ٱلسَّمَكَةَ حَتَّى رَأْسَهَا "I have eaten the fish up to its head", or "even its head", e.g. (from the Holy Qur'ān) :

حَتَّى مَطْلَعِ ٱلْفَجْرِ	97-5 It is till the rising of the morning.

(i) لَكِنْ and لَكِنَّ *lākin* and *lākinna,* "but" the former being followed by a verb, the latter by a noun in the accusative, or pronominal suffixes: لَكِنَّكُمْ ، لَكِنِّي ، لَكِنَّهَا ، لَكِنَّهُ etc.

Examples from the Holy Qur'ān :

مَا كَانَ مُحَمَّدٌ أَبَا أَحَدٍ مِنْ رِجَالِكُمْ وَلَكِنْ رَسُولَ اللهِ وَخَاتَمَ ٱلنَّبِيِّينَ	33-40 Muḥammad is not the father of any man among you, but he is the Messenger of Allah and the last one among the prophets.
فَلَمْ تَقْتُلُوهُمْ وَ لَكِنَّ اللهَ قَتَلَهُمْ وَمَا رَمَيْتَ إِذْ رَمَيْتَ وَ لَكِنَّ اللهَ رَمَى	8-17 Ye (Muslims) slew them not, but Allah slew them. And (O' Muḥammad) thou threwest not when thou didst throw but Allah threw.

(j) إِمَّا *'immā,* "either", followed by أَوْ or (إِنَّمَا) "self", e.g. (from the Holy Qur'ān) :

فَإِمَّا مَنًّا بَعْدُ وَ إِمَّا فِدَاءً	47-4 and afterwards either grace or ransom.

(k) أَمَّا *'ammā,* "as for", with a following nominative, the predicate always being introduced with a ف , e.g. (from the Holy Qur'ān) :

أَمَّا ٱلسَّفِينَةُ فَكَانَتْ لِمَسَاكِينَ	18-79 As for the ship it belonged to poor people.
وَ أَمَّا ٱلْغُلَامُ فَكَانَ أَبَوَاهُ مُؤْمِنَيْنِ	18-80 and as for the lad, his parents were believers.

The particles إِمَّا and أَمَّا are not endorsed by authentic grammarians like **Ibn 'Aqīl** and **Ibn Hishām al-'Anṣārī**, among conjunction particles.

2. Interjection (Vocative) حُرُوفُ ٱلنِّدَاءِ

It is expressed by the particle يَا followed by a noun in the nominative without article and without nunation in the singular, e.g. يَا وَلَدُ ، يَا فُلَانُ ، يَا اللهُ , etc.

If the person addressed is absent or the noun is covered by some word or words after it, then the noun is put in the accusative, e.g. يَا دَاعِيًّا إِلَى ٱلْخَيْرِ "O' caller to the good", يَا غَافِلًا "O' careless".

Likewise, in case of *'iḍāfah* constructions the *muḍāf* (the possessed one) will be put in the accusative : يَا عَبْدَ اللهِ "O' Abdallah", يَا أَمِيرَ ٱلْمُؤْمِنِينَ "O' chief of believers".

Sometimes, pronominals are omitted and replaced by a *kasrah* showing the omission, or a ت to denote emotional feelings towards the addressed one, e.g. :

"يَا رَبِّ = O' my Lord" – here a ي of 1st person is omitted,

"يَا أَبَتِ = O' my father" – here a ت is replacing the omitted ي , e.g. (from the Holy Qur'ān) :

يَا أَبَتِ آفْعَلْ مَا تُؤْمَرُ	37-102 O' my father do as thou art commanded.

(a) Often, the vocative يَا is omitted along with the pronoun; only a *kasrah* which replaces ي indicates the type of inter- jection structure, e.g. (from the Holy Qur'ān) :

قَالَ : رَبِّ إِنِّي دَعَوْتُ قَوْمِي	71-5 He said : O' my Lord! I have called my people.

(b) يَا أَيُّهَا and أَيُّهَا are followed by the noun in the nomina- tive with the article. When addressing a gathering أَيُّهَا is used, as : أَيُّهَا الْإِخْوَةُ "O' brothern!". Otherwise most often it will be preceded by يَا to become يَا أَيُّهَا , e.g. :

يَا أَيُّهَا النَّاسُ	O' people.
يَا أَيُّهَا الْكَافِرُونَ	O' desbelievers.

(c) To express feelings or affections towards someone or something يَا followed by a verbal noun or a nominal sen- tence is used, e.g. (from the Holy Qur'ān) :

يَابُشْرَى هٰذَا غُلَامٌ	12-19 Good luck! here is a youth.

يَا أَسَفَىٰ عَلَىٰ يُوسُفَ	12-84 Alas, my grief for Yūsuf (Joseph).

Sometimes an *'alif* replaces the 1st person pronoun ي to denote deep sorrow, e.g. وَا حَسْرَتَا , "O' sorrow!", وَا أَسَفَا "O' grief!".

(d) To express grief or anguished feelings towards someone, the particle وَيْلٌ always followed by a ل is used in an indirect speech, e.g. (from the Holy Qur'ān) :

وَيْلٌ لِّلْكَافِرِينَ	14-2 Woe unto disbelievers.
وَيْلٌ لِكُلِّ هُمَزَةٍ لُمَزَةٍ	104-1 Woe unto every slanderer fault-finder.

In direct speech, the pronouns take place of ل , as وَيْلَكَ "woe to you", وَيْلِي "woe to me", وَيْلَنَا "woe to us". Also وَيْكَ is used for the same purpose, e.g. (from the Holy Qur'ān) :

وَيْكَ أَنَّ اللهَ يَبْسُطُ الرِّزْقَ	28-82 Ah! woe unto you! Allah enlargeth the provision.
وَيْكَ أَنَّهُ لَا يُفْلِحُ الْكَافِرُونَ	28-82 Ah! woe unto you! The disbelievers never prosper.

Besides the above ones, يَا وَيْلَتَىٰ (with fem. ending ة) and with *'alif maqṣūrah*, instead of ي of 1st person pronoun, is used for the same type of expressions, e.g. (from the Holy Qur'ān) :

يَا وَيْلَتَىٰ أَأَلِدُ وَأَنَا عَجُوزٌ	11-72 She said: Oh, Woe unto me! Shall I bear a child while I am an old woman ?

EXERCISE

1. **Translate into Arabic :**

To translate is one thing; to speak about the art of translation is another thing, but with Allah's help, I shall attempt to outline certain considerations and suggest certain principles on this subject. However, since the material of our craft is language, I must begin by briefly examining the nature of speech, or words, of language itself.

Language is a compassionate gift of God to man in his fallen state :

Then Adam learnt from his Lord words of inspiration, and his Lord forgave him, for He is often-Returning, Most Merciful.

Now man in his fallen state – or in other words, after Adam's expulsion from The Garden – remains God's vicegerent up on the earth, and has not only been granted the distinctive gift of speech, but also the gift of revelation through the medium of **Divine Speech** : "Then We said Get ye down all from here and if, as sure there comes to you guidance from Me, whosoever follows My guidance, on them shall be no fear nor shall they grieve".

2. Translate into English :

مَثَلُهُمْ كَمَثَلِ ٱلَّذِي ٱسْتَوْقَدَ نَارًا فَلَمَّا أَضَاءَتْ مَا حَوْلَهُ ذَهَبَ ٱللَّهُ بِنُورِهِمْ وَتَرَكَهُمْ فِي ظُلُمَاتٍ لَا يُبْصِرُونَ ، صُمٌّ ، بُكْمٌ ، عُمْيٌ ، فَهُمْ لَا يَرْجِعُونَ أَوْ كَصَيِّبٍ مِنَ ٱلسَّمَاءِ فِيهِ ظُلُمَاتٌ وَرَعْدٌ وَبَرْقٌ يَجْعَلُونَ أَصَابِعَهُمْ فِي آذَانِهِمْ مِّنَ ٱلصَّوَاعِقِ حَذَرَ ٱلْمَوْتِ وَٱللَّهُ مُحِيطٌ بِالْكَفِرِينَ .

وَمَثَلُ ٱلَّذِينَ كَفَرُوا كَمَثَلِ ٱلَّذِي يَنْعِقُ بِمَا لَا يَسْمَعُ إِلَّا دُعَاءً وَنِدَاءً صُمٌّ بُكْمٌ عُمْيٌ فَهُمْ لَا يَعْقِلُونَ.

مَثَلُ ٱلَّذِينَ يُنْفِقُونَ أَمْوَالَهُمْ فِي سَبِيلِ ٱللَّهِ كَمَثَلِ حَبَّةٍ أَنْبَتَتْ سَبْعَ سَنَابِلَ فِي كُلِّ سُنْبُلَةٍ مِائَةُ حَبَّةٍ وَٱللَّهُ يُضَاعِفُ لِمَنْ يَشَاءُ وَٱللَّهُ وَاسِعٌ عَلِيمٌ.

VOCABULARY

مَثَلٌ	parable, example.
ٱسْتَوْقَدَ	kindled, X, from وقد (3rd Pers. Masc. Sing. Perf.).
أَضَاءَتْ	illumined, IV, from ضَوء (3rd Pers. Sing.).
حَوْلَ	around.
ذَهَبَ بِـ	to take away.
ظُلُمَاتٌ	darkness, pl. of ظلمة
يُبْصِرُونَ	to see, IV, from بَصُرَ (3rd Pers. Masc. Plural).
صُمٌّ	deaf, pl. of أَصَمُّ

بُكْمٌ	dumb, pl. of أَبْكَمُ
عُمْيٌ	blind, pl. of أَعْمَى (see Chapter 10).
صَيِّبٌ	abundant rain.
رَعْدٌ	thunder.
بَرْقٌ	lightning.
جَعَلَ	to put, to make.
أَصَابِعُ	fingers, pl. of إِصْبَعٌ
آذانٌ	ears, pl. of أُذُنٌ
حَذَرَ	for fear of.
الْمَوْتِ	death.
مُحِيطٌ	imcompasser, (IV, Act. Part.).
يَنْعِقُ	calls out.
دُعَاءٌ	a call.
نِدَاءٌ	cry.
يَعْقِلُونَ	to understand, from عَقَلَ (3rd Pers. Masc. Plu.).
يُنْفِقُونَ	to spend, IV (3rd Pers. Masc. Plu.).
أَمْوَالٌ	wealth, pl. of مَالٌ
سَبِيلٍ	way.

حَبَّةٍ	grain.
أَنْبَتَتْ	to grow, IV, (3rd Pers. Sing. Perf.).
سُنْبُلَةٌ	ear of grain, pl. of سَنابِلُ
يُضَاعِفُ	to make double, III, from ضَعَفَ
وَاسِعٌ	ample-giving.

translation	اَلتَّرْجِمَةُ
thing	شَيْءٌ
with Allah's help	بِعَوْنِ اللهِ ، بِإِذْنِ اللهِ ، بِمَشِيئَةِ اللهِ (Use one of the phrases)
attempt (V.N.)	مُحَاوَلَةٌ
to attempt (V.) III I shall attempt	أُحَاوِلُ
outline	الخُطُوطُ العَرِيضَةُ
however,	عَلَى كُلِّ حَالٍ
consideration	اَلتَّأَمُّلُ ، اَلإِعْتِبَارُ
to suggest, (V.) VII	إِقْتَرَحَ
itself, himself	نَفْسَهُ
The Compassionate	اَلرَّحِيمُ

Compassion	المَـرْحَـمَـةُ
gift	هَدِيَّةٌ ، عَطَاءُ ، عَطِيَّةٌ
fallen-state	النُـزُولُ
inspiration	إِلْـهَامٌ
turned towards (man), forgave	تَابَ عَلَىٰ . . .
oft-Returning	التَّـوَّابُ
expulsion	طَـرْدٌ ، إِخْـرَاجٌ
vicegerent	الخَلِـيفَـةُ
distinctive	المُـمَـيَّـزُ
geting down, descending	النُـزُولُ
guidance	الهُـدَىٰ – الهِـدَايَـةُ
fear	الخَـوْفُ
grieve, sorrow	الحُـزْنُ

CHAPTER 30

SOME DIFFERENT TYPES OF THE VERB

1. **The verb** لَيْسَ **"not to be"**. Only perfect tense of this verb is used. The conjugation is as following :

	Sing.	Dual	Plural
3rd Pers. Masc.	لَيْسَ	لَيْسَا	لَيْسُوا
3rd Pers. Fem.	لَيْسَتْ	لَيْسَتَا	لَسْنَ
2nd Pers. Masc.	لَسْتَ	لَسْتُمَا	لَسْتُم
2nd Pers. Fem.	لَسْتِ	لَسْتُمَا	لَسْتُنَّ
1st Pers. Masc. & Fem.	لَسْتُ		لَسْنَا

This verb is used to negate equational sentences (i.e. sentences which have no verbs). Once a form of لَيْسَ is introduced, the predicate changes to the accusative case (منصوب). This rule, however, applies only to nouns and adjectives, and not to prepositional phrases, as only the former have varying case endings.

Example from the Holy Qur'ān :

وَيَقُولُ ٱلَّذِينَ كَفَرُوا : لَسْتَ مُرْسَلًا	13-43 And those who disbelieve say: Thou art not a Messenger.

The predicate of an equational sentence negated by لَيْسَ is frequently introduced by the preposition بِ , which is written as part of the predicate. In this case, the predicate will be in genative since it is directly covered by the preposition.

Example from the Holy Qur'ān :

أَلَيْسَ اللهُ بِأَحْكَمِ ٱلْحَاكِمِينَ	5-8 Is not Allah the Best of the Judges.

2. **The verbs of praise and blame** أَفْعَالُ ٱلْمَدْحِ وَٱلذَّم , are represented by نِعْمَ and بِئْسَ . Like لَيْسَ , they occur only in the perfect, and have the meaning of imperfect. Moreover, the only existing forms of this verb are of the 3rd person : نِعْمَ masc.; نِعْمَتْ fem., e.g. :

نِعْمَ زَيْدٌ	Zaid is good.
نِعْمَ زَيْدٌ مُعَلِّمًا	Zaid is good as a teacher.
نِعْمَتْ فَاطِمَةُ	Fāṭimah is good.
نِعْمَتْ فَاطِمَةُ زَوْجَةً	Fāṭimah is good as a wife.
بِئْسَ ٱلْكَلْبُ هٰذَا	The bad dog is this. (this is a bad dog)
بِئْسَتِ ٱلْقِطَّةُ هٰذِهِ	The bad cat is this. (this is a bad cat)

If second person is meant to be addressed by one of these verbs it will be used as :

نِعْمَ ٱلصَّدِيقُ أَنْتَ	Really, you are a good friend.
نِعْمَتِ ٱلْأُمُّ أَنْتِ	Really, you are a good mother.

Examples from the Holy Qur'ān :

نِعْمَ ٱلْمَوْلَىٰ وَنِعْمَ ٱلنَّصِيرُ	8-40 (He is) The best Guardian and the best Helper.
وَنِعْمَ أَجْرُ ٱلْعَامِلِينَ	3-136 the good reward of the workers.
لَبِئْسَ ٱلْمَوْلَىٰ وَلَبِئْسَ ٱلْعَشِيرُ	22-13 Certainly an evil guardian and an evil associate!

3. The Verb عَسَىٰ

This verb, which has no imperfect or any form except some of the perfect tense, is used as a supporting verb and means: "it may be, perhaps, it is very likely to be" or "it is well hoped to". Therefore, it is followed by a sentence in the subjunctive introduced by أن ; the subject of which is also the subject of عَسَىٰ :

Examples from the Holy Qur'ān :

عَسَىٰ أَنْ يَبْعَثَكَ رَبُّكَ مَقَامًا مَحْمُودًا	17-79 It may be, thy Lord will raise thee to a position of great glory.
عَسَىٰ أَلَّا أَكُونَ بِدُعَاءِ رَبِّي شَقِيًّا	19-48 May be I shall not remain unblessed in calling upon my Lord.

This verb gives the sense of 'nearness', and in the rare instances in which it occurs in 1st or 2nd person it means: 'nearly' as عَسَيْتُم أَن تَقُولُوا ذَلِكَ "You are nearly saying that...".

4. The Verbs of Wonder أَفْعَالُ التَّعَجُّب

It is formed on the pattern of derived form IV (i.e. with a pre-fixed *hamzah*) from an adjective :

from	حَسَنٌ	"good"	أَحْسَنَ
from	طَيِّبٌ	"good"	أَطْيَبَ
from	كَرِيمٌ	"noble"	أَكْرَمَ

and used with a preceding مَا, while the noun is put in accusative :

مَا أَحْسَنَ زَيْدًا	How good is Zaid.	Note that the same pattern is used for Masc. Fem., Singular and Plural.
مَا أَحْسَنَ فَاطِمَةَ	How good is Fatima.	
مَا أَكْرَمَ الرِّجَالَ	How noble are the men.	
مَا أَطْيَبَ ٱلْمُعَلِّمَاتِ	How good are the teachers.	

Examples from the Holy Qur'ān :

قُتِلَ ٱلْإِنْسَانُ ، مَا أَكْفَرَهُ	80-17 Man is (self) destroyed; how ungrateful !
فَمَا أَصْبَرَهُمْ عَلَىٰ ٱلنَّارِ	2-175 How constant are they in their strife to reach the fire!

A most beautiful form found in the Holy Qur'ān is of singular masculine imperative of form IV, followed by a suffix pronoun to which the preposition بِ is prefixed (thing or person).

Examples from the Holy Qur'ān :

أَبْصِرْ بِهِ وَأَسْمِعْ	18-26 How clear of sight is He and keen of hearing!

أَسْمِعْ بِهِمْ وَأَبْصِرْ يَوْمَ يَأْتُونَنَا	19-38 How clearly will they hear and see on the day when they come to Us.

5. **The Verb مَا زَالَ and its sisters :**

Perfect	Imperfect Indicative	Subjunctive	Jussive
مَا زَالَ or لَا زَالَ	لَا يَزَالُ	لَنْ يَزَالَ	لَمْ يَزَلْ
مَا بَرِحَ	لَا يَبْرَحُ	لَنْ يَبْرَحَ	لَمْ يَبْرَحْ
مَا فَتِئَ or فَتِئَ	لَا يَفْتَأُ يَفْتَأُ	لَنْ يَفْتَأَ	لَمْ يَفْتَأْ

These verbs mean that the action is still continuing, e.g.:

ذَاهِبًا مَا زَالَ حَسَنٌ يَذْهَبُ لَمْ يَزَلْ		Ḥasan is still going. (Lit. did not cease to go)
عَامِلًا مَا بَرِحَ عَلِيٌّ يَعْمَلُ لَمْ يَبْرَحْ		'Ali is still working.
ذَاكِرًا مَا فَتِئَ حَامِدٌ يَذْكُرُ يَفْتَأُ – لَا يَفْتَأُ		Ḥāmid still remembers.

Examples from the Holy Qur'ān :

فَمَا زَالَتْ تِلْكَ دَعْوَاهُمْ حَتَّى جَعَلْنَاهُمْ حَصِيدًا خَامِدِينَ	21-15 And this cry of theirs ceased not till We made them cut off, extinct.

فَلَنْ أَبْرَحَ ٱلْأَرْضَ حَتَّىٰ يَأْذَنَ لِي أَبِي	12-80 So I shall not leave this land until my father permits me.
قَالُوا : تَٱللهِ تَفْتَؤُا تَذْكُرُ يُوسُفَ	12-85 They said : By Allah! Thou wilt not cease remembering Yūsuf (Joseph).

6.   **The Verb** كَادَ means "to be on the point of", but it is used to mean 'nearly' or 'almost', followed by the imperfect indicative or occasionally, by أَنْ plus the subjunctive :

كَادَ أَنْ يَقْتُلَ عَدُوَّهُ	He nearly killed his enemy.
كِدْتُ أَقْتُلُهُ	I nearly killed him.

When used in the negative, it means 'scarcely' :

مَا كَادَ يَنْظُرُ إِلَيَّ	He scarcely looked at me.
لَمْ يَكَدْ ٱلْعَرَبُ يَعْرِفُونَ عَدُوَّهُمْ	The Arabs scarcely knew their enemy.

Examples from the Holy Qur'ān :

وَإِنْ كَادُوا لَيَسْتَفِزُّونَكَ مِنَ ٱلْأَرْضِ	17-76 Surely they proposed to unsettle thee from the land.
لَقَدْ كِدْتَ تَرْكَنُ إِلَيْهِمْ	17-74 Thou mayest have indeed inclined to them.
تَكَادُ تَمَيَّزُ مِنَ ٱلْغَيْظِ	67-8 Almost bursting with fury.
يَكَادُ زَيْتُهَا يُضِيءُ وَلَوْ لَمْ تَمْسَسْهُ نَارُ	24-35 The oil whereof gives light, though fire touches it not.

تَكَادُ ٱلسَّمٰوَاتُ يَتَفَطَّرْنَ مِنْهُ	19-90 At it, the skies are ready to burst.
وَلَا يَكَادُ يُسِيغُهُ	14-17 And he is scarcely able to swallow it.

7. The Verb كَانَ and its sisters

As already dealt with in Chapter 5 & 9, the verb كَانَ "to be" takes a predicate in the accusative, e.g. :

كَانَ ٱلنَّاسُ أُمَّةً وَاحِدَةً – "Men used to be one nation"

Certain other verbs, termed "its sister" – كَانَ وَ أَخْوَاتُهَا, do the same as لَيْسَ "not to be".

The following are the most common used verbs of this group :

بَقِيَ	to remain
دَامَ	to last
زَالَ	to cease
صَارَ	to become
أَصْبَحَ IV	to become
أَمْسَى IV	to become
بَاتَ – يَبِيتُ	to become

Example :

بَقِيَ ٱلإِسْلَامُ دِينًا لِلْعَالَمِينَ.	"Islam remained as a religion for all the worlds".

Example from the Holy Qur'ān :

وَأَصْبَحَ فُؤَادُ أُمِّ مُوسَىٰ فَارِغًا	28-10 And the heart of the mother of Mūsā (Moses) became free.

8. **The Verb** صَارَ "to become", أَخَذَ "to take", جَعَلَ "to make, or do, or put", also mean "began to", if followed by a verb in the imperfect.

Notes: (a) All these verbs render the meaning of the action in the past.

(b) These verbs are known in Arabic as أَفْعَالُ ٱلشُّرُوع that is, 'verbs to initiate the action'. They are auxiliary verbs.

Examples :

صَارَ ٱلْمُسْلِمُونَ يَدْخُلُونَ . . .	Muslims began to enter
أَخَذُوا يُنَفِّذُونَ كِتَابَ ٱللهِ وَسُنَّةَ رَسُولِهِ	They started executing the Book of Allah and the tradition of His prophet.
جَعَلُوا يَرْجِعُونَ إِلَى ٱلدِّينِ . . .	They started turning to the religion.
أَخَذْنَا نَتَعَلَّمُ لُغَةَ ٱلْقُرآنِ ٱلْكَرِيمِ	We began to learn the language of the Holy Qur'ān.

A. Translate into Arabic :

"Muslims are brothers in religion; and they must not oppress one another, nor abandon assisting each other, nor hold one another in contempt. The seat of righteousness is the heart; therefore, that heart, which is righteous, does not hold a Muslim in contempt; and it is wicked to hold a Muslim in contempt; and the things that are unlawful for a Muslim to do to another regarding his blood, property and reputation; he must not act or speak that by which the blood of a Muslim might be spilt, and his property destroyed; and reputation lost. The people of paradise are three; the first, a just king, a doer of good to his people, endowed with virtue; the second, an affectionate man of a tender heart to relatives and others; the third, a virtuous man".

"The duties of Muslims to each other are six. "It was asked: What are they, O' Prophet?", He said: When you meet a Muslim, offer *salām* to him; and when he invites you to dinner, accept it; and when he asks for advice, give it to him; and when he is sick visit him; and when he dies, follow his bier".

B. Translate into English :

١ - كُتِبَ عَلَيْكُمُ ٱلْقِتَالُ وَهُوَ كُرْهٌ لَكُمْ وَعَسَىٰ أَنْ تَكْرَهُوا شَيْئًا وَهُوَ خَيْرٌ لكُمْ وَعَسَىٰ أَنْ تُحِبُّوا شَيْئًا وَهُوَ شَـرٌّ لَكُمْ وَاَللهُ يَعْلَمُ وَأَنتُمْ لَا تَعْلَمُونَ .

٢ - كُتِبَ عَلَيْكُمُ ٱلْقِصَاصُ فِي ٱلْقَتْلَىٰ الْحُرُّ بِالْحُرِّ وَٱلْعَبْدُ بِالْعَبْدِ وَٱلْأُنْثَىٰ بِٱلْأُنْثَىٰ . فَمَنْ عُفِيَ لَـهُ مِنْ أَخِيهِ شَيْءٌ فَٱتِّبَاعٌ بِالْمَعْرُوفِ وَأَدَاءٌ إِلَيْهِ بِإِحْسَانٍ . ذَٰلِكَ تَخْفِيفٌ مِّن رَّبِّكُمْ وَرَحْمَةٌ فَمَنِ ٱعْتَدَىٰ بعدَ ذٰلكَ فَلَـهُ عَـذَابٌ أَلِيمٌ . وَلَكُمْ فِي ٱلْقِصَاصِ حَيَاةٌ يَا أُولِي ٱلْأَلْبَابِ .

٣ - كُتِبَ عَلَيْكُمْ - إِذَا حَضَرَ أَحَـدَكُمُ الْمَـوْتُ - (إِنْ تَركَ خَيْرًا) الْـوَصِيَّةُ لِلْوَالِدَيْنِ ، وَٱلْأَقْـرَبـينَ بِٱلْمَعْرُوفِ . حَقًّا عَلَى ٱلْمُتَّقِينَ .

٤ - وَقَالَتِ ٱلْيَهُودُ لَيْسَتِ ٱلنَّصَارَىٰ عَلَى شَيْءٍ وَقَالَتِ ٱلنَّصَارَىٰ لَيْسَتِ ٱلْيَهُودُ عَلى شَيْءٍ وَهُمْ يَتْلُونَ ٱلْكِتَابَ .

٥ - كُتِبَ عَلَيْكُمُ ٱلصِّيَامُ ، كَمَا كُتِبَ عَلَى ٱلَّذِينَ مِنْ قَـبْلِكُمْ ، لَعَلَّكُمْ تَـتَّـقُونَ .

C. State the patterns of the following words :

القِصاص ، القَتلى ، الأُنثى ، الإحسان ، تخفيف ، الوَصيَّةُ .

D. In the verse given in Chapter No. 4 for translation, state in وَهُمْ يَتلون الكِتَاب what the (و) stands for.

E. Turn the following phrases from plural to the singular and vice versa :

كُتِب عليكم . ليست النصارى على شَيْءٍ . ليست اليهودُ على شَيْءٍ . وَهُم يتلون الكتاب . ولكم في القصاص حياة .

F. It is assumed that by reaching this stage a laborious student can start understanding the meaning of the Holy Qur'ān. Now at the end of this book, you are invited to examine your Arabic knowledge by yourself through rendering into Arabic the first 10 verses from the Surah 12, namely "Yūsuf" (Joseph).

brotherly	الأَخَوِيُّ
love	الحُبُّ الأَخَوِيُّ – الحُبُّ Brotherly Love
mutual assistance	أَلتَّعَاوُنُ
inculcate	يَطْبَعُ ، يَغْرِسُ فِي الذِّهْنِ
emphatic	ٱلْمُؤَكَّد
to oppress	يَظْلِمُ (3rd pers. sing. imperfect)
one another	بَعْضُهُمْ بَعْضًا
wicked	فَظِيعٌ – شَرٌّ
contempt	الإِزْدِرَاءُ ، التَّحْقِيرُ
righteous men	الصَّادِقُونَ
unlawful	الْحَرَامُ
blood	الدَّمُ pl. دِمَاء
property	المِلْكُ pl. أَمْلاك
endowed with virtue	مُلْتَزِمُ العِفَّةِ / المُتَّصِفُ بالفَضِيلَةِ
virtuous man	اَلعَفِيفُ

to invite	يَدْعُو (3rd pers. sing. imperfect)
dinner	عَشَاء (المَأْدُبَةُ)
to advice	يَنْصَحُ (3rd pers. sing. imperfect)
sick	مَرِيضٌ
he dies	يَمُوتُ
the bier	الجَنَازَةُ

كُتِبَ	has been written (Passive of كَتَبَ).
القِتَالُ	fighting.
كَرِهِ – يَكْرَهُ	to dislike.
حَضَرَ	to arrive, to approach.
خَيْرًا	(Acc.) Lit. "good", but here is meant "wealth".
الصِّيَامُ	fasting.
(nom.) الوَالِدَانِ	the parents (acc./gen. الوَالِدَيْنِ).
الأَقْرَبِينَ	relatives.
المَعْرُوفُ	according to the tradition.

حَقًّا	duty bound (Acc.).
المُتَّقِينَ	God-fearing people, pl. of مُتَّقِي (doubled radical verb) VII
القِصَاصُ	the retaliation, the punishment.
الحُرُّ	the free.
الأُنْثَىٰ	the female.
عُفِيَ لَهُ	was forgiven.
إِتِّبَاعٌ	following, (v.n. from إِتَّبَعَ).
إِحْسَانٌ	beneficence, charity, performance of good deeds.
تَخْفِيفٌ	alleviation.
أَلْبَابٌ	heart, mind, intellect, reason. pl. of لُبٌّ

CONTENTS

إيضاحــات حـول هـذا الكتاب

١ - الآيات القرآنية التي استشهد بها لتطبيق القواعد مرقمة برقمي السور والآيات حيث يشير الرقم الأول لرقم السورة والثاني لرقم الآية .

٢ - لم يلتزم المؤلف بنقل الآية بكاملها في كل مكان ، بل أحياناً يأتي بفقرة أو جملة تفيد الغرض ، وهو « الشاهد » للقاعدة النحوية أو الصرفية .

٣ - عندما ذكرت الشواهد من القرآن الكريم يذكر بوضوح « مثال من القرآن الكريم » : Examples from the Holy Qur'ân .

٤ - في بعض التمارين تختلط الآيات بغيرها من الجمل المختارة ، وتفصلها الفواصل والأرقام الخاصة بالقرآن الكريم والتي لا توجد مع الفقرات الأخرى .

٥ - ترجمة الآيات القرآنية نقية صافية « روعيت فيها الصحة والدقة ومطابقة لمـا حواه تفسير الطبري » .

كلمـة شــكر وتـقديــر

يطيب لي أن أذكر بالشكر والتقدير والاعتراف بالجميل معالي الشيخ محمد صالح القزاز الأمين
العام لرابطة العالم الإسلامي (سابقًا) حيث عهد إلى في رمضان عام ١٣٩٤هـ أن أتولى إصدار مجلة
رابطة العالم الإسلامي باللغة الانجليزية ، وكان من بين الأبواب الثابتة التي اخترتها للمجلة « تعلم
لغة القرآن » (Learn the Language of Qur'ān) عنوانًا لباب كنت أكتبه متوليًا لإعدادها إلى
أن انتظمت في هيئة أعضاء التدريس بجامعة الملك عبد العزيز بمكة المكرمة ، ثم بدا لي أن أتناول
هذه الدروس بالزيادة في الايضاح وجمع الشواهد من القرآن الكريم وأن أضيف إليها فصولًا جديدة
فكان هذا الكتاب .

ظهرت الطبعة الأولى لهذا الكتاب من مطابع دار الشروق بالقاهرة ، روعيت في إخراجها الجودة
والاتقان ، غير أن الأخطاء المطبعية كانت كثيرة ، فعمدت إلى الطبعة الثانية بعد التصحيح ، وهذه
الطبعة الهندية وإن كانت على ورق عادي ولكنها مصححة . وإني أشكر الأخوة الذين ساعدوني في
التبييض الأول والتصحيح للطبعة الثانية ، أخص منهم الأستاذ الأديب محي الدين ونجله السيد
معين الدين والسيد أختر نسيم الندوي ، حفظهم الله ، تقبل الله منا ومنهم صالح الأعمال .

د. عبـد الله عبـاس نـدوي
مدرس بجامعة الملك عبد العزيز
مكة المكرمة ، المملكة العربية السعودة

وطريقة تعليم يستطيع وحده أن يرشد الطالب ويأخذ بيده إلى هدفه .

وبما يجدر بالذكر أن هذا النهج الذي اتبعه ليس من ابتداعي ، بل سبقني إليه أستاذي في تاريخ الحديث النبوي الشريف ، **الأستاذ عبد السلام القدوائي** مدير التعليم لجامعة ندوة العلماء بالهند ، فقد أجرى التجربة على عدد كبير من المثقفين من المشتغلين بالتجارة والوظائف الحكومية فثبت نجاح هذا المبدأ وشوهد الطلبة وقد قطعوا مسافات سنوات في شهور .

أما الأمر الذي قمت به وهو أني وَسَّعْتُ هذا المنهج ليشمل أكثر القواعد النحوية المحتاجة إليها في تلقي العربية ، واللغة التي اخترتها للتأليف هي الانجليزية لأن أغلبية من يريد تعلم العربية من غير العرب هم ممن ينطقون هذه اللغة أو تثقفوا بها فأصبحت الانجليزية لغة علم وفهم لديهم .

ويرجع الفضل في إخراج هذا الكتاب إلى المربي الكبير الأستاذ محسن أحمد باروم مدير عام دار الشروق بجدة الذي تولى مشكورًا طبع هذا الكتاب ، فله مني أصدق الامتنان والعرفان بالجميل .

يسر الله أمورنا وهدانا السبيل وآخر دعوانا أن الحمد لله رب العالمين .

د . عبد الله عباس ندوي
مدرس بجامعة الملك عبد العزيز
مكة المكرمة ، المملكة العربية السعودية

للعرب والإسلام ، ففي ثنايا إيضاحهم القواعد وشرحهم لأصل من أصول اللغة يستعملون لغة تقنع الطالب أن اللغة العربية لغة عويصة معقدة تعتمد على الشذوذ أكثر من اعتمادها على الأصول . وإذا صادف أن ذكروا قاعدة تخص اللغة العربية الفصحى فقط نبهوا طلبتهم إلى عدم جدواها ومثال ذلك أن كتاب النحو العربي الجديد الذي ألفه هيري وود وناهمد (Harywood & Nahmad) عندما يذكر المفعول معه ويأتي بمثال له « سافر زيد وأخاه » يقول :

This usage is rather antique; it is found in poetry and the Qur'ān, and is not recommended to the student for general use.

أي « أن هذا الاستعمال قديم مهجور يوجد في الشعر والقرآن ولا يقترح على الطالب اتباعه للاستعمال العام » .

ومن الفقرات التي أتى بها المؤلفان لتطبيق القواعد كشواهد نجد على صفحة ٣٩٢ (طبع لندن عام ١٩٦٥م) :

« حسبت محمداً كذاباً »

« أخبرت حسناً محمداً كاذباً »

وإني لم أعثر على كتاب ألفه أحد هؤلاء « الأعلام » إلا وفيه أمثال هذه الضغائن تجسدت في كتاباتهم .

ومن المؤسف أن المثقفين من المسلمين ممن تعلموا الانجليزية لأنها كانت لغة المستعمرين في بلدانهم إذا أرادوا تعلم العربية لم يجدوا أمامهم إلا ما كتبه هؤلاء الأساتذة المتحيزون ، مما ترك وما يزال – فراغا يحتاج إلى أن يملأ من قِبَل المسلمين أنفسهم فكان هذا الشعور دافعا إلى وضع هذا الكتاب الذي توخيت فيه :

١ – الاعتماد على شواهد من القرآن الكريم ليكون الطالب المسلم الذي يريد تعلم العربية لأجل الإسلام والقرآن منسجمًا مع لغة القرآن الكريم منذ أول خطوة يخطوها نحو تلقي العربية ، وللأمثال تأثير في الفكر أقره علماء التربية ولا يختلف فيه اثنان !

٢ – تبسيط القواعد واختصار الطريقة حتى يستطيع كل من يتفرغ لساعة أو ساعتين من النهار أو الليل أن يدرس العربية في مدة وجيزة .

٣ – جعل القرآن الكريم أداة لتعليم العربية وفتح المجال له للتوسع في دراستها واتقانها إلى أقصى حد ممكن .

وما يجدر الإشارة إليه أن الكاتب لا يؤمن بالطريقة التي تدعى عَلِّمْ نَفْسَكَ (Teach yourself) ويرى أن اللغة كائن نام حي لا يمكن تلقيها إلا من كائن حي فالمدرس الخبير بالعربية لغةً ونحوًا

مقــــدمــــة

الحمد لله ولي النعم وسلام الله على نبي خير الأمم سيدنا محمد وآله وصحبه أولي المكارم ومحاسن الشيم وبعد :

فقد عكف كاتب هذه السطور ردحًا من الزمن على دراسة ترجمات لمعاني القرآن الكريم إلى اللغة الانجليزية ومقارنة بعضها ببعض ، وقد انتهت به هذه الدراسة إلى أن الترجمات - مهما تحرَّى أصحابها الدقة والإجادة - عاجزة عجزًا كليًا عن استيفاء المدلولات الكاملة لأي الذكر الحكيم فضلاً عن نقل ما في كتاب الله من الروعة والجمال وما فيه من قوة التأثير في القلوب والنفوذ إلى العقول كما تبين له أن القاصد إلى فهم كتاب الله العظيم من خلال ترجمة من الترجمات في خطر ، فقد تعمّد المترجمون من غير المسلمين إلى تشويه جمال القرآن وتقويض دعائم الإسلام والتشفي لأحقادهم على المسلمين عن طريق ترجماتهم كما أن آخرين منهم أرادوا من القرآن الكريم أن يجعلوه مطيّة لبيان عقائدهم الشاذة وآرائهم التي ينفردون بها معرضين عما كان عليه السلف الصالح وما عليه جمهور المسلمين من أهل السنة والجماعة .

وليس مما يحل هذه المشكلة أن تضاف ترجمة أخرى إلى مجموعة ترجمات موجودة فإن طبيعة الترجمة تأبى أن تكون أمينة ومستوفية حيث أن كل لغة تمتاز في صياغة ألفاظها وتراكيبها النحوية التي تلبس الكلمات حللاً في المعاني والأساليب البيانية مما لا يمكن نقله إلى أية لغة أخرى على الإطلاق .

فكان الحل الوحيد أن يُدعى المسلمون إلى تعلم هذه اللغة التي خصّها الله للوحي الصادق وهذا المطلب - أن يتعلم المسلمون العربية حتى يفهموا القرآن الكريم مباشرة بدون وسائط الترجمات - سهل قولاً ، وصعب عملاً ، فإن المسلمين منتشرون في شرق الأرض وغربها ، ولهم ما لغيرهم من مشاكل الحياة ومشاغل الكسب ومعالجة شؤونهم المحلية فأنى لهم أن يتفرغوا لتعلم العربية وقضاء عدة سنوات لدراسة هذه اللغة وقواعدها النحوية .

ومن أجل ذلك اتجه تفكيري إلى وضع منهج يراعى فيه التبسيط والتيسير ويمكن تلقي العربية عن طريقه في مدة وجيزة والبحث عن مثل هذا المنهج الذي يلائم عقول الطلاب الأجانب والمثقفين بثقافة انجليزية جعل الكاتب يلقي نظرة على المناهج الموضوعة باللغة الانجليزية لتعليم العربية فوجد أصنافا من الكتب وضعت باللغة الانجليزية لهذا الغرض واطَّلع على عدد كبير منها فوجد أن الأمر الذي يشترك فيه جميع المؤلفين هو أنهم يهدفون إلى تعليم أبناء بلادهم اللغة العربية لأغراض دبلوماسية سياسية وتجارية فكان تركيزهم على أساليب الصحف السيارة ولغات الأفلام والروايات كما لاحظ أن هؤلاء مع مقدرتهم العلمية لم ينجحوا في إخفاء ما في صدورهم من غل وحقد وكراهية

بِسْمِ اللهِ الرَّحْمَنِ الرَّحِيمِ

ٱلْحَمْدُ لِلَّهِ ٱلَّذِى هَدَىٰنَا لِهَٰذَا وَمَا
كُنَّا لِنَهْتَدِىَ لَوْلَا أَنْ هَدَىٰنَا ٱللَّهُ

[صدق الله العظيم]

تعلّم
لغة القرآن الكريم

دكتور عبد الله عبّاس النّدوي

INTERNATIONAL DISTRIBUTOR

IQRA' Book Center, 6408 North Campbell, Chicago, IL 60645
Tel: (312) 274-2665, 1-800-521-4272 Fax: (312) 274-8733

بسم الله الرحمن الرحيم

تعلّم
لغة القرآن الكريم